NATIONAL
GEOGRAPHIC
TRAVELER

hawaii

NATIONAL
GEOGRAPHIC
TRAVELER

hawaii

by Rita Ariyoshi

National Geographic
Washington, D.C.

CONTENTS

Pages 2–3: Surfer on the Banzai Pipeline on Oahu's North Shore
Left: A coconut palm on the beach of Ala Moana Beach Park, Honolulu, Oahu

TRAVELING WITH EYES OPEN

Alert travelers go with a purpose and leave with a benefit. If you travel responsibly, you can help support wildlife conservation, historic preservation, and cultural enrichment in the places you visit. You can enrich your own travel experience as well.

To be a geo-savvy traveler:

- Recognize that your presence has an impact on the places you visit.

- Spend your time and money in ways that sustain local character. (Besides, it's more interesting that way.)

- Value the destination's natural and cultural heritage.

- Respect the local customs and traditions.

- Express appreciation to local people about things you find interesting and unique to the place: its nature and scenery, music and food, historic villages and buildings.

- Vote with your wallet: Support the people who support the place, patronizing businesses that make an effort to celebrate and protect what's special there. Seek out shops, local restaurants, inns, and tour operators who love their home—who love taking care of it and showing it off. Avoid businesses that detract from the character of the place.

- Enrich yourself, taking home memories and stories to tell, knowing that you have contributed to the preservation and enhancement of the destination.

That is the type of travel now called geotourism, defined as "tourism that sustains or enhances the geographical character of a place—its environment, culture, aesthetics, heritage, and the well-being of its residents." To learn more, visit National Geographic's Center for Sustainable Destinations at *national geographic.com/travel/sustainable.*

ABOUT THE AUTHORS

Rita Ariyoshi is the author of *Maui on My Mind* and *Hula Is Life*. She served for ten years as editor of *Aloha Magazine*. Her travel articles, fiction, and memoirs have appeared in a variety of international magazines and literary journals, including *National Geographic Traveler*. She is a five-time, first-place winner in the prestigious Lowell Thomas Travel Journalism Competition. Her stories have been commended by the Hawaii Visitors and Convention Bureau, the Pacific Asia Travel Association, the Hawaii Publishers Association, and the National Catholic Press Association. She is a grand-prize winner in the annual National Steinbeck Center Short Story Competition, and recipient of the Pushcart Prize for Literature. Ariyoshi's work has been collected in anthologies and made into television productions. She lives in Honolulu with her family. A short story about Molakai won the University of Hawaii 2011 Ian MacMillan competition and a novel in progress was a finalist for the 2011 James Jones Literary Fellowship.

Hawaii-born journalist **Thelma Chang** updated and wrote new features for the 2009 edition.

Charting Your Trip

The Hawaiian Islands rise like big green dreams in the middle of the vast Pacific Ocean. The quintessential tropical paradise, they pack surprises too. How about Earth's tallest mountain? Snow? Cowboys? Acclaimed cuisine? The world's most active volcano? Its tallest sea cliffs? Designer boutiques? Hawaii has them all, and more. The unique ambience is Polynesian, Asian, and thoroughly American. You will encounter ancient and exotic cultures, yet feel right at home.

Many Islands, Many Experiences

Before you plan your trip, you should determine which Hawaii and what kind of experience you want. Sorting through the array of possibilities can be overwhelming, especially for a first-time visitor. However, thoughtful choices regarding budget, time, space, and your own personality and interests will reward you with the time of your life and a legacy of happy memories.

The six major islands are known for certain features: Oahu (Gathering Place), Maui (Valley Isle), Kauai (Garden Isle), Hawaii (Big Island and Orchid Isle), Molokai (Friendly Isle), and Lanai (Getaway Isle, for lack of a defining identification).

Time is a key factor in selecting the right island for you. It would be a mistake to hop from island to island for hurried tours or visit more than two islands if you're going to be in Hawaii for only a week. Some would argue one week is barely enough time for one island. It depends on the traveler. Seasoned visitors often bypass Oahu and head straight for the neighbor islands—say, Kauai for hiking, Lanai for peace and quiet, the Big Island for sportfishing and volcanoes, or Maui for beach life and whale-watching.

Traveling There & Getting Around

Almost all flights from the U.S. mainland, as well as international flights, go through Oahu's Honolulu International Airport. From there, five regional airlines handle interisland flights: Hawaiian Airlines, Pacific Wings, Mokulele Airlines, Island Air, and go!, a discount carrier. Look for "triangle route" deals, in which you arrive at one airport and leave from another.

The best way to see an island is by car. Gas, however, is expensive in Hawaii—prices are 10 to 25 percent higher than the national average. If you opt to rent a car, make your reservations early for a better deal. Visit *gohawaii.com* for a list of preferred rental companies.

Oahu

Oahu, including busy, historic Honolulu and sunny, pleasure-packed Waikiki, are musts for first-time visitors, despite the island's reputation as "too crowded," "too commercialized," and "too concrete." Oahu's landmarks include Waikiki, Diamond Head, Pearl Harbor, and the North Shore. Using Waikiki as a home base while exploring the rest of the island is a practical way of experiencing island life and sights. Kapahulu is a neighborhood of local shops and restaurants just minutes away from the lights of Waikiki, while the slopes and beaches of nearby Diamond Head are home to Gold Coast residents. You could skip Waikiki if your temperament dictates quiet and seclusion. But give the area a chance. Its ocean views are fabulous, the water sports thrilling, the people colorful, and the shopping runs from tacky to elegant.

Beyond Oahu, visitors seeking a neighbor island to visit for a day or two should focus on a specific area or activity.

Maui & Kauai

Despite its ever growing traffic snarls, Maui remains popular for its beautiful wilderness and beaches, whale-watching, golf courses, deep valleys, mountain "zipping" (see p. 141), cool heights, fern forests, summit of Haleakala, and more.

Seaside Lahaina, an old port of call for whalers, sailors, and Bible-toting missionaries in the 19th century, is today a waterfront town of souvenir shops, boutiques, art galleries, interesting characters, and marvelous views of Lanai and Molokai. The village of Hana, on the other hand, highlights nature's gallery of fern forests, waterfalls, and pristine swimming spots. The scenic journey there includes a hairy, twisting drive on a narrow cliff-side road. Going slowly and carefully is a must.

Like Hana, Kauai is lush and green. The island, which lies at the northern end of the island chain, endures its share of traffic headaches. Kauai nevertheless prevails as a relaxing place, with gardens, warm people, the magnificent Na Pali coastline, Waimea Canyon, hiking trails, gentle beaches, kayaking spots, and a whimsical weather pattern of rain on one side of the island and sunshine on the other.

NOT TO BE MISSED:

A glimpse of the lives of monarchs at Iolani Palace **59–63**

The summit of Diamond Head for a breathtaking view of Waikiki **98**

A respectful visit to Pearl Harbor, the U.S.S. *Arizona,* & the U.S.S. *Missouri* **114–117**

A scenic drive to Hana for tropical tranquillity **144–145**

Insight into the lives of ancient chiefs and commoners at Puuhonua o Honaunau National Historical Park **155–156**

Nature's breathtaking power at Hawaii Volcanoes National Park **168–177**

The stunning beauty of Na Pali ("the cliffs") **198–199**

Beauty and tragedy at Kalaupapa **212–213**

Packing for Hawaii

Prepare for unexpected weather. Bring comfortable, closed-toe shoes; boots and a backpack for rugged activities. Light, casual dress such as shorts, swimsuits, T-shirts, and long pants are the norm. Add a simple dress or nice shirt and trousers for upscale places. Shop when you get here for sophisticated resort fashions, Island dresses, and aloha shirts. Pack a sweater, windbreaker, insect repellent, sunscreen, and a hat.

Warm & Unpredictable

Tropical Hawaii is usually warm, with an average temperature between 75°F and 85°F. Features include northeasterly trade winds and moderate humidity. The leeward (south and west) sides of islands tend to be dry, while rain keeps the windward (north and east) sides lush and green.

Hawaii has two seasons: summer (May to October) and winter (November to April), a rainy period. Flash floods happen most often in October and November.

The months from August to November may feel not only warmer, but also muggier. The lack of strong trade winds during the transition from summer to the wet season explains part of it. And temperatures in Hawaii have been rising over the past 30 years, especially at night.

Island weather is anything but boring. You may be standing in sunshine one moment and drenched in rain the next. Pleasant days can turn cold at night.

The Big Island

People who wish to find virtually every kind of vista—including a venting volcano, deserts, sunny coastlines, snowy mountaintops, fern forests, and rainbows—will likely fall in love with Hawaii. Anchoring the island chain's southern end, the Big Island dominates through sheer size—more than 4,000 square miles of diversity and still growing. The island has been compared to the Wild West, with features of rough terrain, jagged coasts, and real-life cowboys who were wrangling long before the American West's heyday. Today's Hawaii also reveals an expansion of luxury resorts and homes that dot the Kohala Coast and elsewhere.

The island has a mystique about it and needs to be explored in "chunks," as in north, west, east, south, and inland. The cooler, northern Kohala Coast attracts history buffs who explore petroglyph fields and thick black lava layers, while coffee lovers and fishing fans will delight in the sunny, western Kona Coast. The east side of Hilo is known for its easygoing pace, a place where nature lovers find their niche in the area's fern forests, rain, rainbows, waterfalls, and colorful orchids and anthuriums.

Head south of Hilo and inland, and experience nature's power at Kilauea, a fiery volcano that has spewed its bloodred eruptions continuously since 1983. You can take a fascinating drive around the crater rim, walk among odorous fumes, and, if you're lucky, see lava flow into the sea. The spectacular volcanoes of Mauna Kea (white mountain) and Mauna Loa (long mountain) are also inland, in the central part of the isle.

Safety in General

Hawaii is generally a safe place to visit. As in any city or country, however, you can help to ensure a pleasant, safe trip.

- Do not take valuables to the beach. Bring only essentials and keep an eye on them or use a buddy system of watchful eyes.
- Lock your car.
- Park in lighted or well-populated areas. Avoid parks at night.
- Ensure the sliding glass door of your room's lanai or balcony is locked.
- Ask the hotel concierge or visitor center about unsafe areas.
- Keep handbags or shoulder bags close to the chest.

More Islands

If you prefer respite and seclusion, consider the islands of Molokai and Lanai for a day, a week, or longer. Molokai is slow-paced, with a town

Hanauma Bay, a natural aquarium on Oahu, was formed when the seaward wall of a volcanic crater collapsed.

where people hitch their horses, "talk story" (converse), and enjoy nature. It's also an island to explore with an expert guide on rugged hikes or a swim on the remote, lush east side.

And Lanai? Here, visitors will find few paved roads along with quiet bliss and privacy. You may never leave your hotel grounds, but the island is tempting for hikers, swimmers, snorkelers, golfers, art lovers, whale-watchers, and people who relish early morning or sunset walks on a beach that feels like your very own.

No matter which island you choose, you can enhance the time you spend there. Slow down, absorb the beauty, and linger awhile. Respect the natural elements, have a snack at a small bakery or noodle shop, or talk to the locals and learn about island foods, culture, or history. Think "Aloha."

With that attitude, Hawaii will be more than a place of physical beauty. The islands will become a priceless experience. ∎

Visitor Information

- **Hawaii Visitors and Convention Bureau, Honolulu:** tel 800/464-2924 or 808/923-1811; *gohawaii.com*
- **The Big Island Visitors Bureau, Hilo:** tel 808/961-5797; **Waimea:** tel 808/885-1655; *bigisland.org*
- **Maui Visitors Bureau, Wailuku:** tel 800/525-6284 or 808/244-3530; *visitmaui.com*
- **Kauai Visitor Bureau, Lihue:** tel 800/262-1400 or 808/245-3971; *kauaidiscovery.com*
- **Lanai Visitors Bureau, Lanai City:** tel 800/525-6284 or 808/244-3530; *visitlanai.net*
- **Destination Molokai Visitors Bureau, Kaunakakai:** tel 800/525-6284 (U.S. and Canada) or 808/553-3876 (interisland); *molokai-hawaii.com*

History & Culture

Male dancer at Molokai's Ka Hula Piko festival
Opposite: Walking the lava at Kilauea Volcano, Big Island

Hawaii Today

Farther from a landmass than any other place on earth, the Hawaiian Islands rise as green beacons of life in the middle of the vast Pacific Ocean. From the very beginning, this single factor of isolation has defined Hawaii. The distance from Honolulu to California—the closest point—is 2,397 air miles; to Tokyo, 3,847 miles; to Papeete, Tahiti, 2,741 miles.

The Hawaiian archipelago of 137 islands, islets, and atolls is strung like uneven pearls across the Tropic of Cancer in a 1,523-mile line draped from Kure at latitude 28.5° north to the island of Hawaii at 19° north. The eight main islands lie in the tropics and share the same latitude as Mexico City, Havana, and Hong Kong. Cooling trade winds breeze in from the northeast ocean about 300 days a year.

All the islands, with the exception of the five Midway Islands (which are part of Papahanaumokuakea nature preserve, administered jointly by the U.S. Department of the Interior, U.S. Department of Commerce, and the State of Hawaii) compose the 50th state of the United States of America. The capital of Hawaii, Honolulu, on the island of Oahu, is the only large city in the state. More than a million people have settled in the islands, with more than 75 percent living on Oahu. The major industry is tourism, followed by defense and agriculture.

> **The Hawaiian archipelago of 137 islands, islets, and atolls is strung like uneven pearls across the Tropic of Cancer in a 1,523-mile line.**

Different Isles, Different Styles

Each island is different, not only in appearance but in personality. Oahu is schizophrenic, busy, sophisticated, and urbane, with a surprisingly rural twin personality. Maui is the dreamer. Here the arts flourish in galleries, art schools, and the forward-looking Maui Arts and Cultural Center. In small towns there are still hippie sightings. The Big Island is raw, with room to spare; it bristles with creative energy. Silver-spoon resorts sprout from obsidian lava flows. Kauai is ancient and wise and green. It has the state's only navigable river, the broad Wailua. Golf courses, hiking trails, and a grand canyon make this an isle for outdoor adventure. Molokai defies the times, remaining obstinately out of the mainstream, and that is precisely its charm. Lanai right now seems to have lost its identity. When it was the world's largest pineapple plantation, it was called the Pineapple Island. Since the closure of the plantation, the island's promoters have thought up new names, such as the Private Isle and the Secluded Isle, but nothing seems to stick. Niihau is privately owned and remains largely closed. Its population consists exclusively of native Hawaiians who still speak the Hawaiian language as their primary tongue. Kahoolawe, once an island of temples and ranches, was emptied of people to become a practice bombing target for the U.S. military prior to World War II. In 1990 President George Bush called a cease-fire, and in 1994 the Navy surrendered jurisdiction of the island to the state.

A surfer achieves the ultimate thrill, riding in the tube of a great wave.

Aloha spirit is a powerful part of Hawaiian culture, practiced even by young children.

Aloha Spirit

Aloha. It's a word that does not translate easily, yet it defines and encompasses a race of people. In Hawaii, it's a common word, used in greeting and farewell. Taken to its roots, *alo* means "in the presence of" and *ha* means "the breath of life," with its implications of divine gift.

Egged on by tour guides, tourists delight in drawing out the word, "A-loooooo-HA." They are seldom told that aloha is not just another way of saying hello. When you say "Aloha" to someone you are acknowledging that the two of you are standing in the presence of God, and so all your words, thoughts, and deeds should be virtuous.

It is a tender word that has the power to shape a life. It is the single word that sets Hawaii apart from any place else in the world, enabling many races to come together in one place and live peaceably side by side, not just in tolerance but in mutual appreciation and celebration. Aloha says, "Come, bring your heritage, your family. Learn aloha."

The late and revered Pilahi Paki defined aloha letter by letter:

A is akahai, *kindness*

L is lokahi, *unity*

O is oluolu, *pleasantness*

H is haahaa, *humility*

A is ahonui, *patience.*

People worry about aloha. Is Hawaii losing it? Do we have enough of it? How can we make sure the aloha spirit is not overwhelmed by the waves of newcomers to the islands? Like any relationship, aloha takes care and commitment. It reflects the inner spirit of a person and society. To practice aloha, you must love your neighbor as yourself. It's life-giving.

Happily, it is very much in evidence today. It's there in the smiles that greet even the grumpiest, jet-lagged visitor, in the kindness in which an elderly woman stepping gingerly down from a tour bus is treated as if she is a princess. And "Aloha aina," love of the land, is an environmental cry.

The biggest festival in the state is the Aloha Festival, which takes place annually from mid-September to mid-October. Like the word itself, the statewide party ignores boundaries and overflows into a weeks-long multicultural celebration marked by parades, hula performances, luaus, and exhibitions of traditional arts and crafts. Joyfully included in all the Hawaiiana may be marching bands from the mainland United States or an army of Japanese samurai in full regalia astride their steeds. Personified, aloha has many faces.

The aloha spirit comes naturally to most people. It is layered over every transaction and relationship like the mist that clings to the mountains bearing life-giving water. It binds the whole diverse Hawaii into one brilliant mosaic of life.

A Rainbow of People

With interracial marriages at around 50 percent, it becomes more and more difficult to tell not only who's who, but also who's what. Are you Hawaiian if you are Hawaiian-Filipino-Japanese? A child, upon hearing that a classmate is part Japanese and part Irish is likely to express their condolences—"That's all?"—then proceed proudly to proclaim his own heritage of seven ethnicities. Surveying the faces in an average classroom, it is clear that a new race of island children is emerging. Known as *hapa,* meaning "a part" or "a half," they are a bright and beautiful blend of East and West.

This usually happy mixing of races would probably not have happened if the people had been, at the outset, any race but Hawaiian. It took the generosity and value system modeled by the host culture, that of the Hawaiians, with their unique spirit of *aloha.*

Immigrants: The first immigrants to arrive in any numbers were the Chinese, who came as contract laborers in 1852. The first Japanese laborers stepped ashore in 1868 to claim their plantation contracts, which paid six to nine dollars a month. By the turn of the century there were more than twice as many Japanese living in Hawaii as any other ethnic group. Because most of the immigrants were hardworking and enterprising, they left the pineapple and sugar fields as soon as the contracts were up. They founded small businesses, bought land, and sought education for their children. The plantation owners, in their constant search for cheap labor, brought in workers from the Portuguese Azores and the Philippines. Later, significant immigration to Hawaii came from Korea, Samoa, and the American mainland.

Children of the Land: As for the Hawaiians, their population was decimated by contact with the outside world. It is estimated that within a hundred years of the arrival of British explorer Capt. James Cook in 1778, 90 percent of the native people were dead from introduced diseases to which they had acquired no immunities, having lived in isolation for centuries. In 1892, the last full year of the Hawaiian nation (see pp. 33–34), native Hawaiians numbered 40,000. Today, 5.9 percent

> When you say "Aloha" to someone you are acknowledging that the two of you are standing in the presence of God.

of the population self-identify as Hawaiian, but part-Hawaiians are a fast-growing ethnic group in the islands. No matter what their mix, most identify, culturally, with their Hawaiian heritage. They are proud to be *keiki o ka aina,* children of the land.

Where East Meets West: In addition to the Hawaiians, part-Hawaiians, and other Pacific Islanders who are 26.2 percent of the population (according to the 2010 U.S. census), today's racial tapestry is woven of 38.6 percent Asians, including Japanese, Chinese, Korean, and Filipino, and 24.7 percent Caucasian, both local-born and mainland transplants. Hispanics, Latinos, and African Americans comprise the remaining portion of the population.

English author Somerset Maugham wrote of Hawaii in 1921: "It is a meeting place of East and West, the new rubs shoulders with the immeasurably old. . . . All these strange people live close to each other, with different languages and different thoughts; they believe in different gods and they have different values."

Living side by side, neighbors celebrate each other's holidays, whether Kamehameha Day, Chinese New Year, Obon Season, the Fourth of July, or Christmas (see p. 54).

Misunderstandings: People bring not only their colorful traditions and festivals, their faiths and foods, but their attitudes, too. It sometimes takes the *malihini* (the newly arrived) a while to settle down to "Hawaiian time," to realize he or she can't have it "now!" and possibly not even tomorrow. Traffic is often the proving ground. The sensitive malihini learns to wave a thank-you when a car in traffic makes room to allow him in front. Ethnic humor is pervasive and often hurtful, but in the past it helped defuse racial confrontations and misunderstandings. Recent arrivals tolerate it less these days, and it has even inspired lawsuits.

Too often newcomers, rather than integrating, set up parallel communities, never learning island ways and expecting islanders to change. And with almost 22,000 tourists a day in rent-a-cars, easygoing island ways can be severely challenged.

Understanding Through Culture: A movement toward Hawaiian sovereignty finds both Hawaiians and non-Hawaiians united in recognizing that an injustice was done when the Hawaiian monarchy was overthrown in 1893 and that some form of restitution must be made. A hundred years later, President Bill Clinton formally apologized for the participation of the United States and signed a joint congressional resolution acknowledging the illegitimacy of the 1898 annexation of Hawaii.

The Hawaiian cause suffered a setback in 2000 when the U.S. Supreme Court struck down the state of Hawaii's practice of permitting only people with Hawaiian blood to vote in elections for trustees of the Office of Hawaiian Affairs (OHA). The law also allowed only native Hawaiians to serve as trustees. OHA was created by a state constitutional amendment in 1978 to help improve the lives of native Hawaiians using funds generated by "ceded lands," which are the 1.8 million acres of former crown lands taken by the U.S. government after annexation and later transferred to the state of Hawaii.

In 1996, Harold "Freddy" Rice, a Caucasian rancher from the Big Island whose family has lived in Hawaii since the middle of the 19th century, attempted to vote in an OHA election and was denied a ballot. He sued, claiming violation of his rights under the 14th and 15th amendments to the U.S. Constitution, which guarantee equal protection of voting rights regardless of race. The U.S. Supreme Court eventually ruled in Rice's favor.

After nearly 30 years of working toward an agreement with OHA, Governor Neil Abercrombie signed into law a compromise measure that settles OHA's unresolved claims to income and proceeds from ceded lands. Under the law, the state conveyed to OHA adjacent parcels of park, commercial, and residentially zoned lands along Honolulu's waterfront, valued at approximately $200 million.

In spite of many assaults on its integrity, and even on its own validity in modern Hawaii, the Hawaiian culture, traditionally based on sharing and *lokahi,* the principle of making peace and unity, continues to be the glue holding a diverse population together.

Ironically, tourism has also enabled people to earn a living as cultural practitioners. Hotels sponsor schools, create staff positions for cultural directors, hire consultants, buy native arts, stage cultural performances, and contract with instructors in various crafts such as lei making and *lauhala* (pandanus leaf) weaving. Programs to incorporate Hawaiian values into the visitor industry have been successful, reminding local people of their heritage and instructing malihini employees about their responsibilities, an almost sacred responsibility as hosts in a land whose best known word, *aloha,* means, among many beautiful things, "love." ∎

A scuba diving lesson begins in the swimming pool of the Four Seasons Resort Lanai at Manele Bay.

History of the Land

The Hawaiian Islands are actually the tops of a massive oceanic mountain range that rises from the ocean floor to protrude above the waves. What is seen is only a fraction of what exists. Mauna Kea and Mauna Loa, on the Big Island, are so tall they are often crowned in snow, two giant incongruities presiding over a tropical landscape.

Wind, rain, and catastrophic prehistoric landslides have shaped Hawaii's volcanoes into dramatic peaks and valleys. The mountains are cloud catchers, drawing rain and making these islands lush and habitable. Rainwater seeps through volcanic rock into underground cisterns, providing some of the purest fresh water on the planet. The islands are ringed in beaches. Volcanic activity and coral erosion color the sand.

Birth from Fire

Geologically, Hawaii is a baby. Before it was born, the rest of the world had settled into stable continents. In the Hawaiian creation chant, the "Kumulipo," the islands emerged from the dark depths of primeval night. Other legends tell of how Maui, Superman of the Hawaiian pantheon, fished up the islands from the ocean floor. Both reflect the truth. In the mid-Tertiary period, a rift opened in the floor of the Pacific Ocean, and fires from the molten core of the earth began spewing magma through the fissure. The fires, still raging, were so intense they burned unquenched in the cold perpetual night of the ocean at depths of 2,600 fathoms (15,600 feet).

Magma erupted from the fissure slowly, building mound by mound until the volcano

EXPERIENCE: Observing an Active Volcano

Visitors to the Big Island's Hawaii Volcanoes National Park have referred to their experience as "truly awesome," "primeval," and "getting in touch with our beginnings." Kilauea (Hawaiian for "spewing") is a flat shield volcano, presently the most active on Earth.

Kilauea's continuous lava flow was sparked by a 1983 eruption from the Puu Oo and Kupaianaha vents. The fireworks became more intense when Halemaumau, a large pit crater, erupted in 2008 and emitted sulfur dioxide.

Maps and safety tips are available at the visitor center (see p. 171). Highlights include the Thurston Lava Tube, Kilauea Iki Overlook, Devastation Trail, and the Thomas A. Jagger Museum. Watching an active flow treading its way to the sea and meeting the ocean with searing force is unforgettable.

Any safe exploration, guided or unguided, depends on weather and other conditions. Guided tours offer personalized treks; some tour restrictions may apply.

Hawaii Forest and Trail's Kilauea Volcano Adventure offers a full-day tour, with pickup from Kona and Kohala Coast hotels, breakfast, and gear such as day packs (tel 808/331-8505, hawaiiforestand trail.com, $$$$$). Hawaiian Walkways offers tours that leave from the visitor center at 10 a.m. and finish at 4:30 p.m. (tel 800/457-7759 or 808/775-0372, hawaiian walkways.com, $$$$$).

Helicopter flight-seeing tours are a popular way to view the islands' magnificent sea cliffs and valleys.

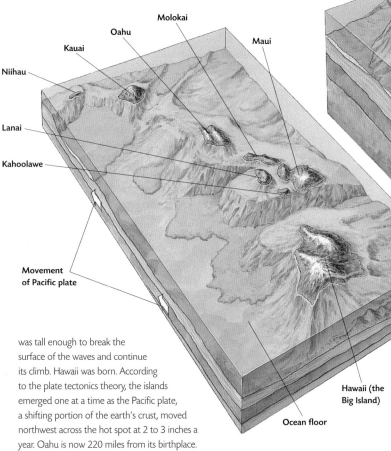

The Hawaiian Islands have all been formed from volcanic activity over a hot spot in the Earth's crust. As the Pacific plate moves northwestward, the islands move with it and new volcanoes form.

Big Island

Molokai

Oahu

Maui

Kauai

Niihau

Lanai

Kahoolawe

Movement of Pacific plate

Hawaii (the Big Island)

Ocean floor

was tall enough to break the surface of the waves and continue its climb. Hawaii was born. According to the plate tectonics theory, the islands emerged one at a time as the Pacific plate, a shifting portion of the earth's crust, moved northwest across the hot spot at 2 to 3 inches a year. Oahu is now 220 miles from its birthplace.

Over the past 44 million years, this hot spot has made the 82 volcanoes of the Hawaiian archipelago. It continues to bubble. Since 1983, Kilauea Volcano has added 550 acres to the Big Island. An embryonic island, Loihi (see p. 234), is forming 20 miles southeast of Hawaii—divers have seen its birth flames glowing beneath the sea. At Hawaii Volcanoes National Park (see pp. 168–169, 171, 173–177), it's often possible to walk right up to a red-hot lava flow.

As new islands rise, old ones slowly sink. The coral reefs, which form around the massive girths of middle-aged islands, become fringe reefs as the aging islands erode and succumb. Eventually, all that's left is a ring of reef, which forms its own uneven circle of islets known as an atoll. Kure in the north is a classic example of a Pacific atoll. Most main islands offer fine examples of fringe reefs, easily accessible from shore. The Big Island reefs are still in infancy.

The Language of Lava

Many of the terms in modern volcanology are Hawaiian. Lava is hot liquid rock ejected by a volcano. *Aa* is rough, rocky lava, and *pahoehoe* is smooth, ropy lava and is hotter. Magma is lava beneath the earth's surface. A caldera is a large, round, or oval volcanic

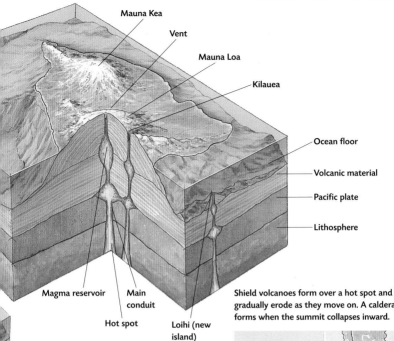

Mauna Kea

Vent

Mauna Loa

Kilauea

Ocean floor

Volcanic material

Pacific plate

Lithosphere

Magma reservoir   Main conduit

Hot spot   Loihi (new island)

Shield volcanoes form over a hot spot and gradually erode as they move on. A caldera forms when the summit collapses inward.

depression; a crater is smaller and bowl shaped. Lava tubes are formed by molten lava as it travels; its crust cools and hardens, while lava flows beneath. Tephra is airborne fragments of hardened lava ejected by lava fountains, also called Pele's tears. Pele's hair is cobweb-like filaments of glass, formed when volcanic gas blows through highly fluid lava.

Formation   Shield building

Flora & Fauna

When the islands emerged from the ocean, they were barren. Life came in the ocean currents and the jet streams or as gifts of migratory birds, evolving into an astonishing biota. All of Hawaii's native forest birds are endemic, existing nowhere else. All the insects and 95 percent of the flowering plants are endemic, as are 65 percent of the ferns. With no predators, plants developed neither

Caldera   Erosion

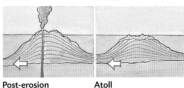

Post-erosion   Atoll

thorns nor noxious odors. Some birds and insects lost the ability to fly. A species might live on one island and not another, or in just one valley. Upland native forests, such as Kamakou Preserve, Molokai (see p. 219), offer a unique environment of plants and birdsong unlike anything else in the world.

The impact of humans and introduced species has been lethal to native wildlife, and conservation groups struggle to preserve what's left of native species. Tropical flora have made themselves at home in this hospitable climate. The result is a fragrant, green, and blooming Hawaii with its fiery origins still visible. ■

History of Hawaii

The history of Hawaii reads like a good novel, with heroes, gods, villains, kings, and queens. There are epic voyages of discovery, an idyllic isolation that is practically paradise, the rise of a star-crossed kingdom, treachery, greed, intrigue, and an overthrow with the U.S. Marines onstage. The past is present in the culture and aspirations of *Hawaii nei,* Hawaii today.

Polynesian Voyages & Settlement

Eia Hawaii, he moku, he kanaka!	Behold Hawaii, an island, a people!
He kanaka Hawaii e!	A nation is Hawaii!
He kanaka Hawaii,	The people of Hawaii
He kama na Kahiki ...	Are the children of Tahiti ...

"Eia Hawaii" is considered by most scholars to be the oldest existing Hawaiian chant. It accounts for the origin of the people. Without a written language, the Hawaiians kept their records in a rich store of oral history composed of chants, hula, and epic stories of gods, kings, and migrations. Oral history is, of course, subject to question and becomes clouded by the loss of the specific to the poetic and by changes in language over the centuries.

The prehistory of Polynesia was further blurred by the ravages a tropical climate inflicts on material objects, and a prevailing Eurocentric attitude that discounted non-Western achievements. Also, traditional radiocarbon dating of artifacts was rendered unreliable by nuclear testing done by both the United States and France in the Pacific.

> **"How shall we account for this nation spreading itself over this vast ocean?"**
>
> —CAPT. JAMES COOK, *1778*

Capt. James Cook, the first Westerner to find the Hawaiian Islands, asked in his log of 1778: "How shall we account for this nation spreading itself over this vast ocean?" Cook knew the rigors of ocean voyaging, and he could not comprehend how a race of people in canoes fastened together with coconut fiber rope, and possessing no maps or navigational gear such as compass and sextant, could have colonized such widely separated island groups.

In 1947, Norwegian explorer Thor Heyerdahl (1914–2002) set out from Peru in a balsa raft, the *Kon Tiki,* to prove that the Polynesians had drifted west from the Americas in prevailing winds and currents and that settlement of the Pacific was largely accidental. He captured the popular imagination and believed he had solved an important question.

Heyerdahl's answer, however, conflicted with the Hawaiians' understanding of themselves. In 1976, using oral history and sketches of early canoes, the members of the Polynesian Voyaging Society in Hawaii built and launched a 60-foot voyaging canoe, the *Hokulea.* They sailed it to Tahiti using ancient Polynesian navigational skills, guided only by the stars, wind, waves, and seabirds. They arrived to a big welcome,

The traditional ceremonial garments of nobility—once made of feathers—are now made of velvet and plush.

having proved that the oral history could be true. Their achievement launched a cultural renaissance.

In 1981, a construction crew bulldozing for a resort tennis court on the Tahitian island of Huahine discovered what has come to be called the Polynesian Pompeii. Evidence shows that around A.D. 850, a tidal wave swept across a coastal village, burying it in just the right mixture of sand and silt to preserve its material culture. In it, archaeologists found the hull of an 80-foot canoe, along with artifacts connecting the site to New Zealand and the Marquesas. Further digging revealed that the village had been a thriving community of about 200 people who engaged in ship manufacture for trade. The evidence to prove the truth of the chants and hula finally existed.

Scientists now believe, from linguistic and archaeological research, that the Polynesians originated in Southeast Asia. Following the trail of a unique pottery, called Lapita, they trace the migrations to the Bismarck Archipelago between 3000 and 2000 B.C. From there, people ventured to the Solomon Islands, Vanuatu, Fiji, and Tonga. By 1200 B.C., they had settled in Samoa, where they spent a thousand years, becoming culturally the Polynesian people, and developing the navigational experience for the long voyages ahead of them to the Marquesas, 1,000 miles to the east, to Tahiti, Aotearoa (New Zealand), Hawaii, and Rapa Nui (Easter Island). It is estimated that the first voyagers to reach Hawaii set sail from the Marquesas about A.D. 500. Later settlers came from Tahiti.

By the time of Western contact, these epic voyages had, for some reason, ceased, and the stories and chants were consigned to myth. A new generation of Hawaiians—taught by Mau Piailug, a traditional master navigator from Satawal, Micronesia—has revived the art of Polynesian navigation, and voyagers are again crisscrossing the Pacific, retracing the ancient ocean highways. The distinctive claw-shaped sail of the Polynesian voyaging canoe is once more filled with the trade winds.

Petroglyphs

Picture writings on rocks, which the Hawaiians called *kaha kii*, are found on all the islands. Some images are obvious—dogs, people, canoe paddles. Others are obscure—concentric circles, geometric shapes, lines that might be charts, even images of men with wings. The meanings are a mystery. Some petroglyphs may mark a person's passing by; others are thought to be astronomical diagrams for navigators or to have religious significance.

Many are from prehistoric times, but those depicting horses were obviously made after the horse was introduced in 1803. The earliest human representations are stick figures, with the unique triangular-shaped torso coming later.

The best examples are on the Kona-Kohala Coast—at Puako and the Waikoloa Resort.

Life in Precontact Hawaii

Early life in Hawaii was mostly good. The climate was benign and predictable, the land fertile, and the sea bountiful.

The Hawaiians were very aware of the finite resources of their island environment and became excellent stewards of nature. They gave hundreds of names to wind and rain, each highly descriptive and poetic. *Ua hanai* is the rain that nurtures the earth; *ua awa*, a cold drizzling rain. They named and classified each creature, and divided the land into pie-shaped segments called *ahupuaa*. Usually an ahupuaa stretched from a mountain summit, down through fertile valleys, and to the outer edge of the reef in the sea. This provided the families living on the land access to every elevation for the cultivation of various crops, plus fishing and gathering rights in the ocean. A freshwater stream ran through the ahupuaa with strictly regulated areas for various functions such as bathing and irrigation. No one was permitted to enter the water above the area designated for drinking water. Below the agricultural terraces, the stream was ingeniously engineered into a series of traps to catch silt so the water entered the ocean clean, thus maintaining the reefs.

Society was well organized and allowed ample time for leisure pursuits, such as sports and the arts. Politically, the larger islands of Kauai, Oahu, Maui, and Hawaii were each ruled by an *alii nui,* or high chief. He divided his island into regions called *mokupuni,* each ruled by a lesser chief. The smaller islands of Lanai, Molokai, and Kahoolawe were ruled by the Maui high chief, while Niihau was assigned to Kauai. War sometimes broke out between one island and another over land or family conflicts among the *alii* (nobility).

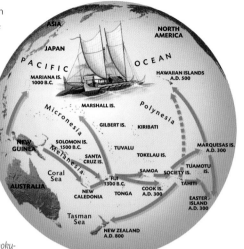

Polynesian voyagers first reached Hawaii from the Marquesas. Later travelers came from Tahiti (broken arrow).

Religion & Education

A strict system of *kapu,* or religious law, governed every aspect of life, from conservation practices to the status of women. Loosely translated, it means "forbidden." The law was administered by the nobility and the *kahuna* (priests). Death was the penalty for violation of the kapu. So deeply rooted was this system that offenders were mortified—sometimes literally dying of shame before they could be apprehended and executed.

The primary gods of the ancient Hawaiian religion are Lono, Kane, Kanaloa, and Ku. Like most Polynesians, Hawaiians also believed in a Supreme Being, sometimes referred to as Io. Little is known about this god above all gods because much of the priestly knowledge was held in secret.

No daily task was begun without prayer. Every beauty beheld, every gift received was acknowledged as coming from the gods. Communion with the divine was not just an act of worship but a way of being. Every family had an *aumakua,* or guardian spirit, often represented in animal form such as a shark, lizard, owl, or turtle. More formalized aspects of religion were conducted at large temples, called *heiau.* The Tahitians introduced human sacrifice at some temples.

Education was conducted primarily by the family in the home. Gifted children were apprenticed to masters in arts such as healing, canoe building, navigation, and hula. Family relationships were strong and often embraced *hanai* (informally adopted) members. Rather than occupy a single thatched house, a family built as many as six houses, including separate sleeping houses and eating houses for men and women. There would be a chapel, a house for beating *kapa* (tree-bark cloth) in bad weather, and a house of confinement for menstruating women. Fortification walls were unknown.

An annual four-month holiday called Makahiki was a time when warfare and work ceased, and taxes in the form of produce and animals were collected. After elaborate ceremonies, the temples closed, and according to Hawaiian scholar and historian David Malo (1793–1853), in his book *Hawaiian Antiquities,* there was a break even in formal religious practices. Makahiki, which began in Ikuwa, the month roughly corresponding to October, was considered to be the time of Lono, god of the harvest. Today's Aloha Festival (see p. 17) is a direct descendant of Makahiki.

Contact

On the evening of January 20, 1778, some fishermen at Waimea, Kauai, saw two large and very strange silhouettes moving across the dark ocean, carrying lights. They hurried ashore and reported their sighting. By dawn, a large crowd

Capt. James Cook, with his ships *Resolution* and *Discovery*, was the first Westerner to reach Hawaii, in 1778.

had gathered along the shore to see two huge ships riding at anchor. All of Waimea Valley rang with excitement. Historian Samuel M. Kamakau (1815–1876) wrote that some people were frightened. "One asked another, 'What are those branching things?' and the other answered, 'They are trees moving on the sea.' "

Captain Cook, in command of H.M.S. *Resolution* and H.M.S. *Discovery,* en route from the South Pacific, had stumbled upon the Hawaiian Islands, breaking centuries of isolation for the Hawaiian people. Life was to change forever.

Cook put the islands on his maps, naming them the Sandwich Isles after his patron, the Earl of Sandwich. During the two weeks Cook and his men spent there, they inadvertently introduced European diseases to which the native people had no immunities. Between that first contact and 1799, some 45 foreign ships called. They brought more disease, hard liquor, tobacco, material goods, weapons of war, and grazing animals. In less than 100 years, 90 percent of native Hawaiians are thought to have died, their culture eclipsed.

> **Kamehameha . . . launched a campaign of conquest that eventually united all the islands into one nation.**

Rise of the Kamehameha Dynasty

On a night in 1758 when Halley's comet streaked across the Hawaiian sky, Chiefess Kekuiapoiwa gave birth at the sacred stones of Kohala, near Mookini Heiau, Big Island (noble women customarily gave birth on special rocks in sacred places). Because of the omen in the sky, a prophet predicted the child would become "a killer of chiefs and ruler of all the islands." Accordingly, the ruling chief ordered him killed. Loyal retainers hid the infant in Waipio Valley, where he was raised in secret and schooled in the arts of warfare and statesmanship. His name was Kamehameha.

A brilliant strategist and courageous warrior, he launched a campaign of conquest that eventually united all the islands into one nation. Kauai alone was not conquered, but voluntarily joined the union.

As was customary, Kamehameha had many wives. Keopuolani (1778–1823) was his sacred wife, the one through whom the kingship passed. But Kaahumanu (1772–1832) was his favorite wife, whom he likened to a lehua blossom. He said: "She rides the waves like a bird; she knows the heartbeat of the people."

Kamehameha I proved as wise in peace as he was ferocious in war. His subjects said of him, "He is our Father. He is the taro of the land." He was also known as Kamehameha the Great.

Upon his death in 1819, his son Liholiho (1796–1824) succeeded him as Kamehameha II (r. 1819–1824), with Queen Kaahumanu reigning as co-regent. Kaahumanu invited the young king to dine with her publicly, thus violating the law against men and women eating together. Her motive may have been to improve the status of women or to break the power of the priests. Kamehameha II hesitated for days before accepting. When the people saw that divine retribution did not fall upon the pair, they rose up throughout Hawaii, destroyed their temples, and overnight became a people without a god and without the structure of religious law that had governed them for centuries (see p. 151).

Missionaries & Whalers

Into this vacuum, the first party of Christian missionaries from New England unsuspectingly and fortuitously sailed. They had come at the request of a group of Hawaiian students studying in New England at that time. Prominent among them was Henry Opukahaia (1792–1818), a Hawaiian Christian convert and author who had wanted to accompany the mission party back to his homeland, but died beforehand. Opukahaia's autobiography, *Memoir*, was a best seller of that time.

The band of 14 men and women, headed by dedicated evangelist Hiram Bingham (1789–1869) of Bennington, Vermont, arrived in 1820 to "bring the heathens to the mansions of eternal blessedness." When Kamehameha II saw that the men had brought wives and families, he welcomed them and gave them permission to preach and build their churches. Foreigners in Hawaii at that time were mostly shrewd sandalwood traders, sailors, whalers, and rank opportunists.

The first whaling ship, the *Balena*, out of New Bedford, Massachusetts, had arrived the year before. Word of Hawaii's pleasurable ports quickly spread among the Yankee captains working the newly discovered whaling grounds off the coast of Japan. Thousands of men, at sea for years at a time, were soon carousing in the streets of Honolulu and Lahaina. They said there was "no god west of the Horn," and behaved accordingly. Honolulu was considered a hellhole of grog shops, gambling dens, and houses of ill repute. Inevitably, their value system, which consisted of the pursuit of demon rum and willing women, clashed with the beliefs of the missionaries. The battles are legendary.

The first serious riot erupted in 1825 in Lahaina on Maui, when the men of the British whaler *Daniel* learned that the missionaries had succeeded in influencing Governor Hoapili of Maui to prohibit women from visiting the ships. Another English whaler actually fired its cannon at a missionary home. In response, cannon were mounted along the Lahaina waterfront, trained seaward.

Scrimshaw

Between whales, life aboard a whaler was boring. To pass the time, whalemen took to carving, etching, and whittling the bones, teeth, and baleen of their prey. In the process, they created what many regard as the only nonaboriginal American folk art—scrimshaw.

Predictably, the most common subjects the sailors chose were women and the sea. It is estimated that half the pieces were pornographic and were later destroyed. In contrast, more noble themes, such as religion and patriotism, were other favorites. Often the men made practical items such as nautical gear, belt buckles, and combs. For sweethearts back home they crafted hairpins, clothespins, pie crimpers, and corset stays.

When the Endangered Species Act of 1973 put whale ivory off-limits, scrimshanders turned to fossilized walrus, wooly mammoth bone, and plastic imitations.

Before this, King Kamehameha II had left on a state visit to England, where both he and the beautiful young Queen Kamamalu (1802–1824) died of measles. He was succeeded by his younger brother, Kamehameha III (r. 1824–1854), who took the helm of a land-rich and cash-poor kingdom. On every front, his people were confronting vast changes. They were also dying at an unprecedented rate. In an attempt to modernize his government and help the common people, and also to raise revenues, he established a legislature consisting of an upper house of royalty and a lower house of representatives.

A bronze-and-gilded statue of King Kamehameha the Great stands in downtown Honolulu.

In 1848, he instituted the Great Mahele, releasing millions of acres of land for sale for the first time. Before he died, he designated a nephew to rule as Kamehameha IV (r. 1854–1863). He and his wife Queen Emma (1836–1885) were known for their great works of charity, including the establishment of the Queen's Medical Center. Their only child, Prince Albert, died at the age of four. The king's older brother, Lot, a bachelor, inherited the throne and was the last of the Kamehameha dynasty (r. 1863–1872).

The missionaries have been pilloried by casual historians, most notably by author James Michener (1907–1997) in his epic novel *Hawaii.* Yet they did establish schools; transliterate the Hawaiian language, assigning it the 12-letter alphabet still in use; import a printing press; publish the first books and newspaper in the Hawaiian language; and offer a religion whose ideal of brotherly love was completely consistent with the Hawaiians' basic philosophy of aloha (see pp. 16–17).

It has been said that the missionaries came to do good and did very well, but that is only partly true. Most of the missionaries did indeed work tirelessly as doctors, ministers, and teachers. Usually it was their children who rose to positions of power and influence, and eventually overthrew the monarchy, establishing themselves as a ruling oligarchy.

Rise of American Business

The Great Mahele was intended to help commoners own their own land. Instead, huge tracts ended up going to foreigners, primarily Americans. These entrepreneurs, many of them descended from missionary families, set up the vast sugar plantations that influenced every facet of life in Hawaii for the next century.

Sugarcane, *ko*, was brought to the islands by the early Polynesians, who planted it for its sweet taste and its use as a natural stimulant. The first Hawaiian sugar to be commercially processed was extracted by a Chinese immigrant on the island of Lanai. After making enough money to retire comfortably in China, he closed down and left. A few years later an English agriculturist started raising cane in Manoa Valley, Oahu. In 1826, his fields were sold to rum distillers. The first successful plantation was established in 1835 at Koloa, Kauai (see p. 188), and by 1900, sugar was the primary industry of the islands.

Pineapple, Hawaii's other plantation crop, was probably brought by Polynesian settlers from Tahiti. The first record of it is an 1813 entry in the diary of Don Francisco de Paula y Marin (1774–1837), a Spanish horticulturist and adviser to King Kamehameha I: "This day, I planted pine-apples [*sic*] and an orange tree." But the name Dole eventually became synonymous with pineapple. James Dole (1877–1958), fresh from Harvard, arrived in 1898. Three years later, he sowed 12 acres with 75,000 pineapples at Wahiawa, Oahu. His first crop, harvested by family and friends, produced 1,893 cans of pineapple chunks.

The Baldwin Home, Lahaina, Maui, shows how frugally the first Yankee missionaries lived when they came to Hawaii.

Labor was a problem for the fledgling plantations. The Hawaiians, accustomed to self-sufficiency and independence, had no interest in the long hours, harsh working conditions, and low pay of plantation work. Besides, there were few men left. Ninety percent of native Hawaiians died of newly introduced diseases. King Kamehameha IV stated in 1855: "The decrease of our population is a subject in comparison with which all others sink into insignificance." The shortage of labor led to an era of population politics that set the stage for Hawaii's multiracial society.

Immigration

The first indentured workers came from China in 1852. They had five-year contracts offering free passage, food, clothing, housing, and wages of three dollars a month. By the time the Chinese government prohibited immigration to Hawaii in 1881, due to reports of abuse, Hawaii had a population of 18,000 Chinese.

> **"The decrease of our population is a subject in comparison with which all others sink into insignificance."**
>
> —KING KAMEHAMEHA IV, *1855*

To further augment the labor force, planters next turned to Portugal. Between 1878 and 1887, 17 ships brought 12,000 Portuguese workers and families from Madeira and the Azores. The Portuguese became the *luna* (foremen) of the plantations. Until recently, they were not grouped with Caucasians in census data, but enjoyed their own category; they were also more accepted into the local culture than other Caucasians. Workers in smaller numbers were recruited from Scandinavia, Germany, Russia, and Puerto Rico.

Walter Murray Gibson (1822–1888), an eccentric American immigrant and a politician so influential he was known as the Minister of Everything, addressed the Chamber of Commerce of Hawaii in 1872: "You have considered the races that are desirable, not only to supply your needs of labor, but to furnish an increase of population that will assimilate with the Hawaiian.... A moderate portion of the Japanese, of the agricultural class, will not conflict with the view that I present, and if they bring their women with them, and settle permanently in the country, they may be counted upon as likely to become desirable Hawaiian subjects."

King David Kalakaua (1836–1891; see p. 34) went to Japan to negotiate labor agreements. Japanese workers were offered three-year contracts providing for free steerage passage, a food allowance, lodging, medical care, fuel, no taxes, rice at no more than five cents a pound, and wages of nine dollars a month for men and six dollars for women. By 1900, they were, at 40 percent of the population, the largest ethnic group in the islands.

Seeking cheap labor, the plantation owners in 1906 turned to the Philippines. The flow of labor was initially two-way, with many workers returning home; nowadays, however, few go back. In the 1970s, Filipinos were the largest group immigrating to Hawaii.

Later immigrants have come from Korea, Southeast Asia, and other Pacific islands. In all, approximately 385,000 workers from around the world were brought to Hawaii to feed the plantations. They became the rainbow of races visitors find so intriguing today.

The Passing of a Kingdom

As King Kamehameha V lay dying in 1872, he begged his childhood sweetheart, Princess Bernice Pauahi Bishop (1831–1884), great-granddaughter of Kamehameha I, to accept the throne. When she declined, he left the question of succession to the legislature, as provided by the Hawaiian constitution. They elected Prince William

Lunalilo (1835–1874), a grandnephew of Kamehameha I. Known as the People's King, he reigned for a little more than a year.

Upon Lunalilo's death of a lung disease, the legislature voted for High Chief David Kalakaua to succeed him. The foreigners, who were very influential by this time, supported the election of the man they considered a scholar and gentleman. His wife, High Chiefess Kapiolani (1834–1899), was of the royal family of Kauai.

King Kalakaua's reign (1874–1891) was marked with triumph and turmoil. He breathed new life into the dispirited Hawaiians by reviving their culture, restoring the hula to a place of prominence, and writing down many ancient chants for posterity. Hoping to secure respect in international circles for his small nation, he modeled his court on the courts of Europe. He built the beautiful Iolani Palace (see pp. 59–63), became the first reigning monarch of any country to circumnavigate the globe, and was the first Hawaiian monarch to visit Washington, D.C. He negotiated the Reciprocity Treaty with the United States, which allowed Hawaiian sugar to enter that country duty-free. In return, he gave the U.S. rights to use Pearl Harbor as a military base. In doing this, the king known as the Merrie Monarch sealed Hawaii's fate, marrying the lovely little Polynesian kingdom to the mighty Uncle Sam.

In 1887, a group of Caucasians, grown prosperous on their sugar, led an armed revolt and forced the king to accept what became known as the Bayonet Constitution, which severely constricted his powers. Its key provision required that voters have an annual income of at least $600 a year or ownership of at least $3,000 in property. Voters who qualified by property did not need to be citizens. Most native Hawaiians, who had formed the majority of the electorate, were effectively eliminated. By allowing foreigners to vote, political power shifted to the Caucasian minority. Four years later, the king, in poor health, journeyed to San Francisco to seek medical help, and died there.

He named his sister, Princess Lydia Kamakaeha Liliuokalani (1839–1917), to succeed him. A strong, brilliant woman with a deep love for her people, Queen Liliuokalani was destined to be the last Hawaiian monarch. Seven months after her ascension to the throne, her American husband, John Owen Dominis (1851–1887), died, leaving her alone to face the monumental task of holding her country together.

The insurgents, who called themselves the Committee of Safety, marched into Iolani Palace and demanded the queen's abdication.

To redress the injustices of the Bayonet Constitution and limit voting privileges to citizens, both native Hawaiians and naturalized foreigners, the queen announced she would promulgate a new constitution. This was used as an excuse by antiroyalist foreigners, primarily American, to launch a revolt. John B. Stevens, the U.S. minister in Hawaii, ordered the landing of Marines from the U.S.S. *Boston*, anchored in Honolulu Harbor on January 17, 1893. The insurgents, who called themselves the Committee of Safety, marched into Iolani Palace and demanded the queen's abdication.

To avoid bloodshed, Liliuokalani complied, saying: "I yield my authority until such time as the Government of the United States shall, upon the facts being presented to it, undo the action of its representatives and reinstate me in the authority which I claim as the constitutional sovereign of the Hawaiian Islands."

Immigrant plantation workers survey a bountiful pineapple harvest.

A "Miserable Business"

A provisional government was imposed, headed by Sanford Dole (1844–1926). President Grover Cleveland sent an investigator, James Blount, to Honolulu. He immediately ordered American flags removed from public buildings and the withdrawal of the Marines. President Cleveland ordered the restoration of the monarchy, but the revolutionaries defied him. They set up what they called the Republic of Hawaii, continuing the voting injustices and excluding Asians, even if born in Hawaii, from voting.

The next U.S President, William McKinley, signed papers annexing Hawaii in 1898, and appointing Sanford Dole as the first territorial governor.

Queen Liliuokalani, after a period of imprisonment in her palace, was permitted to retire to her home, Washington Place (see p. 64), where she continued to work for the welfare of her people until her death in 1917.

In his memoirs, President Cleveland wrote: "Hawaii is ours. As I look back upon the first steps in this miserable business and as I contemplate the means used to complete the outrage, I am ashamed of the whole affair."

The Territory of Hawaii

A year after Hawaii was incorporated as a territory of the U.S. under the Organic Act of 1900, the Moana Hotel opened in Waikiki. In 1903, James Dole harvested his first pineapple crop at Wahiawa on Oahu, and three years later he opened a cannery in Honolulu. By 1908, sugar exports—at the root of the revolution—doubled, reaching 538,785 tons, even though contract labor ended under the U.S. labor laws.

Japanese laborers, protesting against poor wages and working conditions, initiated the first of Hawaii's major, and often bloody, labor strikes in 1909.

The first interisland air flight took off for Molokai from Oahu in 1918 and returned safely. The first commercial interisland flight to Maui from Oahu in 1920 took an hour and a half and cost 150 dollars.

Under the American umbrella, Hawaii contributed 9,800 men to World War I and suffered 102 fatalities.

The islands became more prosperous with the expansion of the plantations and the rise of tourism. The Depression was barely felt in Honolulu, as the major business corporations enjoyed unprecedented power and profits.

In 1920, the population of Hawaii was 256,000 people; almost half lived on Oahu.

War Comes to Hawaii

"WAR!" screamed the headlines of the *Honolulu Star Bulletin,* in an extra edition. "OAHU BOMBED BY JAPANESE PLANES. Wave after wave of bombers streamed through the clouded morning sky from the southwest and flung their missiles on a city resting in peaceful Sabbath calm."

At first, most people, hearing the aerial artillery, thought the American military was on practice maneuvers. They could not believe that anyone would attack

December 7, 1941: Pearl Harbor is under attack, propelling America into the war in the Pacific.

Hawaii—until the enemy aircraft flew low over Honolulu and the red emblem of the rising sun could be seen on the wingtips.

The attack came in four waves, beginning at 7:55 in the morning. Three hundred sixty Japanese aircraft, launched from carriers, devastated the U.S. Pacific Fleet anchored in Pearl Harbor and left behind 2,323 American dead, including civilian casualties. Japanese submarines sank cargo and passenger vessels and shelled Hilo, Nawiliwili, and Kahului harbors.

The next day, in an address before Congress that was broadcast across the United States, President Franklin D. Roosevelt declared war on the empire of Japan, calling December 7, 1941, "a date which will live in infamy."

The territory of Hawaii was placed under martial law for the duration of the war. Military censorship was imposed on all outgoing messages, and a total blackout for Oahu was ordered; barbed wire was rolled out along the beaches in case of invasion.

Young Japanese Americans who naively volunteered their services to their country—thousands already belonged to the Hawaii Territorial Guard—were rejected by the military. On the American mainland, Japanese Americans were rounded up and confined to desert internment camps. Although massive incarcerations were economically and physically impossible in Hawaii, the Japanese Americans lived under a constant cloud of official suspicion.

When the young *nisei* (second-generation Japanese Americans) were finally admitted to military service, they were assigned to special combat units, the Army's 100th Infantry Battalion, which expanded to become the 442nd Regimental Combat Team. Nearly 3,000 Japanese Americans were inducted in a single day on the grounds of Iolani Palace in Honolulu. They served with uncommon valor, even while the constitutional rights of their families were abrogated at home. They were the most highly decorated units of their size in American military history, and their story is chronicled in the book *I Can Never Forget* by Thelma Chang.

When the nisei soldiers came home, they took advantage of the education benefits provided by the G.I. Bill of Rights. They maintained their close ties and became a formidable force in every aspect of island life. They virtually seized control of the Democratic Party and, with the support of now-powerful labor unions, instituted a political revolution that weakened the power of the Caucasian establishment. With statehood, two of their own went to Congress: Masayuki "Spark" Matsunaga as representative and Daniel K. Inouye as senator.

America's Sweetheart Resort

Two things happened in the 1950s that made Hawaii what it is today—America's sweetheart resort. The first, the start of jet travel, put the islands four and a half hours from the U.S. West Coast, and the second was statehood.

Wartime Waikiki

After December 7, 1941, darkness and martial law ruled the islands. Required blackouts after sunset meant that darkness prevailed over an area that once shone with lights and laughter. World War II forever changed a way of life.

Waikiki became a military zone. Barbed wire served as fences along the beach, wealthy residents moved into hotels, and luxury resorts became headquarters for military brass. Even a low-ranking sailor could finally afford the elegant hotels, as 40-dollar suites went for 25 cents a night.

Tourism as a business had actually begun in the 1920s, when most passengers arrived aboard Matson luxury liners. Air travel began in 1936, when Pan Am's *China Clipper* seaplane flew from San Francisco to Honolulu in a time of 21 hours and 33 minutes. Passengers dined on consommé and chicken fricassee served on white linen with wine and silver. After dessert, they retired to their staterooms, and the steward shined their shoes and pressed their clothes while they slept. They paid $720 for their round-trip ticket—at a time when a top executive's salary was $5,000 a year.

Statehood & Sovereignty

For 50 years, beginning with the overthrow of the monarchy, various statehood petitions were placed before Congress. All were rejected due to stiff opposition from Dixie legislators (Hawaii had a majority nonwhite population). Finally, after a vote for statehood was held in Hawaii, and Congress passed the Hawaii State Bill, President Dwight Eisenhower added another star to the American flag on August 21, 1959.

Statehood triggered an immediate building boom as tourists began pouring into Waikiki. The Boeing 747, which began service in 1969, could economically carry hundreds of passengers, putting a Hawaii vacation-of-a-lifetime within grasp of the average person. The following year, two million tourists arrived; a decade later the numbers doubled. In the 1980s, tourism's economic success obscured all else. Everyone was buying and building. The Japanese invested more than $15 billion in a decade, acquiring hotels, resorts, and high-end homes.

It wasn't all good news, especially for the locals. At the opening of a luxury Maui resort, when the dignitaries were introduced, they were a Japanese owner, Canadian developer, Irish general manager, and Austrian chef. Banquet wait help were primarily tanned, surf-blissed Californians. Local people found themselves no longer able to afford homes, even though the husband and wife might be working two or three jobs. Favorite beaches became crowded with tourists.

> **The Boeing 747, which began service in 1969, could economically carry hundreds of passengers, putting a Hawaii vacation-of-a-lifetime within grasp of the average person.**

The whole boom fizzled in the 1990s as tourism fell during the Gulf War. Asia's financial crisis in the late 1990s added to Hawaii's woes, plunging the economy into a recession from which it is just recovering.

Complicating the picture was—and is—Hawaii's messy land ownership situation. Only slightly more than 50 percent of the land on inhabited islands is privately owned. Forty landlords own 75 percent of this. The largest private landowner is Kamehameha Schools estate, formerly known as Bishop Estate. Princess Bernice Pauahi Bishop (see pp. 33–34) left the vast lands of the Kamehameha family for the education of Hawaiian children; worth approximately $10 billion, it is one of the wealthiest foundations in the United States. Its five trustees, who earned close to $1 million each annually, were, in the late 1990s, embroiled in a storm of controversy and scandal that none survived.

Native Hawaiians had begun to raise their voices, demanding reparation for the loss of their nation, as well as some form of sovereignty for the Hawaiian people. John Waihee, the state's first governor of Hawaiian ancestry, wrote in the *Honolulu Advertiser:* "The overthrow of the Hawaiian monarchy on January 17, 1893, was a

Crowds gather for a rock concert at the Maui Arts and Cultural Center, Kahului, Maui.

hostile act against a native people who were organized as a sovereign nation and recognized by the United States of America. It was an international act of aggression conducted, if not with the tacit agreement of the U.S. government, then at least with the United States turning to look the other way." A lot of steam went out of the separatist movement following the September 11 attacks on the United States, when most people in Hawaii felt solidarity with their fellow Americans and the American flag was flown over Iolani Palace.

Some people seek a complete break with the United States, but Ka Lahui Hawaii, the most vocal of the sovereignty groups, proposes "nation within a nation" status, similar to that enjoyed by Native Americans on the mainland. Polls show that the majority of people in Hawaii support greater efforts toward self-determination, while hoping that when it comes, there will still be a place for them beneath the rainbow. ■

Arts & Culture

The Polynesian arts enjoyed their greatest flowering in Hawaii. With the discovery of the islands by the outside world, Hawaii became a cultural crossroads of East and West. Today, it's easier to find good art in places like Maui than it is to find chilled coconut milk. And while no visitor seeks out Hawaii for its art, it is there to be found in a great abundance of beauty and truth.

A student maestro conducts her classmates in a Lei Day concert at Kahala Elementary School, Oahu.

Hawaiian Music

Music was sacred. It celebrated the beauty and bounty of the islands, recorded genealogy, and recounted the deeds of kings and gods. It was woven into the fabric of life. Musical expression in the early Hawaiian Islands was through the chant, the *mele hula* (chanted in the rhythms of the dance) and *mele oli* (free-flowing chant). Instruments were primarily percussion, and included gourd drums; the sharkskin-covered, carved hula drum; gourd rattles; and the conch-shell horn. Various bamboo instruments developed, such as the haunting nose flute, which is played by blowing down one end through the nostril and manipulating sound holes with the fingers.

In 1820, when Yankee missionaries aboard the brig *Thaddeus* arrived in Hawaii, they brought not only their faith, but their music. Mission journals note how pleased the

Hawaiian people seemed with the new music and how they came by the hundreds to hear the hymns. The rising and descending scales were completely different from the Hawaiians' traditional system of tones and pitches, and initially caused difficulty. The resourceful Reverend Hiram Bingham established an evening singing school, where his eager pupils not only practiced Western musical scales, but also learned the Bible by chanting its verses in their traditional *mele* rhythms. It was the birth of modern Hawaiian music, a harmony of New England hymns infused with the beautiful poetic form and ancient rhythms of Hawaii.

The singing schools spread throughout the islands and Hawaiians were quickly composing their own songs in the new genre. The first hymnal, *Na Himeni Hawaii: He Me Ori Ia Iehova, Ke Akua Mau (Hawaiian Hymns and Songs to Jehovah, the Eternal God)*, was published in 1823 and contained 47 songs, including the classic "Iesu Me Ka Kanaka Waiwai" (Jesus and the Rich Man).

Missionary Lorenzo Lyons of Imiola Church, Waimea, Big Island, became the dominant influence in the emerging music when he introduced Gospel songs in the 1830s. These melodies were more compatible with native music, and the sincere, unpretentious sentiments more akin to their own notions of man's relationship to a God of bounty. Lyons was a gifted composer whose "Hawaii Aloha" is one of the most beloved Hawaiian songs. The other is "Aloha Oe," composed by Queen Liliuokalani.

Foreigners continued to influence music. Cowboys of Spanish and Mexican heritage (see p. 163) introduced the guitar, and Hawaiians made it their own with a unique styling called *ki hoalu* (slack key). This and the steel guitar replaced early percussion instruments. Plantation laborers from Portugal introduced the viola, a fiddle, and their *branguiha,* which evolved into Hawaii's famous ukulele.

In the 1930s and '40s, Hollywood discovered Hawaii, and a new song form erupted. Called *hapa-haole,* it was fun, witty, and naughty, largely reflecting an outsider's impression of the culture. "Lovely Hula Hands" and "The Cockeyed Mayor of Kaunakakai" are two classics that emerged from the period. Falsetto, a popular form of singing in the islands, has uncertain origins, possibly in Mexican song stylings or German yodeling.

Hawaiian music is enjoying its greatest popularity in decades with a whole new generation of gifted composers and performers taking their music to the international stage. Among the musicians who called world attention to Hawaiian music and whose work lives after them, played daily on the airwaves of the islands, are Gabby Pahinui and Israel Kamakawiwo'ole.

Hawaii enjoys many music forms. Honolulu supports a symphony orchestra. There are opera and ballet seasons, and niches for jazz and chamber music. Country music has never really caught on, but a few places frequented by military personnel feature it. Top rock and pop stars drop in on their way to bigger gigs, and Broadway road musicals, Chinese opera, Indonesian gamelan, and Irish groups come to town.

> **The painters who came to the islands during the period of discovery by the Western world rendered fascinating glimpses of old Hawaii.**

Arts & Crafts

The early Hawaiians were skilled artists who lived in an orderly society that allowed and encouraged the meditation and reflection necessary for art. They used the limited materials in their environment with skill and sensitivity, and at the core of all they produced—including their orally transmitted literature (see pp. 45–46)—was their deep sense of spirituality.

A woodcarver held the status of priest: Because he sculpted sacred images, he was expected to know the prayers and rituals surrounding the deity as well as the properties of each of the fine native hardwoods. Unlike other Polynesian woodwork, Hawaiian objects were not heavily carved, but relied on the grain, polish, and idiosyncrasies of an individual piece of wood for beauty. Ancient artisans carving with stone adzes created simple household goods, intimidating temple images, powerful hula drums, sleek outrigger canoes, and fine decorative pieces. Contemporary sculpted work in native woods such as koa *(Acacia koa),* milo *(Thespesia populnea),* and kou *(Cordia subcordata)* can be found in galleries today.

Featherwork was also a sacred art. Brilliant scarlet, yellow, and black feathers of native birds were woven into cloaks, capes, helmets, leis, and *kahili* (the feather standards of royalty). Sometimes they even formed images of gods. In his journal on January 21, 1778, Capt. James King, who took part in Cook's historic voyage (see pp. 28–29), wrote of "a particular sort of cloak and cap, which, even in countries where dress is more particularly attended to, might be reckoned elegant. . . . Feathers are so closely fixed that the surface might be compared to the thickest and richest velvet, which they resemble, both as to the feel and the glossy appearance." People who have inherited feather capes wear them on ceremonial occasions. Feather leis are still being made, now employing a range of imported feathers.

Kapa, or tapa (cloth made from tree bark), was a women's art; the *wauke* (paper mulberry) tree yielded the best fiber. Often fragrant flowers and herbs were pounded into the material for a permanent perfume, and the sheet was then painted or stamped in decorative designs using natural dyes. Hawaiian kapa, which had the suppleness of finely woven material, was used for clothing and bed linen. Most kapa is now imported from Tonga and is almost universally decorated in bold, earth-toned, geometric patterns.

The leaves of the *hala* tree (pandanus or screw pine) were woven into pillows, fans, sandals, toys, floor mats, and even canoe sails. The finest mats, called *makaloa,* were woven of a sedge called *ahuawa (Cyperus laevigatus).* The favored plant for making baskets and fish traps was *ieie (Freycinetia).* Many shops today carry *lauhala* hats and bags, sometimes lined in kapa.

Personal adornment took the form of jewelry made from shells, dog teeth, whale ivory, feathers, and flora (see p. 80). Both men and women tattooed their bodies.

The Hawaiian quilt, adapted from missionary needlework, has become its own art form. Families treasure these graphically strong quilts based on patterns from nature. After the overthrow of the monarchy, people made quilts after the Hawaiian flag was forbidden, and hung them as bed canopies so they could at least sleep under their beloved emblem.

Painting

The painters who came to the islands during the period of discovery by the Western world rendered fascinating glimpses of old Hawaii. John Webber, the official artist with Capt. James Cook, executed the first paintings of the Hawaiian Islands and its inhabitants after he went ashore with Cook on January 21, 1778, at Waimea, Kauai. Credit for the first recorded view of Hawaii goes to the ship's surgeon, William Ellis, a gifted amateur who sketched the shoreline of Kauai from the deck of the ship. But it is Webber's body of work, his paintings of temples, habitations, and landscapes,

Iolani Luahine

Iolani Luahine (1915–1978) was a premier hula artist of the 20th century. Her dances have been described as "mystic, spiritual, one with nature." Ted Shawn, a modern-dance pioneer, described Luahine as "an artist of world-class stature."

Born Harriet Lanihau Makekau in Napoopoo on the Big Island, Luahine's contributions to hula are significant, considering that she came of age at a time when missionary attitudes suppressed the dance. Nevertheless, she learned the ways of hula starting at the age of four, under the guidance of her aunt, Keahi Luahine.

Some of Luahine's most memorable dances have been performed near Hawaii's natural wonders, including Kilauea Crater on the Big Island. Her interpretation of the hula speaks to a powerful connection with nature, and she was also known for her wit, free spirit, and sense of humor.

A respected *kumu* (teacher) and performer of ancient Hawaiian hula and chant, she was invited to perform at the National Folk Festival in Washington, D.C., served as a longtime curator of the Hulihee Palace in Kailua-Kona, and advised the islands' annual Merrie Monarch Festival in Hilo.

Her legacy lives on in the kumu hula who studied with her and passed her teachings down to the next generation.

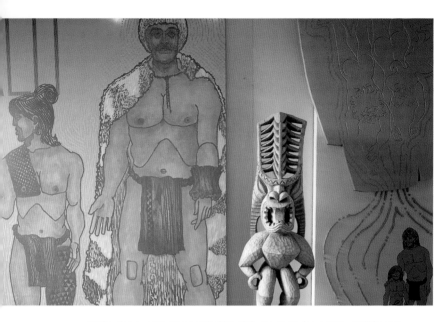

Contemporary artists interpret traditional themes in art shows at Hawaii Volcanoes National Park on the Big Island.

and his portraits of people, that provides the record, sometimes in precise detail, of life in Hawaii at the moment of contact with the outside world.

In the years following Cook's arrival, more British, American, Russian, and French ships called in Hawaii. Many had artists on board to accurately record the bays, shorelines, and landmarks and to satisfy the curiosity of their patrons and countrymen at home regarding these splendid "new" islands.

Louis Choris, artist aboard the Russian brig *Rurick,* did a portrait of Kamehameha I in 1816, three years before the king's death. It hangs in the Honolulu Museum of Art (see pp. 75–78). The great conqueror looks grandfatherly and is already wearing Western clothes, most notably a bright red vest.

English artist Robert Dampier, who arrived in 1825, is known for his portraits of Hawaiian royalty. His portraits of a young Kamehameha III, and his beloved sister Princess Nahienaena, in their red-and-yellow feather cloaks, are hauntingly beautiful and hang now at the Honolulu Museum of Art.

The missionaries and whalers kept diaries and letters, but left few visual records. Edward Bailey (see p. 133) was the exception. Residing at Wailuku, Maui, he didn't begin to paint until 1865, about 28 years after he came to the islands. His landscapes are mostly of Iao Valley, close to his home.

Hawaiian artist Joseph Nawahi left behind only six known paintings, apparently too busy to pursue his art—he served in the legislature of Hawaii from 1872 to 1892, founded a newspaper, and worked vigorously against annexation by the United States.

In the late 19th century, the first distinctive school of Hawaii painting evolved. Known as the Volcano School, it is most widely recognized in the almost fantastic, dramatically lit interpretations of the Big Island volcanoes by Paris-born artist Jules Tavernier.

Contemporary Art

By the time the 20th century dawned, Hawaii was no longer an isolated paradise, but a multicultural corner of America in touch with contemporary art trends. Reflecting the vast changes and the artistic climate of the times, a modernist school developed, which included locally born artists and foreign painters. Prominent among this group were Juliette May Fraser, Isami Doi, Madge Tennent, Reuben Tam, Mabel Alvarez, Lloyd Sexton, Keichi Kimura, Juanita Vitousek, Arman T. Manookian, Hon Chew Hee, and John Young.

The Honolulu Museum of Art and the Bishop Museum (see pp. 72–73) have fine examples of Hawaii's distinctive genres of painting. David W. Forbes, an expert in the field, has written a lavishly illustrated book on the subject, *Encounters with Paradise,* published by the Honolulu Museum of Art.

Literature & Language

The early Hawaiians produced a vast body of literature, passed on orally from generation to generation. Epic in scope, poetic in expression, and vibrant with drama, it explored the great themes of life: passion, sexuality, romantic love, birth, death, ambition, jealousy, the forces of nature, love of home, and cataclysmic battles between good and evil. It is peopled with gods, goddesses, great heroes, and villains. If it were better known, it would take its place beside the Homeric epics, the Norse sagas, the adventures of Cuchulainn, and the Ramayana.

The favorite stories are of Maui, who fished up the islands from the ocean floor; Pele, the tempestuous goddess of volcanoes (see p. 174); and Kamapuaa, the earthy pig-god and lover of Pele, whose rootings created the valleys and springs.

Hawaiian poetry is characterized by vividness of visual image and depth of thought. A poet was called *haku mele,* a weaver of song, and held an honored position in royal courts. Irish poet Padraic Colum said: "The Hawaiian poet has anticipated effects that the cultivated poets of our tradition have been striving for; he is, for instance, more esoteric than Stéphane Mallarmé and more imaginistic than Amy Lowell."

> A whole generation . . . had been forbidden to speak [Hawaiian] . . . Today, Hawaiian is making a spirited comeback.

The Hawaiian language is Austronesian in classification and similar to other languages of Polynesia. It was rendered into written form by the American missionaries, who based their work on that done by French Catholic priests in Tahiti, employing Latin phonetics. The softness of the language comes in its repetition, and from the fact that there are only seven consonants (h, k, l, m, n, p, w).

In modern times, the Hawaiian language fell into disuse. A whole generation, now elderly, had been forbidden to speak it, even though their parents were fluent; it was thought to be a handicap, perhaps even a stigma, in an American society. Today, Hawaiian is making a spirited comeback. Some schools offer language-immersion programs beginning at the preschool level, where parents are required to study with children. It is proving to be highly successful not only in forming a new generation of native speakers, but also in raising Hawaiian academic performance levels in all fields.

Hawaiian and English are the official languages of the state of Hawaii. The unofficial language is pidgin, academically called Hawaiian English Dialect, which is a blend of

Local Lingo

"Eh, I wen da kine place, and the food o dea junk, man." (I went to you-know-where and the food over there was lousy.)

Visitors are often perplexed when they hear locals speaking "la dat" (like that). Pidgin represents a history starting in the early 1800s as Chinese immigrants gathered in Hawaii to work the plantations. Later immigrants added to the mix. Common words or phrases include:

Da kine (da KINE): a catchall word, describing everything, everyone, everywhere

Oh da cute (oh da CU-U-U-TE): as in "That dog is very cute"

Go stay go: go, keep moving

No ack: don't act up; don't be so dramatic

Mo' bettah: better than better, as in "My shoes mo' bettah den yours"

No shame: not embarrassed; don't be shy

Talk story: talk awhile; let's share stories

Stink eye: a hostile stare, as in "Eh, da guy giving you stink eye"

Ono (OH no): Delicious; refers to food

K' den (KAY-den): OK, then; agreed

Moi moi (MOY MOY, usually said like a melody): sleep

Ja like: Just like, as in "My kah [car] ja like one junk"

languages that evolved on the plantations. A child, upon waking from a nap, may announce, *"All pau ne-ne,"* saying in English, Hawaiian, and Japanese, "I'm finished sleeping." Once scorned by academia, pidgin is finding its way into contemporary literature of the islands, most successfully through the work of novelist Lois-Ann Yamanaka.

Over the years, the lure of the Pacific drew a cast of literary lions to Hawaii. In *Roughing It,* Mark Twain (1835–1910) described Kilauea Volcano: "It looked like a colossal railroad map of the State of Massachusetts done in chain lightning on a midnight sky. Imagine it—imagine a coal-black sky slivered into a tangled network of angry fire!"

Watching a group of people with leprosy leaving for exile on Molokai, Robert Louis Stevenson (1850–1894) wrote of a young girl in *The Eight Islands.* "The lepers came singly and unattended; the elder first; the girl a little after, tricked out in a red dress and with a fine red feather in her hat. In this bravery, it was the most affecting to see her move apart on the rocks and crouch in her accustomed attitude. But this time I had seen her face; it was scarce horribly affected, but had a haunting look of an unfinished wooden doll, at once expressionless and disproportioned."

Maxine Hong Kingston (1940–) wrote in her best-seller *China Man:* "Chinese take a bit of sugar to remind them in times of bitter struggle of the sweetness of life, and Hawaiians take a few grains of salt on the tongue because it tastes like the sea, like the earth, like human sweat and tears."

Island Style

Lifestyles in the islands are as diverse as the people, but they share certain elements. Most homes are so married to their gardens that the boundaries between house and garden are blurred. Furniture spills onto the lanai (veranda), while palm trees sit potted in the living room.

The home of a *kamaaina* (one who is island born or island rooted) is immediately identifiable, and it's hard to say how. It might be a grouping of seashells in the center of a table, old rattan furniture on the porch, shoji screens in the dining room, Hawaiian quilt pillows tossed on the sofa, a whiff of incense, a dried maile (Pacific vine) lei draped around a grandmother's portrait, or a rack of straw hats and a pile of shoes by the door.

Many of the new homes—concrete, air-conditioned manses—are the antithesis of island style, far removed from the grass houses of the Hawaiians, crafted from lava rock and tree limbs and thatched with long fragrant *pili* grass, set so unobtrusively on the beloved land as to have barely any impact.

Mission Houses Museum (see p. 66) in Honolulu represents the oldest surviving Western-style building in the islands. The original home is a prefabricated New England saltbox, shipped around the Horn. Rooms are cramped and airless.

With the rise of the great plantations, two kinds of homes emerged. One was the small worker's house with a corrugated tin roof. Colorful and sturdy, these old wood cottages are nestled in gardens all over Hawaii, most notably in Lanai City (see p. 230). Visitors can stay in faithfully restored, modernized editions at Waimea Plantation Cottages (see p. 201, p. 257) on Kauai. The other plantation homes were the spacious houses built for owners and managers. They tended to be Western style, built with local materials such as lava rock and native hardwoods. For the most part, these gracious homes remain sequestered on estates. On Kauai, the Wilcox family home at Kilohana Plantation (see pp. 186–187) has been converted to restaurants, shops, and a restored railroad that manages to maintain the integrity and grace of its 1930s era.

Not until the early 20th century did Hawaii develop its own distinct, recognizable architectural style. Pioneered by architect Charles W. Dickey (1871–1942), it is distinguished by the high roofline borrowed from the old Hawaiian thatched house, which

(continued on p. 52)

This Chinese temple stands at Hawaii's Plantation Village, a cultural theme park in Waipahu, Oahu.

The *kalua* pig, unearthed from the underground oven during a luau

Food

Sugar is the key ingredient in Hawaii's food, not in the traditional sense of adding a cup or two in a recipe, but by virtue of the fact that it was sugar that brought to the islands all the different immigrant groups with their pots and woks, their whisks and bamboo steamers. Living in such close proximity, in such isolation, it was natural that the food be shared.

The first colonists, the Polynesians, brought with them about 30 of their favorite plants, among them a dozen food plants. They also brought domestic animals—dogs, chickens, and pigs. Taro (*Colocasia esculenta*) was by far their most important crop, which they grew in a vast system of irrigated agricultural terraces. The spinach-tasting leaves were steamed, and the corm was baked in an underground oven. They also pounded the corm into that purple dietary

staple, poi. It is interesting to note that archaeologists excavating a site and coming upon a skeleton can tell immediately if it's a precontact site by the state of the bones— the early Hawaiians had perfect teeth, probably due to their healthy nonacidic diet.

With the arrival of whalers and traders, the Hawaiian farmers began to grow, at cooler elevations, potatoes, apples, onions, and other new crops for trade. In fact, Hawaii sent food to the forty-niners during the California gold rush (1849–1860). Parts of Maui, in particular, grew rich at this time, benefiting from the fertile soil and temperate climate (see p. 138).

As each new immigrant group added their specialties—Chinese *gao* (a New Year pudding with mochi flour and dates), Japanese sushi and teriyaki, Korean *mandoo* (savory dumplings) and *kook su* (cucumber salad), Portuguese sweet bread, and Filipino adobo (meat simmered in vinegar, garlic, and shoyu, or soy sauce)—a culinary tradition called simply "local food," or "ono grinds," emerged.

Saimin

Probably the most popular and one of the few truly local creations is saimin—a steaming noodle soup that is a remedy for everything from the flu to the blues. Some people claim it's a rube offspring of Chinese *wonton mein.* Others claim a distinguished Japanese lineage, a ramen gone native.

The man everyone called Mistah Saimin, Shiro Matsuo of Shiro's Hula Hula Drive In and Saimin Haven in Pearl City, Oahu, once said, "It's actually a unique Hawaii concoction created by the first generation of sugar plantation cooks."

Often the noodle soup was a family's first step into entrepreneurship. Matsuo explained: "They'd build a little saimin wagon. The wife would knead the noodle dough with a bamboo pole or pipe, then roll it out with a knife and ruler into strips about 12 inches long. She'd cook the saimin over a hibachi (charcoal brazier). The husband would push the little wagon to a likely place and set up shop for the day."

Saimin basics are a soup base of seaweed, dried shrimp, Japanese mushrooms, and bonito shavings. The noodles have more egg than Asian noodles. Extras include chopped green onion, sliced *kamaboko* (pink and white pinwheel fish cake), and strips of either Chinese *char siu* pork or Spam. Often there will be wonton dumplings, Chinese cabbage, or bean sprouts. Actually, almost anything can, and does, go in. Shiro's serves a thousand bowls a day in 60 varieties at bargain prices.

The pièce de résistance of local food is the "plate lunch," which always consists of two scoops of white rice, a scoop of macaroni salad, and an entree of anything, but usually teriyaki meat, curry stew, *tonkatsu* (breaded, fried pork), or fried fish.

EXPERIENCE: Sampling Fresh Seafood

Fresh seafood has been at the heart of Hawaiian cuisine since ancient times. Here are a few of the author's favorite spots that feature seafood to please the palate—from casual to upscale.

Chef Mavro
(1969 S. King St., Honolulu, Oahu
tel 808/944-4714)

Hualalai Grille
(Four Seasons Resort Hualalai,
Kaupulehu, Hawaii
tel 808/325-8525)

Koloa Fish Market
(5482 Koloa Rd., Koloa, Kauai
tel 808/742-6199)

Lahaina Grill
(127 Lahainaluna Rd., Lahaina, Maui
tel 808/667-5117 or 800/360-2606)

Nico's at Pier 38
(1133 N. Nimitz Hwy., Honolulu, Oahu
tel 808/540-1377)

The Seaside Restaurant
(1790 Kalanianaole Ave.,
Hilo, Hawaii
tel 808/935-8825)

Tidepools Restaurant
(Grand Hyatt Kauai Resort & Spa,
1571 Poipu Rd., Koloa, Kauai
tel 808/742-1234)

**Sansei Seafood Restaurant
& Sushi Bar**
(Kapalua Resort, 600 Office Rd., Lahaina,
Maui
tel 808/669-6286,
Kihei Town Center, 1881 S. Kihei Rd.,
Kihei, Maui, tel 808/879-0004)

EXPERIENCE: Feasting Hawaiian Style

When friends and family gather to share an event such as a baby's first birthday, a wedding, a homecoming, or a just-for-fun festivity, they often celebrate with a luau. Some celebrants sing, dance, or play their ukuleles while other guests dine, dance, and enjoy a festive evening. Early Hawaiians called the feast *paina*.

Paina today is also found at a contemporary luau, where visitors are exposed to such delicacies as *lomilomi* salmon (hand massaged raw salmon), *laulau* (steamed meats wrapped in banana or ti leaves), *kalua* pig (pork roasted in an *imu*, or underground oven), and much more.

One luau, on the **Big Island**, is located oceanside in the shadow of a restored ancient Hawaiian temple and features dances of old Hawaii and the South Pacific *(Courtyard King Kamehameha's Kona Beach Hotel, tel 800/367-2111 or 808/326-4969, islandbreezeluau.com, $$$$$)*.

Maui's longtime host for paina is located in the historical town of Lahaina, by the sea *(Old Lahaina Luau, tel 800/248-5828 or 808/667-1998, oldlahainaluau.com, $$$$$)*.

Hawaiian games, net fishing, and 12 oceanfront acres are part of the luau at **Oahu**'s southwest end of Ko Olina *(Paradise Cove, tel 808/842-5911, paradise covehawaii.com, $$$$$)*. Oahu's north side is home to another, with cultural activities from the South Pacific *(Polynesian Cultural Center, tel 800/367-7060 or 808/293-3333, polynesianculturalcenter.com, $$$$$)*.

Hawaii Regional Cuisine

Tourism initially gave local food a bad reputation. Hotel cooks slathered everything in sweet-sour sauce, added pineapples, topped the congealed mass with macadamia nuts, and declared it Hawaiian. It wasn't until the late 1980s that the first stirrings of a fine regional cuisine were felt, when Peter Merriman, chef de cuisine at the Gallery Restaurant, Mauna Lani Resort on the Big Island, noticed that his kitchen help often brought their own lunch to work. Invited to try, he liked it and began to experiment. Hawaii's fusion cuisine moved to the front burner.

In 1992, it came to a full rolling boil when the top-ranked chefs working in the islands, many of them European, got together formally to promote "Hawaii regional cuisine" and to publish its first cookbook as a charity benefit.

Not only have these talented chefs raised local food to a culinary art form, they have revolutionized the agricultural industry, contracting with farmers to grow fruit, vegetables, and herbs in the quantity, quality, and variety needed to make the cuisine commercially viable.

A centerpiece of the new cuisine is seafood, the sweet-tasting, non-oily fish found in pure tropical waters. The most common found on menus are: *ahi* (yellowfin tuna), *kajiki* (Pacific blue marlin), mahimahi, *onaga* (red snapper), *ono* (wahoo), *opah* (moonfish), *opakapaka* (pink snapper), and *ulua* (jackfish).

Fruits found in abundance in the islands include: guava (grainy pink fruit with a hint of honey taste), *lilikoi* (passion fruit), lychee (sweet, silky fruit), mango (far superior to mangoes from elsewhere), mountain apple (crispy and tasting like a cross between a flower and an apple), papaya, pineapple (the sweetest are the small "sugarloafs"), and star fruit (carambola).

Coffee is harvested now on most islands, but pure Kona coffee remains the standard against which all others are measured. Read the label when purchasing coffee: Some blends contain as little as ten percent Kona coffee.

The Luau

With food and wine festivals all over the calendar, the premier feast on every visitor's menu remains the luau. People lament that they've gotten too big and too commercial. They always were big. And they erupt for almost any reason—a wedding, graduation, political candidacy, fund-raiser, *hula uniki* (graduation), or, most popular of all, to celebrate a child's first birthday. A baby luau was probably the first luau and was given by Chief Hawaii Loa, who came to Hawaii from Tahiti and gave the feast to honor the birth of his daughter Mahealani.

American missionary Charles S. Stewart in 1823 described his first luau, given by King Kamehameha II to celebrate both Kamehameha Day and his own ascension to the throne. It lasted almost three weeks. "All the natives present wore the European costume . . . Tamehamaru (Queen Kamamalu) in satin and lace sustained the part of mistress of ceremonies. She personally saw that no one of the company was in any degree neglected; and extended her kindness even to those who had no claim to special civility. For instance, seeing a crowd of American seamen . . . she immediately gave orders to have refreshments served to them."

Traditional luau fare centers around *kalua* pig, sweet potatoes, and *lau lau* cooked in the *imu* (underground oven). Lau lau are bundles of ti leaves encasing taro tops, pork, and fish. Some other dishes are *lomilomi* (salmon grated with onion and tomato), raw *ophihi* (limpet) and crab, *haupia* (coconut pudding) and *kulolo* (taro pudding), and poi. Today the menu includes everything from fried chicken to tossed salad.

Understanding Hawaiian & Other Local Foods

Here are some foods and culinary terms that you are likely to find in Hawaii:

Char siu: A Chinese dish of sliced roasted pork, with red food coloring added.

Chicken long rice: A Chinese dish made with chicken and long rice, a thin, clear Asian noodle that is a staple at most luaus.

Chicken luau: Chicken cooked with spinach, coconut milk, and other flavors.

Huli huli (hoolee hoolee) chicken: Hawaiian-style barbecue chicken.

Kalua pig: The main dish at a luau. Done properly, the pig is cooked over many hours (sometimes more than half a day) in an *imu,* or underground oven.

Kimchi: A cabbage dish with Korean origins. Sliced cabbage marinated in a stew of garlic, chili peppers, and other spices.

Kulolo: A Hawaiian pudding made of taro, brown sugar, and coconut milk.

Lau lau: At first glance, a steaming, round, green, leafy ball tied with string. Stuffed inside the ti leaf are taro leaves, chicken, pork, beef, or fish, such as butterfish.

Pineapple, a hallmark of Hawaiian cooking, may have been brought by settlers from Tahiti.

Lomilomi salmon: *Lomilomi* means massage, which also applies to salmon that is sliced, diced, and combined with Hawaiian salt, lime juice, chopped tomatoes, onions, and other flavorings. Ideally, served chilled.

Pipikaula (pee-pee-cow-lah): Hawaiian-style beef jerky.

Poi: A staple in Hawaiian diets. A thick, purple-colored paste made by pounding taro.

Poke (poh-kay): Fresh raw *ahi* (tuna), often used as a *pupu* (appetizer) before a meal.

Teriyaki beef, chicken, or fish: Marinated in teriyaki sauce (heavy on garlic, ginger, and soy sauce); a dish with Japanese origins.

Aloha shirts are a fashion staple, with antique shirts commanding sky-high prices.

allows for maximum air circulation. Eaves are wide so windows can stay open, sun or rain. Appearances are inspired by other sunny climes, such as those of the Mediterranean and Southeast Asia. Details often reflect the multiethnic culture, with an antique obi running the length of a dining room table, an entryway that passes over water in the Chinese manner, art deco wood accents, or Japanese screens.

Furniture

Rattan furniture, and lately bamboo, emphasize the tropical ambience. The most prized and expensive furniture is crafted of native hardwoods, especially koa. Much of the native forest has succumbed to development, making koa pieces even more valuable. In 1793, Archibald Menzies, a naturalist aboard H.M.S. *Daedalus* on Capt. George Vancouver's Hawaii expedition, wrote of koa: "Its wood is very hard and close grained, and it takes a fine polish as may be seen by their canoes."

The Yankee missionaries were practical people, some of them good enough carpenters to build their own furniture. When Queen Kaahumanu admired a rocking chair the Reverend Hiram Bingham built for his wife, he made one for her, of koa and koaie *(Acacia koaie)*. Both chairs are at Mission Houses Museum (see p. 66). When Hawaiian and immigrant woodworkers began creating regional furniture from native woods for the monarchy, the pieces were outstanding. Some of the best may be seen at Queen Emma Summer Palace (see p. 69 & p. 72).

Real estate brokers traditionally hold open house for their on-the-market properties every Sunday. If you don't have island friends, it's a good way to peek into homes. Wear shoes that will slip off easily at the door, a local custom.

Fashion

Practically the first thing most tourists do after landing in Waikiki is hit the shops and get in costume—a Halloween aloha shirt exploding in pineapples and hula maidens for men with a matching muumuu (a loose-fitting, long dress), or perhaps another aloha shirt, for women.

Every man in Hawaii has a collection of aloha shirts, and most wear them daily. In fact, a man in a suit and tie is perceived as either heading for a funeral, a court appearance, or a loan office. Businesses observe the weekly "Aloha Friday," when even the stuffiest CEOs don a wicked aloha shirt.

Hollywood seems to like the shirt, too: Bruce Willis and Robert Redford have been spotted in them. John Wayne wore one in *Donovan's Reef,* so did Elvis in *Blue Hawaii.* When Montgomery Clift got shot and fell down dead in the mud in *From Here to Eternity,* shirt fans wailed, "Oh no, he's ruined his shirt."

Vintage aloha shirts, "silkies" with coconut buttons from the 1930s and '40s, have become collectibles, selling for thousands of dollars. The first Hawaiian shirt patterns were based on the geometric designs of *kapa* and colored with natural dyes that quickly mellowed to earth tones. Laser technology has enabled manufacturers to faithfully reproduce vintage shirt patterns. They are currently best-sellers.

Palaka—the earliest mass-produced Hawaiian shirts—were made for plantation workers. They were usually stylized check prints, worn with "sailor moku," denim trousers. In the 1920s, a local firm, Watumull's East India Store, commissioned artist Elsie Das to produce 15 floral designs. These creations were sent to Japan, printed on raw silk, and sewn into shirts. They sold by the boatload and were snapped up by collectors as far away as London. Many people credit designer Ellery Chun for coining the term "aloha shirt" in an ad that appeared in the *Honolulu Advertiser* in 1935.

Traditionally, the female counterpart to the costume is the muumuu and its glorified sister, the *holoku.* The muumuu is an everyday garment, while the holoku, with its small (or sometimes wedding-gown-long) train, goes to parties.

According to Hawaiian historians, Hawaiians had a history of sewing with *olona (Touchardia latifolia)* plant fiber and needles made from bone. They fashioned kapa into *pau* (loin skirts consisting of five layers of fabric), *malo* (loincloths for men), and *kihei,* a toga-like garment. The Russian explorer V. M. Golovnin recorded in 1817, three years before the arrival of the missionaries, that Hawaiian women were wearing robe-like calico dresses. The fabric was no doubt acquired from early traders and valued for its novelty and coolness. Royal women draped themselves in the new silks and brocades.

When Hawaiian and immigrant woodworkers began creating regional furniture from native woods for the monarchy, the pieces were outstanding.

The missionaries undoubtedly popularized the muumuu with the establishment of sewing schools and the introduction of more varied styles based on world fashion trends. Royal attire began to follow European formal dress.

Today, the muumuu ranges from bare-backed mini dresses to tea-length dresses suitable for the office to floor-length dresses. One top designer is Mamo Howell, whose look is known by its strong graphic prints and innovative hem flourishes. A completely different muumuu, more feminine and old fashioned in feel, can be found in the popular Princess Kaiulani line. Another favorite look is the vintage reproduction print in a simple shift.

Festivals

The calendar is crammed with holidays that are so colorful people often plan their vacations around them (see pp. 236–237). Many celebrations center on the Hawaiian culture and feature Hawaiian music, pageantry, crafts, hula—and always food. Anything billed as a *hoolaulea* is a pull-out-all-the-stops party. Waikiki can get so jammed during a hoolaulea that, if you were to fall, there wouldn't be enough room to hit the ground. Rock can be blasting on one stage and steel guitar on the next. The smell of teriyaki meat perfumes the air, and hula dancers hit their gourd drums as they whirl to the beat. The biggest, splashiest of these celebrations are the Aloha Festivals, which are a reflection of the ancient Makahiki (see p. 28). They take place on each island in sequence, beginning with Oahu in September.

Hula festivals and competitions are common, and if there is one happening when you're here, don't miss it. People spare no expense in preparations for these beloved cultural expressions. You'll see authentic dances, both ancient and modern, performed by amateurs who devote themselves to the dance (see p. 170).

Diversity of cultures simply means there's more to celebrate. Regardless of background, everyone celebrates Chinese New Year, with firecrackers and ear-splitting lion dances. Then they don Japanese *happi* coats and fake the dancing at the Buddhist temples during Obon season, honoring ancestors. And of course, there's the Fourth of July, Christmas, and Easter. New Year's Eve is traditionally a blowout of aerial fireworks shows supplemented by all kinds of illegal home fireworks, including spectacular rockets. Recent restrictive legislation has scaled back the mayhem.

> **Hula festivals and competitions are common, and if there is one happening when you're here, don't miss it.**

The Hawaii International Film Festival has won worldwide recognition, showing premier films from all around the globe. The film festival also showcases locally produced features and documentaries.

There's an annual jazz festival, and symphony and opera seasons. Several community theater groups thrive and harbor a surprising depth of talent.

Sports loom large on the calendar with world-class golf tournaments, marathons, triathlons, surf meets, outrigger canoe regattas, and international yacht races to name the big categories.

Many of the hotels and resorts host annual events worthy of a special visit. Often these celebrations are an outgrowth of a hotel's Hawaiian cultural program, and are usually enthusiastically supported and participated in by the staff. The hotels also have ecologically inspired festivals such as Dolphin Days at the Hilton Waikoloa Village on the Big Island, and the Waikiki Aquarium has a full calendar of fun, eco-educational events.

Food and wine festivals come naturally in a place where almost no social intercourse happens without food. The biggest concern even on powerhouse business agendas is always refreshments—who is going to be in charge and who will bring what, or who will cater. Most of the major food events are charity benefits. Some are special promotions designed to fill hotel rooms.

For down-home fun, check the local newspapers. The *Honolulu Advertiser* publishes a weekly guide to entertainment and events in Friday's paper. You may find a fund-raising luau (see pp. 50–51) or "beer bust" sponsored by a church or *hula halau* (school), an arts and crafts event, a school carnival, or even a rodeo. Visitors are always welcomed. ■

Hawaii's most sophisticated and urbanized island, with busy Honolulu, action-packed Waikiki, and, beyond, small towns, lonesome beaches, and plantations

Oahu

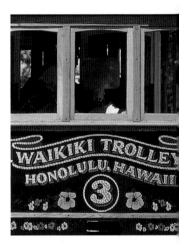

Waikiki sightseeing trolley

Oahu

Oahu is one of the most amazing islands in any ocean. Way out in the middle of nowhere, where no land should reasonably be expected to exist, are high-rises, universities engaged in cutting-edge research, interstate freeways that connect to no other state, a million busy residents, and more than 13,000 tourists a day in bright clothes tucked into an estimated 35,000 hotel rooms.

The visitors are ready to play, counting on their dreams of paradise to materialize, while locals engage in a nightmare struggle to make ends meet at one of the most expensive addresses in the country. Known as the Gathering Place, Oahu is, at 608 square miles, the third largest of the Hawaiian Islands; it measures 44 miles long and 30 miles wide with 112 miles of coastline. It has two mountain ranges: The dramatic Koolau Mountains running north–south for almost the entire

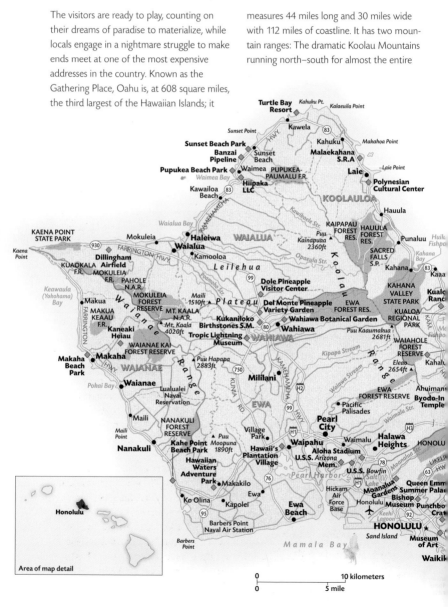

length of the island, and the older, rounder Waianae Range, with the island's tallest peak, Mount Kaala, at 4,020 feet, in the northwest. The vast, fertile Leilehua Plateau forming the interior of the island is planted mainly in pineapple. Three tuff cones (made from rock formed of compressed volcanic ash)—Diamond Head, Koko Head, and Punchbowl—form distinctive landmarks.

Diamond Head looms at the eastern end of Waikiki. The world-famous resort packs into its 681 acres, 152 hotels and holiday condominiums, more than a thousand shops, about 500 restaurants, and more than 300 entertainment venues, all of which pump about five billion dollars into the state coffers.

Honolulu

Downtown Honolulu is the financial center of the Pacific. Women in flowing muumuus and men in aloha shirts flit among the steel and glass towers. At the center of the action is Bishop Street with its banks and power structures, yet one end of the street trails off into green mountains, and the other has cruise ships moored at the waterfront.

The whole island, plus the islets and atolls

stretching 1,400 miles northwest to Kure Atoll, form the City and County of Honolulu, making this the world's longest city and the 11th largest city in the United States.

For all its frenetic activity, parts of Oahu are so wild and rugged that no road completely encircles the island. Windward Oahu is lush and green, some of it suburban, most of it dotted with farms and ranches. The North Shore is where the winter surf comes crashing ashore. Any time of year, the sunsets are magnificent.

Most of the state's cultural events, such as theater, opera, symphony, ballet, and art happen on Oahu. The top commercial tourist attractions are here, and this is where some of the most important moments in Hawaiian history unfolded. There are three national parks, 25 state parks, and 62 county parks. A hundred white-sand beaches soothe the island's sometimes harried soul. ∎

Honolulu

Captain Cook sailed right past Oahu in the night, missing entirely the calm, deepwater harbor of Honolulu and the thatched fishing village of Kou that would become one of the world's great cities.

Honolulu's waterfront is a busy mix of commercial shipping, recreation, and a colorful fishing fleet.

Sixteen years after Captain Cook's 1778 miss, another English skipper, Captain William Brown, aboard the H.M.S. *Jackal,* stumbled upon the bay and renamed it Fair Haven, which coincidentally is synonymous with the name given to it by the people who lived there.

Word of Brown's wonderful bay spread quickly among the traders, and the little fishing village became a port dealing in guns, rum, furs, and sandalwood. King Kamehameha I, after conquering Oahu, briefly took up residence in Honolulu in 1801, but finding the city too loud and crowded, he and his court moved back to Kailua-Kona on the Big Island. Honolulu became the capital of the Hawaiian

INSIDER TIP:

Make sure to spend a few sunsets at a beach facing west to try to see the "green flash" as the sun dips below the horizon.

—MIRIAM STARK
National Geographic field scientist

kingdom in 1845, when King Kamehameha III moved the seat of government from Maui.

Honolulu Today

Honolulu today is a pretty and pleasant city, with the blue Pacific yawning away from its lap and the jagged, mist-haunted cliffs of the Koolau rising behind. The rugged topography of the island places some limits on development; valley walls are so steep they defy

builders. Billboards and aggressive signage are conspicuously absent. Art, trees, flowers, and water features are incorporated into building design. Open space is preserved in parks, conservation areas, and the Honolulu Watershed Forest Preserve, and citizen groups are vigilant in trying to protect views, shorelines, and natural areas.

The city is probably the only place in the world where East truly meets West, not just with tolerance, but with understanding and appreciation. James Michener said that a Honolulu citizen is "a man at home in either the business councils of New York or the philosophical retreats of Kyoto."

Iolani Palace

Iolani Palace is the symbolic and emotional heart of Hawaii. Any understanding of the cultural renaissance and political forces shaping the islands today must

Honolulu

⌂ Map p. 56, pp. 58–59, p. 67, & p. 71

Visitor Information

✉ Oahu Visitors Bureau, 2270 Kalakawa Ave., #801

☎ 808/524-0722

🕐 Closed Sat. & Sun.

Iolani Palace

⌂ Map p. 59 & p. 67

✉ S. King & Richards Sts.

☎ 808/522-0832

🕐 Closed Sun. & Mon.

💲 $$$ (no children under 5)

🚌 TheBus 2 or 13

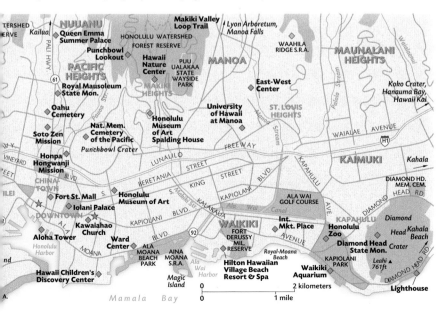

begin here. Even the name, translated as "hawk of heaven," has meaning. The *io* is the highest-soaring Hawaiian bird, said to commune with the gods.

The cornerstone of the palace was laid December 31, 1879, on the birthday of Queen Kapiolani, wife of King Kalakaua, who commissioned the construction.

Iolani took three years to complete and cost $343,595 furnished; the nine-year restoration, completed in 1978, cost seven million dollars. The building was described as "American Florentine." It is crowned with a French mansard roof and embellished with Victorian

INSIDER TIP:

Some of the palace rules are surprising. No pens, only pencils, for taking notes. And you have to wear booties over your shoes.

—RITA ARIYOSHI
National Geographic author

flourishes and Greek columns, but all rooted in Hawaiian cultural expression and modified for the tropical climate. It is two stories high with a basement and attic, and has wide lanais (verandas).

The Approach: With skyscrapers rising around it, Iolani sits like a lovely reprimand in the midst of commerce. Four gates open into the tree-bowered grounds. The **Kauikeaouli Gate** on King Street, once used for state occasions, is the entrance used by most visitors. The coat of arms on the gate

is one of eight cast in bronze at England's Royal College of Arms. They contain the kingdom's motto, now the state's, "Ua mau keia o ka aina i ka pono" (The life of the land is preserved in righteousness). They were the first items removed from the palace, stripped on the very day of the 1893 overthrow of the monarchy, and like everything else that could be pried loose and carried away, they were eventually sold.

The approach to the palace is lined with royal palms. A broad staircase leads to the wide lanai and front entrance: Note the palm tree motif on top of the bright white Corinthian columns. The etched glass doors, made in San Francisco, depict a Victorian woman, taro plants, and, as a nice aesthetic but irrelevant touch, calla lilies. The ornate nickel door hardware with "no-peek" keyholes is from Germany. Windows are high and have 52,000 wooden shutters to admit and control the prevailing trade winds. During the restoration, 28,000 shutters had to be replaced, primarily due to termite damage.

Facing the palace and to your right, in a corner of the grounds, is a fenced mound that was once the royal tomb. In 1865, in a solemn torchlight procession, the bodies were removed to the new Royal Mausoleum in Nuuanu (see p. 68). It is believed that the bones of some chiefs still reside beneath the mound.

Opposite the royal tomb area is the copper-domed **Coronation Pavilion,** built for the coronation ceremonies of King Kalakaua and

Queen Kapiolani and now used for band concerts most Fridays at noon. Behind that are the **Iolani Barracks,** where tour tickets, which should be reserved in advance, are purchased. It's a good idea to arrive in time to see the dramatic 20-minute film about the palace and the monarchy.

The Interior: After a brief talk on the rear lanai, you are swept into the **Grand Hall,** as silent, gleaming, and lovely as a church. The glowing woods are fine native hardwoods—koa, kamani, kou, and ohia—augmented by cedar, black walnut, and bird's-eye maple. Chinese and English urns are tucked in carved niches, and portraits of Hawaiian royalty line the walls.

You are escorted into the **Blue Room.** From here Queen Liliuokalani could see armed U.S. Marines taking up position, and it was here she surrendered her kingdom. William Cogswell's portraits of the queen and her brother King Kalakaua grace the walls. The adjoining **Dining Room** is set for a formal dinner with French china, English sterling silver, and colored Bavarian crystal.

In the bathroom, the queen's copper-lined tub is 6.5 feet long, the king's 7 feet. Iolani was the first palace in the world to install flush toilets. It had the first telephone system in Honolulu and had electricity before the White House, Windsor Castle, or the Imperial Palace of Japan.

A magnificent koa staircase leads to the upper-floor living quarters. The **King's Bedroom** contains a photograph of the

room as it was when King Kalakaua lived in it. When the palace reopened to the public, it was almost empty of furniture, but since then, nearly half of the original furnishings have been

After the 1893 coup, Queen Liliuokalani campaigned vigorously to restore Hawaii's constitutional monarchy.

returned. Still missing is the king's ebony-and-gold bed. A goat-footed Meissen jardiniere is one of the palace's most valuable pieces. The adjoining **King's Office** is completely furnished and contains rare books, including one he wrote himself, *Legends and Myths of Hawaii.* A wooden table that forms the centerpiece of the **Gold Room** is a piece of furniture that never left the palace.

No one is ever quite prepared for the room across the hall, especially after the opulence of all the other rooms. **Queen Liliuokalani's Room** is austerely furnished

The Throne Room at Iolani Palace has been magnificently restored. Great balls and dramas unfolded in this room.

"The Queen's Prayer," and worked on a silk quilt (on display under glass in the room). Into it, the queen stitched her beloved Hawaiian flag and the names of friends who remained loyal to her.

The **Throne Room,** with its sweep of red and gold presided over by two gilt thrones, retains all the pomp of state. A seven-foot narwhal tusk topped with a gold sphere was used as a traditional *puloulou* (tabu stick to create inviolate space around the king). Here King Kalakaua gave fabulous balls, and Queen Liliuokalani was tried for treason by the men who seized her government.

with simple furniture and a crazy quilt she made while imprisoned in this room, after the coup in 1893. The shutters are closed as they were ordered to be for her, so her people could not see her in the window. In the dim light, she composed the elegiac song

Coronation Pavilion   **Blue Room**

The tour ends in the basement **Gallery.** Here the crown jewels of Hawaii are on view, along with a collection of ancient calabashes and *kahili* (feathered royal standards). You also tour the kitchen where formal dinners were prepared.

After Queen Liliuokalani's overthrow, Iolani Palace was used as a capitol by the ensuing governments, until the state capitol was completed in 1969.

State Capitol

This architectural gem, completed in 1969 across Beretania Street from Washington Place, is textured with symbolism: Columns look like palm trees, a major source of food, water, and building supplies; legislative chambers are shaped like volcanoes; and the central courtyard is open to the sky, denoting Hawaii's open society. Support pillars on the top floor are grouped in eights, representing the eight Hawaiian Islands, while other parts of the building appear in fours, to represent the four counties (Hawaii, Kauai,

State Capitol
- Map p. 67
- S. Beretania & Richards Sts.
- 808/586-0178
- Tours by appt.
- TheBus 2

Upper Hall

Koa staircase

Grand Hall

Iolani Palace

Throne Room

Don Ho Remembered

For more than four decades, entertainer Don Ho (1930–2007), Hawaii's own homegrown musical legend, delighted audiences near and far with his warm personality and memorable songs. Whether performing on national television or on a Waikiki stage, he was seen as an enduring symbol of the islands.

Ho, a former Air Force pilot, started his singing career humbly enough in the early 1960s, performing with a band of friends at Honey's, his family-owned bar.

Before long, he was headlining in Waikiki showrooms.

Though "Tiny Bubbles" solidly established Ho, he is known in the islands for other songs as well, such as "Pearly Shells," "Ain't No Big Thing," and "I'll Remember You," the last a haunting melody written by his friend, the late Kui Lee, and exposed to the world by Ho.

Ho suffered a heart attack in 2007 at his Honolulu home, leaving a musical legacy that will long be remembered.

Washington Place

🄰 Map p. 67

✉ 320 S. Beretania St.

☎ 808/586-0248

Oahu, Maui). The complex is surrounded by reflecting pools, just as the islands are surrounded by water.

A statue of Queen Liliuokalani stands between the capitol and Iolani Palace. In front is a statue of Father Damien (see p. 213), who devoted his life to victims of Hansen's disease (leprosy). It was created by Venezuelan artist Marisol Escobar.

Washington Place

Queen Liliuokalani once lived in this stately, two-story Greek Revival house, and until 2002, it served as the Hawaii gubernatorial residence. Named in honor of the first U.S. President, Washington Place was built between 1842 and 1846 by Captain John Dominis, a New England trader and the queen's father-in-law. As a private citizen, Queen Liliuokalani returned to live in the house until her death in 1917. Newly refurbished as a museum, it is open for tours by reservation 48 hours in advance. The home contains many beautiful pieces of her furniture, jewelry,

and other royal possessions. The most prized treasures are the queen's musical instruments. Her grand piano was built of koa logs that had been shipped from Kamuela, on the Big Island, to New York's Fisher Company.

Honolulu Harbor

Fishing boats, tugs, container ships, and cruise liners trace a skein of white wakes in the peacock water of this busy port, located in Mamala Bay. Honolulu Harbor has been sheltering boats for 12 centuries, but it was after Captain Cook put Hawaii on the world map that it became a commercial harbor. Here, fur traders swapped otter pelts from the Pacific Northwest of America for teas, spices, and silks in transit from China. When a particularly fragrant sandalwood was noticed in Hawaii's forests, a brisk trade flourished until the islands were denuded of the wood. The whalers were next, and Honolulu became the largest whaling port in the world. Today, the wharves handle cargo for a burgeoning, sophisticated American city.

The **Aloha Tower,** designed by architect Arthur Reynolds, was the island's tallest building when it opened in 1926. At 184 feet high with a 40-foot flagstaff, it was the pride of the Pacific. Its seven-ton clock was the largest ever made by the Howard Clark Company of Boston, and its light beamed 19 miles out to sea. The largest, most modern pier

The Aloha Tower, designed by architect Arthur Reynolds, was the island's tallest building when it opened in 1926. At 184 feet high with a 40-foot flagstaff, it was the pride of the Pacific.

complex in the Pacific welcomed tourists arriving aboard luxury liners. On "boat day," when the ships docked, local residents flocked to the piers to sell leis, dive for coins, and get their mail; there was music and hula, and flowers everywhere.

The Aloha Tower today is the hub of a smart complex of shops and waterfront restaurants serving everything from sushi to hotdogs. A microbrewery offers free tastings, and music and dancing are around every turn. Ships still ply the waters, and the cruise liners sail away with flower-draped passengers singing "Aloha Oe." Don't miss the panoramic views from the observation deck.

Nuuanu Valley

Caught up in the urban rush of Oahu, it's easy to miss the stunning beauty of the island's green valleys. Nuuanu Valley, whose name means "cool height," stretches from the edge of Honolulu to the Koolau Mountains, and in its folds early Hawaiians and the first foreign settlers chose to build homes.

Today you can drive the Pali Highway right along the valley to a tunnel through the mountains to the **Windward Side** (see pp. 100–107). Along the way, look for "upside-down" waterfalls,

The Aloha Tower, once the tallest building in the state, overlooks downtown Honolulu and the waterfront.

cascades blown upward by strong winds barreling through the pass. At the top of the pass, a well-marked exit leads to the **Nuuanu Pali Lookout** and one of the most spectacular views in Hawaii. Below is Windward Oahu with **Kailua** and **Kaneohe Bays.** Here Kamehameha I defeated the defenders

(continued on p. 68)

Aloha Tower

- Map p. 59 & p. 67
- Pier 9
- 808/566-2337
- TheBus 2, 13, 19, 20

A Walk Around Historic Honolulu

Be seduced by gentle trade winds breezing through flowering trees as you take your sweet Hawaiian time walking around a city that's never in a hurry.

Begin at **Mission Houses Museum ❶** *(553 S. King St., tel 808/447-3190).* The complex includes the home of the first missionaries (see pp. 30–32), and a printing press. Cross crooked little Kawaiahao Street to **Kawaiahao Church ❷** *(tel 808/469-3000),* built of 14,000 large coral blocks cut from the reef with shark-tooth saws. Dedicated in 1842, it was designed by Rev. Hiram Bingham. Royalty worshipped here, and special seating is still reserved for their descendants. Sunday services (9 a.m.) are conducted in English and Hawaiian. The first Hawaiin songs were hymns. Sing along here. The tomb of King Lunalilo is just inside the main church gate.

Cross King Street to **Honolulu Hale ❸,** city hall, built in 1927 by a team of architects including C. W. Dickey and Hart Wood. The courtyard, stairs, speaker's balcony, and open ceiling were modeled after Italy's 13th-century Bargello Palace. Note the ceiling frescoes. The building to the west is the **Hawaii State Library ❹,** a gift from philanthropist Andrew Carnegie and designed by Henry D. Whitfield. Honolulu's first public library, it opened in 1879 and was intended to be a substitute for saloons. The library flourished, but so did the saloons. At the start, it had 130 volumes, and women were not admitted, a ban that was soon lifted.

Cross busy King Street to the gilt-robed **Kamehameha I statue ❺,** in honor of the king who united the Hawaiian Islands into one

---

NOT TO BE MISSED:

Mission Houses Museum
• **Kawaiahao Church**
• **Kamehameha I Statue**
• **Iolani Palace**

---

nation. The original bronze, cast in Italy in 1883, by American sculptor Thomas B. Gould, was lost at sea, so this duplicate was made. Shortly after its arrival in Honolulu, the original was found in the Falkland Islands and now stands in the little town of Kapaau on the Big Island (see pp. 161–162).

Cross King Street again to **Iolani Palace ❻** (see pp. 59–63). Stroll the shady grounds to the huge century-old banyan tree. At the **Hawaii State Archives,** see the exhibit of vintage photographs just inside the front entrance. On the other side of the palace is Iolani Barracks.

Exit the palace grounds and cross to the **Queen Liliuokalani Statue,** sculpted in 1982 by Marianna Pineda. The queen's hand always

Every year on Kamehameha Day, June 11, enormous leis festoon the statue of Hawaii's great king.

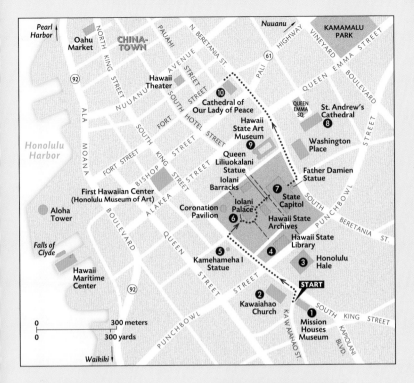

holds fresh flowers, placed there daily by admirers. Proceed up the steps of the **State Capitol 7** (see pp. 63–64), then take the elevator to the second floor for impressive views. In front of the building is a **statue of Father Damien,** the martyr priest of Molokai (see p. 213).

The white mansion set among big trees is **Washington Place** (see p. 64), former residence of Hawaii's governor. Next door is **St. Andrew's Cathedral 8** (tel 808/524-2822), dedicated in 1867. The Anglo-Norman building was designed in England, and much of the construction material, including the sandstone building blocks, was shipped from that country. King Kamehameha IV, and his wife Queen Emma, who supervised the building, were Anglophiles, impressed by the pomp of Church of England rituals they encountered in London.

Nearby Richards Street, a Spanish mission-style structure built in 1928, became the site of

◪	See also map pp. 58–59
►	Mission Houses Museum
⬌	1 mile
◷	2.5 hours
►	Fort Street Mall

the original Royal Hawaiian Hotel. Today it is known as the **Hawaii State Art Museum 9** (tel 808/586-0304), the home of art and culture that reflects the islands' diverse ethnicities.

Down Beretania Street one block and fronting the Fort Street Mall, you'll find the **Cathedral of Our Lady of Peace 10** (tel 808/536-7036). Built by French Catholic missionaries in 1843, it houses the islands' first pipe organ. Father Damien was ordained here.

Fort Street, hub of Honolulu's business district, is a pedestrian mall abounding in eclectic take-out eateries. Dine on benches and watch the parade of people. If you're lucky someone will be strumming an ukulele; if you're not, someone will try to save your soul.

Royal Mausoleum

🗺 Map p. 59
✉ 2261 Nuuanu Ave.
☎ 808/587-2590
🕐 Closed Sat. & Sun.
🚌 TheBus 4

of Oahu, driving them over the cliffs. In the rush of wind, you can almost hear the howls.

The **Royal Mausoleum State Monument** in the lush foothills of the valley is the final resting place for all Hawaii's monarchs but two: King Kamehameha I, whose bones were buried in secret according to ancient rites, and Lunalilo, who asked to be interred at Kawaia-hao Church (see p. 66). The site, which flies only the Hawaiian flag, is considered sacred. Visitors are welcome to this peaceful oasis, surrounded by royal palms, gated with the royal coat of arms, and cradling the bones of kings. If the chapel is open, stop in to see the rich koa-wood interior and ponder the course of nations.

The father of America's pastime, baseball, lies in nearby **Oahu Cemetery** (2162 Nuuanu Ave.), beneath a tombstone bearing the inscription "Alexander Joy Cartwright Jr. Born in New York City April 17, 1820. Died in Honolulu July 12, 1892." After creating the game and launching it in Hoboken, New Jersey, in 1846,

INSIDER TIP:

In the Nuuanu Valley, the Judd Memorial Trail offers a serene world dominated by bamboo, eucalyptus, ironwood, and Captain Cook pine groves.

—MICHAEL PIETRUSEWSKY
National Geographic field scientist

Cartwright sailed to the islands, founded Honolulu's first volunteer fire company, and served as chief.

Other noted departed include Martha Root, apologist for the Bahai faith, several isle governors, missionaries, sea skippers, sugar barons, and casualties of the attack on Pearl Harbor in 1941 (see pp. 36–37).

Two outstanding Buddhist temples reside in Nuuanu. The **Soto Zen Mission** (1708 Nuuanu Ave.) is a faithful copy of the stupa in India where Gautama Buddha first spoke about enlighten-ment. The brilliant white **Honpa**

Robert Wilcox: Hawaii's Forgotten Patriot

He has been called a "freedom fighter of the last Hawaiian Army of the Hawaiian Kingdom." Born in 1855 to a Hawaiian mother and Caucasian father, Robert Wilcox was one of several part-Hawaiian men who sailed to Italy in 1880 for an education at the behest of King Kalakaua (1836–1891), returning with new sophistication and knowledge of military tactics.

In 1889, he led an insurrection against the Reform Cabinet, which sought to strip the monarchy of its powers.

Wilcox's efforts were crushed.

Wilcox and about 200 loyalists planned another uprising in 1895 to restore the queen to power; it failed, and the loyalists were brought to trial for treason but gained clemency when the queen formally abdicated her throne to avoid bloodshed.

Wilcox was later elected as the Independent Party's first Hawaii delegate to the U.S. Congress (1900–1902). This patriot and freedom fighter died in 1902.

The Queen Emma Summer Palace, Hanaiakamalama, in Nuuanu is a remnant of the gracious age of the Hawaiian monarchy.

Hongwanji Mission *(1727 Pali Hwy.)* was built in 1819 for the 700th anniversary of the Shin Buddhist sect.

Queen Emma Summer Palace

Heading northwest along Pali Highway (Hawaii 61), you'll find the Queen Emma Summer Palace. More a home than a palace, the summer palace's real name is Hanaiakamalama, after a goddess who was the foster child of the moon. King Kamehameha IV, Queen Emma, and their little son Prince Albert would retreat here from the heat of the city to the cool uplands of Nuuanu. Built in 1848, and now on the National Register of Historic Places, the airy Greek Revival house, whose frame was built in Boston and shipped around the Horn, has a long Hawaiian lanai and is shaded by huge century-old trees, including a mango

planted on the royal wedding day and still bearing fruit.

The beautifully restored house holds probably the finest exhibited collection of Hawaiian furniture. There are crystal chandeliers overhead and *lauhala* mats underfoot. The canoe-shaped, koa-wood cradle with its wave-patterned overlay in kou wood was commissioned by the king in anticipation of the birth of his heir and is now a state treasure.

Among the notable palace artifacts on exhibit are a well-preserved feather cape; *kahili* (feathered royal standards); the queen's fan collection, hair combs, and jewelry, including a locket with Queen Victoria's hair; and poignant gifts to the prince who didn't survive his fourth year—a ceramic child's bath from the emperor of China, and a silver christening vase from his godmother, Queen Victoria.

(continued on p. 72)

Queen Emma Summer Palace

Map p. 56 & p. 59

2913 Pali Hwy. (Hawaii 61)

808/595-3167

$$

TheBus 4

A Walk Around Honolulu's Chinatown

In the morning, shoppers in Chinatown bustle and bicker when the produce and flowers are freshest. Chinese settlers still come from Taiwan and Hong Kong, but many businesses are now owned by Vietnamese, Laotians, Koreans, Thais, and Filipinos, resulting in a scene that is colorful and dynamic.

Shoppers come from all over the island for Chinatown's food. Here, workers prepare duck.

Your walk begins on the corner of King Street and Kekaulike Street, with instant immersion into the color and delightful chaos of a typical Asian market. The open-air **Oahu Market 1** is crammed with fresh fish, some still swimming in buckets, tropical flowers, local fruit, *char siu,* hanging ducks, thousand-year-old eggs, and vegetables of every stripe. Cross King Street and continue left to **Yat Tung Chow Noodle Factory 2** *(150 N. King St.)* and watch as noodles roll out of the noodle machine amid clouds of flour, destined for city restaurants. Just a little farther on the left, you'll come to the **Hou Ren Tong Chinese Herb & Acupuncture** *(183 N. King St.).* Walls of tiny drawers and rows of scary-looking jars are the backbone of a sophisticated natural pharmacopeia dating back thousands of years.

At River Street, turn right, toward the mountains, enjoying the view. Cross Hotel Street— once notorious for its fleshpots but lately gentrified with shops and galleries—and keep going until the street becomes a pedestrian mall. Here you'll find more shops and some of the best Asian restaurants in town. Lunch lines start at 11 a.m.. At the head of the mall is a **statue of Sun Yat-Sen 3** (1866–1925), who was educated in Hawaii and hatched his plans for the Chinese Revolution here in 1911. On the far side of the stream is a statue honoring José Rizal (1861–1896), a hero of the Philippines.

You'll be passing the **Chinatown Cultural Plaza 4**, with more shops and restaurants around a central courtyard. Locals flock to **Legend Seafood Restaurant** *(100 N. Beretania St., Ste. 108, tel 808/532-1868)* for dim sum,

NOT TO BE MISSED:

Oahu Market • Chinatown
Cultural Plaza • Kuan Yin
Temple • New Lin Fong Inc.

bite-size portions of Chinese dishes that include delicate dumplings. Sit down while waitresses wheel carts to your table stacked with bamboo steamer baskets of dim sum, stuffed with scallops and chives, spicy pork hash, or shrimp. After dining, you may want to give thanks at the little shrine on the third floor of the plaza, the Chee Kung Tong Shrine.

Stroll over the Kukui Street Bridge to **Izuma Taishakyo Mission Shrine ❺**, Hawaii's oldest Shinto shrine, built without a single nail in classic Japanese temple–style architecture. Visitors are welcome, but please remove your shoes after entering beneath the torii gate.

INSIDER TIP:

Be sure to visit Chinatown around the lunch hour. You'll find the most crowded places are the best places to eat. If you prefer to miss the masses, arrive earlier rather than later.

—DOUGLAS PEEBLES
National Geographic contributor

If you haven't had enough of shrines, continue up River Street to Vineyard Boulevard, cross, and turn right for the incense-laden **Kuan Yin Temple ❻** with its jade-colored tile roof and flamboyant architecture. The interior sanctuary is dominated by a 10-foot statue of the Buddhist goddess of mercy.

Continue along Vineyard Boulevard to Maunakea Street and turn right. If you have opted out of the temple, just turn right on

South Kukui Street to Maunakea Street and turn right. Maunakea is lined with lei vendors weaving and stringing their fragrant wares. This Chinatown is the only one in the U.S. with an abundance of lei stands and the perfume of their flowers wafting through the air. **New Lin Fong Inc. ❼** *(1132 Maunakea St.)* will ambush your diet with custard pies and peanut rice squares. If you continue on down Maunakea Street you will come to King Street, where the walk began.

⛰ See also map p. 59 & p. 67
▶ North King St. (Sea Fortune Restaurant)
⟷ 2.5 miles
🕐 3 hours depending on dining and browsing
▶ Maunakea & King Sts.

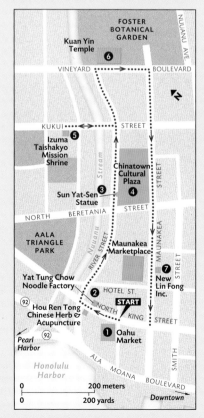

Driving Around Hawaii

Hawaii drivers are typically courteous. Unlike some other major cities, horn honking is rare except for warnings of danger or emergency. In an island community, there is little need to speed. This is Hawaii. Slow down and remember:

- Don't drink and drive.
- Lock your car to avoid burglary.
- Hawaii is a no-fault state. Check your personal insurance coverage and have the telephone number of your company's local claim office handy. Some

credit card and rental companies also offer collision coverage.

- Get free road maps online or in visitor publications. Some car rentals offer a GPS (global positioning system) device.
- Expect to pay a high price for gasoline. Hawaii's gas costs are among the nation's highest, and they are climbing.
- Wear your seat belt. Hawaii state law requires it and levies a fine for those who do not buckle up.

Bishop Museum

- Map p. 56 & p. 58
- 1525 Bernice St. (just off Likelike Hwy., Hawaii 63)
- 808/847-3511
- $$
- TheBus 2
- Closed Tues.

Details like this show the graciousness, hospitality, elegance, and desperate sadness of the monarchy era of Hawaii.

Bishop Museum

The Bishop Museum is about 4 miles southwest of the Queen Emma Summer Palace. The Romanesque-style main building, built from lava rock, is festooned in solemnity. Charles Reed Bishop, husband of Princess Bernice Pauahi Bishop founded the museum in 1889 to honor his late wife and to showcase the treasures of the Kamehameha dynasty for the people of Hawaii.

As the foremost museum of Polynesian culture in the world, its holdings are staggering: 13 million insects, 6 million marine and land shells, 490,000 botany specimens, 115,000 bound volumes, and 2.4 million Pacific and Hawaiian artifacts.

The Museum Complex:

When you are inside and face the museum's riches, the formidable facade outside

is forgotten. Return visitors will notice the extensive renovations Hawaiian Hall has undertaken in phases since 2006. The native koa has been refinished, enhancing the soft gleam of the hardwood used in the trims, railings, and cabinetry at the hall. This complex includes Hawaiian Hall Gallery, Polynesian Hall, the Joseph M. Long Gallery, the Picture Gallery, and the Kahili Room. All have been enhanced with new lighting and the sounds of Hawaii's history.

Cavernous Hawaiian Hall, with its three floors of gallery exhibits, surrounds an enormous center space that includes a traditional grass house. Overhead, the skeleton of a 50-foot sperm whale bears silent witness to the gods, legends, and people of ancient Hawaii in their authenticity. The focus on the first floor is just that—the world of pre-contact Hawaii. The second floor concentrates on the importance of land and nature to Native Hawaiians, while modern-day Hawaiian issues are found on the third floor.

Polynesian Hall honors the Pacific origins of the Hawaiian people, with examples of painted masks, personal adornment items, and other artifacts. The Cooke Rotunda now features Science on a Sphere, including an interactive exhibit on global warming. Castle Memorial Hall houses changing displays and offers programs such as story-telling and an exhibit of royal personal possessions.

In 2005, the museum opened its Richard T. Mamiya Science of Honolulu are so distinct that when people say where they live, you can picture what their house looks like, know which fruit trees thrive in their yard, figure which restaurants they frequent, and guess their incomes.

Kaimuki: A century-old, working-class neighborhood of small homes with front porches, Kaimuki has the sweetest mangoes on the island. The main street, hilly Waialae Avenue, is retro 1940s revved up as an

An authentic grass house stands in the center of Hawaiian Hall at the Bishop Museum.

Adventure Center as a gathering place for people to experience the natural wonders of Hawaii, especially its oceans and skies.

Honolulu Neighborhoods

Whether deep green valleys, impossible-looking hills, or lazy shorelines, the neighborhoods impromptu "restaurant row," with chop suey houses, saimin (noodle soup) restaurants, coffee shops, authentic East Coast pizza at **Boston's North End Pizza Bakery** (3506 Waialae Ave., tel 808/734-1945), and a number of good restaurants, among them **3660 on the Rise** (3660 Waialae Ave., tel 808/737-1177).

Determined—and lucky—shoppers may find vintage aloha shirts, muumuus, or valuable Hawaiian kitsch in the many thrift shops. The 18-seat **Movie Museum** (*3566 Harding Ave., tel 808/735-8771*) screens old films such as *The Blue Gardenia*. It's perfect for this vintage neighborhood, with its 1920s and 1930s storefronts.

Kapahulu: Hugging the hem of Diamond Head, Kapahulu borders Waikiki. Kapahulu Avenue is another string of restaurants, mostly ethnic and inexpensive. **Ono Hawaiian Foods** (*726 Kapahulu Ave., tel 808/737-2275*) is a hole-in-the-wall where locals go for generous portions of fist-clenching food. Nearby, you can schedule a lesson in feather lei making from master artist Paulette Kahalepuna at her shop **Na Lima Mili Hulu Noeau** (*762 Kapahulu Ave., tel 808/732-0865*).

If you didn't have any luck in Kaimuki's thrift shops, you'll definitely find vintage and reproduction aloha wear and dust collectors at **Bailey's Antiques and Aloha Shirts** (*517 Kapahulu Ave., tel 808/734-7628*). On the corner of Kapahulu and Kihei Avenues is a small carriage-trade mall with more antique shops and fashion boutiques. Don't pass **Leonard's Bakery** (*933 Kapahulu Ave., tel 808/737-5591*) without stopping for hot *malasadas*, a Portuguese fried doughnut that's a local passion.

Manoa: The streets of Manoa are lined with big old houses and bigger old trees. The 300-acre **University of Hawaii campus** sits at the mouth of the cool, verdant valley. At the Visitor & Information Center you can pick up a map and find out what's going on in the way of cultural and artistic exhibits and performances, not only on campus but around town. Hour-long tours of the campus are conducted Monday, Wednesday, and Friday at 2 p.m. The center's bookstore and art gallery are worth a visit.

Wander through the sprawling **East-West Center,** a federally funded think tank to promote accord between the United States and the Asia-Pacific Basin. An authentic, solid teak Thai pavilion was personally presented by King

A formal Japanese garden graces the grounds of the University of Hawaii, Manoa.

Bhumibol Adulyadej in 1967; the hand-painted **Center for Korean Studies** was inspired by the Yi-dynasty style of Kyongbok Palace in Seoul. Stone Chinese temple dogs stand sentinel outside **Imin International Center,** while behind the wall is a tranquil Japanese garden bordered by a meandering stream filled with prize ornamental *koi* (carp). The center's Burns Hall features rotating exhibitions of art from Asia and the Pacific.

Way in the back of Manoa Valley, at the very end of Manoa Road, opposite **Lyon Arboretum** (see pp. 83–84), is the trail head for **Manoa Falls,** which is fed by 200 inches of rain a year. The 0.75-mile trail snakes through the thick,

INSIDER TIP:

There is nothing quite like the taste of fish fresh from Hawaiian waters. Jump at the opportunity to enjoy fresh fish at local restaurants.

—VINCENT KHOURY TYLOR
National Geographic contributor

lush rain forest, crossing streams and ending at the plunge pool for the falls; the muddiest parts are covered in boardwalk. Be sure to stay on the trail.

Honolulu Museum of Art

The Honolulu Museum of Art, formerly known as The Honolulu Academy of Arts, is located between Victoria and Ward

---

Spam I Am

"I want a Spam *musubi.***" Visit a diner or fast-food outlet in the islands and chances are high you will hear that phrase or see Spam on the menu, served in creative ways.**

Hawaii, especially its Asian population, has long held an affection for Spam, the humble "mystery meat" that comes in a can. Locals and visitors alike may be seen enjoying the snack, usually under $3. Among the many variations: Spam musubi, a rice block topped with the meat and held together with *nori* **(dried seaweed), or Spam with a slice of scrambled egg atop the rice square and an** *ume,* **a Japanese pickled plum, placed in the center.**

Streets in Honolulu. It was a member of the missionary-descendant Cooke family, Mrs. Charles (Anna) Montague Cooke (1853–1934), whose vision and family generosity launched the museum. She felt it was imperative for Hawaii's children, growing up thousands of miles from the nearest art museums, to have access to fine works of art. The design was a collaboration among New York architect Bertram Goodhue, the Cooke family, and Hardie Phillip, who completed the project after Goodhue's death.

Opened in 1927 to the strains of a concert by the Royal

University of Hawaii at Manoa

🅰 Map p. 57 & p. 59

✉ University Ave. & Dole St.

🚍 TheBus 4

Visitor Information

✉ Campus Center, 2465 Campus Rd.

☎ 808-956-7235

🕐 Closed Sat. & Sun.

East-West Center

✉ 1601 East-West Rd.

☎ 808-944-7111

🕐 Closed Sat. & Sun.

Honolulu Museum of Art

Map p. 56 & p. 59

900 S. Beretania St.

808/532-8700

Closed Mon.

$$ (free 1st Wed. of each month)

Hawaiian Band, the building itself has come to be regarded as a Hawaiian classic, with galleries flowing into courtyards, all of it looking a little Spanish, a little Florentine. You no sooner climb the front steps and enter than you are outdoors again, as spectacular flower arrangements grace the airy stone corridors. In 2005, the museum completed a massive renovation project that began in 1998. It involved expansion, acquisitions, redesign, new galleries, and climate control for the entire collection of more than 50,000 works of art.

The Museum's Collection:

For a museum of its size, the quality of the collection is extraordinary. The **Asian galleries,** to the left of the main entrance, are especially notable, and because their treasures are more perishable, they were the first to be overhauled. In the process, three new galleries were added, the Watumull Gallery of Indian Art, the Christiansen Gallery of Indonesian Art, and the George and Nancy Ellis Gallery of Filipino Arts. Japanese works include 13th-century scrolls, a seventh-century gold-and-silver basket for strewing

 Education Gallery

Fountain Court Gallery

 John Young Gallery

Asian Court

 Central Court

Mediterranean Court

 Luce Pavilion Complex

 Kinau Court

 Fountain Court

Luce Wing

Membership Department

Other areas

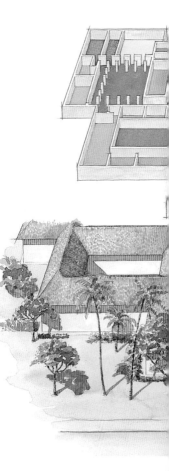

lotus petals, and the acclaimed James Michener collection of 10,000 ukiyo-e woodblock prints. The galleries display Indonesian masks, tribal weavings, third- and fourth-century sculptures from India, and a few examples of Philippine *santos,* wooden carvings of saints from the early Spanish settlement period.

The **Chinese painting collection** boasts one of the finest Ming and Qing painting collections in America. "The Coming of Autumn" was named by James Cahill in *The Compelling Image,* his book on Eastern art, as the finest surviving

INSIDER TIP:

After enjoying the fine collections of art on display, take a break for a relax- ing lunch at the Luce Pavilion Complex.

—DAVID L. MOORE
National Geographic contributor

masterpiece by the great Chinese painter Hong Ren (1610–1663).

While the **Western collections,** to the right of the main entrance, are not as strong or

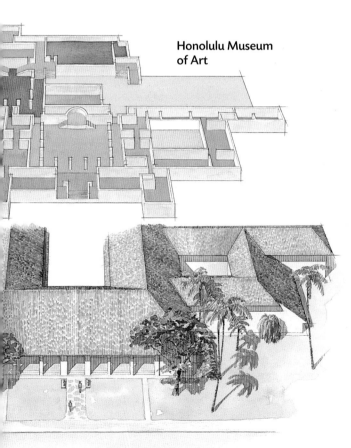

Honolulu Museum of Art

The Honolulu Museum of Art Spalding House

- Map p. 59
- 2411 Makiki Heights Dr.
- 808/526-0232
- Closed Mon.
- $$ (free 3rd Thurs. of each month)
- TheBus 15

Honolulu Museum of Art at First Hawaiian Center

- Map p. 67
- 999 Bishop St., 1st & 2nd floors of First Hawaiian Center
- 808/525-7000
- Closed Sat. & Sun.
- TheBus 56, 57, B & E

INSIDER TIP:

It's worth booking well ahead for a tour of exquisite Shangri La, the 1930s home of Doris Duke, housing her Islamic art collection.

—LOUISE NICHOLSON
National Geographic author

deep as the Asian, there are some remarkable works, including a room of French Impressionism—including van Gogh's "Wheatfield" and Gauguin's painting of Tahiti. Also here is a group of Italian Renaissance paintings, a 14th-century French limestone Madonna and Child, a Georgia O'Keeffe landscape of Hawaii, and works by Pablo Picasso and Winslow Homer.

Hawaii and its people, as seen by the first painters to visit the islands (see pp. 43–44), are on display in the **Hawaiian Gallery,** on the second floor of the Henry R. Luce Pavilion Complex.

The academy is a partner with **Shangri La,** the luxury Diamond Head home of heiress Doris Duke. For tours of the Islamic-style residence and courtyards, tiles, and art, reservations are required, usually months in advance *(tel 866/385-3849, shangrilahawaii.org).*

The Honolulu Museum of Art Spalding House

Mrs. Charles Montague Cooke, who was behind the Honolulu Museum of Art (see pp. 75–78), built Spalding House in Makiki Heights that has become a branch of the museum, dedicated to showcasing the best and brightest art created after 1940. The house was designed by Hart Wood in collaboration with C. W. Dickey, acknowledged as Hawaii's two greatest architects. It underwent expansions and renovations, and was finally transformed in 1988 into a modern museum.

The building sits on 3.5 acres of lush hillside: The exquisite intimate Japanese garden of grottoes and nooks known as

---

Poisonous Beauty

Lush plants, fruits, flowers, and bushes are prevalent in Hawaii. Some of them may be irritating or even dangerous to people, especially for those sensitive to such things. Following a few basic rules may prevent an unpleasant experience:

- In the wilds, do not eat or taste any strange fruit, seed, leaf, flower, or root. Some poisonous plants have berries that appear edible. Flowers such as the sweet-smelling plumeria or the pretty oleander may produce rashes or nausea if ingested.

- Be careful of contact with plants you do not know, especially those with rough hairy leaves, white or milky sap, an unusual shape, or spiny fruit or seed pods.
- Keep plants out of the reach of young children. Berries can choke children; sharp leaves or thorns may injure them.

For more information, contact the Hawaii Department of Agriculture *(tel 808/973-9401, hawaii.gov/hdoa/agresources)* or the Hawaii Poison Hotline *(tel 808/222-1222).*

Nuumealani ("heavenly heights") was designed by a Japanese Christian minister, the Reverend K. H. Inagaki, and took 13 years to complete. Views from the terrace sweep over the city to Diamond Head. Art ambushes you at every turn throughout the manicured grounds: Two stainless-steel kinetic sculptures by George Rickey play on the lawn, while Viola Frey's "Resting Woman No. 2" reclines beside the swimming pool.

The whimsy at the heart of the art at Spalding House camouflages its importance. The first thing visible upon arriving is a strange, bright-red, vaguely Japanese, vaguely Moby Dick sculpture by Jedd Garet. The front door is actually a pair of bronze gates by Robert Graham, each a three-dimensional female form. You won't be sure whether you're entering an art museum or a fun house. James Seawright's "Mirror XV" hanging just inside the entry will confound you—it's a quilt of odd-angled mirrors that reflect your face in dozens of carnival variations.

The **interior galleries** are spare and spacious with sunken floors and bridges. They are devoted to rotating exhibits of the permanent collection and a full calendar of changing exhibitions of predomi-nantly Hawaii artists. A separate pavilion houses a David Hockney walk-in environment inspired by the Maurice Ravel opera *L'Enfant et les Sortilèges*.

Among the artists represented are Josef Albers, Louise Nevelson, Jim Dine, Jasper Johns, Tom Wes-selmann, Deborah Butterfield, Frank Stella, William Wegman, James Surls, and Claes Oldenburg.

Viola Frey sculpted this woman lounging by the pool at the Honolulu Museum of Art Spalding House.

The museum has an excellent café in a garden setting and a gift shop.

More Contemporary Art

The Honolulu Museum of Art operates another satellite in the glass tower of First Hawaiian Center, corporate headquarters of First Hawaiian Bank. The ground and second floors of the ultramodern building have space for island artists' exhibits. The second-floor space is behind a glass curtain made of more than 4,000 panels of stone, glass, and aluminum designed by Jamie Carpenter.

The gallery is part of the vital city art scene. One of the most entertaining times to go is on the first Friday night of the month, when the downtown and Chinatown galleries offer party fare. A self-guided walking tour hits over two dozen hot spots in both downtown and Chinatown.

The Lei of the Land

One of the loveliest aspects of Hawaiian culture is the most fragile. The burden of seasons, the joys of life, the wonders of love, are entwined in the flowers of the lei. Always given with a kiss, the lei speaks eloquently where words might fail.

Origins are uncertain, but flowers have been strung into ceremonial garlands in Asia for centuries, and from there, the custom probably moved, with the people, into Oceania. In Hawaii, it enjoys its greatest flowering.

The beauty and artistry of the lei overwhelmed early visitors, including Isabella Lucy Bird, an intrepid traveler and journalist, who met King Lunalilo in 1873, and reported: "He was almost concealed by wreaths of ohia blossoms and festoons of maile [Hawaiian vine], some almost two yards long." The other guests, she wrote, "wore two, three, four, or even six beautiful lei, besides festoons of the fragrant maile. Lei of crimson ohia lehua blossoms were universal, but beside these, there were lei of small red and white double roses, *pohas,* yellow amaranth, cane tassels, like frosted silver, the orange pandanus, and delicious gardenia, and a very few orange blossoms, and the great granadilla or passion flower."

A lei can be made of almost anything—flowers, fruit, leaves, vine. Permanent leis are crafted from feathers, *kukui* nuts, shells, seeds, even human hair. Contemporary innovations include leis of candy and bubble gum, or the ultimate in tropical tackiness, airline-size liquor bottles. Although every lei is treasured, there is a subtle floral hierarchy: Those made of plumerias (frangipani) are the most common; pansy leis are among the most expensive. Leis fashioned from flowers picked in the giver's garden are probably the most appreciated.

The lei is not above trends; the maunaloa lei and the Micronesian ginger lei, both intricately crafted floral necklaces, were popular in the late 1990s because they complemented contemporary fashion in their simple, unobtrusive appearance. A masculine favorite has been the tailored cigar-flower lei in shades of rust and

Leis for sale are artistically displayed in Chinatown, Moiliili, and at airports and shops throughout the islands.

orange, and also the braided ti-leaf lei, which has the advantage of being inexpensive.

The three most common lei-making techniques are traditional. The *kui* method strings flowers lengthwise with needle and thread; the *haku* approach creates a braided base of ferns or stems; and a *wili* lei entwines the flowers with fiber (purists use softened banana fiber; cheaters use dental floss).

In ancient Hawaii, a lei was worn by a farmer in the field to invoke divine blessing upon his crops. Leis were worn by nursing mothers who believed in their life-giving, life-symbolizing power. Certain leis were used in healing rites performed by the *kahuna lapaau* (medical priest), and the lei was essential for dancers of the hula.

No matter the purpose or the flower, the giving and receiving of a lei has come down through time as a beautiful gesture from one person to another.

The action begins at **The ARTS at Mark's Garage** *(1159 Nuuanu Ave., tel 808/521-2903, artsat marks.com)*, a stylish show space and gallery with poetry slams and performances.

More Galleries: Several prominent artists have their galleries in Chinatown (see pp. 70–71). An international coterie of artists resident in Hawaii exhibit at the **Louis Pohl Gallery** *(1124 Bethel St., tel 808/521-1812)*. Gallery profits go to the Louis Pohl Foundation, which promotes local artists and art education. Pegge Hopper, known for her graphically strong illustrations of Hawaiian women, also

INSIDER TIP:

Visit Pegge Hopper Galleries to see how her paintings of native Hawaiian women have evolved to include women astride motorcycles, symbols of independence.

—THELMA CHANG
Author & National Geographic contributor

has her own **Pegge Hopper Galleries** *(1164 Nuuanu Ave., tel 808/524-1160, closed Sat.– Mon.)* selling originals and limited edition prints. The gallery showcases the work of other leading Hawaii artists as well, and it carries the latest in printmaking.

Sixteen artists exhibit at Hawaii's longest running artists' co-op, the **Gallery at Ward Centre** *(1200 Ala Moana Blvd., tel 808/597-8034)* in the Ward Centre shopping complex. **Native Books/Na Mea Hawaii** *(1050 Ala Moana Blvd., tel 808/597-8967, closed 9 p.m. & Sun. 6 p.m.)* specializes in traditional Hawaiian crafts.

Hawaii Nature Center & Hikes

Surrounded by a 2,000-acre preserve in Makiki Valley, the **Hawaii Nature Center** is a nonprofit environmental education organization that offers a variety of nature-centered activities and hikes to the general public. Most are easily accomplished by children, and hands-on exhibits at the center encourage young people to learn about the plants and animals in their surroundings. The center operates another facility on Maui (see p. 135).

The easy **Makiki Valley Loop Trail,** 2.7 miles long, begins at the bridge behind the environmental education center. Stop at the center to acquaint yourself with the history of the Makiki Valley and what to look for on the trail.

The first thing you'll see are reconstructed taro patches where different varieties of the Hawaiian staple are being propagated. The trail stretches out along a row of Norfolk and Cook Island pines. If you listen, you may hear the clear song of the *shama* thrush, a large black bird native to Malaysia and now resident in Hawaii.

Hawaii Nature Center

 Map p. 59

✉ 2131 Makiki Heights Dr.

☎ 808/955-0100

🚌 TheBus 17

The trees with distinctive silver leaves are *kukui,* whose nuts contain an oil that is used as lamp oil and makes an excellent furniture polish. When polished, the nuts are worn in leis. Other trees you'll pass are avocado (free samples August through October), the lemon-colored guava with its juicy pink flesh, mountain apple (in fruit July, August, and November), mahogany, and the beautiful koa, a native hardwood tree used for fine furniture, art objects, and even outrigger canoes.

You'll smell yellow ginger, eucalyptus, and allspice on the hike. Birds you may see are the spotted dove, mynah, house sparrow, the bright green *amakihi,* the warbling bulbul, and the small, green Japanese white-eye. The trail crosses streams five times and reaches a 760-foot elevation. Through the lush tropical vegetation, you can get fine views of Honolulu.

Gardens of Oahu

The floral heritage of Hawaii is abundant and unique: 95 percent of native flowering plants grow nowhere else on Earth (see p. 23). The first Polynesian settlers brought with them about 30 plants to add to the garden, and later immigrants from Europe, Asia, and the Americas brought their favorite clippings and seeds. It is estimated that about 800 exotic species have become fully naturalized in the islands: What we now think of as a Hawaiian garden is actually, like the people, a composite of many strains. There are more than 5,000 hybrids of hibiscus, the state flower. As for orchids, more than 700 species exist in Hawaii, as well as thousands of hybrids.

West of downtown Honolulu are **Moanalua Gardens.** This private garden, open to the public, as well as the valley behind it, is

Lyon Arboretum is home to more than 5,000 tropical plant species and a number of theme gardens.

Hiking Safety Tips

From time to time, hikers are reported lost, usually in the mountains. There are ways to maximize safety when hiking:

- Travel with a buddy.
- Notify others of your hiking plans, including when you intend to return.
- Do not hike in remote areas without an expert guide.
- Stay on designated trails and observe posted signs.
- Carry a backpack with a fully charged cell phone, an ample supply of water, mosquito repellent, a working flashlight, and snacks, including energy bars.
- Pack a blanket; you can purchase

tightly compacted ones at sporting goods stores.

- Start early, and be cognizant of the time and the distance you will be covering.
- If it is raining or the sky is overcast, postpone the hike. If it rains during your hike, head back. Flash floods are possible in mountain terrain.
- Be aware that the forests, except those on Lanai, are also home to wild pigs. Encounters are rare, but in that highly unlikely situation, climb the nearest tree. It is more likely for the pig to run the other way.
- If you are stuck somewhere and night falls, stay put until daylight.

INSIDER TIP:

Foster Botanical Garden offers visitors several acres of serenity and a rare glimpse of flora from the tropics and subtropics, with some trees planted in the 1850s.

—MICHAEL PIETRUSEWSKY
National Geographic field scientist

steeped in history. The pretty cottage under the trees with a taro patch in front was built in 1853–1854 for Prince Lot, who became King Kamehameha V. When ancient petroglyphs were discovered in the valley, the state, after a long, costly battle with activists, had to reroute a major freeway, with the result that the 16-mile H-3, originally estimated at 70 million dollars, came in at 1.25 billion dollars.

More than a century old and originally planted by the royal physician, Dr. William Hillebrand, **Foster Botanical Garden** (see sidebar p. 84) blooms on the border of downtown Honolulu. Approximately 4,000 tropical species have found a home in this urban oasis of ferns and tall trees. The **Prehistoric Glen** contains some of the oldest plant forms on Earth, some from the dinosaur age, organized and displayed in chronological order. There's also an excellent orchid collection and amazing bromeliads.

Nestled in the verdant folds of Manoa Valley (see pp. 74–75), the **Lyon Arboretum** is a well-planned, 194-acre garden that manages to look unplanned. Its experiments in hybridization, especially of hibiscus, calathea, rhododendron, and ginger, have introduced 148 hybrids to the world. You can trek through a valley of ferns, a rain forest, an herb garden, and beneath towering

Moanalua Gardens

 Map p. 56 & p. 58

✉ 1352 Pineapple Pl.

☎ 808/833-1944

🚌 TheBus 12

Foster Botanical Garden

🅰 Map p. 71

✉ 50 N. Vineyard Blvd.

☎ 808/522-7060

💲 $$

🚌 TheBus 4

Lyon Arboretum

🅰 Map p. 57 & p. 59

✉ 3860 Manoa Rd.

☎ 808/988-0456

🕐 Closed all holidays

🚌 TheBus 5

Koko Crater Botanical Garden
- Map p. 57
- 400 Kealahou St.
- 808/522-7060
- TheBus 23, Kealahou St.

Hoomaluhia Botanical Garden
- Map p. 57
- 45-680 Luluku Rd., Kaneohe
- 808/233-7323
- TheBus 55 or 56

Wahiawa Botanical Garden
- Map p. 56
- 1396 California Ave., Wahiawa
- 808/628-1190
- TheBus 52 from Ala Moana Shopping Center

trees while lily ponds, benches, and pavilions offer quiet places for contemplation. One of the more intriguing areas is the Beatrice H. Krauss Ethnobotanical Garden, with useful Hawaiian plants. The arboretum's gift shop carries books, local crafts, and jams and jellies made from the fruits and herbs grown in the garden.

Koko Crater Botanical Garden lies within the 60-acre basin of an extinct volcano on the southeastern shore of Oahu (see p. 99). The garden is a testing ground for Xeriscape gardening, a system aimed to conserve precious water along this arid coast. Its important collections include climbing cactuses, aloes, sansevierias, euphorbias, and palms. A self-guided walk will take an hour and a half. Bring drinking water.

On the Windward Side near Kaneohe (see pp. 102–103), **Hoomaluhia Botanical Garden** is 400 acres of serenity with a 32-acre lake. The garden was designed and built by the U.S. Army Corps of Engineers to help protect Kaneohe from floodwaters. Labeled plants—many of them endangered and rare—representing the world's tropical latitudes, are grouped by area of origin. There are good hiking trails, and it's a rewarding place for bird-watching. Camping is allowed by permit. Free guided walks are offered on Saturdays at 10 a.m. and Sundays at 1 p.m.

Wahiawa Botanical Garden is set in 27 acres of high-elevation tropical rain forest in the middle of Wahiawa, central Oahu. It has a notable fern collection, a Hawaiian garden, an aroid (plants of the arum family) garden, and 60 exceptional trees from around the world. It is the venerable old trees that give this garden its character. Don't forget to bring insect repellent. ∎

Botanicals

Idyllic settings of Hawaii's gardens may lead one to wonder: Could there be such a peaceful setting near the hustle and bustle of downtown Honolulu? Yes. Busy downtown workers, residents, and visitors from afar can find respite at **Foster Botanical Garden** (tel 808/522-7060, honolulu.gov/parks/hbg/fbg.htm, guided tours: $), part of the Department of Parks and Recreation, City and County of Honolulu.

Outside the range of crowds and traffic noises, more than 13 acres serve as a living museum of tropical plants, including rare and endangered ones, which have been collected from the world's tropics for some 150 years. Majestic trees tower over a garden that features terraces; an orchid garden; a prehistoric glen of primitive plants; an "economic" garden of spices, dyes, herbs, and poisonous plants; and a main terrace that dates back to 1853, when Queen Kalama leased a small parcel of land to William Hillebrand, a German physician and botanist. He planted the trees and later sold the property to Thomas and Mary Foster.

The Fosters bequeathed five acres to the city for use as a public garden that, in time, grew larger through gifts and land purchases.

EXPERIENCE: Sightseeing by Seaplane

The sea runways of the Pan Am China Clippers have been reopened in Keehi Lagoon, which is next to Honolulu International Airport. A seaplane flight-seeing company, Island Seaplane Service, offers airborne tours of Oahu. It has two aircraft: A Cessna 206 that accommodates the pilot and four passengers and a six-passenger DeHavilland Beaver. Book either a half-hour or one-hour narrated flight. Complimentary van service gets you to and from your hotel.

Taking off from water is thrilling, like being in a speedboat revving up to full horsepower and then finding yourself suddenly airborne. On the half-hour flight, you fly over downtown Honolulu and Waikiki at 300 to 400 feet—perfect for aerial photography. Passengers will peer into Diamond Head Crater, see the mansions along Kahala Beach, and head out toward Koko Head Crater, Hanauma Bay, the spouting Halona Blowhole, and along Sandy Beach. Around the mountains, the beauty of the Windward Side bursts upon the senses, and you'll view green palisades, offshore islands, and beautiful Kaneohe Bay.

The one-hour flight follows the same route but continues to the valley where parts of *Jurassic Park, Godzilla,* and *Mighty Joe Young* were shot. You'll get a view of the Polynesian Cultural Center, the old Kahuku Sugar Mill, and the famous surfing beaches of the North Shore. You'll fly over pineapple fields, Schofield Barracks, and then power in over the air path used by the Japanese bombers in the infamous attack on Pearl Harbor. In calm water, you may be able to see the rusting hulk of the U.S.S. *Arizona* beneath the waves.

Landing on Keehi Lagoon is exhilarating, with the plane hovering for the right moment, the right ripple of sea, before you feel the warm breath of the ocean as the plane glides to its pier.

For information contact **Island Seaplane Service, Inc.** *(85 Lagoon Dr., 808/836-6273, $$$$$).*

Pat Magie and his wife, Debbie, operate Island Seaplane Service from the old sea runways in Keehi Lagoon.

Waikiki

Waikiki. The name is magic: It conjures images of moon-drenched surf, Diamond Head, hula maidens, bronze beachboys, and ukulele music. Early Hawaiians gave it this name, which means "spouting water," because of its rushing streams and gushing springs.

From the pink Royal Hawaiian Hotel and other hotels, the views go all the way to Diamond Head.

An Old Retreat

Ancient chants sing of the best surfing spots, including a *kapu* (forbidden) break reserved for chiefs and chiefesses, who rode naked on 18-foot boards. Because surfing was considered a religious activity, temples to the sport once stood along the beach. The principal one, Papae-naena at the foot of Diamond Head, overlooked the popular surfing spot now called First Break. To signal that the surf was up, the priest flew a kite.

In 1804 Kamehameha the Great, having conquered all islands except Kauai, assembled an army of 7,000 warriors on Waikiki Beach to assault this last bastion. The sea bristled with his armada of 27 well-armed schooners, a 20-cannon gunboat, and 500 war canoes. However, the invasion was abandoned when a plague swept through the ranks.

The ruler of all the islands had a villa in Waikiki. Here he married his sacred wife, High Chiefess Keopuolani, from Maui. No Waikiki wedding has matched it.

The first written accounts of Waikiki came from Captain George Vancouver and his crew in 1792. On board was naturalist Archibald Menzies, who described Waikiki as "one of those interesting landscapes which the eye of a meditative mind could long contemplate with new felt pleasure." In his time, it was a land of taro farms and fishponds with thatched homes scattered in the verdure. To set an example of industry for his people, King Kamehameha I personally worked in the taro patches, as did his royal sons.

In 1863, Charles de Varigny, a Frenchman who became prime minister of the Hawaiian kingdom, wrote of visiting the site (near the present Royal Hawaiian Hotel), which was in ruins and "covered with periwinkle." He wrote: "Waikiki is today a charming little village where the people of Honolulu like occasionally to spend several weeks at a time for the pleasure of sea bathing."

Birth of a Resort

About this time the first road made its way around the duck ponds and taro patches from Honolulu to Waikiki. The first public transportation followed—a mule-drawn bus. In 1863, King Kamehameha IV offered to sell a strip of land running from downtown Honolulu to Diamond Head to Eliza Sinclair, a rancher's widow from New Zealand, for $10,000. She turned him down because it wasn't good grazing ground and bought the island of Niihau (see p. 233) instead. That same year, the first Waikiki cottages were opened as guest bungalows and named "Sans Souci." Author

Waikiki

🅝 Map p. 56, p. 59, & below

Visitor Information

✉ Hawaii Visitors & Convention Bureau, Royal Hawaiian Center, 2270 Kalakaua Ave., Suite 801

☎ 808/923-1811

🕐 Closed Sat. & Sun.

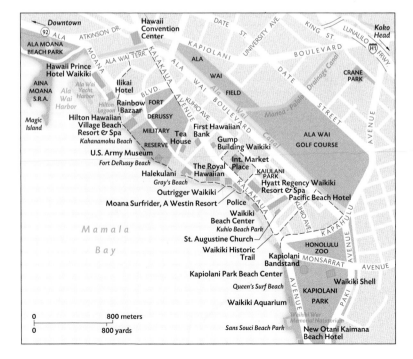

Robert Louis Stevenson came to stay and wrote: "If anyone desires such old-fashioned things as lovely scenery, quiet pure air, clear sea water, good food, and heavenly sunset hung out before his eyes over the Pacific and the distant hills of Waianae, I recommend him cordially to the 'Sans Souci.'"

All those attributes still describe Waikiki, except for "old-fashioned." The 500-acre resort, a mere 2 miles long and a half-mile wide, is the epicenter of a $14 billion tourism industry. A wall of hotels rises behind the people-packed sands, and the waters are dotted with swimmers, surfers, canoes, sailboats, water bikes, rafts—in fact, anything that floats, and some that don't, such as sightseeing submarines. Yet in spite of the crowds, the hustle, and the tacky souvenirs, that old magic asserts itself, and people who haven't been on terms of endearment for years hold hands and stroll through moonlit surf. Waikiki may be high and brash, but it isn't fake, and it's definitely fun.

The Beaches

Waikiki is actually a string of beaches, one flowing into the other in a long line of golden sand with Diamond Head rising to the east in a perpetual

The Duke

The father of modern surfing was Duke Paoa Kahanamoku (1890–1968), who brought the ancient Hawaiian sport of *hee nalu* to California, Australia, and New Zealand, and popularized it around the world.

The Duke was an amazing athlete, whose performances in the water were as impressive as those on top of it. As a young man, his swims were timed and the results sent to the Amateur Athletic Union in New York. The skeptical recipients were unimpressed. "Unacceptable," they replied. "No one swims this fast." In 1912, however, he won a gold and a silver swimming medal at the Summer Olympics in Sweden. He caught Hollywood's eye, too, and was cast in 30 films.

Riding his 114-pound koa board in the long rollers off Waikiki's Diamond Head, the Duke also attracted great attention for the sport of surfing, which had been in decline in the islands where it was born. The sport received a huge boost in 1965 when Honolulu businessman Kimo Wilder McVay, working with the Duke and surfer Fred Hemmings, created the Duke Kahanamoku Surfing Classic and got CBS to film it—the world's first network broadcast of a surfing contest. The top 24 surfers in the world came to Hawaii for the Classic to compete and surf with the Duke. The event was held at Sunset Beach, and it was local surfer Jeff Hakman who was the eventual winner.

The Duke Kahanamoku Surfing Classic helped make surfing a respectable sport, not quite on a par with golf and tennis, perhaps, but certainly elevated above its onetime hippie trappings. Today the ancient sport is televised internationally, and lures people from countries across the globe into its "endless-summer" lifestyle.

In 1990, the centennial of his birth, a bronze statue of the Hawaiian who won the hearts of the world was unveiled in Waikiki, at Kuhio Beach near the spot where he was said to have ridden a 30-foot wave for a full mile.

photo-op moment. Each has its own character and, like all beaches in Hawaii, is open to the public.

Beginning in the west, **Kahanamoku Beach and Lagoon** is calm enough for babies. From a pier at one end, people are water-taxied out to sightseeing submarines and catamaran cruises.

Fort DeRussy Beach, a 20-acre property owned by the U.S. government, is bordered in green lawns and big shade trees with picnic tables beneath.

INSIDER TIP:

Watch the free sunset hula performance at Kuhio Beach. Different *halau* alternate responsibilities for this performance, which adds to the enjoyment.

—MIRIAM STARK
National Geographic field scientist

Gray's Beach, in front of the Halekulani Hotel, is often inundated by tides, but the swimming is grand because of the cool freshwater springs feeding the ocean. The beach was named for Mrs. LaVancha Gray, who operated a boardinghouse where the hotel is now. In ancient times, it was a spot to beach canoes, and *kahuna* (masters, priests) practiced their healing arts here. People still come to these waters for healings.

The best swimming is at **Royal Moana Beach** in front of the Royal Hawaiian, Outrigger Waikiki, and Moana hotels. The Outrigger

Rental surfboards are stacked along Waikiki Beach. First-timers can sign up for lessons.

operates a comprehensive beach activity center where you can sign up for a surprisingly inexpensive outrigger canoe ride, surfing the foamy rollers sweeping in past Diamond Head. Or you can learn to surf—the beachboys guarantee, tongue in cheek, to have even grandmothers standing on their boards, riding the waves like a hotdogger, in one lesson.

The **Waikiki Beach Center,** across from the Hyatt Regency Waikiki, has food concessions, canoe rentals, a bathhouse, benches, and chairs. Locals come to play cards and "talk story." At adjacent **Kuhio Beach Park,** a long wall extends into the ocean: It's a great place to watch surfers, body-boarders, and the tangerine sunsets. The water behind the wave berm looks deceptively safe, but nonswimmers have drowned by falling into unseen holes under the waves. Another danger here is the bacteria count, which can be high because the water is both still and much used.

Queen's Surf Beach on the other side of the pier is a favorite for body-boarding. The grassy lawn and coconut palms make it popular with picnicking families. Check newspapers or your concierge desk for dates for **Sunset on the Beach,** a night of free movies and inexpensive food kiosks from some of the best Waikiki restaurants.

The Rainbow Tower mosaic at the Hilton Hawaiian Village Beach Resort & Spa, in Waikiki, competes with real rainbows.

Kapiolani Park Beach Center, next to Queen's Surf Beach, has restrooms, dressing rooms, and refreshments. The surfing area there is known as Public's. **Sans Souci Beach Park** in front of the War Memorial Natatorium (see p. 98) offers another good, calm swimming area.

Waikiki's Hotels

Hotels along "life's greatest beach" are more than just places to flop at the end of a day of sun, fun, and sightseeing. Many are attractions in themselves.

Riding the glass elevator at the **Hawaii Prince Hotel Waikiki** *(100 Holomoana Street, tel 808/956-1111)* will give you a great view of the Koolau Mountains; the Ala Wai Canal, where outrigger canoes practice for races; and the Hawaii Convention Center. The **Ilikai Hotel** *(1777 Ala Moana Blvd., tel 808/949-3811)* also has a glass-elevator ride and, from the second-floor pool deck, a view of the Ala Wai yacht harbor.

The **Hilton Hawaiian Village Beach Resort & Spa** (see p. 244) is bigger than many small towns. When full, its 3,537 rooms, plus a staff of 2,000, could give the hotel complex a population of almost 10,000 people. The Rainbow Shopping Bazaar incorporates a Thai temple, a Japanese pagoda, an authentic Japanese farmhouse, and two granite lions guarding a Chinese moon gate. The world's tallest mosaic mural splashes up the side of a 30-story tower in rainbow colors. There's a penguin pond, a flamingo lawn, and homes for endangered Hawaiian birds.

The **Halekulani** (see p. 244) is easily the beach's most elegant hotel. Its prized mosaic blooms on the bottom of the swimming pool: The 30-foot orchid is composed of 1.25 million glass tiles. In 1925, author Earl Derr Biggers plotted his Charlie Chan mystery, *House Without a Key,* while staying in a cottage next to the hotel. The new "House Without a Key" is the (see p. 244). The Victorian "first lady of Waikiki," the city's oldest hotel, resides among the high-rises like a big white wedding cake. The beaux arts building, which is now on the National Register of Historic Places, was designed by Oliver P. Traphagen and opened in 1901. For 40 years, the famous

From Cramped Alley to Waikiki Epicenter

Lewers Street in Waikiki was once a narrow road in which cars, vans, trucks, bicycles, and people had to perform some tricky maneuvering. The immediate vicinity, including Beach Walk on the *Ewa* (west) side of Lewers, was like a dark canyon of aging buildings between Kalakaua Avenue and the ocean.

Today the site tells a far different story after undergoing extensive renovations that started in 2005. Now known as Waikiki Beach Walk, its nearly eight acres offer visitors an open, walk-friendly 93,000-square-foot complex of hotels, shops, restaurants, and places for live entertainment. Key features now include an open public plaza fronting Lewers Street where you can take in performances of Hawaiian music and dance. In between, visitors will find just about everything else to suit their taste—from sweets, coffee, and fine dining to clothing, jewelry, and sunscreen. Oh, and also a place to stay.

hotel bar, a great place to watch the sunset. Now you have the added pleasure of Hawaiian music and Kanoe Miller, who weaves a hula magic Earl Derr Biggers would have loved.

Looking like a movie set, the **Royal Hawaiian Hotel** (see p. 244) opened in 1927 with a black-tie dinner costing an exorbitant $10 a plate. The "Pink Palace of the Pacific" was designed by a New York firm, Warren and Wetmore. Its lush landscaping was planned around surviving coconut palms from King Kamehameha the Great's royal retreat. Even after an elegant update, the hotel retains its monarchy-era charm.

You can't miss the **Moana Surfrider, A Westin Resort**

"Hawaii Calls" radio show was broadcast from under the huge banyan tree (planted in 1885) beside the hotel's old-fashioned veranda, where high tea is served in the afternoon and ladies delicately cool themselves with sandalwood fans. Robert Louis Stevenson composed poems beneath the tree, and told stories to Princess Kaiulani. Stop in at the Historical Room to see memorabilia of old Waikiki.

A thousand fish swim in the lobby of the twin-tower **Pacific Beach Hotel** *(2490 Kalakaua Ave., tel 808/922-1233).* A huge 280,000-gallon aquarium rises two stories with two restaurants, **Oceanarium** and **Aloha Center Cafe,** wrapping around it.

U.S. Army Museum

- Map p. 87
- Kalia & Saratoga Rds.
- 808/438-2821
- Closed Sun. & Mon.
- TheBus 8, 19, 54

Tea House of the Urasenke Foundation

- Map p. 87
- 245 Saratoga Rd.
- 808/923-3059
- $
- TheBus 8, 19, 54

Waikiki Off the Beach

The **U.S. Army Museum** at Fort DeRussy has a collection from the darker side of the human psyche, beginning with weaponry of ancient Hawaii, through the American Revolution, the Spanish-American War, both World Wars, Korea, and Vietnam. The museum is housed in Battery Randolf, one of six coastal defenses built on Oahu between 1908 and 1915. On its ocean side, the concrete walls are 22 feet thick; when the

---

Avoid Mr. or Ms. Charming

They may appear friendly and chatty, but beware of hawkers in streetside kiosks who call themselves activities or information centers. The salespeople are usually selling time-shares and offer visitors free or discounted activities, but not before they are persuaded to attend a sales presentation. Once visitors are hooked into such a gathering, they are pressured to part with thousands of dollars for a timeshare investment. As always: "Buyer beware."

---

military attempted to demolish the massive structure in 1969, Battery Randolf broke the wrecking ball. Instead, the Army outfitted it and opened it as a museum on December 7, 1976, the 35th anniversary of the attack on Pearl Harbor and the day before the U.S.'s entry into World War II.

The **Tea House of the Urasenke Foundation,** right across the street from the U.S. Army Museum, seeks to promote international understanding through the Zen of tea. The authentic teahouse was designed by grand tea master Soshitsu Sen of the Urasenke Foundation in Kyoto, Japan, and was a gift to the Japanese Chamber of Commerce in Hawaii in 1952.

On Wednesday and Friday mornings, you may partake of the ancient Japanese tea ceremony (it's a good idea to make a reservation). While you sit on the floor in a tearoom, ladies in kimonos will serve you foamy *matcha,* the chartreuse tea made from the tops of 400-year-old tea bushes. In his book, *Chado, The Japanese Way of Tea,* Soshitsu Sen wrote: "In the practice of tea, a sanctuary is created where one can take solace in the tranquillity of the spirit."

Stop in at **First Hawaiian Bank** *(2181 Kalakaua Ave., tel 808/943-4670, closed Sat. & Sun.)* to see the six massive murals in the lobby by Jean Charlot (1898–1979). Charlot, whose work is represented in the Uffizi Gallery in Florence, Italy, the British Museum in London, and the Metropolitan Museum of Art and the Museum of Modern Art in New York, depicted the peopling of Hawaii and the evolution of the culture.

One of Waikiki's architectural gems is the 1929 **Gump Building Waikiki** *(2200 Kalakaua Ave.),* built in Hawaiian colonial style with its blue tile roof. Restored to its original grandeur, the building today is the home of Louis Vuitton signature luxury goods.

You won't be able to miss the **International Market Place** *(2330 Kalakaua Ave., tel 808/923-9871, closes at 11 p.m.)*. In the face of beautification and upscaling all around it, this hodgepodge acre or so of shops, pushcarts, psychics, wood-carvers, candlemakers, and juice squeezers remains resolutely, defiantly tacky. Looking before departing for home. The ceremonies lasted for a "full moon," wrote historian George S. Kanahele in his book *Waikiki 100 B.C. to 1900 A.D.: An Untold Story.* It's a good thing the police station wasn't there then, because, Kanahele noted, "a sacrifice was offered of a virtuous young chiefess whose body was placed beneath one of the stones."

In Waikiki, luxury boutiques and tacky souvenir stalls offer shoppers a full range of wares.

for dashboard hula maidens, obscene ashtrays, cheap eats, or Mickey Mouse towels? This is your one-stop mini-mall. At night, the sidewalk fronting the market is a magnet for street musicians and others, such as bongo drummers, mimes, and doomsday prophets.

Next to the Honolulu Police substation *(2405 Kalakaua Ave.)*, you'll see four big rocks known as the **Stones of Kapaemahu.** According to tradition, the stones, each weighing thousands of pounds, were quarried in Kaimuki and brought to Waikiki sometime before the 16th century to honor four healing priests from Tahiti who, it is said, transferred their healing powers to the stones

A **statue of Princess Kaiulani,** last heir to the Hawaiian throne, who died at the age of 23, stands in **Kaiulani Park** *(Kaiulani & Kuhio Aves.)*. The 7-foot bronze sculpture is by Jan Gordon Fisher.

The Kuhio Avenue side of Waikiki is a colorful blend of people, noodle shops, discount stores, taverns, souvenir shops, quaint cottages, apartments, hotels, and longtime resident St. Augustine's Church. Kuhio and Kalakaua Avenues offer different contrasts, but they are two sides of the same coin.

New bronze surfboard-shaped history markers have been placed throughout Waikiki to mark significant sites (see p. 118).

(continued on p. 96)

The Outrigger Canoe

The outrigger canoe is as central to Hawaii's identity as the philosophy of aloha (see pp. 16–17), and it is as common around the islands as the coconut palm. Some anthropologists suggest that when the Polynesians set out on voyages of exploration (see p. 24, p. 26), those with fat to spare had the best chance of surviving. By natural selection, Polynesians thus became a race of generously proportioned people.

On Hawaii, they found hardwood trees with girths of 20 feet across, large enough to yield an entire canoe hull from a single trunk. With these, the Hawaiians perfected their shipbuilding techniques, using stone, shell, and wood tools to fashion the craft; braided coconut husk ropes for lashing; and woven plant fiber for sails. In the process, they created what is possibly the most versatile, seaworthy rough-water vessel ever to sail any sea.

The distinct outrigger or arm of the canoe is an ancient design that stabilizes the vessel in the Pacific's notorious swells. It is said that the early Hawaiians trained the branches of young *hau* trees to grow in the curved shape of the outrigger booms (the pieces that hold the small outrigger to the main body of the canoe). For long voyages, a second hull was added and a deck lashed between the two. The romantic upward thrust of the prow of these voyaging canoes, once assumed to be ornamental, was discovered to be essential to "plow" the swells—the sleek vessels were, in fact, conspicuous in their lack of decoration.

Building an Outrigger Canoe

Building an outrigger canoe took more than skill. Historian David Malo wrote in 1836, "The building of a canoe was an affair of religion." Tommy Holmes, in his authoritative book *The Hawaiian Canoe*, lists 26 canoe deities. The *kahuna kalai waa* (master canoe builder) was as adept at ritual as he was at carving. The consecration ceremony and feast for the completion of a canoe was called *lolo ana ka waa i ka halau,* meaning "imparting brains to the canoe," so it would

be "rooted in the sea" and "tear apart the billows of the ocean." Each canoe was said to have a destiny.

The outrigger canoes plying the tourist trade on Waikiki Beach today differ very little from the canoes seen by Captain Cook on his voyage of discovery in 1778. At Kealakekua Bay (see pp. 154–155) on the Big Island, two of Cook's officers estimated that between 2,500 and 3,500 outrigger canoes came out to greet

INSIDER TIP:

One of the best deals in Hawaii is surfing a Hawaiian canoe off Waikiki Beach. Just walk up to one of the canoes on the beach to arrange a ride.

—DOUGLAS PEEBLES
National Geographic contributor

his ships, the *Resolution* and the *Discovery.* When Kamehameha the Great assembled his armada of war canoes on the shore of Oahu, they stretched more than 5 miles solid, from Waikiki to Waialae. Historian and author Abraham Fornander wrote in his *History of the Polynesian People* that an ancient Big Island king, setting out to conquer Maui, assembled a fleet of outrigger canoes so numerous they "covered the ocean from Hawaii to Maui and the people used them as a road to cross over on." That would be an almost unbelievable 30 miles of ocean.

Racing an Outrigger Canoe

Canoe paddling has always been a popular

Paddlers compete in a Maui outrigger canoe regatta.

Hawaiian sport, and with the arrival of Western culture, the races were formalized into regattas. The first recorded outrigger regatta was held in honor of the first birthday of Crown Prince Albert, son of King Kamehameha IV, on May 20, 1859. Two of Hawaii's top racing clubs today, the Outrigger Canoe Club and Hui Nalu, were founded in 1908.

During June and July, canoe races take place almost every weekend somewhere in the state; usually they are listed in the local newspaper. The biggest is the race from Molokai to Oahu, a 40-mile haul through the treacherous Kaiwi Channel. Competition is fierce and race finishes are spectacular—paddlers and canoes, are drenched in kisses and draped in leis.

Outriggers are launched daily along Waikiki Beach as veteran paddlers take visitors to sea in canoes. It's a wild ride down the white crests with sea foam spraying like wings and Diamond Head in the background.

Atop Diamond Head, views stretch from Kapiolani Park, to Waikiki, to the Waianae Mountains.

Honolulu Zoo

- Map p. 59 & p. 87
- 151 Kapahulu Ave.
- 808/971-7171
- $$
- TheBus 2; 8, 19, 20, 47

Separating Waikiki from the rest of Honolulu, the 25-block **Ala Wai Canal** was built between 1921 and 1924 to channel rainwater from the mountains into the ocean and dry out the marshes of Waikiki, setting the stage for the resort you see today. If you stroll beside the canal in late afternoon, you'll usually see rainbows over the mountains, and outrigger canoe paddlers training for races. Watch out for joggers and in-line skaters lost in their headset music.

Kapiolani Park & Diamond Head

Hawaii's first public park was dedicated on Kamehameha Day 1877, and named by King Kalakaua for his beloved wife Queen Kapiolani. The 200-acre sweep of lawns and trees is backed by Diamond Head. In its earliest days, women swathed in yards of satin, and draped in leis, feathers, and hats would parade their flower-adorned horses through the park. *Pau* riders are still a colorful part of every Hawaiian parade. Kapiolani Park once hosted horse races, polo games, and auto races.

INSIDER TIP:

For quick geographical reference, Diamond Head is on Oahu's east side and Ewa is on the island's west side.

—THELMA CHANG
Author & National Geographic contributor

Today's activities include archery, softball, basketball, tennis, martial arts, and family picnics. In December, the annual Honolulu Marathon finishes here.

The **Honolulu Zoo** anchors one end of the park. There are bigger and better zoos elsewhere, but this one is pretty, and where else can you photograph monkeys with Diamond Head in the background or watch an endangered nene (the goose that is the state bird) waddle about? On Wednesday evenings in summer, the zoo offers "The Wildest Show in Town," a free musical entertainment; check local newspapers for particulars. On Wednesdays, Saturdays, and Sundays, look for the **Zoo Fence Art Mart;** many acclaimed local artists got their start hanging on the zoo fence. Much of the work is affordable and certainly makes a better souvenir than some of the Hawaiian vulgarities made in Taiwan and the Philippines.

The Honolulu Symphony and visiting talent perform in the park at the **Waikiki Shell,** and people bring their beach mats and picnic suppers to be serenaded under the stars. The park's other entertainment stage, the **Kapiolani Bandstand,** has been completely rebuilt with more outdoor seating and new landscaping that includes streams and a reflecting pond. It is the site of Sunday afternoon hula shows or concerts by the Royal Hawaiian Band.

The **Waikiki Aquarium,** the nation's third oldest, is oceanside in the park, and built on a coral reef. Opened in 1910, and recently renovated, the facility harbors more than 300 species of Hawaiian and Pacific marine life, including giant 100-pound clams, chambered nautiluses (the only ones bred in captivity), sea horses, and sharks. There's also a special habitat for the endangered Hawaiian monk seal, a touch-me tide pool, a theater with continuously screened short films,

Waikiki Aquarium

 Map p. 59 & p. 87

2777 Kalakaua Ave.

808/923-9741

$$

TheBus 19 or 20

EXPERIENCE: Diving for an Undersea Panorama

Warm waters, brilliantly colored marine life, unusual rock formations, and the challenge of the deep are some of the reasons scuba divers around the world are attracted to Hawaii. Each island exhibits characteristics that lend themselves to the different experience levels of divers, from beginner to advanced.

Certified divers should remember to bring their certificate, along with an ID. Novices would be wise to acquire the necessary skills and earn certification before attempting a dive. However, some beginners may be able to receive instructions and guidance under certain conditions set by the operator.

Most dives run between two and three hours, and for planning purposes you should allow yourself either an entire morning or an afternoon.

There are many extraordinary dive sites off Oahu. Divers can experience an underwater theater of turtles, eels, schools of fish, or shipwrecks that are forming reefs.

Among the many outfitters offering dive charters and courses (including introductory) on Oahu are: **Aaron's Dive Shop** (*307 Hahani St., Kailua, tel 808/262-2333, aaronsdiveshop .com, $$$$$*), in business for 35 years, offers dive charters 365 days a year. **Dive Oahu** (*has five locations around Oahu, tel 808/922-3483, diveoahu.com, $$$$$*) has a deep wreck dive and shallow reef dive, among others.

Diamond Head State Monument

- 🅰 Map p. 59
- ✉ Makapuu & 18th Aves.
- 🚌 TheBus 22

The Kahala Hotel & Resort

- 🅰 Map p. 57
- ✉ 5000 Kahala Ave.
- ☎ 808/739-8888
- 🚌 TheBus 22

Hanauma Bay Nature Preserve

- 🅰 Map p. 57
- ✉ Kalanianaole Hwy. (Hawaii 72)
- ☎ 808/396-4229
- 🕐 Closed Tues.
- 💲 $
- 🚌 TheBus 22, or Hanauma Bay Shuttle, every 30 min., 8:30 a.m.–1 p.m.

and interactive exhibits with a focus on the status of coral reefs.

The nearby **Waikiki War Memorial Natatorium,** built in 1927, has occasioned battles between those who want to tear down the decaying monument and those determined to save it. The swimming pool, the largest saltwater pool in the country and once a training pool for champions, is falling apart and infested with eels.

Diamond Head Hike

You can climb to the 760-foot summit of **Diamond Head** and enjoy panoramic views of Waikiki in one direction and clear out to Koko Head in the other, with the Diamond Head Lighthouse, brightest light in the Pacific, at your feet. The trail head is inside the crater, which you enter by walking or driving through a tunnel—the entrance is well marked on Diamond Head Road. In October 1999, a thousand youth attending the Millennium Young People's Congress planted 900 native Hawaiian plants in a new Peace Garden not far from the park entrance.

Trail signs will tell you the 1.4-mile hike will take an hour, but you can easily do it in half an hour, even with a child in tow. Be sure to bring drinking water, and a flashlight for navigating a dark tunnel. Diamond Head was a military installation in World War II and is headquarters for the island's civil defense. Sirens are tested at 11:45 a.m. the first Tuesday of every month. There is a dollar fee for the hike.

Diamond Head was first called Leahi, meaning "place of fire," by Hawaiians because Pele, goddess

of fire and volcanoes (see p. 174), once sojourned here. However, British sailors in 1825 saw calcite crystals glittering in the sun and thought they had found enough diamonds to marry all the girls in England. The name stuck, and was oddly prophetic because the real estate at the base of the volcanic tuff cone is more precious than crown jewels.

INSIDER TIP:

The hiking trail inside Diamond Head crater offers stunning views of Oahu's southern shore, including a panoramic view of the Waikiki shoreline.

—JOHN SEATON CALLAHAN
National Geographic contributor

East Honolulu

Kahala, Honolulu's most prestigious neighborhood, is lately infested with bizarre statuary by a foreign billionaire. Neglected properties blight the once lovely beach. Kahala Avenue deadends at **The Kahala Hotel & Resort.** Built in 1959, this luxury enclave is the choice of visiting heads of state. Anyone, with or without tiara, can enjoy the spa and gardens or book a dolphin encounter in the hotel's lagoon. Adjacent is the exclusive Waialae Golf Course, where many top tournaments are played.

Hawaii Kai, built around a series of lagoons and canals emptying into Maunalua Bay, is a

Jellyfish Swarms

Like the title of a horror movie, their presence has been called an "invasion." However, box jellyfish typically drift with the currents, show up in Hawaii waters and beaches between 7 and 11 days after a full moon, and literally hang around for several days. Jellyfish tentacles, designed to catch food, deliver painful stings that are random and short-lived. It's rare to find a stung beachgoer who requires an emergency room visit, but the sting can be deadly for some people. It's wise for beachgoers, especially those allergic to stings, to stay out of the water.

Heed posted signs and lifeguard warnings. Lifeguards will shut down a portion of beach when box jellyfish arrive in massive numbers, as in May 2004 when 1,000 box jellyfish arrived at Waikiki Beach sooner than expected.

bedroom community of 30,000 people. The sheltered bay is a mecca for Jet Skiing and parasailing. (You can also rent snorkel gear for Hanauma Bay.)

Six thousand years ago, when a wall of Koko Head Crater fell away, the ocean rushed in and formed a natural aquarium in the crater. A reef stretches across the mouth of Hanauma Bay, separating the shallow interior from deep ocean. In **Hanauma Bay Nature Preserve,** thousands of brightly hued tropical reef fish swim about in this marine sanctuary. Although it is an ideal place for novice snorkelers, do not be deceived by the bay's beauty, as people have been swept from the lava ledges on the sides by sea surges. Also remember that coral is a living organism, so please treat it tenderly. Elvis Presley preened around the bay in *Blue Hawaii.*

A visitor center with interactive, child-friendly exhibits and a seven-minute film educates people about the fragile preserve.

The drive along the lava-lined Halona Coast at the edge of Koko Head on **Kalanianaole Highway** is dramatic, with views, on a clear day, of Molokai and Lanai, and, when atmospheric conditions are right, of Maui. The **Halona Blowhole,** a lava tube (see p. 23) seen from the scenic pullout, is invaded by high surf, which it spits out in salty plumes that may go 50 feet in the air. Be content to watch from the lookout, as people have slipped into the hole and only one lived to talk about it. From early December through May, you can see humpback whales cavorting offshore (see pp. 130–131). To your right, in beautiful Halona Cove, green sea turtles ride the wave surge.

The long golden beach to your left is **Sandy Beach,** the island's most dangerous due to rip currents and a pounding shore break. Note that the swimmers and bodyboarders are all young and local, and even they are not immune to the broken necks and backs Sandy inflicts. On weekends, teenagers congregate around their cars to watch the wave warriors—and the bikinis.

Environmentalists have waged fierce, and so far successful, battles to preserve this wild stretch of Oahu coastline from various development schemes. ■

The Windward Side

The magnificent natural beauty of Windward Oahu never sneaks up on you, but bursts upon your senses, whether you see it from the Nuuanu Pali Lookout (see p. 65) with the Koolau Mountains rising in jagged green ramparts all around, or from Makapuu Point where suddenly the world opens up into a glorious opulence of sea and sky, mountains and islands. Wind blows about your body filling your lungs with some of the cleanest air on the planet, sweeping in from thousands of miles of open ocean.

A hang glider enjoys a bird's-eye view of Sea Life Park and all of Windward Oahu.

The Windward Side runs from Makapuu Point along Waimanalo Bay to Kahuku Point, the north point of Oahu. Makapuu is a black lava thumb protruding into a teal-and-cerulean sea, lashed by white-crested waves. A white lighthouse stands at its tip. Legends claim that a lava tunnel, its entrance now beneath the water, once ran from Makapuu to Molokai, and that people walked through it from island to island. In Waimanalo town there is a hill called Puu o Molokai, named, it is said, for the Molokai people who settled there. Hike to the lighthouse for spectacular views.

The two offshore islands are Manana, an off-limits bird sanctuary commonly called Rabbit Island because it was once a rabbit ranch, and the smaller Kaohikaipu Island. In the blue hazy distance, the turtle-like land formation lying on the horizon is Mokapu Peninsula, home to the Kaneohe Marine Corps Base Hawaii. The rugged volcanic peak is 1,643-foot Olomana, in whose shadow Queen Liliuokalani wrote her love song "Aloha Oe." Hang gliders can often be seen drifting in the thermal currents.

Makapuu Beach is practically a pilgrimage spot for bodysurfers, but it can be dangerous for the novice, especially in winter when the waves break close to shore.

Nearby **Sea Life Park** (41–402 Kalanianaole Hwy., 0.2 mile past Makapuu Beach Park, tel 808/259-2500, sealifeparkhawaii.com, $$$$$) is nestled between the mountains and the sea. This is the only place where you'll see Keikaimalu, the famous wholfin and love child of a dolphin and false killer whale who met on the job. The park features diverse shows, exhibits, and educational programs that focus on marine life, including turtles, stingrays and dolphins. Learn about the park's conservation efforts, sit at an open-air aquatic "theater," and experience the intelligence of penguins, dolphins, and sea lions as they perform.

About 3.5 miles northwest of Sea Life Park, you find Oahu's longest strand of sand. **Waimanalo Beach,** almost 4 miles long, is backed by the magnificent Koolau Mountains that run the length of this side of the island. If you swim here, be careful, as the beach is frequented by young toughs who can break into a car and disappear in seconds.

The former sugar plantation town of **Waimanalo** is "downtown" for the local banana, corn,

organic greens, and flower farmers. Make sure you pick up some sweet white corn from roadside stands. Waimanalo's two most famous sons are the late slack-key guitar virtuoso Gabby Pahinui (1921–1980) and champion sumo wrestler Chad Rowan (1969–), known to the world as Akebono, the first non-Japanese *sumotori* to earn the exalted rank of *yokozuna,* grand champion.

It's hard to believe this rural area shares the same island with Waikiki and Honolulu.

Kailua

Kailua is only a 15-minute drive from downtown Honolulu (30 minutes during rush hour), but crossing through the tunnel from town to the Windward Side is like crossing a frontier from routine into freedom. Although most of Kailua's wage earners work in Honolulu,

Kailua Beach Park

- 🅰 Map p. 57
- ✉ Kawailoa & Alala Rds.
- 🚌 TheBus 56 or 57 to Kailua, then 70

Naish Hawaii

- 🅰 Map p. 57
- ✉ 155-A Hamakua Dr., Kailua
- ☎ 808/262-6068
- 🚌 TheBus 56 or 57

the most famous winter resident works in Washington, President Obama.

Everything revolves around the 2-mile strand of sand, **Kailua Beach.** Hobie Cats with colorful sails whip across the bay in the gusty on-shore winds; windsurfers skim the waves; stand-up paddlers plough the deep. From the dunes of **Kailua Beach Park,** kayakers set out for the offshore islands. Due to new restrictions on commerce, lessons are no longer available, but equipment rentals

INSIDER TIP:

The Kaiwa Ridge Trail offers views of Kailua Beach, the exclusive residential area of Lanikai, turquoise waters dotted with kite surfers and kayakers, and the offshore Moku Lua islands.

—JOHN SEATON CALLAHAN
National Geographic contributor

can be had in town. Windsurfing champion Robby Naish has his own shop **(Naish Hawaii).** Two presidents have dined at **Buzz's Steak House** (413 Kawailoa Rd., tel 808/261-4661), the rickety little restaurant with the tree growing out of the porch; plaques mark the tables of Presidents Clinton and Obama.

Nearby **Lanikai Beach** packs a lot of scenery into a 1-mile strand. The shore is lined with million-dollar houses, and the

horizon is dotted with offshore islands. Swimming is safe in sheltered waters, but protective seawalls are causing serious erosion of this little gem.

South of Kailua town, behind the YMCA (1200 Kailua Rd.), stands a well-preserved ancient *heiau* (temple) called **Ulupo.** The name means "night inspiration," and it is said that Menehune (Hawaii's little people; see p. 187) built it in a night of a full moon. It may well predate the Hawaiians. Note the skilled workmanship in the 30-foot-high flat-topped pyramid. The temple stands at the edge of **Kawai Nui Marsh,** which is the largest freshwater marsh in the islands. Millennia ago it was a vast open lagoon. Those who settled here used it as a *loko wai* (inland stream-fed fishpond). Still a major fish nursery, it is home to four rare species of waterbirds: the Hawaiian coot *(alae keo keo),* the gallinule *(alae ula),* the Hawaiian duck *(koloa maoli),* and the long-legged Hawaiian stilt *(aeo).*

Kaneohe

About 5 miles northwest of Kawai Nui Marsh, you'll find Kaneohe, which is largely a bedroom community where residents' homes creep as close to beautiful Kaneohe Bay as their finances permit. On calm days the blue waters of the bay mirror the grandeur of the surrounding mountains. The island that opened the popular television series *Gilligan's Island* is, in reality, **Mokuoloe,** better known as Coconut Island, home to the University of Hawaii's Institute of Marine Biology.

Anyone actually marooned there is close enough to town to order take-out Chinese food. The other distinctive island in the bay is **Mokolii,** which everyone insists on calling Chinaman's Hat. When you see it, you'll know why.

Kaneohe Bay harbors three of the last five ancient fishponds remaining on Oahu. A fourth passing canoes lowered their sails in salute. From this beach, the *Hokulea,* a reproduction Polynesian voyaging canoe, set out on its historic voyages of rediscovery. Sleek outrigger canoes are still beached on Kualoa's shores. At low tide you can walk on a shallow reef out to Chinaman's Hat. Wear a hat of your own for the sun, and shoes

Heeia State Park

- Map p. 57
- 46-465 Kamehameha Hwy. (Hawaii 83) at Kealohi Point
- 808/247-3156
- TheBus 55

Boaters rendezvous at the sandbar, Kaneohe Bay.

is in nearby Kahana Bay, and the fifth at Pearl Harbor. These aquaculture facilities (see p. 217), amazingly advanced for their time, once numbered almost a hundred and circled the island. The biggest and best preserved is at **Heeia State Park.** The 5,000-foot-long wall once enclosed an 88-acre fish nursery.

The area that is now **Kualoa Regional Park** was once so sacred to the local people that

for the sharp coral, and check the tide table in the newspaper so you won't be cut off by inrushing currents on the way back. There's a sandy cove on the ocean side of the islet, but swimming is dangerous. Views of the bay and mountains from the island are spectacular.

Koolau

The sheer, green palisades of the Koolau Mountains

Kualoa Regional Park

- Map p. 57
- Kamehameha Hwy. (Hawaii 83)
- 808/768-3440
- TheBus 55

Byodo-In Temple

- Map p. 56
- 47-200 Kahekili Hwy. (Hawaii 83)
- 808/239-8811
- $
- TheBus 65

Senator Fong's Plantation & Garden

- Map p. 56 & p. 57
- 47-285 Pulama Rd., Kaneohe
- 808/239-6775
- Closed Sat.
- $
- TheBus 55

dominate the Windward Side, shortening its days by hiding the setting sun, catching the clouds, and making the land bloom. It was thought that rain and wind had sculpted the cliffs, but the latest sonar imaging has revealed a different story. In prehistoric times, half the island of Oahu fell into the ocean, and the cliffs were formed and gouged by the landslide. The resultant tidal wave covered the island of Lanai. Commuters on the Pali Highway (Hawaii 61), Likelike (Hawaii 63), and H-3 Freeway are treated to mist-haunted vistas every morning.

At the foot of the mountains at **Haiku,** a vermilion temple sits beside a lake. The enormous bronze bell echoes against the Koolau ramparts, and there is no

more peaceful place on the island than the **Byodo-In Temple.** The faithful copy of a temple of the same name at Uji, Japan, is surrounded by meditative gardens and little bridges. Ten thousand prize golden *koi* (carp) swim in its ponds, and peacocks strut about like runway models.

In the shadow of the great Koolau, several gardens have sprung up in this lush environment. If you go to **Hoomaluhia Botanical Garden** (see p. 84) in the morning, when the fish are sleeping and the water is still, the lake perfectly reflects one of the best views of those spired mountains. Free guided nature hikes are held on Saturday and Sunday. **Senator Fong's Plantation & Garden** offers guided strolls through the estate of the late Senator Hiram Fong

People come to the Byodo-In Temple for the beauty of the setting and to gaze on the huge golden Buddha.

(1906–2004). Or, if you'd like to lunch in the company of the mountains, the **Haleiwa Joe** restaurant *(46-336 Haiku Rd., Kaneohe, tel 808/247-6671)* sits over a tropical garden right in the heart of the mountain's embrace.

A working cattle spread, **Kualoa Ranch** is situated in Kaaawa, a valley deeply etched

> In ancient times, Laie was a *puuhonua* (place of refuge), where a person who had trespassed against another was given the chance to earn forgiveness.

into the Koolau. You may recognize it—it's been in movies like *Jurassic Park, Godzilla,* and *Mighty Joe Young.* The Morgan family, owners of the ranch, have branched out from cows to tourists, and have come up with a mix of activity packages that includes hiking, horseback riding, kayaking, snorkeling, sailing, ATV and Jeep expeditions, or just beaching it on their private island on the far side of ancient Molii fishpond.

Kahana Valley State Park is just around the bend, fronting Kahana Bay. The **Huilua Fishpond** here has been designated a National Historic Landmark. A hiking trail follows beside Kahana stream and goes into the forested valley. If you hike, obey all warning signs and make sure to let someone know when you are setting out and when to expect you back. Some valley trails, such as those in Sacred Falls State Park, have been closed as a result of tragic accidents. The valleys slice into the deepest part of the mountains, and they are therefore subject to rock slides and flash flooding. Enjoy Kahana from a picnic table in the coconut grove, or on the shady beach.

Laie

In ancient times, Laie was a *puuhonua* (place of refuge), where a person who had trespassed against another was given the chance to earn forgiveness. Mormon missionaries settled here in 1883, and King David Kalakaua (*r.* 1874–1891) came for the dedication of the Mormon chapel.

In 1919, the first Mormon temple outside the continental United States was dedicated at the site. Built of pulverized coral and volcanic stone, it overlooks formal gardens and a pool. The church has been the cornerstone of the Hawaii Campus of Brigham Young University, attracting students from all over the Pacific.

Laie town is a quiet, mostly Mormon community. Drive toward the ocean on Anemoku Street then to the end of Naupaka Street to see a natural lava sea arch and a bird sanctuary on a nearby islet. Just beyond Laie, **Malaekahana State Recreation Area** *(Kamehameha Hwy. at Kalanai Point, tel 808/587-0300)* is a good swimming beach with a shady picnic area and scenic views.

Kualoa Ranch

⛰ Map p. 56

✉ 49-560 Kamehameha Hwy. (Hawaii 83), Kaaawa

☎ 808/237-7321

$ $$$$$

🚌 TheBus 55

Kahana Valley State Park

⛰ Map p. 56

✉ 52-222 Kamehameha Hwy. (Hawaii 83), Kahana

🚌 TheBus 55

Polynesian Cultural Center

- 🅰 Map p. 56
- ✉ 55-370 Kamehameha Hwy. (Hawaii 83)
- ☎ 800/367-7060 or 808/293-3333
- 🕐 Closed Sun.
- 💲 $$$$$
- 🚌 TheBus 55 or PCC coaches from Waikiki

Polynesian Cultural Center

In 1963, the church founded the Polynesian Cultural Center as a visitor attraction to give students an opportunity to live out the brotherhood embodied in both the Mormon faith and the Polynesian tradition, and to earn their tuition by sharing their various cultures with the public. The center brought elders from the home islands to teach the history and culture of the region, and to oversee a way of life consistent with the students' Polynesian backgrounds. The formula has really worked, and now the center is the largest paid visitor attraction in Hawaii.

From the minute you clear the box office, you are in the colorful world of Oceania. Enthusiastic students in native garb greet and direct you to where the action is—shows, films, craft demonstrations. Everything is arranged in villages around a series of lagoons.

The **Fijian Village** is the easiest to spot because of the high thatched roof of the chief's house.

EXPERIENCE: Bon Dancing in Hawaii

Summer means bon dance season for many Hawaii residents. It's a time when Buddhist temple grounds come alive with festive evenings of dancing, food, music, and lighted paper lanterns, some marked with family names.

Although there is no required attire at most places, dancers wear kimono or hapi coats as they circle around a *yagura* (musicians' wooden tower) with stylized hand motions, steps, and claps, moving to the beat of Taiko drums, flutes, gongs, and singers. One dance, the Fukushima, is a 20-minute song that involves the execution of five basic motions, though embellishments and clapping are permitted when the fun becomes contagious.

Bon dances have their roots in Hawaii's early Japanese immigrants who brought their religious traditions, including the belief that the souls of ancestors eventually visit Earth for a while, then return to their spiritual home. The dances have also evolved into social affairs and members of the public are welcome to attend.

In Hawaii, the months of June, July, and August are filled with bon festivals.

It's not uncommon, for example, to find at least 30 festivals on Oahu alone during one season.

Most start after 7:30 p.m. Arrive earlier to meet the bon community. Bring an appetite because bon dances also feature food booths that sell noodles, sushi, teriyaki BBQ sticks, and "shave ice" (snow cones).

For islandwide schedules, visit *gohawaii.com/about_hawaii/plan/events_in_hawaii.* Check the local papers online for bon dance schedules (*staradvertiser.com, hawaiitribune-herald.com, mauinews.com, thegardenisland.com*).

Temple telephone numbers are useful, too:
Oahu: Honpa Hongwanji Hawaii Betsuin (*tel* 808/536-7044) or Haleiwa Joda Mission (*tel* 808/637-4382)
Kauai: West Kauai Hongwanji Mission (*tel* 808/338-1537) or Kapaa Hongwanji Mission (*tel* 808/822-4667)
Maui: Wailuka Hongwanji Mission (*tel* 808/244-0406) or Paia Mantokuji Mission (*tel* 808/579-8051)
The Big island: Kona Hongwanji Mission (*tel* 808/323-2993) or Hilo Meishoin Mission (*tel* 808/935-6996)

Here you can learn ropemaking, lei weaving with dried material, or watch a fashion show of traditional styles in unusual fabrics. Follow the drums to the **Tahitian Village** and learn the *tamure,* the Tahitian version of the hula.

The **Samoan Village** seems to be the most fun. Handsome young men climb 40-foot palm

INSIDER TIP:

Watch the elderly dance at a bon festival. They are the ones with the most history and understanding of bon traditions.

—THELMA CHANG
Author & National Geographic contributor

trees, start fires, and crack open coconuts to share the milk and "spoon" out soft coconut meat. And they do it all with such warmth and good humor that visitors are infected with their enthusiasm. If you see people walking around with *lauhala* woven hats and visors stuck with jaunty flowers, the wearers probably wove them here.

Altogether there are seven villages that offer different crafts, dances, and music. In the regularly scheduled, highly photogenic "Pageant of the Long Canoes," the music and dances of all the islands are showcased on canoe stages that travel the lagoons.

In the evening, you have your choice of a luau, or an extensive buffet. But remember that no alcoholic beverages are ever

At the Polynesian Cultural Center's Samoan Village, you can watch a man climb to the treetops to harvest coconuts.

served at the center. After dinner, everyone moves out to the open theater for a dramatic 90-minute musical production that is complete with "erupting volcanoes" and lighted fountains of water. The young people who make up the cast are enthusiastic, and the timing and pace are professional down to the last drumbeat. The center also has an IMAX theater and a marketplace. You can travel about the 42-acre complex on foot or by canoe. The center is an expedition all by itself. ∎

The North Shore

The North Shore of Oahu is as much a state of mind as a geographic location. Some North Shore beaches are ragged coves framed in lava promontories. Others are long sweeps of sand scoured by wind. Sunsets sear the soul, cattle graze in oceanfront meadows, houses bravely face the sea only feet from its foam.

With an arsenal of boards behind him, a surfer appraises the waves at Banzai Pipeline, Oahu.

The ocean is the center of life, whether it is gentle and rolling ashore in whispers or whipped up to storm fury. Winter is surf season and sometimes the monster waves roll in at 30 feet. In summer the same beaches can look as placid as lakes. They conjure images of youth, beach, laid-back lifestyle, sand, salt, sunblock, small towns, and big surf.

The quiet end of the North Shore is Mokuleia and sleepy Waialua town. The only reason to head this way is to hop a hang glider (*Mr. Bill's Glider Rides, Dillingham Airfield, Hawaii 930, Mokuleia, 5 miles past Waialua High School, tel 808/677-3404, $$$$*) or to pick up the trail head for a 2-mile, three-hour trek around **Kaena Point,** an area that's so rugged it defies road builders. (To get to the trail head, just drive to the end of Hawaii 930.) People talk about a circle-island tour of Oahu, but the truth is, you can't circle Oahu because of Kaena. Many temple ruins sleep in the brush.

INSIDER TIP:

To see the best waves and professional surfers, catch the Triple Crown of Surf-ing—a series of three events held between late November and Christmas Day.

—JOHN SEATON CALLAHAN
National Geographic contributor

The celebrated beaches of the North Shore begin at Haleiwa town (see pp. 112–113) and stretch to the Turtle Bay Resort. The hotel dining room, which is on a promontory jutting into the high surf, is an excellent place to see daredevil wave jockeys up close. At **Sunset Beach** the surf is so powerful it scoops out whole sections of the 2-mile beach. At sunset, the waves are backlit and surfers riding the wild white crests are silhouetted against a blazing sky. Notorious **Banzai Pipeline** is famous for its "tube" waves caused by a shallow reef just offshore that forces waves to rise dramatically. Snorkelers head for the large protected tide pools at **Pupukea Beach Park** *(59–727 Kamehameha Hwy.)*; in winter, these pools are often inundated by surf. **Waimea Bay** in winter sounds like a war zone. Jumbo rollers come boiling in and their roar, echoing against the walls of the bay, sounds like cannon fire. At such times, spectators gather on the cliffs above Waimea Bay as at a gladiator match to watch the wave warriors in their wild rides down the thundering liquid mountains. At the first weather forecaster's warning of jumbo surf, mothers rush home to lock up their sons' boards, to make sure they aren't among the daring surfers enjoying the ultimate thrill of a North Shore wave at its full height.

Extreme caution is urged, even walking these beaches in winter: Rogue waves have swept many a stroller out to sea, often with tragic results. From a safe place, watching a champion surfer ride down the face of one of these mighty walls of water is thrilling. The surfer paddles furiously into the top of the foamy crest, stands up, then slides down the concave wave, speeding sideways, often being swallowed by the tube, then streaks out the other side, on the exciting ride.

Waimea

When the valleys of Oahu passed from one king to another, only Waimea was reserved for the *kahuna* (priests). It was a major religious center of the ancient Hawaiian civilization. Two temples guard the entrance to the valley; one, **Puu o Mahuka Heiau,** is a state monument and a national historic landmark.

Turn off Kamehameha Highway onto Pupukea Road as it winds up the 250-foot bluff. The 5-acre temple has sweeping *(continued on p. 112)*

Surfing & Love

At least a thousand years ago, Hawaiians mastered the sport of surfing, which they called *hee nalu*. Many great love stories in Hawaii's vast literary heritage begin with or revolve around surfing.

Riding a small wave in Hawaiian waters, a surfer uses her arms for balance.

An ancient *pehuehue* (surf-coaxing chant) collected by historian Abraham Fornander (1812–1887) pleads:

> *Ku mai! Ku mai! Ka nalu nui mai*
> *Kahiki mai,*
> *Alo poi pu! Ku mai ka pohuehue,*
> *Hu! Kaikoo loa.*

> Arise, arise, the great waves from Kahiki,
> The powerful curling waves.
> Arise from the chant.
> Swell up, long raging surf.

Surfing is at the center of many Hawaiian love stories. One tells of a handsome, duplicitous chief of Kauai who complicated his life when he fell in love with a goddess whom he first saw surfing at Puhele near Hana, Maui. In another, a *moo* (lizard) goddess, while surfing, lured an unsuspecting royal surfer on to her own board and carried him away to Kaena Point, Oahu. Yet another surfer abduction took place when a chief of Oahu kidnapped Kelea, a beautiful Maui chiefess, while she was riding the waves.

In 1778, Lt. James King, aboard Captain Cook's H.M.S. *Resolution,* described his amazement at first seeing the sport of surfing: "The boldness and address, with which we saw them perform these difficult and dangerous maneuvers, was altogether astonishing and is scarce to be credited."

John Papa Ii (1800–1870), a leading citizen of the Hawaiian kingdom and an associate justice of its supreme court, reported in *Fragments of Hawaiian History* his delight at entering Lahaina harbor, Maui, and seeing boys "surfing on the north side of Pelekane, with banana trunks for surfboards."

Jack London took a leaf from the ancient tales and wrote a short story of surfer love, "The Kanaka Surf." In his 1908 book *The Cruise of the Snark,* he described learning to surf: "Soon we were out in deep waters where the big smokers came roaring in. . . .When a breaker curled over my head, for a swift instant I could see the light of day through its emerald body; then down would go my head, and I would clutch the board with all my strength. Then would come the blow, and to the onlooker on shore I would be blotted out. In reality, the board and I have passed through the crest and emerged in the respite of the other side."

James Michener must have read these stories. In his novel *Hawaii,* he wrote: "As she stood naked on the board, her handsome breasts and long firm legs seemed carved of brown marble, yet she was agile, too, for with exquisite skill she moved her knees and adjusted her shoulders so that her skimming board leaped faster than the others, while she rode it with a more secure grace."

EXPERIENCE: Riding Hawaii's Wild Waves

Surfing remains a symbol of Hawaii and its endless summers. When or where you surf depends largely on the weather and your skills as an expert or beginner.

On **Oahu,** landmark Waikiki Beach is a place to start, especially if you're a beginner. Surf stands line the beach, each staffed with surfing pros. For lessons or just renting a board try **Aloha Beach Services** (tel 888/955-7873 or 808/922-3111, $$$$$), on Oahu's west side. **Hawaiian Fire** (tel 808/737-3473, hawaiianfire.com, $$$$$) is another option.

During winter, the high surf on **Oahu's North Shore** is meant for professional surfers or the very skilled. But the summers are usually milder, offering inexperienced surfers a better time to learn or improve. **Surf n Sea** (tel 800/899-7873 or 808/637-9887, surfnsea.com, $$$$$), located on the beach in Haleiwa, offers beginning to advanced lessons.

Surfing on the **Big Island** is, well, big. In other words, it pays to be a veteran at the sport because winter swells affect the north and west beaches, such as Lyman's at Kona, while the east side receives its share of swells during summer. However, a few places offer lessons, including Honokohau Harbor, with its small surf; for lessons contact **Ocean Eco Tours** (tel 808/324-7873, oceanecotours .com, $$$$$).

Maui's west side displays a range of possibilities for surfers. Experts head toward Honolua Bay (north of Kapalua), Maalaea Harbor (with some of the fastest waves in the world), or Lahaina (especially for long-boarding). Many students learn at Lahaina, next to Front Street. For lessons (including three- to seven-day surf clinics), try **Maui Surf Clinics** (tel 808/244-7873, mauisurfclinics.com, $$$$$).

Molokai's wannabe surfers on the island's south side may contact a seasoned waterman, **Walter Naki** (tel 808/558-8184, molokaiactionadventure.com).

And Lanai's serious surfing for the experienced happens only with a guide-champion surfer at Lopa, called the "hidden side" of the island. For the rest of us, the **Four Seasons Lanai at Manele Bay** (tel 808/565-2000, fourseasons.com, $$$$$) offers lessons. While advanced surfers head for the large waves of **Kauai's** North Shore, beginners slide the waves on the island's "little Waikiki" south side at **Poipu.** Lessons are available from the **Garden Isle Surf School** at Poipu (tel 808/652-4841, gardenislandsurfschool .com, $$$$$).

Waimea Valley

- ⛰ Map p. 56
- ✉ 59-864 Kamehameha Hwy. (Hawaii 83)
- ☎ 808/638-7766
- 💲 $
- 🚌 TheBus 52

views of the entire North Shore, and the glorious panorama was sometimes the last thing the sacrificial victims saw. Two seamen, perhaps three, from Captain George Vancouver's ship H.M.S. *Daedelus* were offered on the altar in May 1792, after being captured drawing fresh water from the mouth of the Waimea River. In 1819, a year before the arrival of the first Christian missionaries, all the *kii* (god images) in Waimea Valley were destroyed by order of King Kamehameha II.

ATVs, and narrated tram tours. Now it has literally gone back to its roots as a botanical and archaeological treasure. Nature paths meander along a stream and past ancient lava walls and platforms, a prayer tower, and thatched temple buildings.

The park claims 5,000 varieties of plants, many of which are rare and endangered. Many represent the unusual evolutionary paths developed by flora in isolated island environments. A 55-foot waterfall cascades

Children in Haleiwa enjoy the local treat—"shave ice."

The power of the priests was broken (see pp. 29–30).

The sacred site was saved from development in 2006 by public outcry that resulted in a creative government/private partnership, involving the mayor of Honolulu, Mufi Hannemann, the private sector, and the Office of Hawaiian Affairs. The valley had become a tourist attraction with cliff divers,

into an icy plunge pool, where swimming is permitted when conditions are deemed safe.

Waimea Valley is an experience focused on education and a deep appreciation of the valley's natural beauty and cultural heritage.

Haleiwa & Central Oahu

There's now a fast bypass

around the funky little surfer town of Haleiwa, but if you take it you'll miss driving over an art deco bridge for the world's most famous "shave ice" (snow cones). It comes in

INSIDER TIP:

Big winter surf at Waimea Bay is a true spectacle; some of the best views are from the _heiau_ that over-looks the bay.

—JOHN SEATON CALLAHAN
National Geographic contributor

unusual flavors such as coconut, _li hing mui_ (salty and sweet red Chinese spice mixture), and lychee.

The best place to queue up for shave ice is **Matsumoto's** (66-087 Kamehameha Hwy., tel 808/637-4827). If you skip Haleiwa, you'll also miss some of the best active-wear and boutique shopping on the island, several interesting art galleries featuring well-priced works of fine local artists, and the free **North Shore Surf and Cultural Museum** (North Shore Market-place, 66-250 Kamehameha Hwy., tel 808/637-8888, closed when the surf is up). Though not state-of-the-art, it's crammed with unusual ephemera such as beach blanket movie posters starring Sandra Dee and Frankie Avalon. You can also trace the evolution of the surfboard from the early wooden boards to today's sleek fiberglass speed demons.

Return to Honolulu through the pineapple fields of the central Leilehua Plateau. First stop is **Dole Pineapple Plantation** for fresh juice, fruit, and ice cream. You can get lost in one of the world's largest mazes and win a prize if you get out in par time. The Pineapple Express train will take you on a tour of the plantation. Just down the road, at the intersection of Hawaii 80 and 99, you can pull out for the small but interesting **Del Monte Pineapple Variety Garden.** No booths, no souvenirs, just all kinds of pineapple, even pink.

At the intersection of Kamehameha Highway and Whitmore Avenue, you'll see a sign for the **Kukaniloko Birthstones State Monument.** In the middle of the pineapple fields, in a grove of eucalyptus and coconut trees, is a group of stones where early Hawaiian royalty came to give birth (see p. 29). Some historians speculate the site may also have served as an astronomy center, and there are interesting petroglyphs in the rocks. This is probably the most sacred of the ancient sites on Oahu.

The U.S. Army's Schofield Barracks in Wahiawa is worth a stop if you enjoy military curiosities. In the base's **Tropic Lightning Museum** (tel 808/655-0438, closed Sun.–Mon.) is a reproduction of a section of the notorious Cu Chi Tunnels in Vietnam. During the Vietnam War, the tunnel network was used to secretly move large numbers of Viet Cong into and out of South Vietnam. ∎

Dole Pineapple Plantation

 Map p. 56

✉ 64-1550 Kamehameha Hwy. (Hawaii 99)

☎ 808/621-8408

$ Maze: $. Train: $$

🚌 TheBus 52

The Waianae Coast

Heading for the Waianae Coast doesn't look very promising as the H-1 Freeway zips past crowded suburbs and malls, but there are a few interesting stops on the way—Pearl Harbor, Hawaii's Plantation Village, and some of Oahu's best beaches.

Fishermen fold away their nets on the Waianae Coast.

To remember plantation days, **Hawaii's Plantation Village** *(94–695 Waipahu St., Waipahu, tel 808/677-0110, closed Sun.)* has created a 3-acre hamlet of replicated ethnic dwellings representing the eight major groups that immigrated to the Hawaiian Islands as sugar workers (see pp. 32–33). Plantation owners kept ethnic groups segregated, so cultural links to the old country remained strong.

From the freeway you can see the rusting **Aloha Stadium** *(99–500 Salt Lake Blvd., tel 808/486-9300),* where the National Football League all-pros come for the Pro Bowl every winter. On Wednesday, Saturday, and Sunday the parking lot becomes a huge **flea market.**

Pearl Harbor

World War II seared Pearl Harbor into the American consciousness.

For the United States, it began on a sunny Sunday morning, December 7, 1941, when, in a daring air raid, the forces of imperial Japan devastated the American fleet in the harbor and killed 2,300 people. It all happened with such surprise that the U.S.S. *Arizona* went down with 1,102 men, who are still entombed in the metal hull today. The dead are honored by the lyrical white concrete *Arizona* **Memorial** erected above the sunken ship.

Designed by Honolulu architect Alfred Preis, the monument was made possible in large measure by the late Elvis Presley, who gave a benefit concert for the *Arizona* in 1961. The monument draws almost 1.4 million visitors a year, so try to arrive early and then immediately secure a number for the launch ride that takes you out to the memorial. Lines have been known to last three hours.

Visiting the Memorial:

Before you board the launch, you will be ushered into a theater for a dramatic documentary of the infamous attack.

The **Visitor Center** has a museum of battle photographs and Navy paraphernalia, a gift shop with a good selection of books on the attack, and a snack shop.

There are tour companies offering boat rides to the *Arizona*, but only designated vessels of the U.S. Navy can dock at the memorial.

Across the parking lot from the Visitor Center, the **U.S.S. *Bowfin* Submarine Museum and Park** is a tribute to the vital role of the submarine in warfare and national security. You can

Pearl Harbor
 Map p. 56

U.S.S. *Arizona* Memorial
Map p. 56
1 Arizona Memorial Dr.
808/422-0561
TheBus 20 & 42 or Arizona Memorial Shuttle from Waikiki

Respecting the Water

Hawaii's gorgeous ocean is inviting. However, visitors occasionally underestimate its power, especially its waves and currents. Generally speaking, an average of 61 people drown in the Hawaiian Islands yearly. For Oahu alone, about 700 to 850 people need an ocean rescue each year.

Caution and common sense will ensure fun in the sun:

- Do not turn your back to the ocean. Waves can take you by surprise.
- Do not go out alone; know your limits.
- Swim at beaches with lifeguards. Talk with them about water conditions before entering the water. Observe posted signs.
- Recognize that waves mean there are rip currents, which can be a source of

major trouble for swimmers in Hawaii.
- If you are caught in a rip current, don't try to fight it. Swim diagonally until you are out of the current; then make your way back to shore with the waves. Keep calm and wave your hand for help.
- Know that hazards such as slippery rocks exist in coastal areas.
- Watch children carefully; keep them within reach.
- Shark attacks are rare, especially when you're swimming in well-populated waters. Do not swim too far out, beyond others. Certain spots such as Maui's Olowalu Beach, the Lahaina area, and the west side of the island are known for their tiger shark numbers.
- When in doubt, don't go out.

U.S.S. *Bowfin*

- Map p. 56
- 11 Arizona Memorial Dr.
- 808/423-1341
- $$

study wartime posters with their jaunty victory slogans, examine the innards of a Poseidon missile, and see a Japanese one-man kamikaze suicide sub. You can even board the U.S.S. *Bowfin* and poke around a submarine that was responsible for 44 enemy sinkings in the war.

A shuttle takes you to "Battleship Row" on Ford Island and the **U.S.S. Missouri.** The 58,000-ton battleship, launched in 1944, provided firepower in the battles of Iwo Jima and Okinawa, and it saw action in the Korean War and

Three years, eight months, and 25 days after the attack on Pearl Harbor, Gen. Douglas MacArthur received the unconditional surrender of Japan on the deck of the *Missouri.* A plaque marks the spot, and from there you can look up and see, 1,000 feet away, the *Arizona* Memorial. The two ships bookend America's part in World War II.

You can wander about the ship on your own or sign up for a guided tour. At the rear of the ship, you'll learn about the Tomahawk missile system that

Throngs of people come every day by Navy launch to pay their respects at the *Arizona* Memorial, Pearl Harbor.

the Gulf War of 1991. In June 1998, "Mighty Mo" was greeted by thousands of islanders as it was towed into its final berth at Pearl Harbor to begin a new life as a museum ship.

The event that has enshrined Mighty Mo in history occurred in Tokyo Bay, September 2, 1945.

was employed so effectively during the Gulf War. From the top deck, the views of Pearl Harbor, the *Arizona* Memorial, and the island of Oahu are breathtaking.

Hangar 37, also on Ford Island, was heavily shelled during the Japanese attack, but found new life as the **Pacific Aviation Museum.** Vintage aircraft such as the Dauntless Dive Bomber and the Japanese Zero are displayed against dramatic dioramas. Climb aboard Vietnam-era attack helicopters and walk the newest exhibit, Mig Alley, from the Korean Conflict. Using a

INSIDER TIP:

So many Japanese visitors come to the memorial at Pearl Harbor that tour-boat loudspeaker announcements are in both English and Japanese.

—RON FISHER
National Geographic author

flight simulator, land aboard an aircraft carrier or defend the skies above Guadalcanal. A gift shop and restaurant round out this top-flight attraction.

Some of the best swimming on Oahu is tucked away at **Ko Olina Resort,** a manicured enclave centered around four accommodation properties, including Aulani, Disney's first non-theme-park hotel; a Ted Robinson–designed golf course with academy, pro shop, and club restaurant; a full service marina where you may book dive and snorkel tours and sunset cruises; restaurants; shops; and best of all, five placid lagoons fringed in coconut palms. The only negative is a shortage of public

parking. Get there early.

Oahu changes character as you reach **Kahe Point Beach Park:** It's like landing on an outer island—laid-back, local, and unspoiled by sophistication. The beaches that punctuate the six miles of sunny shoreline are uncrowded and idyllic, but in winter the surf can be treacherous and extreme caution should be exercised. The beauty of this region is compromised by its tough-guy reputation, so don't linger after sundown.

About 11 miles northwest along Farrington Highway (Hawaii 93), surf meets happen at **Makaha Beach.** The most famous event is the annual Buffalo's Big Board Surfing Classic, initiated by legendary waterman Buffalo Keaulana to revive old-time big-board surfing.

At the next beach along Farrington Highway, **Makua Beach,** commercial operators run dolphin encounters. In summer when these waters are normally calm, the playful mammals frequent the pretty bay.

The last beach before rugged **Kaena Point** is a long, treeless swath of sand baking in the sun. It is popularly called **Yokohama Bay** because so many immigrant Japanese laborers fished here during the plantation era. It is popular with young people who come for the surf and scene. The real name is Keawaula (red harbor) because great schools of shrimp once congregated here in such numbers that the water appeared to turn red. Old stories abound on this laid-back Waianae Coast. ∎

Battleship Missouri Memorial
✉ Pier 5
☎ 808/423-2263
💲 $$$

Pacific Aviation Museum
✉ 319 Lexington Blvd.
☎ 808/441-1000
💲 $$$$

More Places to Visit on Oahu

Hawaii Children's Discovery Center

Don't go there with an agenda. Let your children's curiosity lead you through a pint-size village where they can shop, bank, pump gas, and star in their own theater production; through a digestive system; aboard an airplane; inside a kaleidoscope. They can play house in a Japanese teahouse and dress up in kimono.

Map p. 59 111 Ohe St., Honolulu 808/524-5437 Closed Mon. $$ TheBus 19, 20, 47

Hawaiian Waters Adventure Park

Faux sands aside, this $14-million water-themed amusement park entices with such novelties as two seven-story free-fall water slides, a multilevel activity pool, a children's lily pad walk, an 800-foot-long fake river with a current for floating in an inner tube, a megawave pool, water-toboggan slides, and a tube ride down a 130-foot tunnel from 50 feet in the air.

Map p. 56 400 Farrington Hwy., Kapolei 808/945-3928 $$$$$ TheBus 51

National Memorial Cemetery of the Pacific

The cemetery and Honolulu Memorial are cradled in an extinct volcanic crater known as Punchbowl. Its ancient Hawaiian name is oddly prophetic: Puowaina, "hill of sacrifice." Among the first to be buried there were 776 casualties from the 1941 attack on Pearl Harbor. One of the last to be interred was Ellison Onizuka, the Hawaiian astronaut who died in the 1986 *Challenger* explosion. The Honolulu Memorial honors those who fought in the Pacific in World War II, the Korean War, and the Vietnam War. You can see one of the best views of Honolulu from the overlook on Memorial Walk.

Map p. 59 2177 Puowaina Dr. 808/532-3720 TheBus 15

Old Pali Road

Ten minutes from the financial district of downtown Honolulu, you can do a 2-mile drive-in rain-forest tour. Take the Pali Highway (Hawaii 61) to the stoplight at Nuuanu Pali Road and turn right. Immediately, you will be enveloped in a jungle where it rains 300 inches a year. Great trees form a leafy canopy, while fragrant wild ginger blossoms bloom beside the road. The road rejoins the Pali Highway where you can continue to Kailua, return to Honolulu, or proceed to the Nuuanu Pali Lookout (see p. 65).

INSIDER TIP:

Visit Kaniakapupu—off the Pali Highway—to see an enchanting ruin from King Kamehameha III's summer palace. A few portions of the home stand in the middle of a rain forest.

—DOUGLAS PEEBLES
National Geographic contributor

Waikiki Historic Trail

Waikiki's colorful past comes alive as you walk on a self-guided tour along the Waikiki Historic Trail. The trail was the vision of historian George S. Kanahele, who wanted to restore "*mana* [power] in Waikiki." Visitors on the trail follow bronze surfboard-shaped markers that highlight great events. You'll learn how Princess Kaiulani's pet peacocks screamed so loudly upon her death that they awakened people miles away; and you can almost peek in on Queen Liluokalani's lavish little dinners. You can take a virtual tour at *waikikihistorictrail.com*. Guided tours are available by appointment.

Map p. 87 Native Hawaiian Hospitality Assoc., 808/628-6370 $$$$

Miles of sandy beaches, with well-planned, well-spaced resorts that complement the island's natural beauty

Maui

A Lahaina T-shirt says it all.

Maui

Everything about Maui is young—its attitude, its orientation, and even its actual age. Haleakala, the massive dormant volcano that dominates the island, rose from the ocean only a million years ago. Its older sister, Mauna Kahalawai, broke the surface of the waves two million years ago.

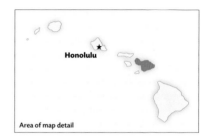

Area of map detail

The lava flows from these mid-ocean giants were so profuse, they connected with other submarine volcanoes that later became the separate islands of Lanai, Molokai, and Kahoolawe. In early times, they were all one landmass, which scientists refer to as Maui Nui, or Big Maui. The islands still maintain their ancient ties, all being governed as part of Maui County.

The island of Maui is the second largest in the Hawaiian chain with a land area of 727 square miles, measuring 48 miles long and 26 miles across at its widest. The shoreline runs a linear 120 miles with 81 accessible beaches, whose sands may be white, gold, black, salt and pepper, green, or garnet, due to ancient volcanic activity. It has more swimmable beaches than any other island—and more color.

Maui's Allures

Beaches dominate the lifestyle of not only the two million visitors who arrive in Maui every year, but the island's estimated 144,000 residents who plan their calendars around outrigger canoe regattas, fishing seasons, and family picnics at favorite strands of sand. Many people come to Maui and experience what they can only call "rebirth." Scratch the surface of a restaurant waiter in Kihei and you may find a former lawyer who now rides a bicycle to work after surfing all day.

Artists are drawn to Maui for the beautiful natural canvas it provides, for the ready art market that comes courtesy of the well-heeled tourists, and for the creative energy born of its youth.

The island is blessed with a wonderful natural diversity that runs from tropical lowlands and rain forest to cloud forest and high mountains.

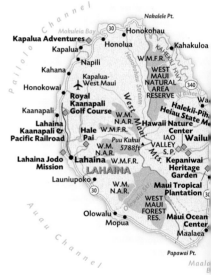

Because of the height of the mountains, Maui has areas with something approximating a temperate zone climate, making the island suitable for ranching and farming a variety of crops.

Less than 25 percent of Maui is inhabited or developed. Resorts are primarily limited to particular, and rather choice, parts of the island. These include Kaanapali and Kapalua in West Maui, the

Kihei-Wailea-Makena sun corridor in East Maui, and little Hana, which sits all by itself on the far side of Haleakala. The Hotel Hana–Maui, the island's first resort, opened in 1961.

Demigods, Kings, & Hippies

The island is named for the demigod Maui, Superman of the Hawaiian pantheon. The capital of the united Hawaiian kingdom was Lahaina, until it was moved to Honolulu in 1845. Kamehameha the Great married a young woman from Maui named Kaahumanu, and appointed her co-regent of the kingdom on his deathbed.

Maui's history is rich and colorful with a cast of Hawaiian royalty, Yankee whalers, missionaries, immigrant plantation workers, hippies, New Agers, surf rats, and ordinary people living their lives in an extraordinarily beautiful part of the planet. ■

NOT TO BE MISSED:

A stroll along the pier and a luau in historic Lahaina **123, 125–128**

Kaanapali, Kapalua, and Wailea, loved by golfers, known for beautiful beaches **128–129, 137–138**

Windsurfers and birds at Kanaha Beach Park **132**

Breathtaking vistas at Iao Needle and Valley **133, 135**

The walk through a tunnel at the Maui Ocean Center for a look at Hawaii's sea life **137**

Fresh flower farms in Kula **138–140**

A golden sunrise at Haleakala and hiking the park trails **140–142**

Browsing through hip Paia town, where surf culture thrives **144**

The scenic drive to Hana **144–145**

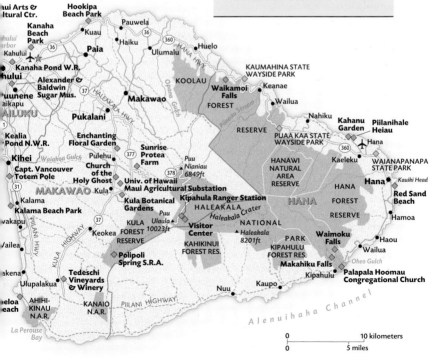

West Maui

The green mountains roll down to the sea, and rainbows crown the misty peaks. The highest is Puu Kukui, "the hill of light," once regarded as the juncture between heaven and earth.

The promontory of Kahakuloa is part of the range known as the West Maui Mountains.

The great gods Kane and Kanaloa are said to have pierced the earth with their spears and created Manowai, a lake filled with the last waters from the Great Deluge. Its lip, from which many waterfalls flow, was called Omaka, "the beginning." Mauna Eke is where the Hawaiians who survived the flood landed their canoe as the waters receded.

Parts of the West Maui Mountains are so wild they have never been explored, yet they are within 10 miles of hotels and holiday condominiums. The shoreline is scalloped in pristine bays and beaches with names that resound like a chant borne on the wind—Honokowai, Honokeana,

Honokahua, Honolua, Honokohau, and Hononana. Honolua and neighboring Mokuleia Bays are home to so many jewel-toned tropical reef fish they have been declared a Hawaii State Marine Conservation district.

The town of Lahaina, the resorts of Kaanapali and Kapalua, and a string of little hamlets between them sit basking on lovely beaches, sheltered by the magnificent hills.

Much of the land is set aside in vast nature preserves, laced with hiking trails. The 9,000-acre **Puu Kukui Watershed Preserve** (see p. 129), managed by the Nature Conservancy of Hawaii, is the largest private preserve in the state and shelters a biologically diverse ecosystem containing hundreds of flora that exist nowhere else on earth. Even the part of West Maui that is developed is green. There are five championship golf courses (see pp. 228–229) at two resorts, Kaanapali and Kapalua, and 9,000 acres of pineapple plantation.

There are still functioning *ahupuaa* in this district, a holdover system of land stewardship in which the land was divided into pie-shaped wedges running from the tops of the mountains to the sea (see pp. 26–27).

A long line of Maui kings and queens, and later the scions of the Kamehameha dynasty, made their homes in West Maui.

The Western Coast

The Kahekili Highway (Hawaii 340) connects the remote areas of the West Maui Mountains with the resorts of Kapalua and Kaanapali on one end and the city of Kahului on the other. Driving this narrow, twisting shoreline route is a white-knuckle experience in places and the scenery is spectacular. It's a 20-mile road that will take you two hours to drive. Sometimes you'll crawl around cliffs that plunge down to the sea only inches from your car window.

As you leave the resorts of Kaanapali and Kapalua, the road winds around the wonderful litany of bays. If it's winter, you may see some mighty waves at **Mokuleia Bay,** which is known to surfers as "Slaughterhouse." If it's summer, the snorkeling will be pristine.

Nakalele Point looks like a hunk of alien turf that was flung in fury from some other galaxy, at odds with its lush surroundings.

This weird lava landscape hisses and moans as the ocean worms its way under the lava and erupts into geysers, one of which sprays 50 feet in the air when the surf is up.

Look for the U.S. Coast Guard lighthouse *(18 miles W of Lahaina),* which is really more like a toy light stick than a fully fledged lighthouse. Walk down for half a mile toward the shore, keeping to the right side of the beacon, to reach the lava formations. You will hear the geyser

INSIDER TIP:

Original pieces of furniture in the Baldwin Home give it a lived-in feel, and its shady porch overlooks the harbor at Lahaina.

—RON FISHER
National Geographic author

rumbling before you see it; be careful of surging surf and incoming tides.

Kahakuloa ("the tall lord") is a huge promontory 636 feet high that rises dramatically from the sea, offering refuge to great seabirds: the frigatebird, shearwater, and *koae kea* (white-tailed tropic bird). The pretty little village of **Kahakuloa** nestled beside it is just the kind of place that makes you want to kiss your job good-bye and settle down in paradise.

Lahaina

Picture a trim, tidy New England coastal town: white picket fences, widow's walks, gray clapboard houses. Move it to the middle of the Pacific. Add rainbows,

EXPERIENCE: Sportfishing in Hawaii

Hawaii is a wonderful place for fishing. Of course, factors such as weather, sea conditions, luck, and skill will determine whether it will be a day of fishing or not. Here is a sampling of charter trips that can help you make sure the "big one" doesn't get away.

Fishing charters can be arranged throughout the Hawaiian Islands.

A Hawaii fishing veteran expressed his vocation this way: "Fishing is similar to gambling. The odds run in our favor when we're playing the quarter machine, as opposed to the $20 one. Action usually translates into fun, so we go where we see action—birds flying, little fish jumping. If nothing's happening, we switch gears and try another level of depth."

Sportfish Hawaii *(tel 877/388-1376 or 808/396-2607, sportfishhawaii.com, shared or private full-day trips: $$$$$)* is at once a handy resource and booking desk that will provide tips, charter boat information, and reservations for all of the islands.

Maui's Lahaina Harbor is the launching site for fishing trips that also provide lots of scenery—from Lanai straight ahead to tiny Kahoolawe just off the boat's port side *(Luckey Strike Charters is a family-run operation: tel 800/474-4606 or 808/661-4606, luckey strike.com, shared or private full-day trips: $$$$$).*

Oahu's "fishing central" is in Kewalo Basin, Honolulu, the main location for chartering boats on the island. Waters here are known for marlin and mahimahi, among others *(Sportfish Hawaii, half- or full-day trips, six-person maximum: $$$$$).*

Deep waters surround **Kauai,** enhancing the chance you'll find Hawaii's favorite fishes—mahimahi, *ono,* and *ahi (Sportfish Hawaii, full-day trips, six-person maximum: $$$$$. Deep Sea Fishing Kauai, tel 808/634-8589, deepseafishingkauai.com, shared or private half- or full-day trips: $$$$$).*

Fishing on **Molokai** offers bonuses galore such as the island's splendid sea cliffs and dolphins cavorting about *(Molokai Action Adventure, tel 808/558-8184. Molokai Fishing, tel 808/567-6789, molokaifishing.com, half-day or private trips, six-person maximum: $$$$$).*

Sunday fishing trips on **Lanai** start from Manele Harbor *(Hotel Lanai, tel 808/565-7211, hotel lanai.com, half-day shared or private trips: $$$$$).*

high green mountains, palm trees, and the biggest Buddha outside Asia. Give it a history that reads like a novel and a cast of characters: kings, queens, a young star-crossed princess, stern Bible-thumping missionaries, scoundrels, and sailors. Now you've just about got Lahaina.

On October 1, 1819, the *Balena* out of New Bedford, Massachusetts, was the first American whaling ship to call in Hawaii (see p. 30). The port was Lahaina, a thriving coastal village and capital of the Hawaiian nation. The 2,400 residents engaged in fishing, farming, and foresting for the lucrative sandalwood trade with China. King Kamehameha II sat on the throne, with his stepmother, Queen Kaahumanu, ruling beside him.

INSIDER TIP:

Experience a fascinating undersea ecotour aboard the *Atlantis* submarine in Lahaina Harbor.

—DEB ANTONINI-CEFARATTI
National Geographic contributor

It was a year of great portent. King Kamehameha the Great had been buried. The ancient *kapu* (taboo) system was overthrown by the people, leaving them without their traditional system of religious law. The first American missionaries were on their way.

Between the 1820s and the 1860s, the Lahaina Roadstead became the principal anchorage of the Yankee Pacific whaling fleet,

and the town took on a distinctive New England flavor. The peak year was 1846 when 429 whalers called, and the harbor was described as a forest of masts. Up to 1,500 sailors at a time rampaged in the streets of the small town. Among them was Herman Melville, gathering material for his novels *Moby-Dick, Typee,* and *Billy Budd.*

Governor Hoapili, influenced by the missionaries, shut down grog shops and outlawed everything from spitting in the street to women boarding the ships. Riots ensued, with whaler cannon firing on the town, targeting the home of the spoilsport the Reverend William Richards. The missionary Lorrin Andrews wrote, "The devil is busily engaged at Lahaina."

The missionaries were busy. They transliterated the Hawaiian language (see pp. 31–32) and taught an eager populace *palapala* (writing); built Lahainaluna, the first high school west of the Rocky Mountains; installed the first printing press in Hale Pai (the house of printing); published the first newspaper; held singing classes; and translated the Bible into Hawaiian. The Hawaiians, a deeply spiritual people, bereft of their old religion, flocked to the new faith. In a decade, the Hawaiians became literate and Christian.

Visiting Lahaina: Lahaina today is a salty survivor. Approximately 55 acres have been set aside as historic districts with several sites designated as national historical landmarks. In place of ships' chandlers and grog shops, the weathered
(continued on p. 128)

Lahaina

🅜 Map p. 120 & p. 127

Visitor Information

✉ Lahaina Courthouse, 648 Wharf St.

☎ 808/667-9193

A Walk Through Lahaina's History

Walk through history in the footsteps of whalers, missionaries, and royalty. But be distracted, too, by ice cream parlors, shops, and restaurant decks over the water.

Art festivals often take place beneath the broad shade of the Lahaina's banyan tree.

Begin at the **Baldwin Home** ❶ *(696 Front St., tel 808/661-3262)*, where you can pick up a free historical map of the town. The original four rooms, built in 1834, have walls 24 inches thick to minimize the heat coming from outside and the high times in the streets. Note the old medical instruments and flag quilt. Next door is the **Masters' Reading Room,** built in 1836 to elevate the spirits of seamen with something other than grog. Pick up another free (walking) map here at the Lahaina Restoration Foundation *(120 Dickenson St., tel 808/661-3262).*

Cross Front Street and head toward the harbor on Market Street. At the edge of the seawall, there's a fine view of the waterfront. For a panorama of the picturesque old town with the majestic green West Maui Mountains rising behind, stroll out on the breakwater and look back. Lahaina appears to be a town from another, sleepier era. Right on the waterfront, the **Pioneer Inn** *(658 Wharf St., tel 808/661-3636)*, built in 1902, is still a salty saloon. The tidy white building next door is the 1859

NOT TO BE MISSED:

Baldwin Home • Pioneer Inn
• The Banyan Tree

Lahaina Courthouse ❷ *(649 Wharf St., tel 808/661-3636).* It has an art gallery and gift shop inside. Upstairs, there's an exhibit of old photographs and artifacts from early Lahaina. The visitor information desk provides maps and brochures. Behind the courthouse, stroll beneath the immense boughs of what is reputed to be the largest **banyan tree** in the United States, shading almost an acre. You might be surprised by a crafts fair here.

Turn toward the mountains on Canal Street, walk to Front Street, and turn right. The softball field, **Maluuluolele Park** ❸, was once the most important site on Maui. Intrigued by stories of a "lost island," volunteers began excavation in 1993. They found confirmation of a one-acre island and its 17-acre lake. The island was home and burial site for Maui royalty. In the 1880s, Princess Pauahi, the great-granddaughter of King Kamehameha I, had the royal bodies moved to nearby Wainee Cemetery, and in the early 20th century, with a disregard of Hawaiian culture that wouldn't be tolerated today, the lake was filled in.

Turn left on Shaw Street and left again on Wainee Street for **Wainee Cemetery** ❹ (*535 Wainee St., tel 808/661-4349*), which contains headstones for Keopuolani, sacred wife of Kamehameha I, and Princess Nahienaena, who died at age 21 in 1836.

Continue on Wainee Street, passing the **Hongwanji Mission** (*551 Wainee St., tel 808/661-0640*), a Buddhist temple built in 1927. On the corner of Prison and Wainee Streets is the old jail. **Hale Paahao** ❺ ("stuck-in-irons house") was built by convict labor in 1852. After visiting, keep walking on Wainee Street two blocks to Dickenson Street. Adjacent to the **Maria Lanakila Church** is the **Seamen's Cemetery.** A cousin of Herman Melville is buried here, as well as a shipmate who died, according to the marker, "of a disreputable disease."

At Lahainaluna Road, turn left two blocks and you'll be back on Front Street. Turn right and find the exotic **Wo Hing Temple** ❻ (*858 Front St., tel 808/661-5553*), built in 1912 by the Chee Kung Tong, a fraternal society dating from the 17th century. The adjacent cookhouse shows a 15-minute film about Hawaii made by Thomas Edison.

Continue along Front Street to the 1833 **Seamen's Hospital** (*1024 Front St.*). You can end your walk here or push on for another ten minutes, turning down Ala Moana Street to see the largest **Buddha** outside Asia at the **Lahaina Jodo Mission** ❼, sitting outdoors with a pagoda beside him and the mountains behind.

> 🗺 See also map p. 120
> ▶ Baldwin Home
> ↔ 2.5 miles to Seamen's Hospital, 0.3 mile more to Lahaina Jodo Mission
> 🕐 3 hours
> ▶ Seamen's Hospital

INSIDER TIP:

The best time to photograph or walk around Lahaina is late in the day. Start about an hour before sunset at one end of Front Street.

—DOUGLAS PEEBLES
National Geographic contributor

Kaanapali

 Map p. 120

Visitor Information

✉ Kaanapali
Beach Resort
Association, 34
Kupuahi St.

☎ 808/661-3271

🕐 Closed Sat. &
Sun.

wooden buildings along **Front Street** and its byways now house boutiques, along with dozens of art galleries offering the works of both local artists and masters such as Dalí, Chagall, and Miró, and restaurants showcasing Hawaii's seafood and regional cuisine. The art market is so successful the galleries host a weekly "Friday Is Art Night in Lahaina," featuring hors d'oeuvres, wine, music, and art demonstrations.

Where whaling ships once lay at anchor, an armada of pleasure boats now waits to take you snorkeling, diving, whale-watching, on a sunset dinner cruise, or on a picnic sail to other islands.

Lahaina might be called the Williamsburg of Hawaii. The whalers are long gone but, ironically, the whales are still around (see pp. 130–131).

Kaanapali

When American Factors designed the world's first master-planned resort in the 1950s, they already knew the best location—Kaanapali. This was where Hawaiian royalty came to surf the long rollers and race their swift outrigger canoes in the channel between Maui and Lanai. On what is now the **Royal Kaanapali Golf Course,** they would play *ulu maika,* a form of lawn bowling. Come evening, there'd be luaus along the perfect three-mile beach, with succulent pigs lifted ceremoniously from the underground ovens. The beat of the *pahu* drums would call the dancers to begin telling the old stories in chant, gesture, and step. When the capital of the

kingdom moved to Honolulu, Kaanapali, like Sleeping Beauty, began a long slumber.

In 1849, Hawaiian scholar David Malo began experimenting with raising sugar. It proved to be an excellent crop. A narrow-gauge railroad was laid from the Pioneer Mill in Lahaina through the new

INSIDER TIP:

At the Hyatt Regency in Kaanapali, you'll find exotic wildlife on the grounds as well as in the lobby and an atrium that opens to the sky.

—RON FISHER
National Geographic author

sugar plantation to a ship landing constructed at what was once a sacred site, Kekaa Point, the towering black lava promontory at the end of the beach.

Kaanapali today is a 1,200-acre resort with five luxury hotels, six condo and vacation club resorts, two 18-hole championship golf courses, 40 tennis courts, a tennis stadium, 20-plus restaurants, and more than 75 shops.

The skeleton of a 40-foot sperm whale welcomes you to **Whaler's Village** *(2435 Kaanapali Pkwy.),* a shopping complex at the resort. Up on the second floor, the **Whale Museum** *(tel 808/661-5992)* has a fascinating collection of memorabilia recalling Maui's 19th-century whaling heyday. Videos and self-guided audio tours tell you all about the nasty business of hunting the world's largest living mammal. There are weapons, ship models, a life-size diorama of the miserable living quarters aboard ship, and a collection of intriguing diaries and letters written by the sailors.

The old sugarcane train, the **Lahaina Kaanapali & Pacific Railroad,** is still running the six miles into Lahaina, though sacred Kekaa, now popularly called Black Rock, is no longer on the route.

Kapalua

Situated amid a 23,000-acre working pineapple plantation, Kapalua is fringed by five exceptional bays, all open to the public. In 1992, Maui Land & Pineapple dedicated 8,661 acres of native forest to the Nature Conservancy of Hawaii, creating **Puu Kukui Watershed Preserve** in memory of Colin C. Cameron (conservationist and former ML&P president). This is home to three native bird species; five very rare snail species; 20 rare native plants, 18 of them endemic and unique to West Maui; fragrant species of sandalwood; rare violets; and the world's only *Lobelia gloria-montis,* a white-and-purple blossom.

The **Kapalua Resort's** offshore waters are a vast underwater park, ideal for snorkeling. **Kapalua Beach** is a dream tropical beach, a perfect smile of sand bordered by palm-fringed promontories on either end. Waves are usually gentle and the water exceptionally clear. Both the beach and the marine sanctuary are accessible to the public.

Kapalua Resort has a number of holiday homes and condominium rentals, most prominently the luxurious Ritz-Carlton Kapalua (see p. 247), which mixes in residential communities, three championship golf courses (see p. 228), 20 tennis courts, 16 restaurants, and more than 20 shops. The Kapalua Villas Activities Desk *(tel 808/669-8088)* runs tours of the surrounding pineapple plantation.

Several notable events take place at Kapalua Resort. Acclaimed artists gather over Easter weekend and conduct free classes for the public. The **Kapalua Wine & Food Festival,** the state's longest running food festival, in June, has been

A kayaker at Napili Bay heads to sea on a calm, clear day.

attracting leading chefs for more than two decades. Throughout the year, the resort hosts major international golf and tennis events.

An ancient burial place was discovered when ground was broken for the Ritz-Carlton. At great cost in both time and money, new plans were drawn up and the hotel was moved to higher ground. The original site remains a vast tranquil memorial. ■

Lahaina Kaanapali & Pacific Railroad
- Map p. 120 & p. 127
- Lahaina Station; Kaanapali Station; Puukolii Station
- 808/661-0080
- $$$

Kapalua
- Map p. 120

Kapalua Resort
- 700 Village Rd., Lahaina
- 800/665-5400 or 808/665-3747

Majestic Mammals

"In 1820 the American came with a rush and a wildness as violent as storms from the sea, as brutal as harpooners closing in upon a herd of sleeping whales."
—O. A. Bushnell (co-author), *Hawaii: A Pictorial History*, 1969

A humpback whale breaching the waters off Hawaii. These endangered creatures are a magnet for whale-watchers.

In an ironic twist, the very waters that ran red with their blood more than a century ago now embrace and protect these splendid creatures of the sea, especially the humpback whale.

Though the whales may be seen at a distance from the shores of every island from early December through May, the protected Auau Channel and shallow warm waters off the west coast of Maui are particularly good. Humpbacks announce their presence by breaching, slapping the water with their tails, spouting streams of water from their blowholes, or in some other dramatic way. Whale-watchers who have seen them "up close" from boats (kept at a required distance away) describe the experience as "jaw dropping."

Generally speaking, whales and dolphins are mammals and belong to one of two classifications of the order Cetaceans: Odontoceti (toothed whales) and Mysticeti (toothless). Humpbacks belong to the baleen whale suborder Mysticeti, a fitting classification because it remains a mystery how they are able to travel 3,000 miles of open ocean from frigid Alaskan seas to the tropical waters of Hawaii within two months. In fact, Mysticeti refers to the whales' feeding mechanism, the baleen, which can trap shoals of krill, fish, plankton, and shrimp. Amazing, when you consider that the largest animals on Earth survive by eating the smallest. Though their numbers vary from season to season, an estimated 4,000 to 5,000 humpbacks arrive in the islands and display their majesty. That number is particularly impressive given that the total North Pacific whale population is 6,000 to 10,000.

Females tend to be larger than males, ranging from 45 to 60 feet, and weighing from 40 to 45 tons. Mature humpbacks are dark, though some sport splotches of white; their pectoral flippers are the longest among whales. And the one distinguishing hallmark of humpbacks that gives these whales their name is seen in the way they curve their backs and tail region when launching a dive.

Whale Behavior

Among other characteristics that mark these splendid mammals are their social interactions. For one, humpbacks display a cooperative feeding strategy in which fellow whales share the food at the dinner table. Several individuals, by swimming in ever tighter concentric circles, "herd" the fish into a kind of net, a bit like the way a border collie herds sheep into a corral. For another, male humpbacks produce wistful, almost haunting sounds beneath the ocean, whale songs that communicate more than romance because the sounds are known to carry on from male generation to male generation in a whale's version of oral history.

What exactly would the whales tell us if they could? Possibly more than we could imagine, considering the fact that whales possess the largest brains on Earth.

The Hawaiian Islands Humpback Whale National Marine Sanctuary was designated in 1992 for the protection of the whales and for educating the world about the grace and intelligence of these creatures.

You may enhance your whale-watching experience by sticking to a few basics. First, the humpbacks arrive around December and head north to Alaska in late May, so plan your visit during that time. Second, Maui, Kauai, and the Big Island are the most popular sites for sighting the whales. Though whales are in Oahu waters, their numbers aren't as large. Most important, respect the whales' space; observers must maintain a distance of at least 100 yards between themselves and the whales. Education and awareness are keys in the preservation of these gentle giants of the sea.

EXPERIENCE: Watching Whales

Whether you choose to watch for whales from the shore or from the ocean, Hawaii offers many good choices, with **Maui** an ideal place to start. You can see whales off the island's west and southern shorelines from numerous points, including Wailea in central Maui and Olowalu Reef in west Maui.

Tours from Lahaina Harbor are available for closer looks *(Safari Boat Excursions, tel 808/661-7670, safariboatexcursions.com, hour-and-a-half to two-hour tours: $$$$$, online discounts available. Captain Steve's Rafting, tel 808/667-5565, captainsteves .com, two-hour tours: $$$$$).*

Whales may be seen off the **Big Island's** Kona coastline while you are driving south from the main airport *(Ocean Eco-Tours, tel 808/324-7873, oceaneco*

tours.com, two-and-a-half-hour tour: $$$$$).

Kauai also enjoys many offshore whale sightings, especially from Kilauea Point National Wildlife Refuge, the North Shore's Kalalau Trail, the shoreline along the Ahakuni Landing by the airport to Anahola, and, of course, Poipu Beach.

Poipu is your launching site if you decide to take an ocean tour *(Blue Dolphin Charters, tel 877/511-1311 or 808/335-5553, kauaiboats.com, two-hour Poipu sunset trip: $$$$$, online discounts available).*

Oahu-only visitors may see the giants from the west side's Waianae Coast, or you can splash out on an ocean tour *(Wild Side Specialty Tours, tel 808/306-7273, sailhawaii.com, four-hour morning cruise or three hours, with a six-person maximum, ages 12 and older: $$$$$).*

Central Maui

Kula-o-ka-Mao-Mao, "the land of mirages," is what Hawaiians called the broad central isthmus between the verdant West Maui Mountains and the massive flanks of Haleakala. Shimmering with heat, teased by almost constant winds, this land belongs neither to East Maui nor West, yet it is the heart of the island, where locals live and tourists land.

The airport was originally built by the U.S. Navy during World War II, to supply the Pacific armada. The military also developed a beach that is now **Kanaha Beach Park** *(Hawaii 380, one mile N of Kahului International Airport),* a protected shallow-water shoreline that is the best beach on this part of the island. Windsurfers like Kanaha for the steady, strong onshore trade winds.

Nearby, directly in the flight path of silver birds with their noisy jet engines, endangered Hawaiian birds, such as the *koloa* and Hawaiian stilt, have set up housekeeping in and around former royal fishponds, playing host to annual migrations of Alaskan birds. Actually, the birds were here first. In 1971, the area was declared a national natural history landmark, and is known as **Kanaha Pond Wildlife Refuge** *(2 miles W of jct. of Hana Hwy. & Haleakala Hwy. Extension, tel 808/984-8100).*

In spite of the glut of commerce around the airport, much of the central plain is carpeted in pineapple fields and acres of emerald sugarcane waving their silver tassels in the breezes. Workers wear colorful protective gear when laboring in the fields.

You can visit a working plantation at the touristy **Maui Tropical Plantation** *(1670 Honoapiilani Hwy., tel 808/244-7643).* Admission is free. There's a restaurant, gift shop, attractive garden and ponds, and tram tour ($$$).

The **Alexander & Baldwin Sugar Museum** *(Puunene Ave. & Hansen Rd., Puunene,*

A bridge across a stream affords excellent views of Iao Valley and its famous Needle.

tel 808/871-8058) chronicles the heyday of King Cane in photographs and artifacts. Located in the former residence of the manager of the state's largest sugar company, it is next to a working sugar mill with all its clatter and wonderful molasses smell.

Kahului & Wailuku

The contrasting towns of Kahului and Wailuku are three miles apart. Kahului was built in the 1950s by the plantation company Alexander & Baldwin to provide housing for workers. Ships once carried away sugar and pineapple. Kahului has the impressive **Maui Arts & Cultural Center** (see p. 146), but otherwise its landmarks are pedestrian—three shopping malls as well as chain stores and discounters.

All these new arrivals have hurt little old **Wailuku.** Much of Main Street is shuttered as small businesses have caved in. Still, the streets are charming and invite walking, and there are antique shops, home furnishings stores, and odd little galleries.

Wailuku is the perfect setting for **Kaahumanu Church** *(103 S. High St., tel 808-244-5189, closed Mon.–Fri.).* Built in 1837 on the site of a former grass chapel and an adobe church, it is named for the favorite wife of Kamehameha I, who precipitated the overthrow of the old religion and paved the way for Christianity (see pp. 29–30).

Caroline and Edward Bailey, missionaries turned sugar growers, lived happily for 45 years in what is now **Bailey House Museum.**

Built in 1833, the house still feels like a cozy home, with its porches, angled staircase, comfortable old furniture, dolls, books, and bed quilts. There are also fascinating precontact artifacts, including an unusual replicated temple image— the Bishop Museum in Honolulu (see pp. 72–73) collected the original. One room is devoted to Edward Bailey's oil paintings of Maui done between 1866 and 1896 (see p. 44).

Iao Valley

The Valley of the Kings, Iao, is named for the god above all gods, the Supreme Light. In ancient days, the Hawaiians carried their royal dead into the valley for secret burial. A natural altar, Iao Needle, rises 1,200 feet from the stream at its base.

INSIDER TIP:

Iao Valley State Park is a must-see! It's a short hike to the lookout for spectacular views of the Iao Needle and the valley.

—VINCENT KHOURY TYLOR
National Geographic contributor

As recently as 1959, old rituals were reenacted during an Aloha Week pageant when, at night, a pathway of bamboo torches blazed all the way to the Needle, where a chanter called out almost forgotten prayers across the dark and deep valley.

One of the bloodiest battles in Hawaiian history took place here

Central Maui

🅰 Map pp. 120–121

Visitor Information

✉ Maui Visitors Bureau, 1727 Wili Pa Loop, Wailuku 96793

☎ 800/525-MAUI or 808/244-3530

🕐 Closed Sat. & Sun.

Kahului

🅰 121

Wailuku

🅰 120

Bailey House Museum

✉ 2375-A Main St., Wailuku

☎ 808/244-3326

🕐 Closed Sun.

💲 $$

EXPERIENCE: Hawaiian Healing

The traditional Hawaiian healing art of *lomilomi* is difficult to characterize. Mary Kawena Pukui, a respected Hawaiian cultural expert, defined "lomi" in her landmark Hawaiian dictionary: "To rub, press, crush . . . rub out; to work in and out as claws of a contented cat."

A *lomilomi* practitioner meditates near a beach in Honolulu.

This ancient healing art starts with a prayer and may make use of the practitioner's palms, hands, fingers, forearms, elbows, knees, feet, even sticks and stones, all in the name of enhancing wellness.

Lomilomi, as a multidimensional way of healing, differs in philosophy and approach from person to person and family to family. However, one underlying principle applies universally: a deep reverence for the healing traditions of old, steeped in authentic Hawaiian spirituality, as handed down from generation to generation.

Maui

A historic neighborhood and resorts on Maui are known for their lomilomi

massages (*Wailuku's Green Ti Boutique & Massage*, tel 808/242-8788, green timaui.com, $$$$$. *Hyatt Regency Maui*, tel 808/661-1234, hyattregencymaui.com, $$$$$. *Four Seasons Resort Maui at Wailea*, tel 808/874-2244 or 808/874-8000, fourseasons.com/maui, $$$$$).

Oahu

The stresses and strains of busy Oahu motivate many to seek lomilomi (*Lomilomi Hana Lima Healing Center & Spa*, tel 808/263-0303, lomi lomihanalima.com, $$$$$. *The Kahala Hotel & Resort*, tel 808/739-8888, kahala resort.com, $$$$$).

Kauai

Kauai's greenery lifts lomilomi to a feeling of oneness with nature, where

therapists have knowledge of old (*Angeline's Lomi Kauai at Anahola*, tel 808/822-3253, angelineslomikauai .com, $$$$$. *Aloha Manalima Lomilomi*, tel 808/639-0893, e-mail: paka16@hotmail .com, $$$$$. *Alexander Day Spa & Salon at the Kauai Marriott*, tel 808/246-4918 or 866/932-9772, alexanderspa .com, $$$$$).

Hawaii: the Big Island

Hawaii's Big Island has its own paths to wellness, including Dane Silva, a co-founder of the Hawaiian Lomilomi Association (*Hale Ola*, tel 808/895-1949, hale ola.com, $$$$$. *Mauna Lani Resort*, tel 800/367-2323 or 808/881-7922, maunalani .com, $$$$$. *Kalaekilohana*, tel 888/584-7071 or 808/939-8052, kau-hawaii.com, $$$$$).

Molokai

Molokai—the Friendly Isle—features the therapy at Hotel Molokai, where lomilomi is accompanied by heated stones (*Molokai Acupuncture & Massage*, tel 808/660-3334 or 808/553-5347, hotel molokai.com, $$$$$).

Lanai

And lomilomi is an important part of the getaway experience at Four Seasons Resort Lanai (*The Lodge at Koele*, tel 808/565-4555, fourseasons.com/lanai, $$$$$).

in 1790, when the army of King Kamehameha I thundered across the plain in pursuit of Kalaniku-pule, defender of Maui and son of Kamehameha's archenemy King Kahekili. With a terrible new weapon—cannon salvaged from a defeated American ship, the *Elea-nora*—Kamehameha took a terrible toll on the Maui forces, their bodies choking the red-running Wailuku River. The cannon was forever called Waha-ula, "the red mouth," and the battle was Kepaniwai, meaning "the dam-ming of the waters."

Kepaniwai Heritage Garden *(Hawaii 32, 2 miles from Wailuku)*, named for the battle, is a cool and peaceful sanctuary. Designed by local architect Richard Tongg, it contains homes and gardens representative of the major ethnic groups that settled Maui. Among them are a New England saltbox, a Japanese teahouse, a Chinese pagoda, and the proverbial "little grass shack." It's quite photogenic

and a good place to have a picnic.

Just up the road, farther into Iao Valley, is a sign pointing out a natural profile of President John F. Kennedy, etched into the mountainside. Such profiles often require a generous imagination, but this one is startling.

Iao Valley State Park is a 6.2-acre park within the 4,000 acres of the valley. You can take in the most breathtaking vistas on an easy 0.3-mile loop trail that crosses the stream. From the bridge you can see the Needle. Other trails go deeper into the valley, but they enter private land and are posted.

To learn more about the val-ley's natural history, stop in at the **Hawaii Nature Center.** This Maui branch of the Oahu-based envi-ronmental education group (see p. 81) has more than 30 hands-on exhibits in the Interactive Science Arcade, plus dioramas, games, and a solarium with stunning views of the valley. On weekends they offer guided hikes into Iao. ∎

Iao Valley State Park

🄰 Map p. 120
✉ Hawaii 32, Iao Valley Rd.
☎ 808/984-8109

Hawaii Nature Center

🄰 Map p. 120
✉ 875 Iao Valley Rd.
☎ 808/244-6500
💲 $$

The Chinese pavilion at Kepaniwai Heritage Garden

East Maui

Haleakala, the world's largest dormant volcano, dominates eastern Maui. Its highest peak, Puu Ulaula, stands at 10,023 feet and towers a mile higher than any other mountain on the island. Arrayed at its feet on the sunny southwest shore is a series of resort areas that die away into dry lava-strewn wilderness surrendering to the sea. Rain is rare in this ideal holiday climate.

Windsurfers line up for a race from Wailea to Molokini Island.

From this leeward shore, you can see Lanai, Kahoolawe, Molokini, and West Maui, which appears to be a separate island from here.

Day-trip boats beat a path to Molokini, a moon sliver of an islet whose volcanic crater has slipped beneath the waves creating a natural aquarium where colorful reef fish swim with pelagic species from the open ocean—and with the snorkelers who arrive on the excursion boats. Molokini is a Marine Conservation District so the fish are plentiful.

The shore road (South Kihei Road) is lined with condominiums, strip malls, inexpensive restaurants, relaxing mai tai spots, activity centers, and farmers' markets. Accommodations range from luxe to "cheap and cheerful." Don't be surprised to see the flag of Canada flying from many a pole. This is snowbird country: Beleaguered northerners come here to sit out the winter in their time-shares.

Beyond the resorts, Oneloa Beach spreads out in golden splendor. The water is exceptionally clear,

INSIDER TIP:

Go by boat to Molokini
—a tiny, eroded volcano
off Maui's southwest
coast—where snorkelers
see rainbows of tropical
fish, manta rays, and
octopuses sheltered by
the coral reefs.

—JERRY CAMARILLO DUNN, JR.
National Geographic author

here and at La Perouse Bay, because
of the absence of development.
Both have been incorporated into
the Makena-La Perouse Bay State
Park. Nudists still tiptoe into the
little cove on the other side of Puu
Olai promontory, risking jail if they
get caught.

Around a corner to the
northeast, Maui remains rugged
and remote, but becomes lush and
green, beribboned with waterfalls,
veiled in mists. Hana lies pinioned
on a lonely road both picturesque
and precarious. This is the most
genuinely Hawaiian part of the
island, gentle in spirit, unpretentious, and happy to be pretty much
left alone.

Kihei, Wailea, & Makena

This is a wonderful area for
budget travelers, and it happens
to be one of the finest coasts of
the state. Don't be put off by the
dike of condos. Once you're in
one, the views are glorious, with
more isles sitting on the horizon
and Haleakala rising in the back.
The beach at **Kihei** runs for
6 miles and is easily accessed in
a string of beach parks. **Kalama**

Beach Park *(Kihei Rd., 4 miles S of
Kihei village)* is 36 acres of shady
lawn and coconut palms. It's a great
place to picnic, and you can take
out local-style food such as Loco
Moco and a "Hawaiian plate" at
The Kitchen *(2439 S. Kihei Rd., tel
808/875-7782).*

Across from the Maui Lu Resort
(575 S. Kihei Rd., tel 808/879-5881)
is a totem pole. Brought from British Columbia by a former manager
of the resort, it was placed to com-
memorate the Hawaiian voyages of
Capt. George Vancouver.

Endangered Hawaiian stilts,
coots, and ducks, as well as sand-
erlings and Pacific golden plover
congregate at 700-acre **Kealia
Pond National Wildlife Reserve.**
A boardwalk through the ponds
begins near Milepost 2 on
Piilani Highway.

At the **Maui Ocean Center**
you walk in a clear tunnel through
a 600,000-gallon aquarium while
tiger sharks cruise past, eyeball to
eyeball. The 5-acre facility is about
the world beneath the waves, and
features tanks and ponds with
some very strange creatures.

The jumble of Kihei stops
abruptly where the meticulously
tended lawns and gardens of
Wailea begin. Even though billions
of dollars built the 1,500-acre resort
and its three championship golf
courses (see pp. 228), there are
some moderately priced accommodations amid the conspicuous
luxury. All the beaches are public,
as they are throughout Hawaii.
You can walk the shore on a paved
nature path for one and a half miles
from the Fairmont Kea Lani Hotel
(see p. 248, *4100 Wailea Alanui, tel
808/875-4100)* to the Andaz Maui

**Kealia Pond
National Wildlife
Reserve**

Map p. 121

Jct. of Piilani
Hwy. (Hawaii
31) & Mokulele
Hwy. (Hawaii
350)

808/875-1582

**Maui Ocean
Center**

Map p. 120

192 Maalaea
Rd., Maalaea

808/270-7000

$$$$

at Wailea *(3550 Wailea Alanui, tel 808/879-1922)*. Many of the Hawaiian shoreline plants are labeled. Take time to explore the fantastic Grand Wailea Resort Hotel and Spa (see p. 249, *3850 Wailea Alanui, tel 800/888-6100 or 808/875-1234)*. Their Spa Grande is bigger than all other Maui spas

---

What Remains in Hawaii

Certain plants and animals harbor pests, diseases, and other microscopic dangers that threaten American agriculture. Before departure for the mainland, passengers and their baggage will be screened at all Hawaii airports. U.S. Department of Agriculture officials *(tel 808/861-8490)* **will confiscate fresh fruits and plants, including:**

- **mangoes, bananas, papayas, sweet potatoes;**
- **berries of any kind, including coffee berries;**
- **fresh flowers of gardenia, jade vine, and Mauna Loa orchids;**
- **live insects and snails;**
- **seeds with pulp and fresh seed pods; and**
- **soil or plants in soil, as well as cactus plants or parts.**

---

combined. There's a river pool with a swim-up bar in a swim-in cave, waterfalls, water slides, a water elevator, a fake beach, gardens, sculptures, and lily ponds.

Beyond Wailea is the resort of **Makena,** a quiet, dignified retreat before the island goes wild again.

At Makena Landing, cowboys mounted on Percherons once drove cattle from the Upcountry ranches into the sea (see p. 163).

Upcountry

Take Montana, move it to Maui, crown it with a crater that looks like the face of the moon, and you have Upcountry, one of Hawaii's biggest surprises. Girdling the mid-slopes of 10,023-foot Haleakala Volcano, the area—also known as Kula—is blessed with a temperate-zone climate, making it ideal for agriculture and ranching. During the whaling era, Hawaiian farmers switched from traditional crops of taro and sweet potato to feed the crews on Irish potatoes, corn, wheat, apples, peaches, plums, and pears. During the California gold rush, they shipped the same fare to the forty-niners and grew so prosperous the area was called Nu Kaliponi, New California. Kula cotton clothed the Union Army during the American Civil War.

Today's food crops range from big plump strawberries to the famous Maui onion, so sweet it can be eaten like an apple. The bumper crops, however, are flowers, from roses to the exotic protea, huge and otherworldly, looking more like a bloom of the moon than anything an earthly garden could grow. Many of the flower farms welcome visitors and will ship bouquets home for you. **Sunrise Protea Farm** *(416A Haleakala Crater Rd., tel 808/876-0200)* has rows of various protea from king to mink, growing just feet from picnic tables and a snack shop.

The **University of Hawaii Maui Agricultural Research** *(209 Mauna Place, off Copp Rd., tel 808/878-1213, closed Fri.–Sun.)* pioneered the protea as a cash crop and offers free walking maps of their 34-acre garden. Thirty varieties of protea grow at the **Enchanting Floral Garden,** which has 1,500 species of flora in 8 charming acres, including the world's only white pineapple. After strolling the gardens, you'll be offered a fruit cup of whatever is in season—orange, star fruit, banana, papaya, guava. **Kula Botanical Gardens** is primarily 5 acres of orchids, bromeliads, and trees, including koa, king of the Hawaiian forest. They also grow 11 acres of fat, fragrant, and fluffy Monterey pines for Christmas trees.

Upcountry's biggest surprise is the grape. On the sprawling **Ulupalakua Ranch,** a former Napa Valley vintner, Emil Tedeschi, experimented with 140 different grapes to find what grew best in Maui's rich volcanic soil. He's now producing respected white, red, and sparkling wines, one of which

was served at Ronald Reagan's 1985 inauguration. **Tedeschi Vineyards & Winery** *(end of Hawaii 37, tel 808/878-6058)* offers a tour, a shop, and a tasting room.

Stitched into the patchwork quilt of farms and ranches are country towns with mom-and-pop stores, trendy boutiques, and galleries—and more surprises. In **Kula,** the white octagonal **Church of the Holy Ghost** is like an exquisite Fabergé egg. Built in 1897 by Father James Beissel, it is home to a magnificent baroque-style altar and a reproduction of the crown of Queen Isabella of Portugal, a gift to former subjects living here.

If a beautiful church inspires the spirit, Upcountry's **Alii Kula Lavender Farm** *(1100 Waipoli Rd., tel 808/878-3004)* inspires the senses. Visitors are greeted with fresh-from-the-fields fragrances that reflect 31 varieties of lavender growing on the slopes of Haleakala. They bloom profusely during the summer and are used in versatile ways—from lotions to aromatherapy products.

Enchanting Floral Garden

- Map p. 121
- Hawaii 37 at Milepost 10, Kula
- 808/878-2531
- $

Kula Botanical Gardens

- Map p. 121
- Hawaii 377, uphill from jct. with Hawaii 37
- 808/878-1715
- $

Church of the Holy Ghost

- Map p. 121
- Hawaii 37 and Lower Kula Rd., Kula
- 808/878-1091

Exotic protea have become a cash crop in Hawaii and flower farms grow dozens of varieties.

From the lookout, the moonlike crater of Haleakala spreads to the horizon.

Makawao is a town in transition. Once known as Macho-wow, it used to be the domain of the rugged cowboy: Stores sold feed, saddles, and ammunition. Now they dispense fashion, books, art, crystals, and gifts. But the old **Komodo Store and Bakery** *(3674 Baldwin Ave., tel 808/572-7261, closed Wed. & Sun.)* is still, after 60 years, selling its yummy cream puffs. The biggest local event is the Fourth of July Rodeo.

Haleakala National Park

Haleakala means "House of the Sun." Looking across the crater from the summit lip at dawn, the sun appears to rise from inside the caldera to ignite the world into daylight. According to legend, Maui, Superman of Hawaiian myth, climbed to the top of Haleakala and lassoed the sun to force it to move more slowly across the Hawaiian sky. La, the mighty sun, as a compromise agreed to slow his pace for half the year, granting people longer summer days.

The summit has always been sacred. Hawaiians came to the land above the clouds to quarry stone for adze heads and to worship their gods. The Specter of the Brocken, a natural phenomenon of the volcano that allows a person to see his own shadow in a halo of rainbow-hued mist, they called *aka-ku-anue-nue*—the seeing of one's own soul.

The summit area of Haleakala was declared a part of Hawaii Volcanoes National Park in 1916 and acquired full status of its own as a national park in 1961. Eight years later, the ecologically fragile lower slopes at Kipahulu (see p. 143) were added to the park. The crater dimensions are awesome: 21 miles in circumference, 3,000 feet deep. Thousand-foot cinder cones that once spewed lava lie napping in its lap. The volcano last erupted in 1790. Looking into its silent depths, Mark Twain wrote: "I felt like the last Man, neglected of the judgment and left pinnacled in mid-heaven, a forgotten relic of a vanished world."

Some of the life-forms you'll encounter in the park are among the rarest on Earth. The nene, the Hawaiian goose, was rescued from the brink of extinction. Even though it's still endangered, you will probably see some in the park, maybe even with goslings in tow. Once plentiful, they are being bred in captivity and successfully returned to the wild. The strangely beautiful *ahinahina,* or silversword, is an evolutionary descendant of the sunflower. For up to 20 years it sits like a spiked silver crown and then throws out hundreds of blooms on a stalk up to 9 feet tall. On close examination, the individual blossoms resemble their sunflower ancestor. The easiest place to see the silversword is the enclosure at the **Kalahaku Overlook.** At the **Leleiwi Overlook,** just beyond Milepost 17, there's a good lunar-like view of craters and shale. Around sunset, if the clouds are low, you may experience the Specter of the Brocken. Haleakala's highest peak, the **Puu Ulaula Overlook,** is near the visitor center and is the most popular stop, especially at sunrise, because the panorama is so broad. Be careful when stepping out of your car. Not only will it be cold, but at 10,023 feet the altitude could make you dizzy. If you experience drowsiness or headache, have someone drive you to a lower elevation.

For a more intimate experience of the park, there are 36 miles of hiking trails in the crater, although rangers warn that only those in excellent physical condition should attempt them. Allow twice as long to come back out as it takes to go in. An easy solution is the quarter-mile **Hosmer Grove nature walk,** which doesn't go into the crater but will introduce you to the unique ecology of the park. There are two campgrounds and three cabins in the crater. The latter are awarded on a lottery basis. **Pony Express Tours** (tel 808/667-2200) offers horseback rides to the floor of the caldera.

The place that's off-limits is one that you can't help seeing—the domed white buildings called **Science City,** sitting on the crater lip. They do spacey things here like bouncing laser beams off prisms

Haleakala National Park

- Map p. 121
- 808/572-4400 or 808/871-5054 (recorded weather forecast)
- Daily nature talks, hourly 9:30 a.m.–11:30 a.m. from Park Headquarters (1 mile from entrance) & Summit Visitor Center (11 miles from entrance)
- $

EXPERIENCE: Zipping Above It All

Ever imagine the thrill of zooming through the air while looking at the world through a bird's eyes? Get that rush by zipping via steel cable lines over rain forests, cliffs, valleys, gorges, and waterfalls. Two islands feature guided zip tours: Maui and Kauai.

On **Maui,** zipping at Haleakala's cool heights involves a number of different experiences: a forest hike, more than 2 miles of ziplines, views of an Upcountry area, and an introduction into Hawaii's fragile landscape. Allow at least three hours for the tour, and make sure to dress warmly before setting off. When you return, keep moving and see the rest of the House of the Sun (Skyline Eco-Adventures, tel 808/878-8400, skylinehawaii.com, $$$$$, online discounts available).

Kaanapali is a less chilly spot, and presents an adventure deep into the rugged lands where eight ziplines allow vistas from the mountains to the sea while soaring above streams, waterfalls, and treetops. Plan for a full day of adventure (Skyline Eco-Adventures, tel 808/878-8400, skylinehawaii.com, $$$$$, online discounts available).

Zipping at Kapalua offers yet another scenic ride as eight dual-track ziplines cross over Maui's mountain ridges. You may choose options of two-, three-, or four-hour tours (Kapalua Adventure Center and Mountain Outpost, tel 877/665-4386, kapaluaadventues.com, $$$$$).

There's definitely a green perspective zipping in **Kauai.** Seven ziplines descend a mountainside and glide over tropical forests and pristine lands, within a spectacular view of Mount Waialeale (Kauai Backcountry Adventures, tel 888/270-0555 or 808/245-2506, kauai backcountry.com, $$$$$).

positioned on the moon by American astronauts.

Getting to the park is a good part of the fun. The entrance is at the 7,000-foot elevation of **Haleakala Highway,** encompassing legs of Routes 37, 377, and 378, and is an amazing drive. Climbing from

Kaahumanu

Born in a cave at Kauiki Head in 1772 during a time of war, Kaahumanu lived her life in a period of great turmoil and seized the reins of power of the Hawaiian kingdom. When she was ten, a prophet told her that she would one day become the wife of a king. Seven years later, she married Kamehameha the Great and was always the favorite of his 21 wives. Capt. George Vancouver called her "the most beautiful woman in the South Seas." She was also brilliant. Upon Kamehameha's death in 1819, Queen Kaahumanu, in a single act called *Ai Noa,* **"free eating," toppled the ancient system of religious law (see pp. 29–30). She died in 1832.**

sea level to 10,000 feet in only 40 miles is like driving from Mexico to Alaska in two hours. Palm trees give way to pine and eucalyptus, and all finally shrink into the lava desolation above the tree line. Summit temperatures average 35°F to 77°F in summer, 26°F to 75°F in winter. Most people start in predawn darkness and sightsee on the way down. Wear layers of clothing.

Hana-Kipahulu

At the end of the long and winding **Hana Highway** (see pp. 144–145) awaits the little town of Hana. There's something about the air here that induces a peace bordering on euphoria. Some claim the thick lush vegetation results in more oxygen. Others know it's the spirit of the place itself. You can drive through the town in five minutes. There's a hotel on one side of the street, cows on the other, plus a couple of glorious old churches and a few stores. As soon as you arrive in this town hugging the bay, you recognize this as one of the world's special places.

Hana is dominated by two forces, the 3,000-acre **Hana Ranch** and the upscale **Hotel Hana–Maui** *(5031 Hana Hwy., tel 808/248-8211),* the first resort built outside of Waikiki. Guests have included Walt Disney, Clark Gable, and the von Trapp family. On top of **Lyons Hill,** a lava stone cross was erected in 1960 in memory of Texas millionaire Paul Fagan, who brought the first tourists to town. It's a 3-mile hike through open cow pasture to the hilltop for panoramic views of Hana. It's especially nice at sunset.

The promontory at the right end of the bay, **Kauiki Head,** looms large in history and legend. When Noenoe Ua Kea O Hana, daughter of the great Maui, fell in love with Kauiki, an adopted son of the Menehune (see p. 187), her enraged father changed the unsuitable lover into the hill and Noenoe into the beautiful, white, misty rain of Hana. Fierce battles, primarily between Hana and Big Island chiefs, were waged on and around Kauiki Head. It was also the birthplace of Queen Kaahumanu.

At the base of Kauiki, on the right side, is **Kaihalulu,** usually called **Red Sand Beach** because its sands, eroded from the surrounding cinder cone, are the color of garnets. The sea, foaming in at the mouth of the cove, is teal and cream. Kaihalulu is at the end of the parking lot for the Hotel

INSIDER TIP:

Hike up to Waimoku Falls above Maui's Oheo Gulch. Protect your camera from sudden tropical downpours and spray from the falls.

—ROBERT HOLMES
National Geographic contributor

Hana–Maui's Sea Ranch Cottages, then left across a field, following a worn footpath along a cliff. The trail is hazardous but mercifully short, about 15 minutes.

Hana's other favorite beach is **Hamoa.** Salt-and-pepper sands line a 1,000-foot shoreline at the base of 30-foot sea cliffs.

Piilanihale Heiau, the largest *heiau* (temple) in Hawaii and a national historic landmark, broods over the Hana coast just north of town. Its walls are 60 to 90 feet high. The temple is maintained by

direct descendants of its builder, King Piilani (late 14th–early 15th century). It is said to emanate such force that pilots approaching nearby Hana Airport refuse to fly over it. Hawaiian ceremonies are still held here. The temple stands within **Kahanu Garden,** 126 acres of tropical flora and lava coastline, with an extravagant background of green mountains.

You can explore the history and culture of the area at **Hana Cultural Center,** a former police station. There are some exceptional Hawaiian quilts, *kapa* (tree-bark cloth), a century-old *olona* fishing net, historical photographs, and a collection of portraits of Hana's people by the late Leslie Eade.

Kipahulu

About 10 miles south of Hana, Haleakala National Park spills down the mountainside to Kipahulu. The dense rain forest has yet to be properly explored, yet trails have been laid to some of the most beautiful segments. The best known is **Oheo Gulch.** If you want to sound like an ignorant tourist, call it Seven Sacred Pools. There are about two dozen pools spilling into each other as they descend to the ocean. Swimming is grand. Hawaii 31 crosses over Oheo Stream, with waterfalls on both sides of the road. You can hike the **Pipiwai Trail** a half mile to **Makahiku Falls** overlook. Continue 1.5 miles through a thick bamboo forest to 400-foot **Waimoku Falls.** Check on weather conditions at the **Kipahula Ranger Station** before setting out. ∎

Kahanu Garden
- Map p. 121
- Ulaina Rd., Mile Marker 31
- 808/248-8912
- Closed Sat. & Sun.
- $$

Hana Cultural Center
- Uakea & Hana Rds.
- 808/248-8622
- Closed Fri., Sat., & Sun.
- $

Kipahulu Ranger Station
- Map p. 121
- 808/248-7375

Hana Drive

The scenic but twisty Hana Highway is only a slight compromise with the impregnability of Hana, whose people maintain a good-natured but determined standoff with modern Hawaii.

Along the road you will drive 53 miles across no less than 56 mostly one-lane bridges and around 617 turns. It's slow-going, so it's good to remember that the purpose of this road is the journey itself. You will be traveling beside waterfalls, through rain forest, and along rugged lava coastline.

The road begins as Hawaii 36 at **Kahului Airport ❶**, heads innocently, flatly through sugarcane fields, then passes the sandy sweep of **Baldwin Beach Park.**

The first—and last—town of consequence is **Paia ❷**, last gas till Hana. This former plantation town went psychedelic in the sixties and has never quite gotten over it. Windsurfers congregate here because it's only two miles to **Hookipa ❸**, a pilgrimage site for the sport.

At Mile 16, the twists, turns, and bridges begin. The name of each bridge and stream is announced with a sign, and the names have lovely meanings, such as Kolea, "happiness that comes on the wind," and Makapipi, "desire for blessings."

Just past Mile 16, Hawaii 36 becomes Hawaii 360 and the mileposts begin again at zero. Between the tiny towns of Huelo and Kailua, you can probably pick up roadside guava, mountain apple, banana, and mango. The trees with the colorfully streaked bark are rainbow eucalyptus.

In 2 miles you will pass three waterfalls: **Waikamoi, Puohokamoa,** and **Haipuaene ❹**. There's a 30-minute nature walk at **Waikamoi** and picnic tables with grand views, but bring mosquito repellent. You can revisit *Jurassic Park* at the **Garden of Eden Arboretum & Botanical Garden** *(Mile 10, tel 808/572-9899, closes 4 p.m. daily)*. Scenes from the dinosaur saga were shot here.

At Mile 11, **Puohokamoa Falls** plunge 30 feet into a good, icy swimming pool. Just beyond Mile 12 you can find restrooms at

---

NOT TO BE MISSED:

Paia Town • Hookipa Beach • Keanae Overlook • Waianapanapa State Park

---

Kaumahina State Wayside Park ❺. The size of the plants attests to the region's fecundity and rainfall—about 300 inches a year. Coastline views are breathtaking.

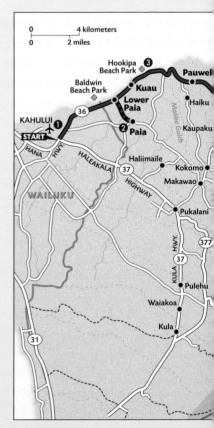

The **Keanae Arboretum ⑥**, free and open 24 hours, is *makai* (toward the sea) and less than half a mile beyond Mile 16. You'll find Hawaiian ethnobotanical gardens, and you can picnic and swim in the pools.

To see Hawaii's traditional food crop, taro, growing in all its emerald glory, turn *makai* at Mile 17 and drive down to **Keanae Peninsula,** where the *kalo loi* (flooded fields) are more than 500 years old. The road dead-ends at the ocean, whose waves tear savagely at the lava shore.

If you don't want to take time to drive down to Keanae, keep going a few feet, just past Mile 17, for an **overlook ⑦** and a splendid photo opportunity. You're now halfway to Hana. One of the roadside fruit and snack stands will be open and selling ice cream or freshly baked banana bread.

Between Wailua and **Puaa Kaa State Wayside Park** at Milepost 22, you'll pass **Waikani Falls.** Gurgling streams and ponds make this a good picnic spot.

Next stop is **Waianapanapa State Park ⑧** *(Mile 51, tel 808/984-8109).* Lava shoreline at its most dramatic is on show in black craggy cliffs, sea stacks, arches, lava caves and tubes, and a gleaming black-sand beach. Campsites and cabins are available by permit. The roads winds down into **Hana** town (see pp. 142–143) ⑨.

🅰	See also map p. 121
▶	Kahului Airport
◀▶	53 miles
🕒	3 hours
▶	Hana town

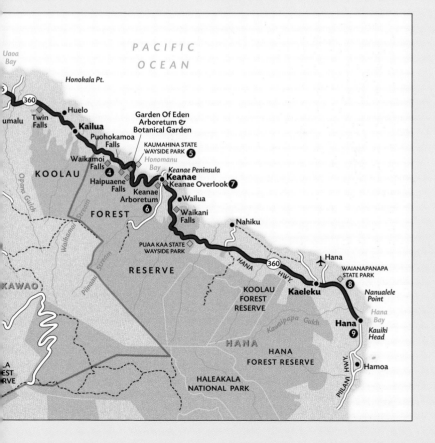

More Places to Visit on Maui

Halekii-Pihana Heiau State Monument

These twin temples just outside Wailuku were once significant religious and governmental sites. Little remains of Pihana Heiau, which was a *luakini*, a place of human sacrifice. Halekii was a royal compound with what were probably thatched guesthouses for noble attendees at the rites. There is a commanding view of central Maui and the Wailuku Plain from this 10-acre park. Take Waiehu Beach Road (Hawaii 350) to Kuhio Place, turn inland to Hea Place, go left to the end.
🅰 Map p 120

Hana Rain-forest Hike

Swim beneath towering waterfalls, listen to bamboo hum in the wind, see ferns as tall as a man, listen to rare Hawaiian birds sing in the forest canopy on a hike in the tropical side of Haleakala National Park, all with experienced guides who know the flora and bring lunch and snacks. With Hike Maui's Full Day Waterfalls and Rain Forest Hike, it's an 11-hour adventure that begins in central Maui. Bonus: You get to ride the scenic, twisting Hana Highway without driving. *hikemaui.com* 🅰 Map p. 121 ✉ Intersection of Highways 350 & 380, Kahului ☎ 866/324-6284 or 808/879-5270 💲 $$$$$

Kapalua Adventure Center

Experience Maui with the help of professionals who can tailor an activity just for you, including kayaking, hiking, mountain biking, scuba diving, snorkeling, and whale-watching. The center's mountain outpost offers 2 miles of ziplines (see p. 141). Before or after a day's activities, visit the Adventure Center Café, which serves premium beers, fine wines, coffee, and organic produce fresh from the farm. *kapalua.com* 🅰 Map p. 120 ✉ Kapalua Adventures, 2000 Village Rd. ☎ 877/665-4386 or 808/665-4386 💲 $$

Maui Arts & Cultural Center

Opened in 1994, the $27 million center demonstrates Maui's commitment to the arts. Entertainers have included Ziggy Marley and Tony Bennett, the Moscow Ballet and hula groups. It's also a showcase theater for local artists and theater and dance companies. In addition to two performing arts theaters, there's a visual arts gallery.
🅰 Map p. 121 ✉ 1 Cameron Way, Kahului ☎ 808/242-2787

Palapala Hoomau Congregational Church

Famed American aviator Charles Lindbergh (1902–1974) fell in love with Kipahulu (see p. 143). He spent the last seasons of his life here with his wife, Anne Morrow Lindbergh. When he was dying, he planned all the details of his funeral, insisting he wanted to be buried barefoot in a rough-hewn eucalyptus coffin at this little country church built in 1857. The inscription on Lucky Lindy's simple granite headstone is from Psalm 139: "If I take the wings of morning and dwell in the uttermost parts of the sea." Up to 500 people a day make the pilgrimage to his quiet resting place.
🅰 Map p. 121 ✉ Hawaii 31, 1 mile S of Oheo Gulch

Polipoli Spring State Recreation Area

Pine trees, a sequoia forest, nippy weather—overnight the grass becomes white with frost. At 6,200 feet, Polipoli is set amid the vast fog belt of the Kula Forest Reserve. The 5-mile **Polipoli Loop** through eucalyptus, plum, pine, and redwood trees takes about three hours. Dress warmly, in layers. To get there, take Kekaulike Avenue (Hawaii 377) from Kula, turn uphill on Waipoli Road to the end. Camping and one cabin available from the DNLR, Division of State Parks.
🅰 Map p. 121 ✉ Div. of State Parks, 54 S. High St., Rm. 101, Wailuku ☎ 808/984-8109

A microcontinent of an island, with balmy coasts, snowcapped mountains, lush rain forest, huge cattle ranches, acres of spectacular flowers, and the active Kilauea Volcano

Hawaii: The Big Island

Kilauea volcano, Hawaii Volcanoes National Park

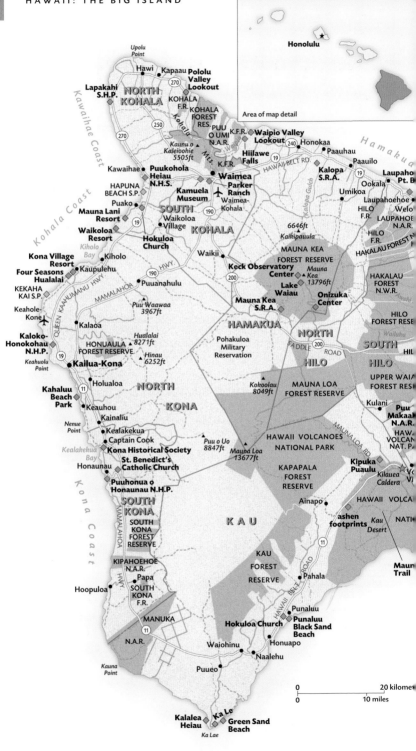

Hawaii: The Big Island

The Big Island, as Hawaii is generally called, is so big that all the other Hawaiian Islands could be tacked onto one half and leave the other half to spare. The island is twice the size of Delaware and it's still growing.

Five enormous volcanoes, Mauna Loa, Mauna Kea, Kilauea, Hualalai, and Kohala, created its bulky 4,028 square miles. Kilauea, the world's most active volcano, is making the Big Isle bigger by the day. There are 266 miles of coastline: You can go to a different beach park every day for a month. Some days you'll go home with purest white sand clinging to your

bathing suit, some days jet black, and some days even glistening green olivine.

With all this room, only 10 percent of the state's population calls the Big Island home; there are more cattle than people.

On this most unusual isle, big is more than a matter of size: It applies to the spirit. Everything seems touched with grandeur—the scope of history, the passionate legends, the heights of the mountains, the opulence of the resorts on the Kona-Kohala Coast, and the creative energy inspired by nature, stripped down and raw, being born before your eyes.

The Big Island is the cradle of the Hawaiian kingdom. Kamehameha the Great was born on the Kohala Coast, and from these shores he launched his campaign of conquest and unification. Remnants of history are everywhere.

The skies above Hawaii are so consistently clear, and clean of pollution, that scientists from all over the world come to study the universe from powerful telescopes atop Mauna Kea. Down below, the towns of the Big Island are rural with a kind of creaky charm. Behind the weathered, often unpromising storefronts are surprisingly sophisticated galleries and delightful restaurants, where your meal naturally climaxes with locally grown Kona, the world's standard for good coffee. ■

NOT TO BE MISSED:

Diving and snorkeling at
  Kealakekua Bay **154–155**

Puuhonua o Honaunau for an
  ocean adventure **155–156**

The lush Kohala Coast **157–159,
  161–162**

A cowboy experience at Waimea
  160, 162, 163

The scenic Hamakua Coast from
  Hilo to Waipio Valley **165**

Hilo and neighboring Rainbow Falls
  and Akaka Falls **165–168**

A hike at Hawaii Volcanoes
  National Park **173, 176–177**

Mauna Kea and the astronomy
  center **178–179**

Kona Coast

The districts of North and South Kona form the sunny 60-mile leeward shore of the Big Island, encompassing resorts, villages, farms, commercial centers, and wide-open spaces. Here the sun seems brighter, intensifying colors.

Outrigger canoes race off Kailua-Kona.

Flowers are so vivid they are almost harsh, the sea seems deeper and bluer than elsewhere, the lava is inky and iridescent, and the sunsets, ignited by volcanic particles, are positively fluorescent in tangerines, golds, magentas, and flashes of brilliant emerald just as the sun sizzles into the sea.

People come to Kona to catch the biggest marlin, or to run the Ironman World Triathlon, consisting of a 2.4-mile open ocean swim, a 112-mile bicycle race, plus a 26.2-mile run. The triathletes end up being absorbed so seamlessly into the balmy climate, the immensity, and the unhurried pace that they barely make an impression as they race across the strange landscape.

Predictably, the flat coastal lowlands are sprinkled with hotels, condominiums, and retirement villas. The hills above wear a lei of small towns that are fun to poke around in: Holualoa, Kainaliu, Kealakekua, Captain Cook, and Honaunau. Higher than that is the forest. Macadamia nuts grow in North Kona, while South Kona excels in coffee.

Weary of war, and sick of eight years of city life in Honolulu, Kamehameha the Great, with his family and court, retired to Kailua. With three ships and accompanied by a fleet of outrigger canoes, they set sail for Kailua on August 12, 1812. Upon landing, the king built a residential compound for his royal relatives and a temple to Lono, god of harvests.

Lt. Otto von Kotzebue, skipper of the Russian trader *Rurick,* wrote in 1816 of his first encounter with the king: "I now stood at the side of the celebrated Tamaahmaah, who . . . inspired me with the greatest confidence by his unreserved and friendly behavior. He conducted me to his straw palace . . . he prefers this simple dwelling, not to forsake the customs of his country . . . as he only wishes to increase the happiness and not the wants of his subjects." The warrior king died in Kailua seven years after his arrival, May 8, 1819, aged 60.

Kailua-Kona

Partly fishing village, partly party town, and—lately—mostly shopping mecca with its new malls and discounters on the fringes of town, Kailua-Kona maintains a castaway charm. Its main street, Alii Drive, follows a 2-mile stretch of waterfront that claims a major chunk of history.

Ahuena Heiau juts into Kailua Bay like a sentinel of another age. The temple has now been restored. The most critical event in Hawaiian history occurred at this site when Kamehameha II, defying the *kapu* (law) against men and women dining together, sat down to eat with his mother and stepmother. According to eyewitness accounts, the king seated himself and "began to eat with a fury of appetite that showed he was doing violence to himself. . . . The whole assembly was struck with horror. . . . but no harm to the king ensuing, they at length cried out with one voice, 'The kapu is broken!'" Word spread like wildfire, triggering minor insurrections and violence that left the old temples

INSIDER TIP:

Coffee trees grow in the rich volcanic soil of the Kona district. Look for white blossoms in spring; cherry red berries in fall and winter.

—JERRY CAMARILLO DUNN, JR.
National Geographic author

in ruins and the *kii* (god effigies) toppled and burned.

One year later in 1820, the brig *Thaddeus* sailed into Kailua Bay. Mrs. Thomas Holman, wife of the physician in the party, described Ahuena Heiau: "It was sure enough in ruins, and such a scene of devastation I never before beheld. There appeared to me to have been stone enough among the ruins of the temple to build a city."

Ahuena Heiau

✉ Public beach on grounds of King Kamehameha Kona Beach Hotel, 75-5660 Palani Rd.

EXPERIENCE: Java Break

Coffee farms today may be found on Hawaii, Oahu, Molokai, Kauai, and Maui, each island producing its own specialty beans and brew. Who would have guessed roughly 200 years ago that coffee would become a popular industry and delicacy in the islands when Don Francisco de Paula y Marin, a Spanish physician, brought the tree to Honolulu in 1813?

Years later, the Reverend Samuel Ruggles transplanted an Oahu cutting to Kona, and the plant flourished in the area's climate and volcanic soil. By the middle of the 20th century, quality Kona coffee was thriving as a result of the hard labor on numerous family-owned immigrant farms.

Gourmet Kona Coffee is sold up and down the Kona Coast.

Big Island

Gourmet coffee aficionados may experience bean-to-brew tours at several well-known sites, with no better place to start than the Big Island's Kona region. **Mountain Thunder Coffee Plantation** *(tel 888/414-5662 or 808/325-2136, mountainthunder.com, VIP tours: $$$),* at an elevation of 3,200 feet, features free or guided tours Monday through Saturday. Call ahead for specific directions.

Hilo Coffee Mill *(tel 866/982-5551 or 808/968-1333, hilocoffeemill.com)* on the Big Island's east side features coffees that have been grown in the fertile rain forest climates of Puna, Hamakua, and Kau. Free tours showcase the production process.

Discover even more coffee farms that dot the Big Island's west corridor by obtaining a detailed brochure *(tel 808/326-7820)* and driving via the picturesque **Kona Coffee Country Driving Tour** *(konacoffeefest.com).*

Molokai

Mules do the pulling at **Coffees of Hawaii** *(Kualapuu on Farrington Hwy., tel 808/567-9490, coffeesofhawaii .com, morning walks: $$$$, mule wagon tour: $$$$$)* in Kualapuu, Molokai, where visitors have a choice between a walking tour or a mule-drawn wagon ride through the fields and around the Kualapuu water reservoir.

Maui

Unlike Molokai's four-footed approach, Maui's java experience at **Shim Coffee & Protea Farm** *(Kula, tel 808/876-0055, shimfarmtour .com, tours Feb.–July, by appt. only: $$)* is touted as a "one-man, working coffee, protea, and botanical farm" with coffee trees, processing machinery, and gardens in the heights of Kula.

Kauai

Not to be outdone, Marin's coffee tree legacy also made its way to the Garden Island, where the **Kauai Coffee Company's** *(off Hawaii 50 near Poipu, tel 808/335-0813, kauaicoffee.com)* estate on the southwest side is open seven days a week for free tours at its visitor center.

In 1836, the missionaries built **Mokuaikaua,** the first church in Hawaii. Its 112-foot white steeple dominates the little town. Across the street, **Hulihee Palace** sits between church and temple, as if still caught between old and new. Built in 1838, it hosted a succession of Hawaiian guests and was eventually purchased by King Kalakaua. After his death in 1891, it was sold and fell into disrepair. In 1927, it was turned over to the Daughters of Hawaii, a group concerned with preserving Hawaii's cultural legacy. They faithfully restored it and opened the palace as a museum. It has many of the original furnishings, including a koa-wood bed whose beautifully carved posts came from Kamehameha's grass palace. The furniture indicates the size of the noble residents. Kamehameha I was probably close to 7 feet tall. Hawaiian music and hula events are held at the palace the last Sunday of the month at 4 p.m.

A simple thatched chapel marks the site of the first Catholic Church in Kona, **St. Michael's.** It's all the congregation has left after an earthquake in 2006 forced demolition of the church's historic 1840 incarnation, leaving the faithful to hope and pray in tents and under the trees *(75-5769 Alii Dr., tel 808/326-7771).*

Keauhou & South

Once it leaves Kailua, Alii Drive becomes a meandering country road. About 4.5 miles from town you come to **Kahaluu Beach Park,** a fascinating place to snorkel, made special by its black-sand bottom against which the myriad jewel-hued reef fish look like Vegas dancers. On the north end of the bay, tiny, white **St. Peter's Catholic Church,** its blue tin roof framed by sea and palms, makes a perfect photo. The diminutive chapel, which was built in 1839 on the site of an old

Mokuaikaua Church
- ✉ 75-5713 Alii Dr.
- ☎ 808/329-5179

Hulihee Palace
- ✉ 75-5718 Alii Dr.
- ☎ 808/329-1877
- 💲 $$

Botanicals

The Big Island's 15-acre **Amy B. H. Greenwell Ethnobotanical Garden** *(808/323-3318, bishopmuseum.org/ greenwell, $)* highlights content and thoughtful design. Located at Captain Cook, high above Kealakekua Bay on the slopes of Mauna Loa, the garden focuses on Hawaiian ethnobotany—the study of interrelationships among Hawaiian people, their cultural traditions, and their plants before Capt. James Cook's arrival in 1778. The plants lend glimpses into the ways early Hawaiians utilized them, whether as food, building materials, clothing, adornments, medicinal remedies, or religious purpose.

Home to more than 250 species of trees, shrubs, and ferns, the garden is organized in a way that displays different cultivation zones used in traditional Hawaiian agriculture: coastal, lowland dry forest, and upland forest. Foods range from taro and *kukui* (an oil-producing nut) to *ko* (sugar cane) and *awa* (a relaxant), to name a few.

Remnants of stonework, part of a vast agricultural complex, are preserved on 7 acres of the garden. Amy B. H. Greenwell (1921–1974), an author of botany books and a member of a prominent west Hawaii ranching family, bequeathed the site to the Bishop Museum in 1974.

Kona Historical Society

⛰ Map p. 148

✉ 81-6551 Mamalahoa Hwy. (Hawaii 11), Kealakekua

☎ 808/323-3222

🕐 Closed Sat.–Sun.

💲 $

Kealakekua Bay

⛰ Map p. 148

heiau (temple), always has fresh flowers on the altar.

Along Alii Drive at Keauhou Bay is a sacred bathing pool once reserved for royalty. Look among the shoreline rocks for ancient petroglyphs. The historic site is near where the Keauhou Beach Resort once stood at 76-6740 Alii Drive. There are plans for a Hawaiian cultural center here, but nothing has happened yet.

A very worthwhile stop is the **Kona Historical Society** in Kealakekua, which has a small museum with Hawaiian artifacts, and memorabilia and photographs from the early days of ranching and coffee plantations. It's housed

site on the National Register of Historic Places.

Kealakekua Bay is where Captain Cook met his demise at age 49, February 14, 1779. To expedite the return of a stolen rowboat, he attempted to kidnap a Kona chief as hostage. A fight ensued and Cook was killed. David Samwell, assistant surgeon aboard Cook's flagship, H.M.S. *Resolution,* reported the death at the water's edge: "He endeavored to scramble on the rock when a fellow gave him a blow to the head with a large club and he was seen alive no more." Heavily outnumbered, the British retreated to their ships. A 27-foot white obelisk on the far

Fierce *kii*, god images, guard the sanctuary of Puuhonua o Honaunau, an ancient refuge.

in the old stone Greenwell Store, built in 1875 and now on the State and National Registers of Historic Places. The nonprofit society conducts walking tours of Kailua, Kealakekua Bay, and Keauhou. You can also tour the **D. Uchida Coffee Farm,** founded in 1925, another

north shore of the bay marks the spot where he fell. The Hawaiians took his body and accorded it the mortuary rites of a great chief. Fifty years after his death, American missionaries, perhaps wary of British influence in the isles, began to publish a cautionary tale about how Cook was deified by the Hawaiians as the god Lono, his collaboration incurring the wrath of Jehovah. Cook's deification came to be accepted as fact, although there is no evidence, either in journals of the time or in Hawaiian oral history. The bay is reached via Napoopoo Road, about 4 miles south of Captain Cook town.

INSIDER TIP:

Look for spinner dolphins frolicking across the bay from the Puuhonua shores— an added magical touch to a visit to the sacred Puuhonua o Honaunau.

—BARBARA A. NOE
*National Geographic Travel
Books editor*

Kealakekua today is a state marine life preserve. The crystal-clear water runs from teal to jade. Most people come by boat for the snorkeling, and hoping to see sea turtles and dolphins. The ruins of **Hikiau Heiau** mark the approach to the bay. On New Year's Day, 1779, Cook conducted the first Christian service in the islands when, with the permission of the chief, he conducted a burial rite atop the temple platform for his valet, William Watman.

St. Benedict's Catholic Church, "the painted church," once stood along the shore near Kealakekua, but was moved to its present location around the turn of the 20th century. Behind the white latticework and beneath the Gothic Revival steeple is a grand cathedral in miniature. Between 1899 and 1904, Belgian priest Father John Berchmans Velghe created a masterpiece, now on the State and National Registers of Historic Places. He created the sense of depth and size in his church by painting a trompe l'oeil version of the cathedral of Burgos, Spain, behind the altar. The ceiling represents the Hawaiian sky; the church pillars sprout palm trees, whose branches growing toward the altar are green while those growing away are dry brown. Biblical scenes glow on the walls, illustrating Scripture for the faithful who had not learned to read. On the second Sunday of the month, Mass is in Hawaiian and everyone is invited to breakfast afterward.

The small towns you pass through in this region are worth exploring for their art galleries, boutiques, and restaurants (see pp. 250–254, 260–261). Many of the coffee farms welcome visitors, and there is a great variety of roadside stands.

Puuhonua o Honaunau National Historical Park

For longer than anyone can remember, Puuhonua o Honaunau was a sacred site, a place of refuge. To the Hawaiians of old there was no more powerful word than *kapu*, meaning the laws based on spirituality, environmental stewardship, and civil order. Punishment for violation of kapu was severe, often death. Justice, however, was tempered with mercy: On

St. Benedict's Catholic Church

🅰 Map p. 148

✉ 84-5140 Painted Church Rd., Honaunau

☎ 808/328-2227

Puuhonua o Honaunau National Historical Park

🅰 Map p. 148

✉ Park entrance on Hawaii 160, 3.5 miles from jct. with Hawaii 11

☎ 808/328-2288

💲 $$

every island there were *puuhonua* (places of refuge). If a lawbreaker or defeated warrior could reach one ahead of his pursuers, he was put through atonement and purification ceremonies by the resident priests. When he left the puuhonua, no one could harm

INSIDER TIP:

The "City of Refuge" in South Kona is one of the best preserved Polynesian religious sites in Hawaii. Capture an image of the wooden *kii* as the sun sets.

—JOHN SEATON CALLAHAN
National Geographic contributor

him under penalty of breaking a kapu themselves. The puuhonua were also refuges for the elderly, conscientious objectors, women, and children during times of war.

When Puuhonua o Honaunau's great stone walls were built around 1550, it was already old. One legend credits a Chief Ehu Kamalino with its founding in 1200. A temple, its name lost to time, lay in the middle of the 12-acre enclosure. Next to it, tradition maintains, another temple was built, Alealea Heiau. In 1650, Ka Iki Alealea ("the little Alealea") was built at the north corner of the Great Wall. Now reconstructed and known as Hale o Keawe, it once held the remains of 23 high chiefs, whose bones conferred even greater protection on the refuge.

Visiting the Site: At the visitor desk, pick up a self-guided tour leaflet. Numbered coconuts at the sites correlate with the map. As you walk beside a tile mural, you'll hear taped histories and stories of the puuhonua woven in with the "Kumulipo," the Hawaiian creation chant.

In the park you'll find thatched homes and work areas. Local canoe builders, wood-carvers, and other traditional craftspeople are often working here. Note the canoes, probably the only ones in existence made in the old way from koa with coconut fiber lashings.

Walk around to the far side of the bay, to the enclosed **Hale o Keawe** and its fierce *kii* (god effigies). You can only imagine how this refuge must have looked to the fugitive, heart pounding, running for his life, his enemies crashing through the brush behind him, the gods before him, as with one last superhuman effort he reaches safety.

The temple is at the northern apex of the **Great Wall,** which runs for 1,000 feet, stands 10 feet high, and is 17 feet thick, all constructed without mortar and ingeniously held together by friction. The wall is reflected in the fishpond, an ancient aquaculture facility to supply royal tables. If you enjoy photography, there is not a more dramatic place to frame a sunset.

On the first weekend in July, a three-day Establishment Day cultural festival is held with great pageantry, a *hukilau* (community net fishing), crafts, music, and hula.

The park has a picnic area. ∎

Kohala

Massive and vital, a more powerful landscape than Kohala cannot be imagined. Along the dry sunny coast from Waikoloa to Upolu Point, luxury resorts have been hacked out of old lava flows. More than $2 billion has been carefully bestowed to make this black desert bloom. The Hilton Waikoloa Village, built in 1988, is an attraction in itself: A network of canals, lagoons, and swimming pools splash across 62 oceanfront acres; you can tour it by yacht or mini–bullet train.

Another luxury extravaganza, the **Four Seasons Hualalai** (see p. 250) is an elegant oasis by the sea. Designed with serene themes of Hawaii and Asia, Hualalai features many amenities—from a cultural center to a pool carved out of natural rock. The resort lends itself to pleasant walks around lush greenery in an area marked by ancient lava flows.

The sweep of lava coast is so immense that each resort is a green enclave, tucked around a gleaming white-sand beach, unencumbered by neighbors. Queen Kaahumanu Highway (Hawaii 19) knifes across the eerie landscape, with lava stretching away on both sides.

Away from the tropical shore, the temperature drops a degree a minute and the land becomes green as it rises—tentatively at first, spotted with remnants of the desert (cactus and plumes of ocher grass)—until at Waimea, the mighty volcanic hills and Kohala Mountains are robed in forests and grasslands, thick and plush as an Aubusson carpet. Ranches, including the famous Parker Ranch, spread across the land where rainbows are as common as cows. In fact they sometimes hang in veils of color; the rain comes so lightly that when it falls through sunlit

Canal boats transport guests to their rooms at the Hilton Waikoloa Village.

air, it swirls with the glitter of fine snow. True snow crowns Mauna Kea, towering over everything.

In Kohala, history is your constant companion. Kamehameha the Great was born here; the temples are among the oldest

Four Seasons Hualalai

⬛ Map p. 148

✉ 72-100 Kaupulehu Dr., Kailua, Kona

☎ 808/325-8000

Mauna Lani Resort

⬛ Map p. 148

✉ 68-1050 Mauna Lani Point Dr.

☎ 808/885-6622

in the islands; golfers play amid sacred rocks and prehistoric petroglyphs; and restaurants serve fish raised in ponds built for kings.

Kohala Coast

Seldom are history lessons so beautifully presented as those on the Kohala Coast. The easiest petroglyph viewing (see p. 26), in the most pleasant setting, is from the Waikoloa Resort. You walk the **Ala Kahakai,** a national historic trail popularly called The King's Trail *(from Kings' Shops, tel 808/886-8811, free*

maintained the ancient fishponds to ensure a steady supply of seafood in all weather. It is said that swift runners used to carry fresh fish from the ponds to King Kamehameha the Great in Kona and deliver the fish still alive.

At **Mauna Lani Resort,** informative signs guide you through 15 acres of restored fishponds (see p. 217) and 27 acres of archaeological preserve. The **Kalahuipuaa Fishponds** have been faithfully restored and the ancient aquaculture facility is again providing a steady supply

EXPERIENCE: Manta Rays

Imagine yourself in a wetsuit, sitting on a boat and looking at the blue-black ocean shimmering from the moon's reflection. Upon a signal, you step into the darkness, descend into 30 to 40 feet of water, and head toward an illuminated area of underwater lights. Suddenly, something that resembles a huge butterfly swims by, as if performing an elegant ballet just for you. You have encountered a harmless manta ray *(Manta birostris),* an experience that people have described as "spiritual" and "otherworldly."

Mantas have no teeth, stingers, or barbs, though their appearance may give

another impression. Wingspans range anywhere from 6 feet to more than 20 feet across, though an average is 12 feet to 16 feet. Some have been reported to weigh as much as 5,000 pounds. They live up to 25 years.

Kona is the place for a guided, sunset manta experience. Contact **Dolphin Journeys** *(tel 808/329-3030 or 800/384-1218, dolphinjourneys.com, $$$$$),* which includes dinner; **Sunlight on Water** *(tel 808/896-2480, sunlighton water.com, $$$$$);* or **Kona Honu Divers** *(tel 808/333-4668, konahonudivers.com, $$$$$),* with a choice of deep dive or snorkeling tour.

guided tours Mon.–Fri. at 10:30 a.m., Sat.–Sun. 8:30 a.m.). The ancient shoreline footpath along Anaehoomalu Bay passes many prehistoric house and temple remnants in a parklike setting. The petroglyphs are among the best preserved in the state. Hawaiian families

of seafood. The highlights will take 30 minutes.

From the resort parking lot, you can take a 1.4-mile hike northward on the well-signed **Malama Trail** to a collection of more than 3,000 petroglyphs at **Puako.** Go early morning or late afternoon, wear sturdy shoes, and bring water. The little community of Puako runs along a ribbon of white sand; its crowning glory is **Hokuloa Church** (*Puako Beach Dr., tel 808/883-8295*), built in 1859 by the Reverend Lorenzo Lyons, a missionary who founded 13 other churches. Well liked by his parishioners, he composed the beloved Hawaiian hymn "Hawaii Aloha," which has become an unofficial anthem. Emotionally powerful, the song concludes almost every gathering of import, as all hold hands and lift their voices in gratitude for this place, Hawaii.

E Hawaii e kuu one hanau e
Kuu home kulaiwi nei
Oli no au i na pono lani e
E Hawaii, aloha e.
Hui: E hauoli na opio
o Hawaii nei.
Oli e! Oli e!
Mai na aheahemakani
e pa mai nei,
Mau ke aloha, no Hawaii.

O Hawaii, O sands of my birth, My native home, I rejoice in the blessings of heaven. O Hawaii, my love. *Chorus:* Happy the young of Hawaii today. Rejoice! Rejoice! Gentle breezes blow toward me now, Forever I will love Hawaii.

The best public beach on this coast is **Hapuna,** a half-mile stretch of flat, white sand embraced by lava outcroppings. It gets only 10 inches of rain a year so sunshine is almost guaranteed.

Hapuna Beach is one of the best swimming beaches on the island of Hawaii. Mauna Kea rises behind it.

On the north end of the beach, if you walk across the lawn of the luxe **Hapuna Beach Prince Hotel,** (see p. 250) you'll come to a tiny cove, excellent for snorkeling and visiting with sea turtles. The Prince's pool deck restaurant usually has live music.

North of Hapuna are the ruins of the massive **Puukohola Heiau.** Kamehameha the Great was having little luck in his campaign of Hawaiian unification until Kapoukahi, a powerful prophet from Kauai, told him that if he built a great temple to his war god Kukailimoku, he

Hapuna Beach
Map p. 148
✉ Queen Kaahumanu Hwy. (Hawaii 19), 12 miles N of Waikoloa
☎ 808/880-1111 or 888/977-4623

Puukohola Heiau National Historic Site
Map p. 148
✉ Hawaii 270, 1 mile S of Kawaihae
☎ 808/882-7218

EXPERIENCE: Horsing Around

Feel like a 19th-century Hawaiian cowboy, or *paniolo*, who worked with cattle at Waimea's Parker Ranch long before the 1849 gold rush to California? Many riding stables throughout Hawaii offer guided tours and private rides. Here are a few sites.

At North Kohala on the Big Island, **Naalapa Stables** *(tel 808/775-0419, naalapastables.com, $$$$$)* offers two-hour rides through a 12,000-acre working cattle and sheep ranch or a tropical rain forest of trails and waterfalls.

Paniolo Adventures *(tel 808/889-5354, panioloadventures.com, $$$$$)* has rides starting from another working ranch that extend from the forest to the ocean, with views of the Kona and Kohala coastlines, the volcanoes, and Haleakala on Maui.

Kauai's vivid greens and blues are the backdrop for two- and three-hour rides on the south shore, offered by **CJM Country Stables** *(tel 808/742-6096, cjmstables.com, $$$$$, reservations required)*. Part of the journey goes along the rugged Mahaleapu area. For North Shore vistas, rides at **Princeville Ranch Stables** *(tel 808/826-6777, princevilleranch.com, $$$$$)* highlight 2,500 acres of private lands that include waterfalls, pastures, and a view of the Kilauea Lighthouse.

On Maui, spectacular vistas are the focal point of a two-hour horseback adventure offered by **Mendes Ranch & Trail Rides** *(tel 808/244-7320,*

Parker Ranch cowboys head out for the day's duties.

mendesranch.com, $$$$$), taking in pastures, the west mountain range, the Waihee Valley, waterfalls, and views of the ocean and Haleakala.

Experience paniolo riding in Maui's high country of ranch land, rolling hills, ocean views, and the panorama of the valley below. **Pony Express Tours** *(tel 808/667-2200, ponyexpresstours.com, $$$$$)* has a range of options, including a four-hour trek on the Sliding Sands Trail to the floor of Haleakala Crater. Bring a jacket for this "cool" ride.

Molokai's paniolo adventure with **Puu o Hoku Ranch** *(tel 808/558-8109, puuhoku.com/horseback.html, $$$$$)* includes acres of pastures and forest wildlife.

Horseback riding on restful Lanai means reaching spots even a four-wheel

drive might miss. At the Four Seasons Lanai Resort's **Stables at Koele** *(tel 808/559-4600, fourseasons.com/lanai, $$$$$)*, a two-hour trail ride showcases a diversity of life, from guava groves and ironwood trees to axis deer and wild turkeys. Oh, be sure to bring a raincoat along.

Oahu-only visitors may escape the traffic and crowds by roaming the range at Kahuku, where trails at **Turtle Bay Resort** *(tel 808/293-8811, turtlebayresort.com, $$$$$)* take you through ironwood forests and along the beach.

The family-operated **Gunstock Ranch** *(tel 808/293-2026, gunstockranch.com, $$$$$)* at Kahuku features rides through mountains, trees, groves of wild fruit, and a scenic overlook, as well as a magical moonlight ride.

would be unstoppable. In the hot summer of 1790 he began construction of the temple. Rival chiefs tried to halt the project, but Kamehameha prevailed and fulfilled the prophecy. Even in ruins, the temple is impressive, 224 feet long by 100 feet wide, built of unmortared stones hand carried from Pulolu Valley, 14 miles away.

On a hill below is **Mailekini Heiau,** an older temple dedicated, ironically, to peace. Submerged over time in the offshore waters is Hale o Kapuni Heiau, a temple to the shark gods.

For a look at how non-gods and non-kings lived in old Hawaii, visit **Lapakahi State Historical Park.** It's hot with not much shade, so an early morning visit is best *(park opens at 8 a.m.).* Well-marked paths with good explanatory signs guide you through the detailed remains of this fishing village that thrived from the 14th to the 19th century. Some thatched buildings have been reconstructed, and you'll see many of the small things that are big indicators of a way of life: fishing shrines, nets, and implements, saltmaking pans, a family temple, poi (taro) pounders, a lampstand for burning *kukui* nuts. On an overlook where fishermen gathered to watch for signs of arriving schools is a stone *konane* board, a game similar to checkers.

One of the secrets of Lapakahi is the snorkeling just offshore of the coral beach. Park attendants don't mind people swimming, but they discourage lounging about in bathing suits.

The stones on which Chiefess Kekuiapoiwa gave birth to the baby who would become Kamehameha the Great (see p. 29) are now known as **Kamehameha Akahi Aina Hanau,** and lie a few yards from **Mookini Heiau** where the baby was taken to be blessed before being spirited away (the ruling chief had ordered his death). According to oral historians and the Mookini family, who have been its custodians for eight centuries, the original *heiau* was built in A.D. 480 and was rededicated as a *luakini,* temple of human sacrifice, in the 13th century by high priest Kauamoo Mookini from Tahiti. The stone walls run 267 feet long and 135 feet wide and are, on the perimeter, 35 feet high. Inner walls define altars, ceremonial stones, and the *mu* (body catcher), a sacrificial stone. The 3.2-acre park was the first site in Hawaii to be placed on the National Register of Historic Places.

A **statue of King Kamehameha** stands on Akoni Pule Highway (Hawaii 270) in the little town of **Kapaau,** in front of the courthouse (where they dispense advice and pamphlets to tourists). The statue is the original of the one in Honolulu (see p. 66). When it was lost at sea off the Falkland Islands, a new statue was commissioned. A few weeks after it arrived in Honolulu, in 1883, the 9-ton original turned up, salvaged from a Falklands dump. King Kalakaua bought it for $850 and shipped it to Kapaau, near the king's birthplace. The statue

Lapakahi State Historical Park

- Map p. 148
- Akoni Pule Hwy. (Hawaii 270), 12 miles N of Kawaihee
- 808/587-0300

Mookini Luakini Heiau & Kamehameha Akahi Aina Hanau

- Akoni Pule Hwy. (Hawaii 270) at Milepost 20

Parker Ranch

⛰ Map p. 148

✉ 66-1304
  Mamalahoa
  Hwy., Waimea

☎ 808/885-7311

🕐 Closed Sat.–Sun.

is given a fresh coat of house paint each year in preparation for Kamehameha Day, June 11.

Akoni Pule Highway ends at the **Pololu Valley Lookout** where the rugged land defies civilization. You will see a long blue-green parade of cliffs that is the beginning of the lush, wild Hamakua Coast (see p. 165). It's a 20-minute hike down a switchback trail to the beautiful valley rimmed in black-sand dunes.

Waimea

Waimea is cattle country, but it's been discovered by escapist glitterati who, even in jeans and cowboy hats, exude a tattletale bit of sparkle. High and cool at 2,700 feet above sea level, the town is embraced by the verdant Kohala Mountains. Dominated by the 225,000 acres of Parker Ranch, and other smaller ranches of the area, Waimea, sometimes called Kamuela, is now known for its gourmet restaurants (see p. 253) and sophisticated country stores (see pp. 260–261).

Parker Ranch was founded by seaman John Palmer Parker of Newton, Massachusetts, who first arrived in Hawaii in 1809, at age 19. Hired by Kamehameha I to round up the wild cattle on the island, he married the king's granddaughter Kipikane. His small land grant, plus her own 640 acres, and the best of the wild cattle, formed the core of what grew into the largest privately owned cattle ranch in the United States, producing

10 million pounds of beef a year.

The beautiful old ranch house **Puuopelu,** built in 1862 by John Parker II, now serves as business offices for the sprawling ranch. Some of the stunning private art collection, including exceptional Impressionist paintings and antique Chinese ceramics, are still on display in the reception area, which is open to the public. Also open is the historic original ranch house, **Mana,** built entirely of warm, rich native koa wood. Imagine yourself curling up with a good

INSIDER TIP:

Check out Parker Square off Kawaihae Road in Waimea to find unique creations from local artists and clothing boutiques.

—THELMA CHANG
*Author & National Geographic
contributor*

book in the snug embrace of the precious wood.

The ranch has scaled back most of its visitor activities except for hunting *(tel 877/885-7999)*. Big game species include wild cattle, Spanish and Hawaiian Ibex goats, and the Polynesian boar, which can weigh up to 150 lbs with 4- to 6-inch tusks. With specially-trained dogs, hunters can also go for wild turkeys, pheasant, and other game birds. Arrangements can be made for hunting licenses, guns and equipment, and taxidermy. ■

Hawaiian Cowboys

The Hawaiian cowboy has been celebrated in song, portrayed in lively hulas, and woven into the colorful legends of the islands. He was riding, roping, and branding decades before Texas or any other western state had even one cowboy.

Hawaiians didn't see a cow until the British captain George Vancouver brought the first ashore in 1792. Although he had never tasted a T-bone, Kamehameha recognized a good food source and turned the cattle loose in the verdant valleys of the islands. He placed them under royal protection for ten years so they could multiply. The population exploded. The first horses arrived from Mexico in 1803, also as gifts to the king. They, too, enjoyed royal favor and made themselves equally at home. Twelve to 14 hands high, the wild *kanaka* mustang, descendant of the mounts of the conquistadores, weighed up to 900 pounds.

To control this unbridled bounty, the king sent to California for Mexican *vaqueros* in 1832. The first *paniolo*, as they were called because the word *espagñoles* was not harmonious with the Hawaiian language, were Kossuth, Louzeida, and Ramon. Dressed in their brilliant ponchos, sashes, bandannas, fringed leather leggings, boots, jangling spurs, and sombreros, they were instant heroes.

In 1908, a group of paniolo headed for the big-time—Frontier Day Rodeo in Cheyenne, Wyoming. Wearing their best aloha shirts and floppy leather hats, and riding borrowed mounts, they were a curiosity. When the dust cleared, Ikua Purdy of Hawaii was the new world champion steer roper, accomplishing the feat in 56 seconds flat. Paniolo have been bringing home the trophies ever since.

Working life was not so glamorous. Cattle drives were timed for nights of the full moon because the heat of the tropical sun exacted such a great weight loss from the animals. The cattle moaned mournfully as they moved down the mountains and across the lava flatlands to the shore. The shipping operation would begin with the first light of day. Mounted on well-trained, sturdy Percherons, the men would drive

Hawaiian cowboys were riding and roping before the American West was won.

the cattle into the surf. Once beyond the breakers, each animal had to be lashed to the side of a shore boat, usually a former whaleboat. With five or six tied to the sides, the boats would make their way out to an interisland barge, where the cattle would be hauled aboard by a sling. In addition to the obvious dangers in such work, the paniolo had to be on the alert for sharks. More than once, schools of tiger sharks caused havoc. The last sea roundups were in the 1950s.

Through it all, the paniolo developed their own distinctive style of saddle, wore hats intricately woven from pandanus leaves, and decorated them with bands of flowers, shells, and feathers. They sang their own songs and came up with their own jargon.

Today's paniolo, though enshrined in legend, are still supplying 80 percent of the beef in island markets. On Saturday mornings, driving the country roads of Waimea, you may come across a roundup or branding operation by paniolo from Parker Ranch.

East Hawaii

Considering that you can get grandstand seats at the act of creation in Hawaii Volcanoes National Park, admire the waterfalls, and pick wild orchids by the side of the road, there is not much standard tourism on this huge hunk of the Big Island, stretching from the Hamakua Coast in the north to Ka Lae, the southernmost tip of the United States.

The Hamakua Coast, with its black-sand beach, as seen from the Waipio Valley Lookout

The rain can come in such torrents around lush Hilo that looking out the window you'd think you were in a submarine; in the Kau Desert it comes not at all.

The ultratech eyes of the observatories atop Mauna Kea focus on the far reaches of the universe, while in the deep coastal valleys men knee-deep in the mud of the ancient *kalo loi* (flooded taro fields) focus on pulling enough corms to feed their families.

Flower farms quilt the greenery in bright and delicate colors—anthurium, heliconia, ginger that perfumes the air, and orchids everywhere. When they are at the height of bloom, wild bamboo orchids are so profuse they flower like fields of cotton and creep across lawns to battle home owners (and their Weedwackers) for the turf. And when the African tulip trees are flowering, the hills blaze red as running lava.

Sugar was, until recently, the main agricultural crop, but after a reign of more than a century King Cane fell to foreign competition.

To combat the economic depression left in its wake, farmers are trying new crops, growing vegetables for the chefs of the Kona-Kohala Coast and planting more acres in macadamia trees. The buttery nut has given rise to a whole new industry—candy. Cacao trees have also been planted to meet the need for chocolate.

Towns, with the exception of Hilo, are small, weatherbeaten, tin-roofed, and picturesque—an artist's delight. Hilo claims all the above adjectives, except that it's big.

If you don't see this wildly contrasting side of the Big Island, dominated by massive volcanoes, you will miss one of the most unusual landscapes on Earth.

Waipio & Hamakua

The cliffs of the Hamakua Coast rise in glowing greens from the sea, mist-haunted and streaming with waterfalls. So many Scots settled here to "boss" the sugar plantations, it was once called "the Scottish Coast." They must have felt right at home in the wild gloom with shafts of brilliant sunlight lancing the hills.

Seven magnificent amphithe-ater valleys are carved into the Hamakua Coast, but none are drivable. You can hike to the bot-tom of the largest, **Waipio**, in 30 minutes, or take a shuttle and tour from the **Waipio Valley Lookout.**

Many people are content just to look at the long cobalt rollers washing up on the black-sand beach below and the fields of green taro, grown by the few inhabitants of the area, that stretch into the wild back of the valley. The clear flowing streams that water the taro are fed by the twin cascades of **Hiilawe Falls** plunging 1,300 feet, Hawaii's highest free-falling waterfall.

A long succession of Hawaiian chiefs ruled from Waipio, begin-ning with Pili in the early 14th century and ending with Umi-aliloa, who moved the court to Kona in 1600. Kamehameha the Great spent time here during his youth. **Honokaa** is the only town of note in the rural district, worth a stop if you like to poke around small galleries and shops.

Hilo

Residents claim the rain, for which Hilo has a reputation,

Waipio Valley Lookout

 Map p. 148

Honokaa

 Map p. 148

Hilo

 Map p. 149

Visitor Information

✉ Hawaii Visitors & Convention Bureau, 250 Keawe St.

☎ 808/961-5797

🕐 Closed Sat.–Sun.

Nanaue: The Shark Man

In old times, the Waipio Valley was home to Nanaue, the shark man. The son of a shark god and an earthly mother, he had a shark's mouth on his back, which he concealed under a cape. He spent his days sitting on a rock at Nanaue Falls. When people passed on the way to the sea, Nanaue would warn them of sharks, then arrive first by swimming downstream. In the ocean he devoured a victim, then went back to his waterfall to await the returning mourners. When the peo-ple of Waipio uncovered Nanaue's identity and bad deeds, they burned the shark man alive.

Lyman Museum & Mission House

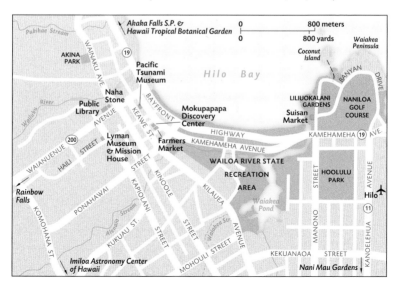

⛰ Map below
✉ 276 Haili St.
☎ 808/935-5021
🕐 Closed Sun.
💲 $$

Imiloa Astronomy Center of Hawaii

✉ 600 Imiloa Place, Science & Technology Park at Univ. of Hawaii-Hilo
☎ 808/969-9700
🕐 Closed Mon.
💲 $$$

falls mainly at night; statistics put the rainy days (or nights) at 278 a year. On the bright side are the gardens—lush botanical gardens, opulent front yards, acres of orchid and anthurium farms, yellow ginger and wild bamboo orchids blooming by the wayside. A town walking map can be obtained from the Hawaii Visitors and Convention Bureau and from Lyman House. Many of its colorful buildings are on the National Register of Historic Places.

At the **Lyman Museum and Mission House** you'll see the oldest wood-frame house on the island, built of koa planks in 1839. Furnishings that belonged to missionaries David and Sarah Lyman provide a window into life almost two centuries ago. This contrasts with the **Earth Heritage Gallery** in the building next door, with its astronomy and geology exhibits. The **Island Heritage Gallery** features reproductions of homes

from diverse cultures, including a grass house.

The **Naha Stone** in front of the public library (*300 Waianuenue Ave.*) is Hawaii's Excalibur. Similar to the story of King Arthur and the famous sword, it was said that whoever could move this stone would be king of all the Hawaiian Islands. When he was 14, Kamehameha the Great is said to have moved the 2.5-ton rock, then went on to fulfill the prophecy.

Explore Hawaii's coral reef system at the **Mokupapapa Discovery Center** (*308 Kamehameha Ave., tel 808/933-8195*). Learn about Hawaii's marine life sanctuaries, many of which can be seen on snorkel and dive excursions. Exhibits introduce you to humpback whales and other denizens of the Hawaiian deep—a fascinating stop for children.

Reach for the stars and encounter the skies at Hilo's **Imiloa Astronomy Center of Hawaii,** a 40,000-square-foot

EXPERIENCE: Discovering Farmers Markets

Start early, don comfortable shoes, wear a hat, bring a tote bag, and head toward one of the many popular islandwide markets open on various days of the week, 41 in Oahu alone.

One of the most popular farmers markets is held on the weekend on **Oahu,** just minutes away from Waikiki at Kapiolani Community College on the backside slope of Diamond Head. You'll find such items as oatcakes, breakfast frittatas, goat cheese, and local foods.

The farmers market in Hilo shows why **Hawaii** is also known as the Orchid Isle. While perusing the fresh produce, jams, ceramics, and clothing, you'll notice the sweet smells and bright colors of flowers, leis, and orchids. Arrange to have approved flowers shipped home.

Kauai's markets usually feature their sunrise papayas, exotic squashes, mangoes, and avocados. Popular ones include the Kapaa Farmers Market and the North Shore's Hawaiian Farmers of Hanalei, the latter also a picturesque experience located as it is near the ocean.

The Queen Kaahumanu Shopping Center *(808/877-3369, queenkaahumanu center.com)* hosts one of many farmers markets on **Maui** (the county includes Lanai and Molokai), where you'll find a bounty of fresh fruits and vegetables, as well as seasonal goodies like Makawao mushrooms and Upcountry jams.

Ask vendors if their plants and flowers originate from certified nurseries whose items may be packaged, stamped, and approved for shipment home. For a general islandwide schedule of farmers markets, call 808/973-9560 or visit *hawaii .gov/hdoa.*

---

exhibition and planetarium complex that works directly with 13 observatories on the summit of Mauna Kea. Science fanatic or not, sample some of everything cosmic—from planetarium shows to the ancient Hawaiian view of cosmology *(IFA.hawaii.edu/mko).*

The 30-acre **Liliuokalani Gardens** *(Banyan Dr.),* named after the islands' last queen, is the largest formal Japanese garden "east of the East." Stroll beneath a crimson torii gate, over a moon bridge, and past a tea pagoda. You can cross the footbridge to Coconut Island and look back at the Hilo waterfront backed by mighty mountains.

Rainbow Falls *(Wailuku River State Park, Waianuenue Ave., past fork to Kaumana Dr.)* are spectacular in the early morning or late afternoon when rainbows gather about the cascade as it tumbles into its 100-foot diameter pool.

Around Hilo

For a region where tourists seldom linger, the Hilo area offers some outstanding attractions, aside from Hawaii Volcanoes National Park (see pp. 168–177).

You can see two glorious waterfalls at **Akaka Falls State Park** *(Hawaii 220, 3.5 miles W of Honomu).* Walk the easy loop trail connecting 420-foot Akaka Falls with the smaller Kahuna Falls. During the half-hour walk, you'll see blue, red, and pink ginger, banks of wild impatiens, orchids, and tunnels of jungle vegetation. Akaka Falls are among the prettiest in the state, and really easily accessible.

Along the **Pepeekeo Scenic Drive,** a 4-mile detour off Hawaii Belt Road 19 *(7 miles N of Hilo),*

Hawaii Tropical Botanical Garden
- Map. p. 149
- 27-717 Old Mamalahoa Hwy., Papaikou
- 808-964-5233
- $$$

Nani Mau Gardens
- Map p. 149
- 421 Makalika St.
- 808/959-3500
- $$

Akatsuka Orchid Garden
- Map p. 149
- Hawaii 11, just after Milepost 22
- 808/967-8234

INSIDER TIP:

Viewing and photographing rainbows at the 900-foot Akaka Falls is best in the early morning before the sun gets too high.

—JACK JEFFREY
National Geographic contributor

you'll pass dramatic lava coastline, surf-drenched coves, streams gushing with waterfalls, and lush stands of jungle. At Onomea Bay is **Hawaii Tropical Botanical Garden,** a sprawling bouquet of tropical flora, complete with lily lake, ginger jungle, banyan canyon, waterfalls, and orchid garden. Everything is labeled.

Nani Mau Gardens *(off Hawaii 11, 3 miles S of Hilo Airport)* is a little more commercial. They've got restaurants, a gift shop, and tram tours—but also some serious

botany, with 2,000 varieties of flora. The orchid collection is outstanding, and there's a botanical museum, Japanese garden, and hibiscus collection.

Farther along Hawaii 11, you can walk for free around the **Akatsuka Orchid Garden** and see one of the largest orchid collections in the state. If Hilo is having one of its rainy days, this nursery has covered walkways.

Hawaii Volcanoes National Park

Kilauea (4,078 feet), the world's only drive-up volcano, is the red-hot heart of Hawaii Volcanoes National Park. It also happens to be the world's most active volcano, having erupted continuously since January 3, 1983, when it came to life in a trembling of the earth and a 40-foot fountain of fire.

The 377-square-mile park was founded in 1916 to protect the amazing natural wonders of

Tsunami

Tsunamis are ocean waves triggered by a major disturbance of the ocean floor caused by earthquakes, volcanoes, or landslides. Only a few feet high when they begin, they can travel thousands of miles undetected in open ocean at typical speeds of 600 miles per hour. As they approach shore, they may slow down and steepen to heights of 100 feet. Since the early 1800s, when records were first kept, about 50 tsunamis have been reported in the Hawaiian Islands.

An Alaskan earthquake in 1946 sent tsunamis south to Hawaii. On the morning of April 1, they sped ashore at Hilo at 57 feet high, destroying half the town

and killing 96 people along the coast. Hilo rebuilt itself after the devastation, only to have another tsunami, this one from off the coast of Chile, slam the city in 1960, taking 61 lives. This time, the town retreated, moving inland, and created parkland along the shore. The tsunami also devastated Waipio Valley and Laupahoehoe.

Visit the **Pacific Tsunami Museum** in Hilo's historic First Hawaiian Bank Building to see fascinating exhibits and videos. On display is a quilt made by students from Laupahoehoe in memory of children and teachers who lost their lives in the 1946 tsunami.

Akaka Falls State Park has an easy nature trail through jungle.

Kilauea and its simmering neighbor, Mauna Loa volcano. It was the first national park in Hawaii, and originally included Haleakala, on Maui (see pp. 140–142). In 1982, the park was named a World Heritage site by UNESCO. It encompasses the summit calderas of both Kilauea and Mauna Loa (currently quiet on the surface) and sections of the Kalapana Coast.

The composition of lava here is such that the eruptions are usually not as explosive as they are in other parts of the world, although history indicates they have that potential. Ashen footprints imbedded beside the **Mauna Iki Trail** are all that's left of 100 warriors of Chief Keoua, who were killed by a 1790 eruption as they marched to do battle with Kamehameha. Still the "good volcano" image persists so that when Kilauea erupts, instead of heading for the nearest escape route, people pack a picnic and

head for the park to see the most spectacular fireworks show on Earth. Saturday crowds can number in the thousands when Kilauea is really pumping. Park rangers help all see the eruption safely, often marking new walking trails several times a day as lava flows change course. One scientist said, "It's like playing with a jigsaw puzzle with moving parts."

The volcano is most awesome at night when the fires rage against the darkened sky. Sometimes lava flows in blazing cascades down the side of the mountain and into the sea, creating great billows of steam for miles along the seething coast.

Since it began its current eruptive phase, Kilauea has added more than 500 acres to the Big Island. As lava flows into the sea, it quickly cools and hardens, building up in the shallows along the coast. It has also covered 16,000 lowland acres in as much as 80 feet of lava, destroying rain forest,

Pacific Tsunami Museum

 Map p. 166

✉ 130 Kamehameha Ave.

☎ 808/935-0926

🕐 Closed Sun.

💲 $$

Hawaii Volcanoes National Park

Map pp. 148–149 & p. 175

✉ Hawaii Belt Rd. (Hawaii 11) 29 miles from Hilo

☎ 808/985-6000 (information on visitor center, Jaggar Museum, park activities, and recordings of latest eruption updates)

💲 $$$ (7-day pass)

Hula

Hula is Hawaii's history book. Without a written language, Hawaiians incorporated their values, tales of gods and kings, epic romances, accounts of great events, and their genealogies from one generation to the next in the chants and dances of hula. In the old days, a dancer could not change a single step or movement under pain of death, for to change the dance was to change history.

Although the dance is the most famous cultural expression of the islands, its importance is often underestimated and its message misunderstood. Missionaries were shocked at its sensuality. C. S. Stewart wrote in his journal of 1823: "The dull and monotonous sounds of the native drum and calabash, the wild notes of their songs . . . and the pulsations, on the ground, of the tread of thousands in the dance . . . fell on the heart with a saddening power, for we had been compelled . . . to associate with them unrivaled licentiousness and abominations which must forever remain untold." Hollywood loved the hula but treated it as a sort of Polynesian go-go dance.

Dressed for the *hula kahiko* (ancient hula), a dancer chants his song.

Hula has evolved so drastically from its ancient religious origins that today it is divided into two distinct categories. *Hula kahiko* is the oldest form; its energy is primal. The costume is a skirt of grass, ti leaf, or cotton imprinted to look like *kapa* (tree-bark cloth), worn with a simple, loose top. Leis woven of flowers, vines, and ferns are worn about the head and shoulders. It is danced to the driving beat of drums, gourd rattles, bamboo sticks, and nose flutes.

Hula auana evolved after Western contact and the introduction of Western musical instruments. In this form, guitars and ukuleles join the ancient instruments. The dancers smile more and use very specific hand gestures to illustrate the message of the dance. Costuming is often rather elegant, reflecting the clothes of the monarchy era, which were modeled after the courts of Europe. Leis and flowers are lavishly worn with slender *holoku* (Hawaiian gowns with trains).

An aspiring dancer does not "take lessons." Rather, he or she joins a *halau*, a group presided over by a *kumu hula* (master teacher). Close bonds of loyalty are formed among the dancers as they study not only the words, music, and movements, but also the language and all facets of Hawaiian culture.

Hula still holds an honored place in the hearts of the people, and is part of the official and daily life of Hawaii. It attends every party and opens the state legislature. Even the palatial megaresorts have found that without the hula, their guests simply don't think they're in Hawaii.

A full calendar of hula festivals and competitions throughout the islands keeps dancers on their toes. Visitors will find hula everywhere—luaus, dinner shows, shopping malls, and cocktail terraces.

The late Maiki Aiu, founder of Halau Hula O Maiki, and the woman considered to be "the mother of the Hawaiian renaissance," summed it up concisely: "Hula is life."

towns, subdivisions, a 700-year-old temple, a park visitor center, and famous Kaimu Black Sand Beach.

The most recent activity centers on Puu Oo, a cinder-and-spatter cone. Although it is in a remote area of the park, the red-hot lava is often visible miles from its source, as it makes its way to the sea.

Volcanoes are notoriously unpredictable, and it is entirely possible that on the day of your visit all the lava will be moving through underground chambers. Even if you don't see red, Hawaii Volcanoes National Park is still an awesome experience. It has 150 miles of some of the most unusual hiking trails in the world. Features range from a 15-minute stroll through an old lava tube to a four-day trek to the top of Mauna Loa. There are also 50 miles of paved roads in the park, although some may be blocked by lava flows. Many of the plants and birds in the park are rare and endangered. In the middle of lava flows are *kipuka,* areas unmolested by the flows and left as pristine islands of life in the bleak, black desert. Some are quite large and offer refuge to endemic species of flora and fauna.

It can be extremely hazardous to stray from marked trails or enter closed areas of the park. People who have disobeyed signs and directives have been fried, steamed, and boiled by the volcano. Infants, pregnant women, and people with health problems, particularly heart and lung, should avoid the park.

Lodging can be found within the park, just outside at Volcano Village, or in Hilo.

Volcano Sites: Every visit to the park should begin at the **Kilauea Visitor Center,** the only surviving center (lava consumed the other), where the day's activities are posted, such as guided nature walks and ranger talks, along with the latest eruption information. If you're planning on taking an overnight backcountry trip, register here so rangers know where you are in the event of an emergency.

Every hour on the hour, the center airs a 25-minute film on the park and the volcanoes' most impressive eruptions. There are also exhibits of volcanology, Hawaiian culture, and park wildlife and flora, as well as maps and books.

INSIDER TIP:

Madame Pele willing, enter one of the Kilauea volcano wilderness runs held every year in late July and experience landscape and flora that are out of this world.

—MICHAEL PIETRUSEWSKY
National Geographic field scientist

The **Thomas A. Jaggar Museum** is a playground of seismometers, computers, videos, and hands-on displays. A million-dollar Vax 11-750 computer, linked to the scientific headquarters next door at the **Hawaiian Volcano Observatory** *(closed to*

Kilauea Visitor Center

⛰ Map p. 175

✉ Just inside park entrance

☎ 808/985-6000

EXPERIENCE: Spelunking

One way of discovering the "real Hawaii" is by literally seeing and touching it from the inside out—underground, in darkness, on your stomach. That "Indiana Jones" experience comes from crawling, walking, and feeling your way through the bumpy, rocky terrain of lava tubes that are the result of volcanic eruptions, lava flows, and hundreds of years of hardening and cooling.

Mother Nature's whimsy can be seen in the fact that some caves are only a few feet in height, while others have high ceilings and stretch out for miles.

Flashlights often reveal a variety of underground life, from silent albino crickets to blind spiders that feed off organisms in the water that emanates from the walls and floors. Wear long pants and comfortable shoes for these adventures, where some physical restrictions may apply.

The Big Island's **Kazumura lava tube system** is an example of a dark and large world of ancient sculpture on the island's east coast that starts at Kilauea and runs downward to sea level. A complexity of tubes extends more than 36 miles, making Kazumura the world's longest and deepest. **Kilauea Caverns of Fire** (tel 808/217-2363, kilaueacavernsoffire.com, $$$$$) offers different tours, including a 75-minute guided walking tour and the more strenuous, three-hour adventure tour (gear provided).

More rock formations are on the menu at the Big Island's **Kula Kai Cave** (tel 808/929-9725, kulakaicaverns.com, $$$–$$$$$), where early Hawaiians once used the tubes as shelter during back-and-forth journeys from the sea to Madame Pele's domain. There, you'll likely encounter a maze of small spaces, spacious chambers, and rock slabs while hearing the sounds of dripping water. Use your imagination and envision the past when Hawaii's first people were stewards of the tunnels.

Receive a free introduction to lava tubes by visiting the **Thurston Lava Tube** at the **Hawaii Volcanoes National Park.** The park also offers a free weekly tour at its own tubing system. These tours fill up quickly, so it is important to register at least a week before your arrival on the Big Island. For more information, contact the visitor center (tel 808/985-6017, hawaiivolcanoesnationalpark .com; see pp. 168–169, p. 171, & p. 173).

Maui also offers a cave and tube adventure of stalagmites, stalactites, and unusual rock formations. The **Hana Lava Tube** off the Hana Highway is actually a pass underneath an old volcanic vent, giving visitors yet another inside-out experience. **Maui Cave Adventures** (tel 808/248-7308, mauicave.com) offers 40-minute self-guided tours ($$$) and longer, more strenuous adventures ($$$$$).

Spelunkers make their way down to the entrance of the Hana Lava Tube.

Historic Volcano House

The only hotel in the Hawaii Volcanoes National Park is perched right on the edge of Kilauea caldera. When there is summit activity, you can dine in its restaurant and watch the show; otherwise watch the continuous-run video in the bar. The lobby fireplace is always burning, and there are people who claim to have seen the face of Pele in the flames. The original Volcano House was built in 1846. After several reconstructions, it was built in its current form in 1941 with major upgrades in 2013.

the public), gives instant printouts of every earthquake on the island, and there are several hundred microquakes a day. A bank of seismographic drums records the pulse of the volcano, registering any movement of the earth. There is also a small seismograph set up to record "people tremors"; when you hop, jump, or leap, the instrument records the shock to the floor as if it were a shock to the volcano's heart.

Videos show past eruptions: fountains of fire, churning rivers, and lakes of lava. A display case with a ragged, singed safety suit testifies to the dedication of the park's volcanologists. It was worn by a scientist who fell knee-deep into lava at 2,000°F, and lived to tell about it. Sharing space

with the technology are murals depicting the legends of Pele, the goddess of volcanoes, painted by Hawaiian artist and historian Herb Kawainui Kane.

The museum is named for Professor Thomas A. Jaggar (1871–1953), who founded the observatory in 1912. He worked tirelessly to have the area declared a national park.

At the **Volcano Art Center** (tel 808/967-8222) more than 200 artisans exhibit their creative work, much of it centering on the volcano and its energy. Lauhala-weaving virtuoso Glenn Okuma sits on the center's porch almost every day, fashioning his acclaimed baskets. You'll also find paintings, jewelry, bronzeware, ceramic, textiles, and photography. There are new shows monthly at this nonprofit arts center housed in another Volcano House building dating from 1877.

Kilauea Trails & Birdlife

Hawaii Volcanoes National Park is best discovered on foot. More than 150 miles of trails explore the various environments of the park, and even if there were no active lava flow, the terrain is unique. You'll encounter some of the rarest flora and fauna on the planet. You'll need sunscreen, a hat, sturdy walking shoes, and drinking water.

The most unusual trail you'll ever walk is **Kilauea Iki.** It will take four hours for the 6.5-mile round-trip from the **Thurston Lava Tube** (see p. 172, p. 175) parking lot. The trail descends 400 feet through rain forest to the crater (continued on p. 176)

Crater Rim Drive

Crater Rim Drive, the road encircling Kilauea's oval summit caldera, 2.5 miles across and 300 feet deep, is the main attraction of the park. On the drive you will pass through lush rain forests with tree ferns, and see raw, steaming craters and vast areas of devastation. Along the road are well-marked trails and overlooks to encourage you to get out of your car periodically and explore this strange landscape.

Leaving the **Kilauea Visitor Center,** go right to begin the loop road. You'll immediately pass **Volcano House** and the **Volcano Art Center** ❶ (see p. 173). If you wish, you can rent a self-guided audiotour of Crater Rim Drive for a nominal fee at the art center.

Next is a sign for **Sulphur Banks** ❷. Follow your nose to a steamy, smelly area where the rocks are mustard color from sulfur carried by volcanic fumes. From the fenced steam vents across the road you can get a good look at the steam vaporized from the groundwater that seeps into lava crevices.

The first big lookout point is **Kilauea Overlook** ❸, with a view onto the crater's crackling, steaming floor. The **Hawaiian Volcano Observatory** and **Thomas A. Jaggar Museum** (see p. 171 & p. 173) are just beyond, and from there, too, you can gaze into the crater. In the opposite direction, massive Mauna Loa looms in the west. This area was sacred to the ancient Hawaiians. Impressive fields of lava mark the **Southwest Rift Zone,** scene of a 1971 eruption.

At **Halemaumau Crater** ❹, you can park and walk to this steamiest, most odorous area of the caldera. On some days the fumes are so toxic the area is closed. Halemaumau last erupted in 1974 but is obviously just napping. In one of the most dramatic moments in Hawaiian history, High Chiefess Kapiolani, a devout convert to Christianity, climbed down onto a ledge in Halemaumau while it was erupting in 1824. She stood just above the lava lake and defied Pele by eating *ohelo* berries (sacred to the goddess), then threw rocks into the pit, shouting, "Jehovah is my God."

Keanakakoi, next crater on the route, spewed 200-foot fountains of fire in the air and poured out the lava that first interrupted the Chain of Craters Road.

A good place to get out and walk is **Devastation Trail** ❺, a half-mile, 15-minute, family-friendly stroll through hell. In 1959, 1,900-foot lava fountains gushed into the air,

NOT TO BE MISSED:

Volcano Art Center • Jaggar Museum • Devastation Trail • Thurston Lava Tube • Kilauea Iki Overlook

Pele

The goddess of fire and volcanoes is said to have sailed in a canoe to Hawaii from a land in the far reaches of the ocean. From Niihau, she traveled southward through the islands, looking for the perfect place of fire. She settled finally in Halemaumau Crater of Kilauea Volcano, where she dwells to this day.

She appears as a beautiful woman, or an old crone. If you pass her by, the sages say, your car will develop trouble. If you pick her up, she will sit quietly in the backseat; when you turn around, she will vanish.

Pele's love affairs, rivalries, and jealousies are the raw material of Hawaii's literature. Her presence is everywhere: in the obsidian stretches of hardened lava, in the fiery rivers of lava flowing to the sea, and in the trembling of the earth.

spilling ash and pumice, wiping out an ohia forest, and leaving white tree skeletons standing in black cinders. Life has begun to proliferate again along the boardwalk, however, so that the name of the trail may have to be changed as it looks less and less devastated.

The next stop is a walk of a completely different nature. The **Thurston Lava Tube 6** is an easy 20-minute loop that descends quickly into a forest of tree ferns. Native birds have begun to nest in the area. With luck, you may see the scarlet *iiwi* or the chartreuse *amakihi*. You will cross a bridge over a small chasm and enter an electrically lit tunnel that once ran red

with magma. It is 450 feet long and in places as high as 20 feet, all of it eerie and awesome.

Last stop on the drive is **Kilauea Iki Overlook 7.** The 1959 eruption that shaped so many of the park's features filled this crater with a lava lake, as fire fountains shot into the air. One of the park's most popular hiking trails ventures into this nuclear-looking wasteland.

> See also map pp. 148–149
> ► Kilauea Visitor Center
> ⇔ 11 miles
> ⧖ 1 hour
> ► Kilauea Visitor Center

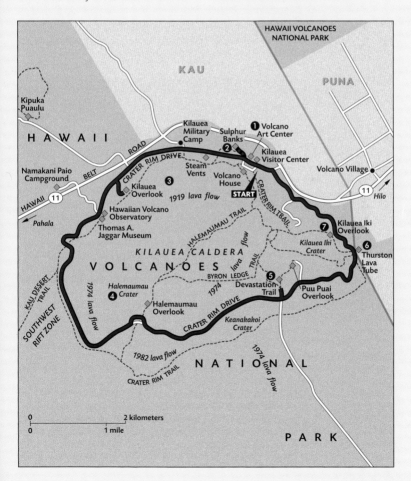

floor. You'll see the scarlet blossoms of the ohia lehua and the cranberry-like *ohelo* berry. Then, as you set out across the crater floor, you'll follow the rock cairns into what looks like a nuclear accident scene. Walking on the brittle, hardened lava is like walking on potato chips; beneath your feet, the ground is toasty warm and steam vents hiss. The graceful white bird you'll see overhead is the *koae kea,* an endemic seabird that nests in nooks of the crater wall; it carries squid dinners 7 miles from its oceanic hunting grounds to its nestlings.

The **Sandalwood Trail** is a good bet for bird-watchers. It's

yourself enveloped in rain forest. Ferns tower 20 feet overhead in a lacy canopy, and dew sparkles like crystal in the scarlet pompoms of the ohia lehua blossoms. All around, if you stop, is the sweet song of birds, unnoticed in the parking lot only feet away.

The brilliant red *apapane* is the endemic bird most likely to be spotted. It has a distinctive whirring of wings as it flies and has about 50 melodious songs. The best strategy for sighting Hawaiian birds is to stake out the flowers they feed on, the bright yellow *mamane,* the creamy bouquets of the giant koa tree, and the red ohia lehua.

The *iiwi (Vestiaria coccinea)* sips nectar from the ohia lehua blossom.

an easy trail, less than a mile, and would take 15 minutes to do, if you weren't lingering to look at birds. The trailhead is right across from the Kilauea Visitor Center parking lot. The first birds you'll encounter will probably be mynahs quarreling in the grass at the entry. In just a few steps, you cross a profound biological divide and find

The trail winds through the forest, in the cool shadow of the crater wall, into rocky crevices, and out to panoramic views across the crater. The *elepaio* frequents the koa trees. In days gone by, canoe-makers seeking suitable trees for their vessels would watch the elepaio carefully. If it landed on a koa tree and began to probe for insects, the tree was rejected.

Some other native birds commonly found in the park are *pueo,* the Hawaiian owl; *io,* the Hawaiian hawk; the crimson *iiwi;* and *omao,* a Hawaiian thrush. The coastal area of the park has populations of *noio,* the black noddy; *akekeke,* a ruddy turnstone; *kolea,* the Pacific golden plover; and *kioea,* the bristle-thighed curlew. The *nene* (Hawaiian goose) struts around the park like an owner doing inventory. Watch the nene from the dining room of the **Volcano Golf and Country Club** (*35 Pii Mauna Dr., tel 808/967-8228*), where they gather on the greens.

Aside from native species of birds, the park has populations of introduced mynah, melodious laughing thrush, Japanese white-eye, northern cardinal, nutmeg mannikin, common barn-owl, California quail, chukar, francolin, and Kalij pheasant.

Rather than drive, you can take a day to hike the 11.6-mile **Crater Rim Trail** (see pp. 174–175). Start in the early morning from the trailhead in front of Volcano House and walk counterclockwise to get the hot, treeless Kau Desert area out of the way before the midday heat. If you want to hike a part of the trail you won't see from the road, pick up the portion that crosses Chain of Craters Road and walk west to Keanakakoi Crater. You'll see eerie tree molds, natural black lava sculptures created when flowing hot lava engulfs a tree and hardens around it while the tree burns inside. Allow an hour's round-trip back to the road.

Mauna Loa & Mauna Kea

Mauna Loa, at 13,677 feet, is second to Mauna Kea as the highest peak in the Pacific, but it is the most massive mountain anywhere on Earth. One hundred times the size of extinct volcano Mount Rainier in Washington State, it's so big

INSIDER TIP:

Skiing on Mauna Kea is not recommended. The slopes are rocky and often icy.

—THELMA CHANG
Author & National Geographic contributor

California's entire Sierra Nevada mountain range could fit inside it. The name means "long mountain"—the summit caldera, Mokuaweoweo, is 3 miles long and 600 feet deep.

Mauna Loa was born three million years ago, 18,000 feet beneath the ocean. Too young to be sculpted by erosion, it is a perfect shield. It has erupted 37 times since 1832, most recently in 1984, when it threatened Hilo but stopped in time.

The hike to the top is a tough four-day round-trip, and you must be equipped for winter mountaineering. Driving up to the 6,662-foot elevation on **Mauna Loa Road** (*from Hawaii 11*) gives a grand experience of the mountain.

One mile up the road is **Kipuka Puaulu,** commonly called Bird Park. About 400 years ago, an eruption from the northeast rift zone of Mauna Loa covered

Onizuka Center for International Astronomy

⚠ Map p. 148

✉ Summit Rd., at the 9,600-foot marker

☎ 808/961-2180

vast areas of 2,000-year-old forest. The erratic flow left *kipuka,* islands of untouched forest in the sea of lava, and Kipuka Puaulu is a vestige of this ancient environment. Allow at least an hour to appreciate the 1.2-mile loop trail through the kipuka. Listen to the arias sung by cardinal, *iiwi, apapane, amakihi,* and *elepaio,* then stroll beneath giant koa trees, ohia lehua, and *mamane.*

Stands of koa line Mauna Loa Road as you continue upward. Watch for the exotically plumed Kalij pheasant; it has crowned itself king of the road, and is disdainful of traffic. A native of Nepal, it was imported in 1962 and is completely at home here.

To really enjoy this drive, pull over occasionally and experience the quiet. Overhead the *io,* once the symbol of Hawaiian royalty, may be surfing wind waves above the trees. At the end of the road, where the arduous trail to the summit begins, there are picnic tables.

Mauna Kea: Driving the 55-mile Saddle Road (Hawaii 200) between Hilo and the Kohala Coast, you cross a high valley with Earth's most massive mountain on one side of the road and its highest on the other. Mauna Kea, at 32,796 feet if you add the 13,796 feet above sea level to 19,000 down to its base on the ocean floor, is higher than Everest. Its name means "white mountain," as its peak is usually mantled in snow.

Mauna Kea hasn't erupted for 3,500 years. During the Ice Age, 15,000 years ago, a glacier locked the heights in ice, leaving a layer of permafrost that exists today.

EXPERIENCE: Nuts to You

Visit virtually any local food or sundry store in Hawaii and chances are high their shelves are stocked with an array of macadamia nuts, brittle, popcorn, crunch, oil, and other selections.

The delicious, hard-shelled nuts from Hawaii, known to be high in the "good" fat that reduces cholesterol levels, have been lauded for their quality and a crisp, "buttery" taste.

Macadamia nut growers number in the hundreds today, employ an estimated 4,000 people, and have struggled to survive the unpredictable effects of weather and economic conditions. The Big Island contains some 90 percent of all macadamia trees in Hawaii. Tours are free, with tastings at the end.

A 600-acre farm founded in 1993, **Hamakua Macadamia Nut Company** (Kawaihae, tel 808/882-1116, hawn.nut

.com) features a tour through its cannery area, where 100 percent of its macadamia nuts are Big Island grown, processed, and marketed.

On the Big Island's east side, 6 miles south of Hilo, the **Mauna Loa Macadamia Nut Factory** (tel 808/966-8618, maunaloa.com; see pp. 179–180) is the world's largest processor of macadamia nuts. It gives tours of a nut-processing plant and chocolate factory.

Molokai's own macadamia farm is located in the heart of Hawaiian homestead land, the central Hoolehua district. At **Purdy's Natural Macadamia Nuts** (tel 808/567-6601, molokai-aloha.com/macnuts), you may crack a few nuts by yourself, sample some fresh from the shell, and taste macadamia nut honey. Call ahead. Tour times and days may be subject to change.

The summit caldera of Mauna Loa, an enormous shield volcano

It feeds Lake Waiau, the third highest lake in the United States, at 13,020 feet.

On top of the mountain, astronomers from eleven nations have set up powerful telescopes, including the world's largest, the Keck Telescope, which is eight stories high with a lens diameter of 33 feet. Proximity to the equator and pollution-free skies make this the premier stargazing location. It's an awesome sight, even to the naked eye.

The road to the top of Mauna Kea begins at Milepost 28 on the Saddle Road. You can easily drive the steep 6 miles to the **Onizuka Center for International Astronomy** (tel 808/961-2180, no children under 16 years, no pregnant women), but only a 4WD can attempt the summit. Free summit tours, in your own vehicle, leave the center Saturdays and Sundays at 1 p.m. You can walk around inside one of the observatories. Stargazing through a powerful telescope into some of the clearest skies in the world is offered nightly from 6 to 10 p.m.

The Onizuka Center is named for Big Island astronaut Ellison Onizuka, killed in the *Challenger* space shuttle in 1986. Memorial exhibits and items of Mauna Kea's geology form most of the display.

Puna

The town of **Pahoa** has never gotten over the 1960s. Third-generation flower children, raised around the peace symbol and confirmed in tie-dyed regalia, can be spotted along the old wooden sidewalks and in the rickety stores reborn as New Age boutiques, funky secondhand emporiums, and health food stores. The 1917 **Akebono Theater** enjoys a crowded calendar of rock and reggae concerts. The town's weekend outdoor market draws an interesting crowd of bead traders and farmers.

Visitors are welcome at the **Mauna Loa Macadamia Nut Factory,** featuring one of the district's chief crops. You approach through 3 miles of orchards. At the factory, you can watch the

Mauna Loa Macadamia Nut Factory

 Map p. 149

Mail End of Macadamia Nut Rd. off Hawaii 11

tel 808/966-8618

Ka Lae

 Map p. 148

✉ End of South
Point Rd. off
Hawaii 11

gourmet nut get cracked, sorted, cooked, and processed into snacks, cookies, candy, and ice cream. Samples? Of course, and there's also a gift shop.

A whole stand of ohia forest got cooked in 1790 when a molten river of red-hot lava surged across the land. When it cooled, the trees had become eerie black

cause illness. Two more thermal pools, near **Isaac Hale Beach Park** *(end of Pahoa-Pohoiki Rd.),* are smaller and unimproved, but that is their charm.

Cape Kumukahi *(end of Hawaii 132),* the easternmost tip of Hawaii, has led a charmed life. The spectacular 1960 volcanic outburst that destroyed the town

Ka Lae, also known as South Point, is the southernmost tip of land in the United States.

sculptures. At **Lava Tree State Monument** *(Hawaii 132, 2.7 miles SE of Pahoa),* pleasant paths wander among 17 acres of these tree molds. The ohia forest has now regenerated, so the park is shady and cool.

The volcano has created several thermal ponds in Puna, where you can simmer in Earth's own bath. The most accessible is a 60-foot seaside pool at **Ahalanui Beach Park** *(look for a chain-link fence and what looks like a private house on Hawaii 137, 1 mile N of Pahoa-Pohoiki Rd.);* be aware that the bacteria count in this warm, popular pond can sometimes be high enough to

of Kapoho shot geysers of fire into the air from a 2,600-foot-wide eruption. The lava stopped 6 feet from the base of the lighthouse and politely went around it.

Kau

For tourists, the most famous thing about the Kau district is **Ka Lae,** also known as South Point, the southernmost tip of the United States. The next stop is Tahiti. For locals, it's the ugly Kau orange, with the sweetest taste of any orange.

Ka Lae is also believed by scholars to be the first landfall of the first Polynesians (see pp. 24–26), probably around A.D. 500.

Here in the fierce winds are the ruins of an ancient temple, **Kalalea Heiau.** Winds are so strong that they support a thriving wind farm along the road. Mooring holes for securing canoes are perfect circles carved into the lava rocks. A fishing village once flourished here, and thousands of bone hooks have been found in the mixed green-and-black sand. Platforms for launching boats dot the high cliffs. Daring tourists jump from there, probably unaware of the notorious currents often lurking below.

Papakolea, popularly called **Green Sand Beach,** is 3 miles east. It's about an hour's hike (or a 2.5-mile trip by 4WD) into the wind to an unprotected beach with dangerous surf. The big draw is the emerald green olivine "sand." Olivine is the first mineral to crystalize as basaltic lava cools. The semiprecious crystal is also found in Iceland and on the moon.

Two quiet towns east of Ka Lae are Naalehu and Waiohinu. There are some small, very agreeable restaurants at **Naalehu** (see p. 254). The island's famous Punaluu Portuguese sweet bread is made here at **Punaluu Bake Shop** *(95-5642 Mamalahoa Hwy., Hawaii 11, tel 808/929-7343).* Stop by for free samples flavored with guava or taro.

Waiohinu's claim to fame is Mark Twain Square *(Hawaii 11, tel 808/929-7550),* a charming pit stop. The famous author planted monkeypod trees here in 1866; surviving offshoots offer shade. All around the luxuriant garden are quotes from Twain, who rode in on horseback and liked it enough to stay awhile.

Farther east at **Punaluu,** the beautiful **Punaluu Black Sand Beach** *(Hawaii 11, 5 miles W of Pahala)* is lined with coconut palms and lapped by turquoise surf. You couldn't find a more picturesque spot to swim. On a hill overlooking the ocean, historic **Hokuloa Church,** rebuilt in 1957, is a memorial to Henry Opukahaia (see p. 30), the young Hawaiian Christian who had been studying in New England and who was most instrumental in persuading missionaries to come to Hawaii. ∎

Health Risks

Most people who walk or hike Hawaii's great outdoors enjoy the experience. Be aware of leptospirosis, however, a bacterial disease lurking in freshwater streams, ponds, and moist soil. The infection is endemic to the islands with 22 to 60 reported cases each year, some of them fatal. Here are some facts and tips:

• Leptospirosis causes flu-like symptoms, including fever, nausea, chills, and body aches.

• People usually get it when wading or swimming in fresh water that has been contaminated with animal waste.

• Observe posted signs.

• Two-thirds of local cases occur after outdoor summer activities.

• See a doctor if symptoms arise.

More Places to Visit on Hawaii: The Big Island

Kalopa State Recreation Area

This little known park, up in the northeast, is one of the loveliest on the island. A hundred acres of ohia forest can be explored at the cool, 2,000-foot elevation. Some of the giant trees are three to five centuries old. This is one of the last and most accessible vestiges of native rain forest left. There's a 4-acre arboretum for native species. In 1979, a stand of koa trees was planted as part of an effort to save the species, which had been dying out. The trees were so at home, some grew from seed to 8 feet in the first year. Many are now more than 75 feet high. An easy 0.7-mile nature

Telescopes of the Keck I and Keck II observatories atop Mauna Kea are trained on space.

trail loops through the rain forest. Many of the rare trees and plants beside the path are labeled. Additional trails go into the forest reserve, and there's also a horseback trail.
🗺 Map p. 148 ✉ End of Kalopa Rd., 0.5 mile SE of Honokaa, 3 miles inland from Hawaii 19 ☎ 808/974-6200

Keck Observatory Center

The first celestial photograph taken with the partially completed Keck Telescope atop Mauna Kea was of Galaxy NGC 1232, about 65 million light-years from Earth. A model of the world's largest telescope is on view here along with a video on the observatory's exploration of the universe. The actual telescope is eight stories high and weighs 270

tons. Most people don't make it to the top of Mauna Kea, so this is an intriguing, educational substitute, right in Waimea town.
🗺 Map p. 148 ✉ 65-1120 Mamalahoa Hwy., Waimea ☎ 808/885-7887
🕐 Closed Sat.–Sun.

Laupahoehoe Point Beach Park

It is said that Poliahu the snow goddess came down from Mauna Kea to go sledding at Laupahoehoe. But Pele, goddess of volcanoes, caused an eruption that drove Poliahu back to the summit. Poliahu sent freezing winds and snow over the lava, forcing it to enter the ocean and form Laupahoehoe Point on the Big Island's east coast, 25 miles north of Hilo. The beach park is reached along Hawaii 19.

On April 1, 1946, a tsunami (see p. 168), swept across Laupahoehoe Point, killing 32 people, most of them schoolchildren. A memorial stands where the school once did. The surf at this point is spectacular as it assaults the craggy black lava shoreline.
🗺 Map p. 148

Taro

In old Hawaii, at least 300 kinds of taro, the Hawaiian staff of life, were cultivated. Its leaves taste similar to spinach. The corm is baked or boiled like a potato, or—more likely—pounded for poi, the bland, clean-tasting purple paste served in big bowls on local tables or in thimbles at tourist luaus.

According to legend, when the first-born infant son of Papa and Wakea, the mother and father of the human race, died, his parents buried him. From his body a new plant, taro, sprang up from the earth to nurture all the siblings who were to come.

Nowadays poi is added to pancakes, muffins, and breads, turning them lavender and sweet.

A fantasy island with Bali Hai peaks, verdant forests, rainbows disappearing into the mist, and waterfalls cascading like shimmering drapes over steep cliffs

Kauai

The exotic bird of paradise, a common plant on Kauai

Kauai

Oldest of the major Hawaiian islands, Kauai was created by a massive volcano now extinct for six million years. Nature has had time to sculpt it into a great beauty, with majestic sea cliffs along the Na Pali Coast, a grand canyon in the heart of the island, an interior blessed with tremendous rains, and coasts bathed in sunshine.

The island is 33 miles long by 25 miles wide and is the only Hawaiian isle with navigable rivers. Much of it may look familiar, cast as it has been in more than 50 feature films and full-length television productions. That lyric waterfall in the opening sequence of *Jurassic Park* is here; in *South Pacific* Mitzi Gaynor "washed that man right out of her hair" at Lumahai Beach; King Kong went rampaging in Honopu Valley; and Elvis swayed beneath the palm trees of the Coconut Coast in *Blue Hawaii* (see p. 192).

Three times in the past century, Kauai has been ravaged by hurricanes, the most recent being Hurricane Iniki in 1992 (see p. 188). Each time, the island bounced back with admirable spirit. Indeed, courage has always been Kauai's guiding light. When the warriors of Kamehameha the Great swept across

the other islands, conquering all in their path, Kauai alone remained stubbornly independent. Eventually, when it was good and ready, Kauai voluntarily joined the fledgling kingdom.

Even developers have had to tiptoe lightly across this landscape, especially after residents passed a law that no building can stand higher than a coconut palm. So what you see when you look at this island is a hundred grades of green. Ninety-seven percent of it remains rural and cast into vast nature preserves.

Kauai may well have been the first island to be settled, perhaps as early

NOT TO BE MISSED:

as A.D. 500, and by some estimates even a few centuries before that. The first wave of colonists came from the Marquesas, some 2,000 miles to the south; later groups sailed from Tahiti. This is the home of the Menehune, the legendary little people (see p. 187).

Known as the Garden Isle, Kauai does, indeed, abound in botanical gardens. Homes are overwhelmed by the flowers around them. If it's Christmas, you'll see poinsettias as high as a house. ■

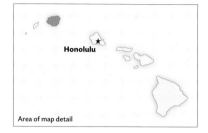

Honolulu

Area of map detail

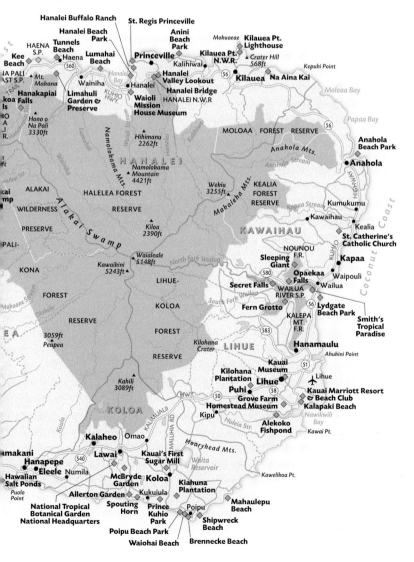

Lihue

The county seat of Kauai is one of those small towns that got big without a lot of planning. Lihue is a confusion of multistreet intersections and small malls, but it's where visits to the island start because the airport is here. Most people get out as fast as they can, heading for the resorts—which is a mistake because some gems are found in and around Lihue.

An interisland cruise ship calls at Nawiliwili Harbor.

Lihue
⬛ Map p. 185
Visitor Information
✉ Kauai Visitors Bureau, 4334 Rice St.
☎ 808/245-3971

Kauai Museum
⬛ Map p. 185
✉ 4428 Rice St.
☎ 808/245-6931
🕐 Closed Sun.
💲 $

If you want to understand Kauai, its people, and its culture, you ought to make at least a brief stop at the **Kauai Museum.** It looks like a library, because that's what it was until 1970, but it has a remarkable collection of ancient Hawaiian artifacts. The museum is also noted for its fine Hawaiian quilts, one of which is fashioned into *holoku* (a Hawaiian gown with train). There are large calabashes of native wood, *kahili* (the feather standards of royalty), and even a hand-carved canoe. You'll see vintage photographs of old Kauai through the eyes of a Japanese immigrant

and a bird's-eye helicopter video of the legendary beauty of the island as it is today.

History that doesn't feel like history can be found 2.5 miles away in Puhi, at **Kilohana Plantation.** Designed for missionary-descended sugar baron Gaylord Wilcox and his wife, Ethel, by Honolulu architect Frank Stewart Potter, Kilohana was completed in 1935, and the grand house quickly became the social center of the island. It still is, although now they let anybody in. You can lounge around the living room with its period furniture and artifacts, or you can dine in a fine restaurant (see p. 254). All the other rooms—even some of the nine bathrooms—are shops crammed with arts, crafts, and gifts. Look for the historic **Kauai Plantation Railway depot** and climb aboard for a ride in a replicated royal Touring Car *(tel 808/245-7245, $$$$)*.

Another legacy of the Wilcox family is **Grove Farm Homestead Museum.** George, the bachelor son of missionaries Abner and Lucy Wilcox (see pp. 196–197), established Grove Farm Plantation in 1864. He put in irrigation, built up a profitable sugar business, and lived there until he died in 1933, a millionaire and still a bachelor at 94. Tours guide you not only through the gracious rooms, but also through a typical day on the plantation, which seems to have been very charming as long as you weren't working hard in the fields.

Lihue's port is the spectacular harbor of Nawiliwili, embraced by brooding mountains. Adjacent to the harbor is **Kalapaki Beach.** Its white sands front a megaresort, the Kauai Marriott Resort & Beach Club *(tel 808/245-5050)*, claiming the biggest swimming pool in the state, which tends to keep Kalapaki Beach relatively uncrowded.

On Hulemalu Road, above the picturesque harbor, is a lookout for one of the aquaculture wonders of ancient Hawaii, the **Alekoko Fishpond.** The walls of this rare inland fishpond run 900 feet long and stand 5 feet above water with another 13 to 30 feet below water. The 39-acre facility for raising mullet is sometimes called the Menehune Fishpond because it was said to have been built in a single night by the little people. You can't go down to see it close up because it's private property, but the view of the huge pond, backed by the Hoaryhead Mountains, is painted in an Impressionist's palette, soft and infused with light. ∎

Kilohana Plantation

 Map p. 185

✉ 3-2087 Kaumualii Hwy. (Hawaii 50)

☎ 808/245-5608

Grove Farm Homestead Museum

 Map p. 185

✉ 4050 Nawiliwili Rd. (Hawaii 58)

☎ 808/245-3202

🕐 Closed Tues., Fri., Sat., Sun. Tours 10 a.m. & 1 p.m.; must be arranged a week in advance

💲 $

EXPERIENCE: Splashing Through History

Mountain tubing is a splash-in-your-face kind of adventure that literally floats you into spectacular vistas and an important part of Hawaii's past. This experience involves a 4WD-vehicle adventure into the former Lihue Sugar Plantation at Hanamaulu, where a guide shares Hawaii's sugar history, especially Lihue's own system of tunnels and flumes that Chinese immigrants built by hand in the 1860s and 1870s.

Pristine, emerald green wilderness and a launch site await visitors, who are supplied with safety equipment, including helmets, waterproof headlamps, and, of course, an inner tube. From there, it's a floating journey along open ditches and a series of five tunnels.

To date, mountain tubing is available only on Kauai. Wear sunscreen, water-friendly shoes, a swimsuit, or other similar attire, and pack a hat, towel, change of clothing, and bug spray. Allow at least three hours for a family-friendly adventure. Age, weight, and other physical restrictions may apply. Lunch is included *(Kauai Backcountry Adventures, 3-4131 Kuhio Hwy., Hanamaulu, 888/270-0555 or 808/245-2506, kauaiback country.com, $$$$$)*.

Koloa

This little sugar town sits beneath spreading banyan and monkeypod trees where Maluhia Road joins Poipu Road. It began as a thriving Hawaiian settlement, whose inhabitants probably grew sugar for their own sweets (the name means "long sugarcane"). After the decline of the sugar industry, Koloa was purchased by a developer who gave it the face-lift it needed.

Koloa
🅰 Map p. 185

Yamamoto Store (Crazy Shirts)
✉ 5356 Koloa Rd.
☎ 808/742-7161

Spouting Horn
🅰 Map p. 185

Take a look at the colorful old wooden storefronts that now house boutiques and restaurants. Each has a story. The Ashida Soda Works Building was once a poi factory. The 1900 **Yamamoto Store,** which may be Kauai's most photographed building, was once the Koloa Hotel catering to traveling salesmen, and is now home to Crazy Shirts, a T-shirt retailer. Pick up a Koloa Heritage Trail map at most shops, or call the Poipu Beach Resort Foundation (*tel 808/742-7444*).

You approach Koloa beneath eucalyptus trees on **Tree Tunnel Road,** aka Maluhia Road. The tattered smokestack of Kauai's first sugar mill lies in the brush at the entrance to town. On the road's right side stands what looks like a war memorial, but it's a tribute to the plantation laborers who came to Koloa from around the globe.

Along the lava shoreline, southwest of Koloa is Kukuiula Bay and **Spouting Horn,** a lava tube that spits salty surf as high as 50 feet. At sunset the geyser becomes incandescent with the colors of the rainbow. You may encounter some unexpected fellow sunbathers on the coast—sometimes rare Hawaiian monk seals haul themselves up on the sand only yards from beach blankets. ∎

Iniki

Hurricane Iniki slammed into Kauai the afternoon of September 11, 1992. The name means "fierce piercing wind"; it was that and more. Winds were clocked at 227 mph before the wind meters stopped working. When the next day dawned, Kauai, the green and beautiful isle, did not have a leaf left on a tree, and barely a branch. Nearly three-quarters of the homes were destroyed or damaged.

Today the island is lush and emerald again, though you can still see a few remnants of the savage storm along the Poipu and Coconut Coasts.

INSIDER TIP:

At Mahaulepu Beach, scientists have found sightless spiders in the shoreline caves and fossils of extinct flightless birds in the coastal sand dunes.

—JOCELYN FUJII
National Geographic writer

The Poipu Coast

Poipu began life as a major resort in 1962, when the beach home of sugar planter Valdemar Knudsen was demolished to make way for the first hotel.

Horseback riding is one of the many activities enjoyed by visitors to Kauai's sunny southern shore.

The plantation manager's home and garden have become the centerpiece of **Kiahuna Plantation** (see p. 255), a holiday condominium. The garden grows more than 3,000 kinds of tropical flowers and has a noteworthy cactus collection. Pick up a map at the front desk.

Poipu is actually several beaches, beginning with Poipu itself. Next is **Waiohai Beach.** Snorkeling here will acquaint you with many-hued tropical fish, and the offshore surfing site is very popular. **Poipu Beach Park**, next in line, is much frequented by families because of its sheltered waters. Bodyboarders and bodysurfers favor **Brennecke Beach;** be careful of a strong rip current. Makawehi Point separates **Shipwreck Beach** from the sands to the east. A dawn

walk along the dunes, cliffs, and nature trails on the western end of the beach is exhilarating. Some people like to bicycle beyond Shipwreck to unspoiled **Mahaulepu Beach,** a 2-mile stretch of golden sand. Lithified dunes contain fossils, and there are also petroglyphs (see p. 26, p. 158, p. 230), as this was the most settled area of Poipu in ancient times.

Prince Kuhio Park commemorates Prince Jonah Kuhio Kalanianaole, a tireless worker for the rights of native Hawaiians, who was born on the coast at Kukuiula, on March 26, 1871. The foundation of the royal home and its fishpond are incorporated into the park. The prince's birthday is a state holiday, celebrated with islandwide cultural events, canoe races, and a ball (see p. 236). ∎

Kiahuna Plantation
- Map p. 185
- 2253 Poipu Rd.
- 808/742-6411

Prince Kuhio Park
- Map p. 185
- Lawai Rd.

National Tropical Botanical Garden

The U.S. Congress gave a green thumbs-up to Hawaii's unique biota in 1964 when it chartered the National Tropical Botanical Garden, with five facilities—three on Kauai, one on Maui, and one (The Kampong) in Coconut Grove, Florida.

Kauai's three gardens—McBryde and Allerton, both on the South Shore at Kalaheo, the headquarters for the National Tropical Botanical Garden (NTBG); and Limahuli, on the North Shore—each with a personality of its own, deserve about two hours of visitor time for a comprehensive tour.

Limahuli Garden & Preserve, tucked into the ramparts that form the beginning of the Na Pali Coast

McBryde & Allerton Gardens

The focus at McBryde is on rare and endangered Hawaiian species and economically important tropical plants. McBryde has the largest collection of native Hawaiian plant species in the world. Some 90 percent of the flowering plants in Hawaii are endemic, a far greater percentage than anywhere else on Earth. More than half are considered threatened, endangered, or extinct in the wild. McBryde Garden also has significant collections of palms, flowering trees, heliconias, and orchids.

The national headquarters for the NTBG overlooks McBryde Garden. The NTBG herbarium contains 56,000 specimens of tropical plants, while its research library holds an impressive collection of 20,000 books, journals, botanical prints, and historical images.

Adjoining McBryde Garden is the oceanfront Allerton Garden. This former estate was originally planted in the 1870s by Queen Emma. Gardening gave a measure of peace to the queen, who had lost both her husband, King Kamehameha IV, and their only child. The queen worked beside her gardeners, planting *lauae* fern, ginger, heliconia, rose apple, bamboo, pandanus, haole lehua, pikake *(Jasminum sambac),* and spider lily. She added trees—tamarind, thornless *kiawe,* the almond-like *kamani,* and mango. Magenta bougainvillea cascade from the cliffs above the queen's cottage.

Emma's garden was expanded during the 30-year proprietorship of Robert and John Allerton. Today it is an enchantment of outdoor garden "rooms," sculpture pools, fountains, miniature waterfalls, and flower gardens set beside a stream along the sea.

Limahuli Garden & Preserve

The other NTBG facility on Kauai is Limahuli Garden and Preserve at Haena. This magnificent, 17-acre site is notched into towering **Mt. Makana** near the end of the road on the North Shore. Its beauty is almost a distraction to the garden's importance.

Within Limahuli are two vital ecosystems: the lowland rain forest and the lower mixed mesophytic (moderately moist) forest. Together, these two systems are the natural habitat of more than 70 percent of Kauai's and 59 percent of Hawaii's endangered plant species. The valley receives an annual rainfall of 80 to more than 200 inches. Adjacent to the garden are approximately 990 acres of preserve. Limahuli Stream is home to the last five species of Hawaiian freshwater fish.

The garden was begun in the 1960s when missionary descendant Juliet Rice Wichman (1901–1987) set out to create a garden that would be a living museum of Hawaiian flora. The garden was honored as the best natural botanical garden in the U.S. by the American Horticultural Society for its rare plant conservation and sound environmental water and soil practices in an overall garden design.

The name, Limahuli, which means "turning hands" in Hawaiian, acknowledges the early Hawaiians who built gardening terraces from lava rock, planted *kalo* (taro), and sustained their community with this food staple. Ruins of terraces and house sites are scattered throughout the beautiful valley. ∎

Healing Gardens

In addition to their awe-inspiring beauty, Hawaii's botanical gardens represent a significant effort to study, interpret, protect, and propagate rare plants that early Hawaiians utilized not only for food but also for medicinal purposes. *Awa,* for example, is a relaxant that is part of mainstream medicine in Europe.

Unfortunately, native plants and other wildlife have disappeared through the years by several stressors, including human intrusion and invasive plants and animals. The crisis has earned the 50th state a dubious title as the nation's "extinction capital." Thus, botanical gardens in Hawaii have become a kind of resistance movement against complete extinction.

McBryde & Allerton Gardens

- 🗺 Map p. 185
- ✉ Visitor Center, Lawai Rd., across from Spouting Horn parking lot
- ☎ 808/742-2623
- 🕐 Guided tours by reservation only, also self-guided tours
- 💲 $$$$$

Limahuli Garden & Preserve

- ✉ Kuhio Hwy., Haena
- ☎ 808/826-1053
- 🕐 Closed Sun. & Mon. Guided tours by reservation
- 💲 $$ ($$$ for guided tours)

Coconut Coast

This breezy stretch of coastline on the east of the island has become the most popular part of Kauai—and it has the traffic to prove it. Kapaa and its neighbors Kealia, Waipouli, and Wailua have become one long oceanfront community linked by hotels, holiday condominiums, restaurants, shops, mini-malls, Kuhio Highway, and a line of beaches. Towering over everything are the hundreds of coconut palms that give the area its name and its charm.

Anahola Beach Park

- ⚠ Map p. 185
- ✉ Anahola Rd., *makai* (oceanside) of Kuhio Hwy. (Hawaii 56)

Kauai royalty once ruled from the Coconut Coast. The island's last queen, Deborah Kapule, favorite wife of King Kaumualii, lived here. In the 1800s, a German immigrant planted one of the largest stands of coconut palms in the Islands. The site later became the Coco Palms Hotel, still mourned after its destruction by Hurricane Iniki. The trees have nicely recovered, however; you'll pass right by them driving along Kaumualii Highway, just beyond Wailua. Walking among them could be dangerous: Those nuts can come down like cannonballs in the wind.

Cove after sandy cove scallops the shoreline, while the Anahola and Makaleha Mountains stage a dramatic backdrop for the towns. The mountain that gives Kauai its verdure, 5,148-foot Waialeale, lies behind Kapaa like a great rain magnet, sucking the clouds away from the coast and leaving it dry and sunny. **Waialeale,** whose summit is almost always swathed in clouds, receives 40 feet of rain a year, making it the world's wettest place. Helicopter tours (see p. 264) drop into the green crater that streams with waterfalls.

Near Milepost 7 on Kuhio Highway, you'll see a sign pointing toward the Coconut Coast's other

famous mountain, **Nounou,** and its natural formation commonly known as the **Sleeping Giant.** He's stretched out flat, faceup, with his head in Wailua and his feet in Kapaa.

The safest swimming beach on this often tempestuous coast is **Anahola Beach Park.** If you're lucky, you may find a glass fishing float from the Japanese fleet. The currents must be just right, for they often wash up here.

Note: A bypass allows you to skip the worst of the area's traffic at Kapaa. However, taking it means that you will also bypass all of the town's shops and restaurants. ∎

Elvis

The King of Rock and Roll, Elvis Presley, came to the Coconut Coast in 1961 to film Blue Hawaii. **Some of the Kauai landmarks seen in the film include the Coco Palms Hotel, Lydgate Park, Lihue Airport, the Wailua River, Anahola, and Opaekaa Falls. The King returned to Kauai in 1966 to shoot** Paradise Hawaiian Style, **later retitled and remarketed as** Girls! Girls! Girls!

Up the Wailua River

This 12-mile-long river was once known as Wailua Nui Hoano ("great sacred Wailua") and had nine temples lining its green banks.

A family sets out to paddle up the Wailua River.

To explore its many fingers, rent a kayak in **Kapaa** and pick up a picnic lunch at the nearby Safeway *(4-831 Kuhio Hwy., tel 808/822-2464)*. Before you launch from the boat ramp at **Wailua River State Park,** take a look at the temple ruins and birthing stones at the park.

Paddle up the river, toward the mountains, keeping to the right to avoid currents and tourist barges heading for **Fern Grotto.** After an hour, take the left fork to the grotto, a huge amphitheater cave. Pull up on the bank past the docks; a few minutes' walk takes you to the grotto.

Back at the fork in the river, take the right branch. In a few minutes you'll be gliding beneath cliffs

as you head into the jungle. Great banyans dangle giant philodendron vines, and the dense foliage overhead forms a canopy. Stop along the riverbank for lunch.

When you come to a small island, you can tie your kayak to a tree and hike to 100-foot-high **Secret Falls.** The kayak company will provide a trail map. It's only a mile, but it takes an hour each way through the tangled forest. Hidden in the jungle are the falls, with their milky jade plunge pool.

Back at the river, turn your kayak around to glide downstream. Explore the little fingers of water that lead into the habitats of rare Hawaiian birds, where you'll hear songs heard no place else in the world. ∎

Wailua River State Park

▲ Map p. 185

✉ Kuhio Hwy. (Hawaii 56) & Kuamoo Rd. (Hawaii 580)

Kilauea & Princeville

Little Kilauea, a former sugar plantation town, is the gateway to Kauai's North Shore. Here, life proceeds at a leisurely pace and the scenery is magnificent.

Kilauea
🔺 Map p. 185

Kong Lung Store
✉ Kilauea Rd., Kilauea
☎ 808/828-1822

St. Regis Princeville
🔺 Map p. 185
✉ 5520 Ka Haku Rd., Princeville
☎ 808/826-9644

Two lava-built churches here are worth a peek: **St. Sylvester's Catholic Church** (tel 808/ 822-7900) displays murals by island artist Jean Charlot, and **Christ Memorial Episcopal Church** (tel 808/828-1825) has 11 stained-glass windows from England.

Kilauea, however, is better known for its commerce than its prayers. For many years, Mr. Lung Wah Chee (1850–1931) operated a plantation general store in Kilauea. In 1902 he moved to the present site of the **Kong Lung Store.** In 1940, his landlord built him the unique lava store, which served as post office, general store, barbershop, and butcher. Everything was sold, from axes to opium (legal at that time). Now, even Honoluluans fly over to shop among the art, home furnishings, designer Hawaiian wear, and thousand-dollar shell necklaces, all with an emphasis on local artisans. The Kong Lung "shave ice" (snow cone) stand appeared in the movie Six Days, Seven Nights, which starred Harrison Ford.

The nearby **St. Regis Princeville** is Kauai's largest resort. Scattered across its 1,000 acres are golf courses, holiday condominiums, residences, restaurants, and shops. To obtain one of the most stunning views in Hawaii, walk into the sumptuous lobby and look out the glass wall at Hanalei Bay and the jagged massifs of Namolokama

streaming with waterfalls, and at Mt. Makana, which was cast as Bali Hai in South Pacific. The same view can be captured from the hotel's terrace and Café Hanalei.

The resort is named for Prince Albert Edward Kauikeaouli, who visited the area with his parents, King Kamehameha IV and Queen

INSIDER TIP:

It's mesmerizing to watch the frothy waves crashing against Mokuaeae, off Kilauea Point. It looks like a sea of whipped cream.

—RITA ARIYOSHI
National Geographic author

Emma, when it was a plantation owned by Hawaii's foreign minister, Scottish-born Robert Crichton Wyllie (1798–1865). The 13-year-old daughter of the plantation manager wrote of a royal birthday party given May 20, 1861: "The celebration consisted of a parade of 200 Hawaiian men and women on horseback dressed alike, the men in red and white shirts and blue pants, and the women in red and yellow pau and maile leis. . . . In the evening the large bonfires were lighted in the lowlands, and on the hilltops, making a fine display and discharging bombs which resembled cannonading." ∎

Kilauea Point NWR

Ka Lae o Kilauea is the ancient name of this wave-lashed bastion of land at the northernmost tip of Kauai. The Hawaiians of old once gathered at such geographically prominent places for night-watch parties to tend the *kukui ahi,* the fires that guided fishermen home.

Kilauea Point Lighthouse is the high-tech end of a noble tradition. The 52-foot-high white tower on a 216-foot cliff dominates the 200-acre refuge. It was dedicated at sundown May 1, 1913, preceded by a day-long luau and shark shoot. To lure the sharks within shooting range, a dead cow was lowered into the offshore waters. The lighthouse has the world's largest clamshell lens, which can shine 90 miles out to sea. In 1927, aviators attempting the first trans-Pacific flight from California to Hawaii suffered instrument failure, and would have flown past Hawaii into oblivion had they not seen Kilauea's beam. They were able to readjust, and landed safely on Oahu after more than 25 hours in the air. The lighthouse is enjoying retirement as a national historical landmark in the midst of a wildlife sanctuary.

Among the birds you'll see are the great frigatebird with its 8-foot wingspan, the red-footed booby, and the nene, Hawaii's state bird. Good signage helps you identify them. In the coves on either side of the point, you may spot the rare Hawaiian green sea turtle, and whales and porpoises often make an offshore appearance. The

small islet at the base of the cliff, **Mokuaeae,** is a sunning spot for monk seals; Mokuaeae means "fragment frothing in the rising tide," and it's easy to see why.

Go to the 568-foot **Crater Hill** to take in grand views of the refuge and lighthouse. ■

Kilauea Point National Wildlife Refuge

Map p. 185

Kilauea Rd. to the end at Kilauea Point

☎ 808/828-1413

$ $

Kilauea Point Lighthouse and the national wildlife refuge

Hanalei

For more than a thousand years, people have farmed at Hanalei. Looking down from the Hanalei Valley Lookout (just past Princeville Shopping Center, on the right), you'll see the Hanalei River flowing through brilliant emerald green *kalo loi* (flooded taro fields).

The river, mountains, and taro fields of Hanalei Valley

Hanalei National Wildlife Refuge

Map p. 185

Brooding, mist-shrouded mountains weep with waterfalls. Interpretive signs tell you about the **Hanalei National Wildlife Refuge.** It's not open to the public, but often you can see gallinule, coot, spindly legged stilt, and endangered Koloa duck in the *kalo loi.*

The district of Hanalei (meaning "crescent bay") is actually three valleys—Hanalei, Waioli ("singing waters"), and Waipa ("touched waters"). Three villages, Hanalei, Wainiha, and Haena, are lost in the greenery.

One reason the area has remained so pastoral is the rusty one-lane **Hanalei Bridge,** too narrow for tour buses. Made in New York, this national historic landmark was installed in 1912.

If you see buffalo grazing, don't be surprised. The **Hanalei Buffalo Ranch** has 200 head of American bison, some of which end up as buffalo burgers on local menus.

Hanalei Town

The **Ching Young Village** mini-mall *(5-5190 Kuhio Hwy., tel 808/826-7222)* on the east end of town was founded by Ching Young and his wife, Man Sing, who arrived from Chungshan, China, in 1896. They raised eight children here and eventually bought a rice mill and general store. Man Sing continued to operate the store after her husband's death, and was so generous in giving food to the poor and needy that, at one point, she had to sell her jewelry to pay her debts. Her descendants now run the center with its shops and healthy restaurants.

On the way out of town, you can't miss the graceful **Waioli Huiia Church** *(Kuhio Hwy., tel 808/826-6253).* Built in 1912, its green shingles blend perfectly into the landscape, and its stained-glass windows shine like the waterfalls. Behind it is the 1836 **Waioli Mission House Museum** *(Kuhio Hwy., tel 808/245-3202),* home of Yankee missionaries Abner and

Lucy Wilcox. Lucy gave birth to eight sons in the main bedroom. The wooden house, designed by the Reverend William Alexander from Kentucky, has a southern generosity to it. With its wraparound lanai (veranda), it is comfortably furnished and still feels like a home. A clock, installed in 1866, is still keeping perfect time.

Beaches

Hanalei has a strand of incredibly beautiful beaches. The first of these is **Hanalei Beach Park** (Weke Rd., between Aku & Pilikoa Rds.). Sheer volcanic palisades rise 4,000 feet behind golden sands, and yachts anchor in the lee. The bay, calm as a lake in summer, reflects the mountains. The swimming is excellent, too.

The most famous strand of sand in the district is **Lumahai Beach** (Kuhio Hwy., at Milepost 33). You can pull over to the side of the road for a good photograph of the beach that starred in South Pacific. There's a steep trail down, just east of the lookout. White surf crashes on high black boulders, creating streaming waterfalls. Riptides and a strong undertow are extremely treacherous, so swimming on all but the calmest summer days is not recommended.

Less famous but equally beautiful is **Tunnels Beach** (Kuhio Hwy., at Milepost 8). Also known as Makua, it has a lacy coral reef that invites snorkelers. The name Tunnels was bestowed by surfers who come for the famous tubular waves in winter.

A lava tube cave known as **Maniniholo Dry Cave** is directly across from **Haena Beach Park,** another extremely dangerous swimming beach. The cave runs several hundred yards under the lava cliff. A mile down the road are two more caves, **Waikapalae** and **Waikanaloa.** It is said that Pele, the volcano goddess, dug here hoping to find a home, and instead struck water so she moved on. The caves and beaches are all part of **Haena State Park** (W end of Hawaii 560). Right at the end of the road is **Kee Beach,** also part of the park's more than 230 acres of scenic wildland and the start of the **Kalalau Trail** (see pp. 198–199). Kee is the prettiest swimming beach in the park. The sandy-bottomed lagoon is fringed in lacy coral. Swimming on the reef can be dangerous in times of high surf. Limahuli Garden and Preserve (see p. 191) is nearby.

INSIDER TIP:

The shops at Ching Young Village offer kayaking and snorkeling equipment rentals.

—THELMA CHANG
Author & National Geographic contributor

Just above the west end of Kee Beach, a path leads to **Ka Ulu o Laka Heiau,** an ancient hula temple. To train themselves in chant, dancers would pit their voices against the surging seas below. Hula dancers from all over Hawaii still visit this shrine in the place where Pele fell in love with Lohiau, a handsome chief of Kauai. She was drawn to Haena by the sound of the hula pahu (drum). ∎

Na Pali Coast

Towering green cliffs rise 2,000 feet out of a turbulent sea. Their fluted ramparts follow that part of Kauai's northern shore called the Na Pali Coast, stretching 15 miles from Kee to Polihale (see p. 201).

The setting sun illuminates the massive sea cliffs of Kauai's Na Pali Coast.

The names of the valleys roll from the tongue like a sacred litany: Hanakapiai, Hoolulu, Waiahuakua, Hanakoa, Kalalau, Honopu, Awaawapuhi, Nualolo, Koahole, and Milolii. Rainbows crown them, and waterfalls feed them. They are deep and green and so remote it is like entering a time warp and seeing the land before it was peopled and priced. The coast has ocean-filled caves with waterfall curtains, sea arches, and five sandy beaches. There is no way to see this remote and magnificent wilderness except by air, boat, or on foot (see p. 264). It is much too rugged for a road.

In **Na Pali Coast State Park** *(8 miles W of Hanalei at end of Hawaii 56, tel 808/274-3444),* the ancient **Kalalau Trail** winds along the *pali* (cliffs) 11 miles from Kee Beach to Kalalau Valley. The trail traverses lofty sea cliffs and lush amphitheater valleys. It dips and drops, gets slippery with fallen guava and rivulets of rain, and all the time rewards you with impressive turrets, pleats, and peaks. In the first half mile you'll have splendid, almost aerial views of Kee and its lacy reef. Looking ahead, you'll get a preview of the long line of fluted cliffs arrayed in sunshine. Sometimes the surf is so powerful the ground trembles beneath your feet, even hundreds of feet above the sea.

The 2-mile, two-hour hike to **Hanakapiai,** the first of the valleys, is a popular day-hike and an overnight stop for backpackers. Once there, you can take a further 2-mile hike into the valley to spectacular **Hanakapiai Falls.** The trail at first seems easy but becomes progressively more difficult.

From Hanakapiai Beach, the trail climbs 800 feet. The strenuous 4 miles to **Hanakoa** will take almost three hours and traverse two hanging valleys—valleys where streams have not yet carved a way to the ocean. A third of a mile into Hanakoa is a 2,000-foot waterfall. Pushing on, it's another 5 miles to the trail end at Kalalau. Beyond that, Na Pali resists even a footpath.

Jack London (1876–1916) wrote a poignant story, "Koolau the Leper," about a Waimea cowboy afflicted with leprosy, who led a band of fellow sufferers into the Na Pali wilderness to escape shipment to Molokai, where all those suffering from the disease were sent (see pp. 212–213).

These remote valleys were once inhabited. Agricultural terraces and *auwai* (irrigation ditches) suggest that Kalalau was the most cultivated valley in old Hawaii. Hawaiians lived here until 1919 when the last were lured away by the dubious comforts of towns. Artifacts carbon-dated back to

INSIDER TIP:

Take a boat tour to Nualolo Kai off the Na Pali Coast. This area—only accessible by the ocean—supported a substantial precontact population.

—MIRIAM STARK
National Geographic field scientist

A.D. 800 show strong cultural links to the Marquesas Islands.

In the 1960s archaeologists exploring Nualolo Valley unearthed a treasure trove of surprisingly well-preserved bows, arrows, fishhooks, poi pounders, adzes, and tattoo needles, as well as fine examples of cord and *kapa* (tree-bark cloth). The researchers cataloged more than 4,000 specimens.

Na Pali abounds with tales of kings, gods, and the little people—the Menehune (see p. 187). And there are more recently born legends. Honopu became the Valley of the Lost Tribe in the 1920s, when an archaeologist found skulls that he declared were not Hawaiian. Speculation as to their origins ranged from Menehune to one of the lost tribes of Israel. The skulls were subsequently proven to be Hawaiian, but the legend persisted.

Na Pali inspires awe, whether you see it from a helicopter, soaring above the windlashed *pali*; from the sea, plunging into its caves and beneath its waterfalls in a Zodiac or more sedately in a motor launch; or from the ground itself, walking its old and mysterious paths. ∎

West Kauai

You can take days to explore the history, towns, and natural wonders on the driest, sunniest side of Kauai.

Waimea Plantation Cottages

⛰ Map p. 184

✉ 9400 Kaumualii Hwy. (Hawaii 50)

☎ 808/338-1625

When you come to a blaze of bougainvillea blooming madly on the side of the mountains, you'll be at Hanapepe, one of Kauai's most colorful towns. Beneath the flowers, the historic old buildings have blossomed into a collection of 16 art galleries, plus several boutiques and restaurants. Pick up a map for a self-guided history walk at any of the shops. In 1.5 miles you'll find 69 key sites, 43 of them on the National and State Registers of Historic Places. One is the site of the 1924 labor strike when 16 laborers and four policemen were killed in the landmark protest against Hawaii's exploitative plantation system.

Hanapepe was Lilo's hometown in the Disney animated 2002 hit *Lilo and Stitch,* and served as the Filipino city of Olongapo in *Flight of the Intruder.* Every Friday between 6 and 9 p.m., Hawaiian musicians stroll the streets, and the art galleries have open houses with refreshments.

Friday is also the only night the gourmet Hanapepe Café *(3830 Hanapepe Rd., tel 808/335-5011)* is open. One gallery worth a peek, even for nonshoppers, is **Kauai Fine Arts** *(3848 Hanapepe Rd., tel 808/335-3778).* They have a fascinating inventory of antique maps, original engravings from Captain Cook's voyages to Hawaii, and rare 19th-century ships' logs. Look for the little **Taro Ko** shop *(tel 808/335-5586)* at the east end of Hanapepe Road. When they sell out of their famous taro chips, they just close for the day.

Hawaiian Salt Ponds *(Hawaii 543),* by the ocean at Hanapepe, reflect age-old salt-gathering practices. People say a luau isn't a luau without Hanapepe salt. The same families have been working the basins for hundreds of years. They were there when the Russians established a fort down the coast

Descendants of ancient Hawaiians still gather salt from the salt ponds at Hanapepe.

on the east bank of the Waimea River in 1816. Built by Dr. Georg Anton Scheffer, and named for the wife of Czar Alexander I, **Fort Elizabeth** *(Hawaii 53, near Milepost 22)* was the most prominent of several Russian forts established in Hanalei and Honolulu. The fort was completed by the Hawaiian army, who

outside Waimea, **Kiki a Ola** *(Menehune Rd., 1.5 miles from intersection with Hawaii 50)* is an unimpressive 2-foot stone wall. But it's all that's left of an aqueduct that once ran 5 miles up the Waimea River, an amazing engineering achievement attributed to the Menehune.

Polihale State Park is where civilization yields to the fortress

Did the Spanish Get There First?

Two centuries before Cook's voyages, Spanish galleons were sailing the 8,000-mile route from Mexico to the Philippines, carrying gold and silver one way, and silks, spices, and porcelain the other. Several Spanish navigational charts, secret in their day, do show islands at the latitude of Hawaii. In 1743, a Manila galleon carrying such a map was captured by the English. Cook carried a copy of that chart. French explorer Jean François de Galaup La Perouse, who sailed to Hawaii in 1786, wrote, "In the charts might be written: Sandwich Islands, surveyed in 1778 by Capt. Cook, who named them, but anciently discovered by the Spanish navigators." Hawaiian accounts support the theory. King Kamehameha II and others told the Reverend William Ellis about white-skinned foreigners who had landed eight generations earlier at Kealakekua Bay and immediately knelt in prayer. On Kauai, Cook's men discovered "many iron utensils," including a broken sword blade, convincing them the Spaniards were first.

occupied it until 1864, when the guns were removed. Nature has done its work on the 17-acre site, and walls once 30 feet thick are mere rubble.

On the opposite bank of the river, a cement slab in the mud marks the spot said to be the first footfall of Europeans on Hawaiian soil when Captain Cook anchored in Waimea Bay, January 20, 1778. A statue of the British explorer stands among palm trees in **Waimea** town.

At **Waimea Plantation Cottages,** actual plantation houses have been moved from all over the island, restored, decorated with period furniture, and rented to vacationers (see p. 257). Just

of Na Pali. To get there, follow Kaumualii Highway (Hawaii 50) to the end, then follow signs through sugarcane fields for 5 miles on dirt roads. The beach actually begins 15 miles away in Kekaha, wraps around the Mana Coastal Plain, and stretches out to the state park at the northwestern end of the beach. And these sands bark: The tiny grains are perforated with small cavities causing them to emit sounds when rubbed together by motion.

Polihale is three football fields wide and backed by 100-foot-high dunes. The safest place to swim is an inlet called **Queen's Pond.** Extreme caution is called for at this beautiful but remote beach. ■

Polihale State Park
Map p. 184

Waimea Canyon

It must have been quite an earthquake, because it almost split Kauai in two. Sometime in the Hawaiian dawn, long before sails appeared on any horizon, before even the Menehune, the earth convulsed and opened, and all the mountain streams that previously had their own paths now flowed into one river, the Waimea.

Helicopter tours are the easy way to explore the Grand Canyon of the Pacific.

As the swollen river swept to the sea, age after age, it carved the cleft in the earth into a magnificent canyon unlike any other in the Pacific.

Waimea Canyon has a continental grandeur to it, a visual scope associated with larger landscapes. You think of Arizona with its buttes, crags, and palette of earthen colors. It invites comparisons to America's Grand Canyon, and is called the "Grand Canyon of the Pacific." It's smaller, of course, 14 miles long and 3,567 feet deep, but the eye cannot see to its limits. It is the domain of wild goats and mouflon sheep, which you can see on precarious perches. Wild pigs inhabit the valley forests. From the rim of the canyon at Puu Ka Pele, the fire goddess is said to have leaped from Kauai to find a home on another island.

INSIDER TIP:

If you're interested in taking an ultra-light flight through the Waimea Canyon or along the Na Pali Coast, make your reservations early.

—SUSAN FIFER CANBY
National Geographic contributor

You can see Waimea Canyon by car from the lookouts, via hiking trails, on horseback, or from a helicopter (see p. 264).

Visiting the Canyon

From Kaumualii Highway (Hawaii 50) at Waimea, turn inland on **Waimea Canyon Drive** (Hawaii 550) for the 20-mile climb that skirts the canyon rim. At 6 miles it joins Kokee Road, from Kekaha. Get your first taste of Waimea by walking the 0.3-mile **Iliau Nature Lookout Trail** (between Mileposts 8 & 9), giving you your first breathtaking vista of canyon walls and waterfalls. Along the way, rare plants are identified on signs, including the *iliau,* a spectacular green relative of Maui's silversword (see pp. 140–141). At **Waimea Canyon Lookout** (between Mileposts 10 & 11), the natural masterpiece of the canyon unfolds, with three tributary canyons adding dimension. You will be impressed with the overwhelming quiet, as if all sound has fallen into the jaws of the gorge. You can see the silver ribbon of river below, and you may spot 800-foot **Waipoo Falls** to the

left, but you won't hear them. Graceful *koae kea* (white-tailed tropic birds) soar silently in the drafts of the canyon. You get another good view at **Puu Hina-hina Lookout** (between Mileposts 13 & 14).

From **Kokee State Park** (see pp. 204–205) several hiking trails explore the canyon. The canyon drive continues another 2 miles past the park to the cool and glorious **Kalalau Lookout,** 4,120 feet above the floor of this broad Na Pali Coast valley. No matter how many times you visit this site, it is never the same. It changes every moment as clouds sail in and out of the valley, and sunlight and shadows steal across the awesome green cliffs. It has the quality of light associated with Ireland, where brooding greenery is suddenly shot through with glowing sunlight. ■

EXPERIENCE:
On Location in Kauai

Hawaii Movie Tour's *(4-885 Kuhio Hwy., Kapaa, 808/539-9400 or 800/831-5541, hawaiimovietour.com, $$$$$)* famous, innovative, five-hour tour takes you to locations where Hollywood filmed major motion pictures on Kauai. On the way to each site, you'll see clips from the film on large video screens in the van, complete with surround sound. Among the sites you'll view are locations from *Jurassic Park, Blue Hawaii, South Pacific,* and that of the TV series *Gilligan's Island.* You can swing on a rope over a river as Harrison Ford did in *Raiders of the Lost Ark.* A picnic lunch is provided at beautiful Anini Beach County Park. The company now has additional tours so you can choose by the films you want to see.

Kokee

In the cool uplands of Kauai, high in the cloud forest above Waimea Canyon, lies a land strange to the tropics. The air is nippy, maybe in the 50s or 60s. No coconut palms here, only eucalyptus, fir, and redwood.

Kalalau Valley, often crowned in rainbows, is visible from the lookout at Kokee State Park.

Kokee State Park
- Map p. 184
- Hawaii 550. Headquarters at park entrance
- 808/587-0400 (Kauai Division of State Parks)

Kokee Natural History Museum
- Map p. 184
- 808/335-9975

Kokee State Park is 4,354 acres of forest, meadows, trout-filled streams, and hiking trails. From here you can look down at the Na Pali Coast, peer into Waimea Canyon, and explore the foggy dew of the Alakai Swamp, the wettest place in the world.

For a crash course in the legends, history, birds, and plants that you'll encounter at Kokee, your first stop is the **Kokee Natural History Museum.** It includes photographs, hiking maps, books, exhibits of flora, the head of a wild boar, and a mounted 6-pound rainbow trout, the Kokee record. You can also get trail maps, and information on weather and trail conditions, at park headquarters. Staff at the Kokee Lodge (tel 808/335-6061) right next to the museum are helpful. There is a restaurant there (closed 3:30 p.m.), and cabins for rent.

The first wildlife you'll meet, probably in the parking lot, are the moa. Though they look like common barnyard chickens, they are rare red jungle fowl, the last descendants of the poultry brought to Hawaii as domestic stock by early Polynesian settlers.

Kokee and the surrounding forest and swamp are the last stand for some of the world's rarest birds, like a honeycreeper called the *nuku-puu* and the *puaiohi,* a thrush that may be saved from extinction through captive breeding programs. The *kauai oo* has not been seen for some time and is now believed to be extinct. Other fauna are so prolific that the park has hunting seasons for wild boar, goats, black-tail deer, and game birds.

Walks in the Park

If you want to hike in the park, be sure to check weather conditions at headquarters and on the bulletin board of the museum. Bring plenty of drinking water and rain gear, and, most important of all, stay on established trails.

The easiest trail is the **Nature Walk** that begins behind the museum and makes a 0.1-mile loop through the rain forest. Plants along the way are identified.

The **Canyon Trail** runs 4.8 miles, skirting the rim of Waimea Canyon, passing through distressed koa forest that has been devastated by hurricanes, and then dipping down to Waipoo Falls with its pool fringed by ginger plants. Parts of the trail are strenuous and scary but the views are awesome. Allow four hours to complete the route.

The **Alakai Swamp Trail** traverses fascinating terrain. Alakai is the soggy bottom of a huge caldera, 13 miles in diameter and 4,000 feet above sea level. Parts of it have never been explored. Thigh-high mud used to be the norm on this 7-mile hike, but a new boardwalk across the swamp makes things easier. Alakai is the source of all the rivers on Kauai. Deep in the bog, trees take on a bonsai look because of the extreme dampness, growing only a foot tall, while ferns and violets tower overhead. Mosses are green, brown, orange, and even white. If the clouds clear, you may be treated to a view into Wainiha Valley, as big as Waimea but much less accessible. All along, you will be cheered by birdsong, a harmonious singing in rarest notes. ∎

Queen Emma's Journey

Queen Emma, intrigued by the descriptions of Alakai, in 1871 mounted an expedition into the wilderness. The 100-strong royal party started out on horseback, but the trail became so impenetrable the animals had to be left behind. Tree fern logs were dropped over the mud for the queen, who insisted on pausing for chants and hula along the way. This slowed things down, so that the party was forced to spend the night, soaked and chilled, in the swamp. The queen kept singing, cheering her companions.

The annual Eo e Emalani i Alakai Festival, which is held every October at Kokee State Park, celebrates Queen Emma's journey with drama and music performances, and hula displays.

More Places to Visit on Kauai

Anini Beach Park

The big attraction here is the 2-mile-long fringing reef that runs up to 1,600 feet out into the ocean. Between the reef and the golden sands of the shore there is a perfect turquoise lagoon. People come to Anini for swimming, windsurfing, snorkeling, diving, and fishing. You'll often see fishermen using the old Hawaiian throw-net technique. Poised on rock or reef, or in shallow water, they'll stand motionless, net carefully pleated under their arms, watching for fish. At the right moment, they whip out the net, arc it over the water like a cloud, then quickly haul it in with their catch. On summer Sunday afternoons, polo matches are held on the broad park lawns.

🅰 Map p. 185 ✉ From Kuhio Hwy. (Hawaii 56) take Kalihiwai Rd., then turn left on Anini Beach Rd.

INSIDER TIP:

Listen to live music as you sample the signature dishes of more than 50 of Hawaii's chefs at Taste of Hawaii, held in June at Smith's Tropical Paradise.

—KEN POSNEY
National Geographic contributor

Historic Waimea Walking Tour

When Capt. James Cook and his crew ventured northward from the South Pacific, they landed on Waimea, marking the beginning of vast changes to come for Hawaii. Missionaries arrived with a different belief system; disease and despair decimated a people; rice and sugar growers changed an economy. A free 90-minute tour begins at the West Kauai Technology and Visitor Center every Monday at 9:30 a.m.

🅰 Map p. 184 ✉ 9565 Kaumualii Hwy. (Hawaii 50), Waimea ☎ 808/338-1332

Na Aina Kai

Sitting on a promontory adjacent to Kilauea Point National Wildlife Refuge (see p. 195), this most unusual botanical garden is actually a collection of 12 gardens combining art and flora. More than 70 sculptures are situated beside and within lagoons, along garden paths, and in banks of flowers. Water features form an integral part of the garden. A hedge maze composed of 2,400 mock orange plants has a statuary surprise at the end of every path. The meat-eaters of the plant world lurk in the Carnivorous Plant House, where Venus flytraps and purple butterworts lie in wait armed with sweet-smelling deadly cocktails. In the middle is a bronze child pulling a water pump by artist Brenda Maltz.

🅰 Map p. 185 ✉ 4098 Wailapa Rd., Kilauea ☎ 808/828-0525

St. Catherine's Catholic Church

Inside this very modern house of worship at Kealia, on the Coconut Coast, are murals by three of Hawaii's most acclaimed artists: Jean Charlot (1898–1979), Juliette May Fraser (1887–1983), and Tseng Yu-ho (1923–). Miraculously, the murals were not damaged by Hurricane Iniki (see p. 188).

🅰 Map p. 185 ✉ 5021-A Kawaihau Rd., Kapaa ☎ 808/822-7900

Smith's Tropical Paradise

The many cultures of Kauai are celebrated in this well-maintained 30-acre garden at Kapaa on the Coconut Coast. You'll find a curved, red Japanese bridge over a stream, a thatched Hawaiian house with a taro patch, a lily pond, and tropical flowers. In the evening, the Smith family, who own the garden, stage a spectacular luau and show, reflecting the multiethnic theme. It features a Chinese Lion Dance with fireworks.

🅰 Map p. 185 ✉ 174 Wailua Rd., Kapaa ☎ 808/821-6896 🕐 Luau: Mon., Wed., & Fri. evenings

A small, undeveloped island with big attractions—Hawaii's tallest waterfall and the world's highest sea cliffs

Molokai

A statue of Father Damien draped in leis

Molokai

The ancient name of the island is Molokai Pule Oo (Molokai of the Powerful Prayer). It is the heart of Hawaii, not only geographically, but in the infinitely larger matters of the spirit. A mere 22 miles across the Kaiwi Channel from Honolulu, Molokai is wild, unspoiled, and very Hawaiian.

Fifth largest of the Hawaiian Islands, Molokai is a mere 38 miles from end to end and 10 miles wide. A fringe of ancient fishponds scallops the shoreline. The highest mountain is Mauna Kamakou at 4,970 feet.

Because of its small size, and its strategic position in the center of the island chain, Molokai would have been a plum in the many interisland wars of old. Its saving grace was the reputation of its *kahuna* (priests), who practiced a fearsome sorcery. The island's largest temple, Iliiliopae, whose altars ran red with human blood, was notorious throughout Hawaii. A grove of *kukui* trees, still regarded as sacred, marks the burial site of Lanikaula, the most powerful of the kahuna.

Molokai's internationally famous man of prayer was Father Damien, a Belgian-born Roman Catholic priest who devoted his life to the victims of Hansen's disease (leprosy), living exiled on Makanalua Peninsula, now Kalaupapa National Historical Park. To reach it, you fly in by small plane, hike down a sheer palisade, or take the Molokai Mule Ride.

Many people believe the hula (see p. 170) was born on Molokai, and the island's biggest festival, Ka Hula Piko, celebrates the assertion every May. Hula groups come from around the state for a day of music, dance, arts, and eating.

Molokai isn't for everyone. If you're looking for nightclubs, gourmet dining, or cute boutiques, you'll be disappointed. As for cuisine,

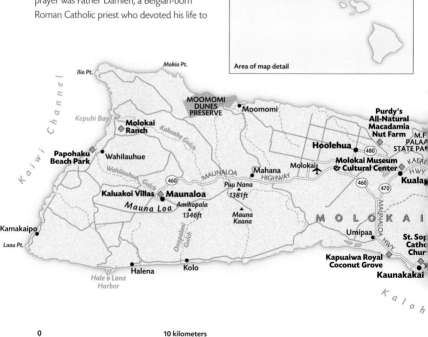

Area of map detail

NOT TO BE MISSED:

fresh seafood and vegetables from local farms will have to suffice. Instead of excitement you get serenity, plus recklessly lovely scenery, small towns, big beaches, and a feeling of incredible freedom.

The first Westerner to set foot on the island was Capt. George Dixon, who landed uneventfully in 1786. Kamehameha the Great's arrival in 1795 was another matter. The warrior chief beached his war canoes at Pakuhiwa and tucked this small island into his kingdom. The missionaries arrived in 1832 and estimated the population to be about 6,000, which is not much under its present count of 7,686.

Molokai entered the 20th century as a quiet island of ranches and pineapple fields. When Del Monte closed its plantation in 1982, the island sank into an economic depression from which it has yet to recover.

If recovery means development, many islanders prefer their poverty, relying on the gifts of land and sea for subsistence, supplemented by various forms of welfare. Activists are outspoken in their defense of the environment and their right to live a traditional culture-based, nature-centered way of life in one of the last places in Hawaii where this is possible.

Despite its problems, Molokai prides itself on being "the Friendly Isle." The majority of people are native Hawaiian, and the spirit of aloha is the governing principle. ■

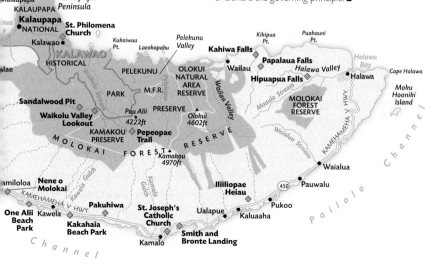

Central Molokai

Molokai's action center is Kaunakakai, in the middle of the south coast. The main street, Ala Malama, is three blocks long, its old wooden storefronts making the place look like a movie set from a vintage Western.

Kaunakakai may be one of Hawaii's smallest towns, but residents still put on an Aloha Week Parade in full regalia.

Kaunakakai

◪ Map p. 208

Visitor Information

✉ Molokai Visitors Bureau, 2 Kamoi St., Ste. 200, Kaunakakai

☎ 808/553-3876

🕐 Closed Sat.–Sun.

Kapuaiwa Royal Coconut Grove

◪ Map p. 208

✉ Maunaloa Hwy. (Hawaii 460), 2 miles W of Kaunakakai

If you want to laugh, visit the **Molokai Fish & Dive shop** *(Ala Malama, tel 808/553-5926, closed Sun. p.m.)* and read what's written on its collection of T-shirts. In late afternoon trucks pull up in front of the post office *(Ala Malama)* selling just caught fish, shrimp raised in local ponds, and homemade *laulau* (ti-leaf-wrapped packets of steamed fish, pork, and taro greens). If you walk out to the end of the big stone jetty and look back toward land, you'll have a wonderful view of the island, from the golden sand beach to the

mountains with gauzy clouds about their heads.

Around 10 at night, people hurry to the back door of **Kanemitsu Bakery** *(Ala Malama, tel 808/553-5855, closed Tues.)*, knock, and whisper the variety they want of famous Molokai sweet bread—pineapple, coconut, taro, cheddar—hot and fragrant from the oven. Condo renters have the adventure of shopping for all their other grocery needs such as fresh fish, taro greens, and bananas at the legendary **Misaki's Grocery and Dry Goods** store *(Ala Malama, tel 808/553-5505)*.

Molokai's only traffic jam of note happens on Sunday morning when all seven Hawaiian churches along Church Row let out about the same time, around 11 a.m. Visitors are always welcome, and attending services in one of these small chapels is an experience in aloha. The singing in Hawaiian is wonderful. The Catholic church, **St. Sophia** (*Ala Malama, tel 808/553-5220*) sits under a blazing orange tulip tree.

Across from the row of tidy churches, by the seaside, you'll see a thousand towering coconut trees planted on 10 acres in 1863 by Chief Kapuaiwa, who was

INSIDER TIP:

The royal grove of coconut trees at Kapuaiwa on Molokai's south shore is a great location for a sunset image. Beware of falling coconuts. A falling coconut can easily shatter a windshield.

—JOHN SEATON CALLAHAN
National Geographic contributor

soon to be crowned as Kamehameha V. **Kapuaiwa Royal Coconut Grove** is a beautiful place to watch the sunset.

The adjacent beach is a popular spot with families, and children are usually paddling and splashing about in the shallow waters. In the evening, outrigger canoes are launched from here as paddlers head out to practice their skills for the highly contested canoe races.

Northwest of Kaunakakai

At Hoolehua near the airport, **Purdy's All-Natural Macadamia Nut Farm** (Na Hua o Ka Aina) is as famous for the quality of its nuts as it is for the aloha spirit of the farm's owner, Tuddie Purdy. Stop by for a free tour conducted by Tuddie, who will tell you all you ever wanted to know about the life cycle of the macadamia nut. He'll do it with charm and humor, and with tasty samples along the way, of course.

The **Molokai Museum & Cultural Center** is housed in Hawaii's smallest sugar mill. Built in 1878, it displays old photos of plantation life and early Molokai, and has been fully restored to working order. It is on the National Register of Historic Places. Festivals and a schedule of crafts classes take place in the adjoining sugar museum. It is a very peaceful and picturesque site.

Two miles farther along, at **Palaau State Park,** you'll find an interesting, even intimidating rock nestled in the cool upland forest, easily reached by a short trail. In ancient times, barren women slept beneath the 6-foot Phallic Rock and reportedly had no infertility problems later. The rock's name is Ka Ule o Nanahoa, and its shape is not entirely natural (ancient stoneworkers skillfully enhanced it). The 234-acre park also has an arboretum and a commanding view of Kalaupapa Peninsula (see p. 217). The trailhead down the cliff is here, and you'll often see mule riders negotiating the sheer route. ■

Purdy's All-Natural Macadamia Nut Farm

- Map p. 208
- Lihipali Ave., behind Molokai High School, Hoolehua
- 808/567-6601
- Closed Sun. & Mon.

Molokai Museum & Cultural Center

- Map p. 208
- Kalae Hwy. (Hawaii 470), just after Ironwood Hills Golf Course sign
- 808/567-6436
- Closed Sun.
- $

Palaau State Park

- Map p. 208
- Kalae Hwy. (Hawaii 470), 3 miles N of Kualapuu
- 808/567-6923

Kalaupapa National Historical Park

A black lava shoreline of tempestuous surf and riptides surrounds the park on three sides. On the fourth is a sheer palisade, 2,000 to 3,000 feet high. It is a magnificent natural prison.

Mule riders brave the hairpin turns of the trail down the face of a cliff to Kalaupapa.

Kalaupapa National Historical Park

Map p. 209

The Hawaiian people had lived isolated from other cultures for so long that they had no resistance to European and Asian illnesses, from the common cold to leprosy. The first authenticated case of Hansen's disease (leprosy) appeared in the Hawaiian Islands in 1840. By 1868, it had cut such a swath through the population that King Kamehameha V, in desperation, decreed a policy of isolation for those infected, and established the remote peninsula of Kalaupapa on Molokai as the place of confinement.

Government officials imagined that the people, who were normally so self-reliant, would farm and provide for themselves. Instead, Kalaupapa became a wild and hostile social environment, for the exiles had nothing to lose; their watchword was "Prepare for Molokai as for the grave." They lived in caves, under rocks, and in

INSIDER TIP:

The plain glass windows of St. Philomena Church are aligned to allow the trade winds to flow directly through the building.

—RITA ARIYOSHI
National Geographic author

trees; a fortunate few had crude huts. They fought over the meager rations sent over from Honolulu.

Although a cure was found for Hansen's disease in 1946, about 60 former patients chose to live out their lives at Kalaupapa. You may visit the colony only on an organized tour.

The **Molokai Mule Ride** will take you on an all-day adventure, riding on a well-trained mule down the cliff trail from "topside" at Palaau to Kalaupapa. In 2.9 miles, this vertiginous route descends 1,600 feet to sea level with 26 hairpin turns, each numbered so you can chart your progress. You can also tell how close you're getting by the volume of the roaring surf. At Kalaupapa, in addition to hauntingly beautiful scenery, including small offshore islands and the tallest sea cliffs in the world, you will see Father Damien's little **St. Philomena Church,** his grave, a museum, the volcanic crater that formed the peninsula, and a memorial to Mother Marianne, a Franciscan nun from Utica, New York, who arrived at the colony in 1888, five months before Father Damien died. She continued his work and died at Kalaupapa in 1918 at the age of 81. Both Father Damien and Mother Marianne have been canonized as saints by the Catholic Church. ■

**Molokai
Mule Ride**

✉ 100 Kalae Hwy. (Hawaii 470)

☎ 808/567-6088 or 800/567-7550

$ $$$$$

**Father Damien
Tours**

✉ P.O. Box 1, Kalaupapa, HI 96742

☎ 808/567-6171 Fax: 808/567-6171

$ $$$$$

Father Damien

The 33-year-old Roman Catholic priest, Joseph de Veuster, who became known as Father Damien, stepped ashore at Kalaupapa leper colony on May 10, 1873. He immediately besieged the Board of Health, the crown, and the church with requests for building supplies, medicine, food, and clothing. He refused to sleep indoors until every patient had decent shelter, curling up under a *hala* (pandanus) tree beside tiny St. Philomena Church. With the help of the patients, he built cottages, roads, a wharf, and an orphanage for infected children. He started farms and laid the pipes for a water system that is in use today. He dressed wounds, built coffins, and almost daily buried the dead, 6,000 of them in

his time. St. Philomena Church became a place of celebration. The church was strewn with leis and fragrant flowers, and though leprosy attacks the vocal chords, he assembled choirs. At times it took two people to play the organ so that there would be ten fingers to make the music.

Damien was diagnosed with leprosy in 1885 and died in 1889. He was buried beneath the *hala* tree. In 1936, amid great lamentations, his body was exhumed and returned to Belgium, his place of birth. In 1995, Pope John Paul II beatified the priest, and the bones of his right hand were given to a delegation of Kalaupapa patients. They were reinterred beneath the *hala* tree with full state honors at a Mass and luau.

East End Drive

Kamehameha V Highway (Hawaii 450) skirts the southeastern and eastern shores of Molokai, with mountains on one side and the ocean on the other, ending at one of the most beautiful valleys in the world, Halawa. When setting out from Kaunakakai, have a full tank of gas, drinking water, and food.

Some 60 fishponds that scallop the shoreline are among the best preserved in Hawaii, although most are in disrepair. On the outskirts of town, you'll see your first one, **Kalokoeli ❶**. It's just past the Molokai Shores Condominium on the oceanside of Aahi Place.

Beyond Milepost 4, at what appears to be two barnlike houses, Hawaii's state bird, the endangered nene, is being raised for release into the wild. The nonprofit **Nene o Molokai ❷** *(tel 808/553-5992, by appointment only)* offers free one-hour tours.

The Kawela area you'll be passing through was the scene of a fierce battle in 1786 for control of Molokai. **Kakahaia Beach Park** *(6 miles from Kaunakakai)* is a national wildlife refuge, and a good place to bird-watch.

The tiny white church with the high white steeple, just past Mile 10, is **St. Joseph's Catholic Church ❸**, built in 1876 by Father Damien (see p. 213). The Damien statue in front of the church always wears a lei of fresh flowers.

About a mile farther, a Hawaii Visitors Bureau sign marks **Smith and Bronte Landing**. In 1927, the first civilian flight from California to Honolulu ended upside down here in a *kiawe* tree. Ernest Smith and Emory Bronte emerged shaken but unhurt. The story is interesting but the site's a shrug.

To see a fishpond that's in working order, stop at **Ualapue ❹**, just after Mile 13, where mullet are being raised.

Father Damien in 1874 built **Our Lady of Seven Sorrows Catholic Church** at Kaluaaha. You'll see its red roof standing out against the lush green background on the *mauka* (upland) side of the road.

NOT TO BE MISSED:

Nene o Molokai • St. Joseph's Catholic Church • Ualapue Fishpond • Iliiliopae Heiau • Halawa Valley

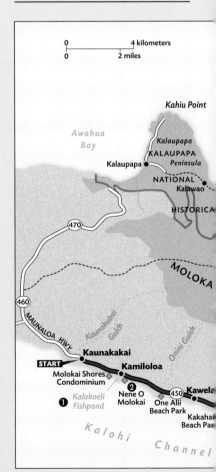

The oldest and largest *heiau* (temple) on the island, and the second largest in the state, is 13th-century **Iliiliopae 5,** now on the National Register of Historic Places. Pick up a five-minute trail between Miles 15 and 16.

At Pukoo, just before Mile 16, is **Manae Goods & Grindz 6** *(tel 808/558-8498),* your last chance for water and food. The roughest and most spectacular part of the drive is in front of you.

The road twists around blind bends, clinging to cliff faces and dipping down to lonely bays such as Honouli Maloo and Honouli Wai. Between the two, the road hugs a huge boulder called **Pohakuloa 7.**

In the last few miles before **Halawa 8,** the road climbs inland through the grasslands and hills of **Puu o Hoku Ranch.** When it comes to the sea again, it makes a hairpin turn, and below you will be the dark sands, the stream, and the waterfalls of **Halawa Valley** (see pp. 216–217). The view from the pullout near Mile 26 is breathtaking.

You can drive down to the beach park. If you wade across the stream, which should be attempted only in summer, there's a nice swimming beach. When the bay is turbulent, beware of the currents and riptides. A guided hike to the 250-foot **Moaula Falls** can be arranged.

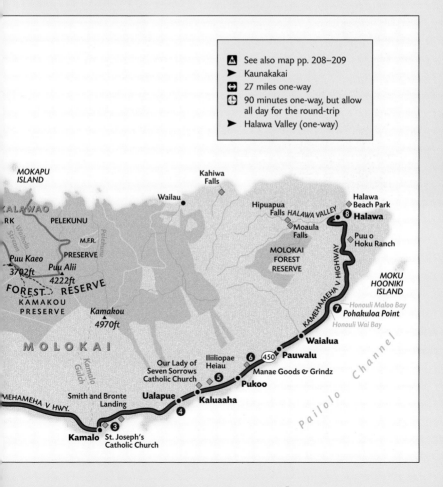

◩	See also map pp. 208–209
▶	Kaunakakai
⬌	27 miles one-way
◷	90 minutes one-way, but allow all day for the round-trip
▶	Halawa Valley (one-way)

Halawa Valley & the North Shore

Molokai looks something like a fish, long and slender, the North Shore its spine and Kalaupapa Peninsula its dorsal fin. Along the coast, from Kalaupapa to Halawa, emerald green sea cliffs rise from an ocean the colors of peacock's feathers. The ramparts tower to almost 4,000 feet, their peaks crowned in mists.

Halawa Valley is the first and most accessible of the magnificent North Shore valleys.

Waterfalls tumble in spectacular columns from their heights. Teased by the trade winds, they live up to the Hawaiian word for waterfall, *wailele* (leaping water), as they leap and dance upward in breeze-tossed veils. The record holder is Kahiwa, "the sacred one," at 1,750 feet. Their names sing like their waters: Puukaoku, Oloupena, Haloku, Hipuapua, and Papalaua.

The nearly vertical forests support some of the rarest plants on Earth. To save them, dedicated botanists rappel down cliffs, thousands of feet above the roaring surf. They have built a fence around the last survivor of a species of *loulu* palm *(Pritchardia munroi)* to protect it from goats. In the absence of pollinators, which are probably extinct, the scientists themselves pollinate the creamy flowers of a succulent-stemmed *Brighamia rockii*. Fewer than 200 survive in the wild, although they are now being propagated at the National Tropical Botanical Garden on Kauai (see pp. 190–191).

Halawa was one of the earliest Polynesian settlements in Hawaii, farmed for more than a thousand years. All that changed on April 1, 1946, when a 45-foot wave roared across the valley, destroying major sections of the ancient *kalo loi* (flooded taro fields). Another tsunami inundated the valley in 1957, finishing off the taro. Most people abandoned the valley. Only recently, a new generation has started reviving agriculture and resettling Halawa (see p. 215).

Wailau ("many waters") is the largest valley. There is no way in but from the ocean. This was no problem for the ancient Hawaiians, who used the ocean as their highway. Fishermen and taro farmers settled the valley, dwelling between green walls that rise to 4,970 feet. Silver ribbons of waterfalls coursing down the mountain walls fed a skein of streams coursing to the sea. The last of the people left for work and a more comfortable life in town, and the public school closed in 1920. The taro still grows untended, and there are mango, banana, guava, papaya, and avocado trees for the plucking.

Pelekunu Valley is so narrow and its walls so high that the sun's rays find it only four or five hours in a day. It rains almost half the time. In the old days, fishermen had to travel to Kalaupapa and Moomomi to find enough sunshine to dry their fish. The lyrical sounding name means "moldy smell." It's so lovely to look at, intrepid people of the 20th century periodically carved little niches for themselves and lived for periods in the glorious gloom. John H. Wilson, the engineer who

built a road over Oahu's precarious Nuuanu Pali (see p. 65) and for whom Oahu's Wilson Tunnel is named, lived here with his wife, Jennie, who was born in Pelekunu. Author Audrey Sutherlin swam

Fishponds

Before Christopher Columbus landed in America, Hawaiians had perfected an aquaculture system that is being examined and restored today. Typically, stone walls were built into the sea in a semicircle from one point of land to another. An ingenious system of gates and grates allowed for circulation of fresh seawater, and the capture of fish on incoming tides. Fish would be raised and fattened in the ponds for a steady supply of seafood.

from Halawa to Pelekunu towing a raft with construction materials for a home, then wrote about life on the North Shore in *Paddling My Own Canoe*.

The waters of Waikolu bring life to **Kalaupapa Peninsula.** It was this stream that Father Damien (see p. 213) tapped to build his irrigation system for crops to feed the leper colony. An irrigation tunnel also carries water to the arid west end of the island.

No roads invade this wilderness of water and cliffs. Kamehameha V Highway gets as far as Halawa and is thwarted by the terrain. ■

Molokai With Native Guides

Exploring the island with islanders offers visitors a personal perspective on Molokai. Native guides are experts in fields such as Hawaiian culture, ocean activities, or hiking. Many of them have access to special places on private lands. Most guides, like the two featured below, will customize their tours to suit visitors' interests.

Walter Naki explains taro growing on one of his cultural tours.

Walter Naki *(Ma a Molokai Action Adventures, tel 808/558-8184, $$$$$)* has been a teacher of marine studies, youth counselor, member of the Army National Guard, decathlon champion, and fitness teacher. He quit his job to share his adventures with visitors, and he enjoys taking people on hikes.

Walter is also a hunting guide for deer, wild boar, and goats—hunting can be done with rifle or bow and arrow. He can skin a deer in 15 minutes, then process and pad the meat on the spot. He offers culture tours visiting taro farms and fishponds. He also has a snorkel and beach-cookout excursion, and, weather permitting, a North Shore boat ride to several waterfalls and a black-sand beach for a picnic. Tours are customized and can be any length from a half day to four or five days.

Anakala Pilipo Solatorio, last Hawaiian native born and still living in Halawa Valley

Anakala Pilipo Solatorio *(Halawa Ohana Loi Kalo, tel 808/567-9292, $$$$)* is the last native Hawaiian who was born, raised, and still lives in magnificent, remote Halawa Valley. He and his family open their home to visitors, by appointment. His Mooula Waterfall Hike begins in the outdoor classroom of the Hawaiian Learning Center and proceeds past ancient archaeological sites to the falls for a picnic, swim, and talk story. Or you can just hang out and work in the taro patch, up to your thighs in mud. It's actually fun. Freshly pounded poi with a clean coconutty taste is your reward.

To learn more about native guides or ocean and land activities, contact **Molokai Outdoor Activities** *(P.O. Box 1236, Kaunakakai, Molokai, 96748, tel 808/533-4477, molokai-outdoors.com)* or Molokai Fish & Dive (see p. 210).

Kamakou Preserve

This 2,774-acre preserve was established to protect the best forests on Molokai. Its terrain ranges from gulch bottoms to summit rain forest, with the crowning glory being the montane bog, Pepeopae, at the top of the mountain.

Within the preserve are at least 250 kinds of plants, 219 of them exclusive to Hawaii. The unique environment shelters rare and endangered birds like the *olomao* (Molokai thrush), and the *kakawahie* (Molokai creeper), whose sole remaining habitat on the planet is Kamakou Preserve.

The preserve is managed by the Nature Conservancy, a nonprofit organization that protects ecologically important lands and waters worldwide. You can hike the **Pepeopae Trail** on your own, but you'll really appreciate the preserve if you go on one of the monthly hikes led by Nature Conservancy staff and volunteers.

To reach the start, you'll need a 4WD vehicle. You hike on a boardwalk surrounded by tree ferns and ohia trees. Birds trill in the trees, and lush, spongy mosses drip at the wayside. The change from rain forest to bog is abrupt. The forest does not diminish, it simply stops, as if on command. Before you is a vast, orderly garden of 4-inch-tall ohia trees with glorious scarlet blossoms as big as the plant, mounds of grasses, and mosses shaded from russet to silver. Tended only by the winds and rains, mist, and sunshine, wild Pepeopae looks as if lovingly nurtured by a bonsai gardener. From the viewing platform here, the rest of Molokai lies below.

A hiker sets up his tripod in the native cloud forest at Kamakou Preserve.

There are two interesting stops on the Forest Reserve Road leading to Kamakou. The **Sandalwood Pit** is a ship-shaped depression in the earth. In the days of the sandalwood trade, Hawaiians would toss the cut timber into the hull-size pit. When it was full, they hauled the fragrant cargo down the mountain to China-bound ships.

Waikolu Valley Lookout overhangs a notch in the mountains where waterfalls plunge into unseen depths and the ocean laps at the lips of the valley. ∎

Pepeopae Trail
 Map p. 209

Nature Conservancy of Hawaii
✉ 923 Nuuanu Ave., Honolulu, HI 96817
☎ 808/537-4508 or 808/553-5236 (Molokai)

EXPERIENCE: Hiking Hawaii

If you want to see Hawaii's glorious outdoors, hear the birds sing, and feel sun, rain, heat, and cold—possibly on the same day—then take a hike. Hikes in the Hawaiian Islands, guided or unguided, range from mild and moderate to strenuous and rugged. Here are some of the best.

Molokai

Remote, wild **Halawa Valley,** on the island's northeast coast, is Molokai's oldest settlement, dotted with temple ruins. It can only be seen by guided hike; contact the **Halawa Ohana Loi Kalo** *(tel 808/567-9202, gomolokai.com).*

The Nature Conservancy of Hawaii provides a monthly guided 3-mile hike of **Kamakou Preserve** *(tel 808/553-5236; see p. 219),* a rain forest alive with more than 250 species of Hawaiian plants.

Lanai

A favorite hiking spot is **Koloiki Ridge,** with its forested uplands giving way to Pacific views. Take a 5-mile loop; or the nearly 10-mile Munro Trail to the island's highest point at Lanaihale for a five-island panorama. The **Four Seasons Resort Lanai, Lodge at Koele** *(tel 808/565-4000, fourseasons.com/koele, $$$$$)* offers guided hikes.

Oahu

Moderate treks include the paved **Diamond Head Trail,** a 0.7-mile ascent up more than 100 stairs and through World War II tunnels. At the top is a 360-degree panorama of Waikiki.

The Clean Air Team *(tel 808/948-3299, unclejackin hawaii.com),* led by Jack Christensen, conducts a free **President Obama's Hawaii Nei** walking tour of young Barry's Honolulu. See the website for other free walks.

The 1.5-mile, round-trip **Kanealole Trail** in the Makiki Forest Recreation Area—one of several trails here—is an excellent way to get to know this verdant forest. The **Hawaii**

INSIDER TIP:

Drive to Oahu's Nuuanu Pali Lookout to hike down Old Pali Road. A small path under Pali Highway leads through lush rain forest.

—YANNIS PAPASTAMATIOU
National Geographic field scientist

Nature Center *(2131 Makiki Heights Dr., tel 808/955-0100)* has trail information and sponsors weekend hikes.

Maui

You'll find fabulous hiking at **Haleakala National Park** (see pp. 140–142). Summit hikers often start at the **Halemauu trailhead;** the trail switchbacks steeply down the spectacular northwest wall of the wilderness area.

Iao Valley (see pp. 133–135) near Wailuku offers some easy, beautiful hikes; for a view of the Iao Needle, follow the paved path from the state park parking lot along the stream.

Kauai

The fabled, very strenuous **Kalalau Trail** (see pp. 198–199) winds 11 miles along the Na Pali cliffs between Kee Beach and Kalalau Beach; the first 2 miles from Kee Beach will give a good feel for the spectacular beauty.

Waimea Canyon (see pp. 202–203) and neighboring **Kokee State Park** (see pp. 204–205) have a plethora of magnificent trails. Try the **Canyon Trail** from Kokee, highlighted by a 360-degree view of the canyon.

Big Island

Hike to an active lava flow at **Kilauea** (see pp. 168–169, 171, & 173–177), off Chain of Craters Road; ask at the visitor center for current lava flow information.

In North Kohola, the 4-mile trail beginning at the end of Hwy. 270 offers breathtaking views of the majestic **Pololu Valley.** To explore the equally gorgeous **Waipio Valley** (see p. 165), hike down from the Waipio Valley Lookout to the valley floor and wander across the wide open expanse of jungle trees and gurgling streams.

Information

For general information: hawaiitrails.org/home; or **State of Hawaii** *(1151 Punchbowl St., Rm. 310, Honolulu 96813, tel 808/587-0300).*

Moomomi Dunes

The Moomomi Dunes rise along the northwest coast of the island, in view of the Kalaupapa Lighthouse. The 920-acre preserve, managed by the Nature Conservancy of Hawaii, is the best remaining area of native strand vegetation in the state.

Wind scours the lonely stretch of beach at Moomomi Dunes.

There is utter isolation and a feeling of freedom here. Moomomi is windswept, salt-sprayed, and uncompromising. There's a rocky ledge offshore, so the ocean arrives in great plumes.

Clinging tenaciously to this wild landscape are tiny, low-to-the-ground plants. The silvery green *hinahina (Heliotropium anamalum)* colonizes the dunes, almost hiding its fragrant, tiny white blossoms. The leaves of the pale silver *enaena (Gnaphalium sandwicensium)* feel as soft as a baby seal's coat. The vine *Pau-o-Hiiaka* is said to have appeared first at Moomomi, to cover the goddess Hiiaka and protect her from the sun as she slept.

The people of Pelekunu (see p. 217) used to come out of their rainy valley to dry fish here, living in the shelter caves lining the beach. Important archaeological sites at the dunes revealed bones of a flightless ibis, a 4-foot goose *(moa nalu)* that laid coconut-size eggs, a long-legged owl, and an oceanic eagle, all long extinct. The area is still visited by native shorebirds, the *hunakai* (sanderling) and *kolea* (golden plover). Endangered Hawaiian monk seals haul themselves out of the ocean for sunbaths, and green sea turtles steal ashore at night to hide their eggs in the dunes.

There's a gold-sand beach here, but the wind often drives the sand about. Bring drinking water, a hat, and sunscreen. The Nature Conservancy offers monthly hikes *(tel 808/553-5236)*. Jeep trails crisscross the terrain; it's a 20-minute walk from the parking area to the beach. ■

Moomomi Dunes

- Map p. 208
- Hawaii 480, 3 miles W of Hoolehua town

Western Molokai

"About 100 years ago the land that is now owned by the stockholders of the Molokai Ranch, Limited, was a cattle ranch belonging to the High Chief Kapuaiwa [in 1863], who later became King Kamehameha V."   — George Paul Cooke, *Moolelo o Molokai*, 1949

Molokai Ranch
Map p. 208

Maunaloa
Map p. 208

Papohaku Beach Park
Map p. 208
Kaluakoi Rd.

Fast-forward to late March 2008 when **Molokai Ranch** and most of its considerable enterprises ceased major operations. News of the shutdown stunned 120 employees and a community of islanders and visitors whose lives had become an integral part of the ranch.

For years, some residents and developers have waged a battle over the nature of development, water for the dry west side, and "keeping Molokai Molokai." This complex struggle has its roots stretching back decades. In the early 1900s, the owners were ranchers and farmers Charles M. Cooke and his son, George P. Cooke. Pineapple became an industry by the 1920s and **Maunaloa** town was developed to house immigrant workers. The pineapple companies closed in 1988, and the Cooke family sold its holdings to Brierly Investments Ltd., later known as GuocoLeisure Ltd., a Singapore-based firm that now owns the ranch's estimated 64,000 acres, roughly 35 percent of the island.

GuocoLeisure's 2004 plan to build 200 seaside luxury homes at Laau Point, on the island's southwest side, was put forward. Those who wanted Laau Point, a jewel by the ocean, preserved in perpetuity opposed the plan. Also, in January 2004 the Hawaii Supreme Court had reversed the ranch's previous (1998) state approval to develop a new water source and to take more than 1 million gallons of water a day from ranch land above Kaunakakai. Molokai Ranch declared itself no more in March 2008, its future in question.

There are, however, signs of life at **Maunaloa,** the once sleepy plantation town. Kites billow from the ceiling of the colorful **Big Wind Kite Factory** *(tel 808/552-2364);* the post office, the General Store, and the **Kaluakoi Villas** *(tel 877/367-1912 or 808/545-3510)* conduct business as usual.

Five miles northwest of Maunaloa, the white sands of **Papohaku Beach** run for 3 miles beside a turquoise ocean; underneath, powerful rip currents render the ocean treacherous for swimmers. In May, the picnic-friendly beach park is the site for **Ka Hula Piko,** the island's biggest festival, in honor of Laka, the ancient goddess of the dance. ∎

A rugged little island with two luxury resorts, two championship golf courses—and plenty of privacy

Lanai

Stone marker at the Garden of the Gods

Lanai

Lanai is shaped like a crusty oyster, but for the few who have discovered its pleasures, Lanai is a pearl. Once the world's largest pineapple plantation, it is now a retreat for the rich and famous, and those who want to try the lifestyle for a while.

Least known of the major Hawaiian Islands, Lanai was formed by a single volcano, giving it a configuration unusual in the archipelago. The single mountain is eroded into deep, red gorges that end in cliffs at the sea or taper into lonely beaches. The only way to get around on your own is to rent a 4WD vehicle. There are few paved roads.

The volcano's caldera is the broad, fertile Palawai Basin, which was once the island's pineapple basket. The fog and mists now look ghostly hovering over empty fields.

Lanai is 17 miles long and 13 miles wide, 89,000 acres of serenity unmatched in Hawaii. There are 47 miles of coastline, scalloped into coves interrupted by 2,000-foot cliffs.

Considered to be the abode of demons, Lanai was uninhabited until the 15th century

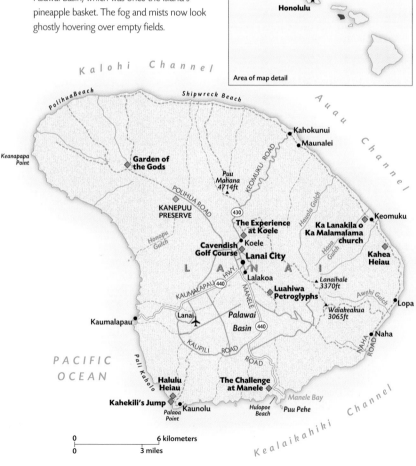

Tourists adventuring along the dirt roads of the island pile rocks upon each other in a kind of natural graffiti.

when Kaululaau, the rebellious son of a Maui king, was banished to the island. With cunning and daring, the young man vanquished the evil spirits residing there and made Lanai safe for habitation.

At least for a while. In 1778, a Big Island chief, Kalaniopuu, raided the island and killed almost everyone. In the party was a warrior named Kamehameha who would one day rule the islands, and return to Lanai to go fishing.

Two attempts were made to establish utopia on Lanai, once by the Mormon Church and then again by Walter Murray Gibson, who arrived in 1861. Both failed.

Others established short-lived sugar and ranching operations. In 1922, James Dole (see pp. 32–33) planted the island's first pineapple, and for the next 65 years the fruit was king, producing about 250 million pineapples a year.

In 1985, Los Angeles entrepreneur David H. Murdock purchased 98 percent of Lanai as part of the assets of a missionary-founded company. Murdock shut down the plantation and built two luxury hotels, forever changing the character of the island.

Billionaire Larry Ellison bought Lanai in 2013, then bought an airline to serve it. His plans for the island include expansion of the Four Seasons Manele Bay Hotel and a new hotel on the remote eastern shore. ■

NOT TO BE MISSED:

The marine sanctuary at Hulopoe Bay, an ideal spot to swim 226

Snorkeling at the sheltered haven of Manele Bay 226–227

Learning Hawaiian history at Kaunolu village 227

A walk along Shipwreck Beach, where ships were driven to shore by roaring winds prevalent between Maui and Molokai 227

The well-preserved Luahiwa petroglyphs outside Lanai City 230

Garden of the Gods, an ethereal moonscape experience without leaving Earth 230

A drive or a hike to the top of Lanaihale for a knock-your-socks-off view of five islands 230

Lanai *Makai*

To see Lanai *makai* (along the ocean), you have to visit the beaches in separate assaults, as there is no road that encircles the island. Hulopoe Beach and adjacent Manele Bay, in the south, form a state marine life conservation district.

A lone hiker ponders the legend of love gone bad at Puu Pehe, Sweetheart Rock.

Snorkeling is excellent, and spinner dolphins often come to play, interacting with swimmers at **Hulopoe,** the island's most popular beach. Most Lanai children learn to swim in the tidal pools of the lava apron on the left of the lovely sandy beach. To get there, go to the end of Manele Road (Hawaii 440), 8 miles south of Lanai City.

Manele, an ancient spatter cone, separates Hulopoe from the boat harbor. The red dirt cliffs fall sharply into a churning teal-blue sea. Offshore is a dramatic sea stack, **Puu Pehe**, or Sweetheart Rock. It takes its name from the legend of a beautiful Maui girl kidnapped by a young Lanai warrior who hid her on the rock. The girl drowned during a storm and the brokenhearted warrior threw himself from the cliff.

There are good views of the coast and Puu Pehe at the top of Manele, easily reached by a trail. Don't go near the edge, however, as the loosely packed cinders often slide away. **Manele Bay**, sheltered by cliffs, is a haven for visiting yachts, pleasure boats, and fishing craft. A cattle-loading chute from ranching days is cemented into the cliff outside the breakwater. Ruins of an ancient fishing village are hidden in the thickets.

To really get a feel for what life might have been like in these fishing villages, visit **Kaunolu,** a national historic landmark. It's reached by taking Manele Road (Hawaii 440) 4.5 miles south of Lanai City to Kaupili Road and then a dirt track; signs mark the

INSIDER TIP:

Along Hulopoe Bay, explore the tide pools filled with marine life, such as sea cucumbers, spaghetti worms, and sea stars.

—THELMA CHANG
*Author & National Geographic
contributor*

way. The site contains house foundations, remnants of trails, and the sacred remains of **Halulu Heiau,** an ancient temple. On the eastern end of the site is a 62-foot cliff called **Kahekili's Jump,** where warriors tested their courage by leaping out far enough over the sea to clear a treacherous ledge at the foot of the cliff. A timid leap ended in certain death.

Abandoned in the 19th century, some village platforms and walls are well preserved, and there's a fishing shrine. This was a favorite fishing retreat of Kamehameha the Great—the *aku*

(skipjack tuna) still run plentifully in offshore waters. To the right is the tallest sea cliff on Lanai, **Pali Kaholo,** rising 1,000 feet.

The island's most notorious strand of sand is 8-mile-long **Shipwreck Beach**—take Keomuku Road (Hawaii 44) to its end at Kahokunui, 8 miles northeast of Lanai City. The wild windswept place has earned its name. The earliest recorded shipwrecks were in the 1820s when an American and a British ship went aground. The reef has trapped hundreds of others over the years. The rusting hull of a World War II ship is still lashed by waves. Look for rocks painted white, marking the way to famous petroglyphs (see p. 26, p. 158, p. 230).

To the South

Along the dirt road to the south are isolated coves, with Maui looming almost close enough to touch. The ghost town of **Keomuku** is along the route. Abandoned when the sugar plantation failed, it once had a population of 2,000. The weathered wooden church, **Ka Lanakila o Ka Malamalama,** built in 1903, rests beneath the coconut trees. A little farther along, you'll see the *heiau* (temple) said to have caused the village to become a ghost town: When plantation managers used stones from **Kahea Heiau** to build a sugarcane railway, the sweet water of the district turned salty within a day, and many laborers died from a mysterious fever. The shoreline road runs 15 miles to Naha village, where you have to turn around and come back. ■

Hulopoe Beach
△ Map p. 224

Kaunolu
△ Map p. 224

Shipwreck Beach
△ Map p. 224

EXPERIENCE: Golfing in Hawaii

With more than 90 golf courses rolling across the hills of Hawaii, you could play two different courses a day for a month and never repeat yourself. The courses range from short and easy to long and tough, and are among the most beautiful anywhere. Special hazards include lava fields and crashing surf. But lucky golfers may spy offshore leaping whales. When making your golfing reservations, ask about special packages and lower "twilight" tee-time rates.

Lanai

Lanai has three golf courses. No reservations are needed for the public, nine-hole **Cavendish Golf Course** (Lanai City, tel 808/565-7300), and there are no greens fees. But golfers can, if they choose, make a donation to the Lanai Golf Association (P.O. Box 630-883, Lanai, HI 96763). The island's first resort course, **The Experience at Koele** (Four Seaons Resort Lanai, The Lodge at Koele, tel 808/565-4653, golflanai.com, resort & nonresort guests: $$$$$), opened in 1991. Its 390-yard eighth hole, with a drop of 250 feet to a wooded gorge, became instantly famous. The other championship course is **The Challenge at Manele** (Four Seasons Resort Lanai at Manele Bay, tel 808/565-2222, golflanai.com, resort & nonresort guests: $$$$$). It was designed by golf legend Jack Nicklaus to live up to its name, but with sets of five tees, players of all levels can enjoy a game.

Maui

On Maui's northwest shore, two 18-hole courses, **The Bay & The Plantation** (Kapalua Resort, tel 808/669-8044, kapalua.com, resort guests: $$$$$), are trendsetters. Championship venues, they are designated Certified Audubon Cooperative Sanctuaries, the only ones in Hawaii. The Kapalua Golf Academy offers a golf school, daily clinics, and practice facility.

Among Maui's many other quality greens: **Kaanapali Golf Resort** (Kaanapali Resort, tel 808/661-3691, kaanapaligolfresort.com, resort & nonresort guests: $$$$$) on the west coast; the **Wailea Golf Club** (Wailea Resort, tel 888/328-6284 or 808/875-7450, waileagolf.com, resort & nonresort guests: $$$$$) on the southern coast; and, also on the southern coast, **Makena Golf Courses** (Maui Prince Hotel, tel 808/891-4000 or 808/879-4000, prince resortshawaii.com, hotel and nonhotel guests: $$$$$).

Hawaii: the Big Island

Some of the Big Island's top courses located on the Kohala Coast include: the newly renovated **Mauna Kea** (Mauna Kea Resort, tel 808/882-5400, maunakearesort.com, resort & nonresort guests: $$$$$); **Waikoloa Golf Courses** (tel 808/886-7888, waikoloabeachresort.com, Waikoloa Beach Resort & nonresort guests: $$$$$); the **Hapuna Golf Course** (tel 888/9-PRINCE or 808/

880-3000, princeresorts hawaii.com, resort & nonresort guests: $$$$$); and **Francis H. Li Brown Course** (Mauna Lani Resort, tel 808/885-6655, maunalani.com, resort guests & nonresidents: $$$$$).

INSIDER TIP:

Koolau Golf Club on Oahu has the most challenging course in the U.S. because of its rugged natural elements, including winding ravines.

—THELMA CHANG
Author & National Geographic contributor

Kauai

Kauai golf courses are set amid some of Hawaii's most extravagant scenery. The **St. Regis Princeville** courses (Princeville Resort, tel 808/826-3580 or 800/826-4400, princeville.com, resort & nonresort guests: $$$$$) are renowned in this regard. The **Prince Golf Course** at (Princeville at Hanalei, tel 800/826-1105 or 808/826-5070, princeville.com, resort & nonresort guests: $$$$$) on Kauai's northern shore is known as a masterpiece. The

Bernhard Langer of Germany tees off at the 11th hole at the 2005 Sony Open, at Waialae Country Club in Honolulu.

Kukuiolono *(tel 808/332-9151, $$)*, a nine-hole course that opened in 1928 at Kalaheo, is a bargain. **Kauai Lagoons Golf Club** *(Kauai Marriott Resort & Beach Club, Kalapaki Beach, Lihue, tel 808/241-6000, marriottgolf.com, resort & nonresort guests: $$$$$)* boasts two championship courses.

Oahu
At Kaneohe, the **Koolau Golf Club** *(tel 808/236-4653, koolaugolf.com, $$$$$)* has three distinct climate zones and features waterfalls, winding ravines, and extreme changes in elevation. Architect Ted Robinson designed the **Ko Olina Golf Club** *(Ko Olina Resort & Marina, tel 808/676-5300, koolinagolf.com, resort & nonresort guests: $$$$$)* on the leeward coast and included his signature water features. The **Hawaii Prince Golf Club** *(tel 808/944-4567, princeresortshawaii.com, $$$$$)*, an hour's drive west of Waikiki, was designed by Arnold Palmer and Ed Seay.

Lanai *Mauka*

Mauka means "upland." Lanai's one and only town, optimistically called Lanai City, sits at a cool elevation of 1,600 feet amid stands of tall Cook Island pine trees. Small, vintage 1920s plantation homes, with exuberant gardens, line the quiet streets and lanes. Almost everyone on the island lives here. The fun of this town is just walking around admiring the charming houses.

Lookouts on the Munro Trail peer into steep ridges and deep gulches.

Garden of the Gods

 Map p. 224

✉ Polihua Rd., 6 miles NW of Lanai City

Lanaihale

 Map p. 224

✉ Manele Rd. (Hawaii 440), 5 miles S of Lanai City

You'll find the **Luahiwa Petroglyphs** in abundance in the hills and brush of a 3-acre field on Lanai. The earliest rock etchings here are about 500 years old; in the 1870s, students from Maui added horses and surfers to the earlier stick figures of men and dogs—and gave the dogs leashes. Look for a group of black boulders and great big century plants off Manele Road, then cut across the old dirt pineapple tracks. Late afternoon is best for photography.

About a half-hour drive from Lanai City is the **Garden of the Gods,** a strange, raw landscape of weird, oddly placed volcanic boulders. Just after dawn and just before sunset, the earthy colors glow and almost vibrate.

On the way there is a self-guided nature trail into **Kanepuu Preserve.** It takes about 15 minutes to reach all eight stations and read the informative signage. Once a month, the Nature Conservancy *(tel 808/565-7430)* conducts guided hikes into this lowland forest, the only known one of its kind left in the archipelago. It owes its existence to rancher George C. Munro, who in 1918 erected fences around it to protect a grove of *lama* (native persimmon) and *olopua* (native olive). A knowledgeable naturalist, he is also responsible for planting the Norfolk and Cook Island pines that have become icons of Lanai.

On a clear day, you can see five Hawaiian Islands from the 3,370-foot summit of **Lanaihale.** You'll need a 4WD vehicle to get there, and don't attempt it unless the weather is clear, for the 5-mile dirt track to the top is rutted and prone to washout. Most people consider the views of deep brooding gorges, misty forests, and the other islands to be worth it. ■

An elongated strand of 132 Hawaiian isles and islets, but only a few you can visit

More Hawaiian Isles

An endangered Hawaiian monk seal

More Hawaiian Isles

Niihau lies in a time warp, 17 miles off the west coast of Kauai across the Kaulakahi Channel. It has no electricity, no paved roads, no privately owned vehicles, and only one town, Puuwai. The 250 inhabitants are largely native Hawaiians who speak their own language and live very much a traditional lifestyle in a close-knit community.

The island is owned by the Robinson family, descendants of Eliza McHutcheson Sinclair, who bought it from Kamehameha V in 1864 for $10,000 in gold. Ranching is the main occupation on this 6-by-18-mile island, but its most famous product is the shell lei. The small lustrous *pupu* (shells) are gathered only on this island and fashioned into exquisite jewelry commanding prices that can run into thousands of dollars.

1994, to the sounds of chants, drums, and conch-shell horns, the federal government returned Kahoolawe to Hawaii, along with promises to clear the military ordnances and replant the largely denuded land. John Waihee, governor at that time, said Hawaii was "whole again." The island cannot be visited.

Papahanaumokuakea Marine National Monument

In 1909, President Theodore Roosevelt established the Hawaiian Islands Bird Reservation, later renamed Hawaiian Islands National Wildlife Refuge. The chain of islands, reefs,

Kahoolawe

The island of Kahoolawe has an interesting past. By A.D. 1250 the island was inhabited, and by 1600 the temple at Hakioawa was built. The island served briefly as a penal colony for Catholics being punished in compliance with an 1829 order of Queen Kaahumanu, a convert to Protestantism, for practicing their faith.

The island was reborn as a ranch in 1858. By 1925, the U.S. Army Air Corps was using Kahoolawe for military exercises. After the 1941 attack on Pearl Harbor, the U.S. Navy took control of the island, beginning the decades-long assault on it for target practice. Protests began in 1969. Finally, on May 7,

and atolls extends 800 miles northwest of the main Hawaiian Islands, reaching to Midway Atoll.

A presidential proclamation by George W. Bush in 2006 established the Northwestern Hawaiian Islands Marine National Monument, later renamed Papahanaumokuakea Marine National Monument, the single largest marine conservation area under the U.S. flag. Encompassing 139,797 square miles of Pacific Ocean, it is larger than all our national parks combined and is the largest fully protected marine

Kure Atoll
MIDWAY ATOLL N.W.R.
Midway Islands
PAPAHANAUMOKUAKEA
Pearl and Hermes Atoll
Northwestern
Lisianski Island
MARINE
Laysan Island
Maro Reef
Gardner Pinnacles
Hawaiian
NATIONAL
French Frigate Shoals
Is

The small island of Lehua lies just off the private island of Niihau in the background.

conservation area in the world. The islands of Nihoa and Mokumanamana have the highest density of sacred Hawaiian sites in the entire archipelago. The monument has been designated a UNESCO World Heritage site.

The northwestern Hawaiian islands that anchor these Pacific paradises are mere dots in the vast blue ocean, yet they provide a vital habitat for endangered Hawaiian monk seals, green sea turtles,

EXPERIENCE: Visit Niihau

The only way to visit Niihau is by a helicopter tour, which may be doubling as the "poi bird," flying in several hundred pounds of the staple *(Niihau Helicopters, Hanapepe, Kauai, tel 808/335-3500)*. Where you land depends on your focus, such as snorkeling, beachcombing, or swimming. You can purchase the island's prized shell lei at the tour company's Hanapepe headquarters.

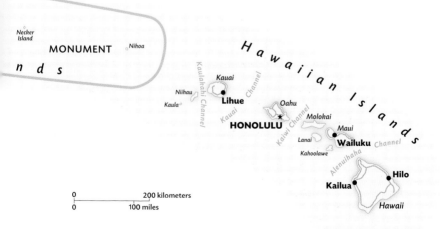

Necker Island

MONUMENT   Nihoa

n d s

Kaulakahi Channel

Hawaiian Islands

Kauai

Niihau

Kauai Channel

Lihue

Kaula

Oahu

HONOLULU

Molokai

Lanai

Maui

Wailuku

Channel

Kahoolawe

Alenuihaha

Hilo

Kailua

Hawaii

| 0 | | 200 kilometers |
| 0 | | 100 miles |

and more than 14 million seabirds of 18 species.

Sooty terns are the most common birds that frequent this pristine, uninhabited niche. Other frequent visitors are albatrosses, shearwaters, petrels, tropic birds, boobies, and noddies. Some endangered finches have found their last refuge on Earth on Nihoa and

---

Loihi

A fire burns 3,775 feet deep in the ocean, as a new Hawaiian Island is born 18 miles southeast of the Big Island's Kau Coast. Named Loihi ("long"), the active volcano has two large craters that loom 500 feet above its summit plateau. The base of the mountain lies 14,000 feet below sea level. Scientists estimate that it may take from 100 to 10,000 years for Loihi to rise above the waves. Aided by mini-submarines, scientists can observe the formation of an island. They say Loihi could grow taller than Mauna Kea.

Laysan Islands, while Midway Atoll (NWR) is said to have the world's largest population of "gooney birds."

One of the most curious creatures here is the frigatebird, which flies continuously at sea, yet has a hard time fishing because its feathers do not repel water like those of other seabirds. Its strategy is to frighten boobies and shearwaters into

surrendering their food. Hawaiians call the frigatebird *iwa*, thief. Another interesting critter, the Hawaiian monk seal rears its pups at **French Frigate Shoals,** sharing the coves with green sea turtles. The turtles roam several hundred miles in search of food.

INSIDER TIP:

Visitors must accommodate the wildlife on Midway Atoll. For example, when gooney birds are nesting, you can't go near the birds.

—THELMA CHANG
Author & National Geographic contributor

In order to protect the fragile environment, visitors are prohibited from entering the lagoon waters or landing on the islands. The only part of the national monument open to the public is the **Midway Atoll National Wildlife Refuge,** and even then visitors are only permitted to visit with a group. A current list of the companies that have been awarded permits, which must be applied for annually, can be found online (*papahanamo kuakea.gov/midway*).

A visit is worth the effort, however—Midway's pristine lagoons and long white-sand beaches provide a relaxing retreat for naturalists, photographers, and escapists in general. ∎

Travelwise

A trolley—open-air transport in Hawaii

TRAVELWISE

PLANNING YOUR TRIP

When to Go

Hotel occupancy and rates are highest mid-Dec.–March. Summer is busy when school is out. The last week of April, a Japanese national vacation, is the most crowded in Waikiki. Off-season is mid-April–mid-June, and again Sept.–mid-Dec. Climate is ideal, and the rates tend to be lower.

Climate

Hawaii has two seasons, summer and winter. Winter is wetter. Average winter daytime temperature is 78°F. Average summer daytime temperature is 85°F but cooled by gentle trade winds. Warmest months are Aug. and Sept. Evening temperatures drop about ten degrees; winter nights can hover in the sixties.

Main Events

Contact the Hawaii Visitors and Convention Bureau (see p. 241), or the telephone numbers listed for further information.

January

Hyundai Tournament of Champions *(Maui, first week, tel 877/527-2582).* The tournament is the PGA's season-opening event, at Kapalua Resort.

Opening of State Legislature *(Honolulu, Oahu, third Wed., tel 808/586-6100, capitol.hawaii .gov).* The annual session opens at the state capitol with ceremonies, lei, music, hula, and speeches.

Lunar New Year *(Honolulu, Oahu, day of the second new moon after the winter solstice in mid- to late Jan., tel 808/953-3181).* It opens the five-week Narcissus Festival of Chinese cultural events, mainly in Chinatown.

Molokai Makahiki *(Molokai, last Sat., tel 808/533-3673 or 800/800-6367, molokai-hawaii.com).* Islandwide celebration of Hawaiian arts, crafts, games, food.

Pro Bowl *(Honolulu, Oahu, Sun. before Super Bowl, tel 808/486-9300).* NFL all-pros battle it out at Aloha Stadium.

February

Waimea Town Celebration *(Waimea, Kauai, fourth weekend, tel 808/338-9957).* Multiethnic entertainment and food, rodeo and sports meets.

March

Buffalo's Big Board Classic *(Makaha Beach, Oahu, first two weeks, tel 808/951-7877).* Surfers compete on traditional longboards. Paddlers surf their outrigger canoes.

Cherry Blossom Festival *(all islands, tel 808/949-2255).* Japanese cultural demonstrations over 11 weeks: flower arrangement, martial arts, food presentation, and tea ceremony.

Polo season opens *(Mokuleia, Oahu, first or second weekend).* Bring a picnic and enjoy Sunday at the seaside field.

Prince Kuhio Festival *(Lihue, Kauai, weekend closest to March 26, tel 808/245-3971).*

April

Easter Sunrise Service *(Honolulu, Oahu, at Punchbowl Cemetery).*

Kapalua Celebration of the Arts *(Kapalua, Maui, tel 808/669-6200).* Weekend of free art classes and Hawaiian cultural events at the Ritz Carlton.

Merrie Monarch Festival *(Hilo, Big Island, tel 808/935-9168).* The most prestigious hula event in the Islands.

May

Lei Day *(all Islands, May 1).* Everyone wears a lei. Lei-making contests and school pageants, with lei day courts and multicultural dancing.

Molokai Ka Hula Piko *(Papohaku Beach Park, Molokai, third Sat., tel 808/553-3876 or 800/800-6367).* Outdoor hula celebration with arts, crafts, and food booths.

Kahikolu *(Honolulu, Oahu, last Monday, tel 808/955-0050).* This down-home, very friendly Memorial Day event honors Maiki Aiu, the mother of the Hawaiian Renaissance, and draws top local entertainers and hula groups.

June

King Kamehameha Celebration *(all Islands, weekend closest to June 11).* Parades, floral floats, street parties, and cultural events. King's statue in Honolulu is draped in massive leis.

Flavors of Honolulu *(Oahu, late June, tel 808/532-2115).* Restaurants and their top chefs participate in this annual fundraiser for Abilities Unlimited, an organization that helps people with disabilities. On the grounds of the Civic Center.

July

Puuhonua o Honaunau Festival *(Big Island, first weekend, tel 808/328-2326, ext. 32).* Pageantry, games, entertainment, traditonal fishing, and crafts in the national historical park.

Makawao Rodeo *(Makawao, Maui, July 4, tel 808/572-8102).* Parade and rodeo.

Parker Ranch Rodeo *(Waimea, Big Island, July 4, tel 808/885-7311).* Cowboys strut their stuff.

Prince Lot Hula Festival *(Moanalua Gardens, Oahu, second Sat., tel 808/839-5334).* Prettiest of the many hula events.

Queen Liliuokalani Keiki Hula Competition *(Honolulu, Oahu, late*

July, tel 808/521-6905). No expense spared in outfitting children for this hula competition.

August

Hawaii State Farm Fair *(Honolulu, Oahu, early Aug., tel 808/848-2074).* Rides, local food, local farm produce including flowers, entertainment.

Koloa Plantation Days *(Koloa, Kauai, last week).* Week-long festival recalling plantation days. Look for a parade, sports, and a variety of cultural events.

Hawaiian International Billfish Tournament *(Kailua-Kona, Big Island, timing based on new moon, tel 808/329-6155).* For ten days an armada of boats search the Pacific for record marlin.

September

Aloha Festivals *(all Islands).* Parades, street parties, major cultural events.

October

Maui County Fair *(Kahului, Maui).* Carnival rides, a parade, enter-tainment, and exhibits.

Eo e Emalani i Alakai *(Kokee, Kauai, second Sat., tel 808/335-9975).* Re-enactment of Queen Emma's visit to Alakai Swamp, plus hula and nature events.

Halloween *(Lahaina, Maui, Oct. 31, tel 808/667-9194 or 888/310-1117).* Annual spook spoof with costume contests and a bawdy street party.

Ironman Triathlon World Cham-pionship *(Kailua-Kona, Big Island, tel 808/329-0063).* The small town erupts for this big swim-bike-run challenge with more than a thou-sand competitors.

Hawaii International Film Festival *(Oahu, last week, tel 808/528-3456, hiff.org).* Various neighboring islands the following week. Draws top films focused on cross-cultural themes. Mini-festival in April.

November

Kona Coffee Festival *(Kailua-Kona, Big Island, early Nov., tel 808/326-7820).* Farm tours, parade, pageantry, coffee tasting, recipe contest.

Mission Houses Museum Christmas Fair *(Honolulu, Oahu, end of Nov., tel 808/531-0481).* Hawaiian crafters sell local arts and Christmas decorations.

December

Honolulu Marathon *(Oahu, early Dec., tel 808/734-7200).* Runners race from Aloha Tower along the eastern shore and back to Kapiolani Park, Waikiki.

Honolulu City Lights *(Oahu).* Downtown becomes a fantasia of lights, trees, and displays.

Christmas *(all Islands).* Most hotels are lavishly decorated, have special lobby displays. Santa often arrives by outrigger canoe.

What to Take

You should be able to buy anything you need in Hawaii, but prices are about 18 percent higher than on the U.S. mainland. Pharmacies offer a wide range of drugs, medical supplies, and toiletries, but bring any prescrip-tion drugs you might need. A second pair of glasses or contact lenses is a good idea. You will need sunscreen and a hat. Dress is casual, but top-end restaurants request "dressy resort wear." Take a light waterproof jacket and sweater in winter or if staying in the mountains. Most sports equipment can be rented. Lastly, don't forget the essentials: passport (if coming from outside the U.S.), driver's license, ATM cards or traveler's checks, and docu-mentation for medical insurance.

Passports

Non–U.S. citizens tend to forget Hawaii is a state of the U.S. Visi-tors from most foreign countries need a valid passport with a U.S. tourist visa. Canadian citizens need only proof of residence. **U.S. Customs** *(tel 808/356-4100);* **U.S. Immigration** *(tel 800/375-5283).*

What Not to Bring

You cannot bring any fresh fruits or vegetables to Hawaii even if you are coming from the U.S. mainland and do not have to go through customs. You will be asked to sign a declaration form and be warned that fees for noncompliance are high. Also, because there is no rabies in Hawaii, there is a strict animal-quarantine law requiring all ani-mals to be held for four months at the state quarantine station on Oahu. Under a carefully regulated program of inoculations prior to arrival in the islands, your animal may qualify for a 30-day quarantine. Snakes are strictly for-bidden. **Hawaii Department of Agriculture** *(tel 808/973-9560).* **Animal Quarantine Station** *(tel 808/483-7171, hawaii.gov/hdoa).*

Further Reading

Hawaii by James Michener, Random House, 1959, is a popu-lar novel encompassing much of Hawaiian history.

Hawaiian Heritage by Kathleen Dickenson Mellon, Hastings House, 1963, is a small book of brief biog-raphies of Hawaiian royalty.

Hawaiian Mythology by Martha Beckwith, University of Hawaii Press, 1970, a collection of impor-tant Hawaiian mythology.

Holy Man, Father Damien of Molokai by Gavan Daws, University of Hawaii Press, 1973, a biography of the priest who worked among the lepers.

Hula Is Life by Rita Ariyoshi, Maiki Aiu Building Corporation, 1998, is the most important book about hula to be published.

Journal of a Residence in the Sandwich Islands, University of

Hawaii Press, 1970, is the diary of an early missionary.

Maui on My Mind by Rita Ariyoshi, Mutual Publishing, 1985, is a lavishly illustrated portrait of Maui.

Plants and Flowers of Hawaii by S. H. Sohmer and R. Gustafson, University of Hawaii Press, 1987, photographs and text about the unique flora of the islands.

Shoal of Time by Gavan Daws, University of Hawaii Press, 1968, is the best history of Hawaii.

HOW TO GET TO HAWAII
Airlines
Most major U.S. and many international airlines service Honolulu International Airport. Overseas flights also fly direct to Kona and Hilo airports on the Big Island; Kahului, Maui; and Lihue, Kauai.

Useful Numbers
American Airlines, tel 808/833-7600 or 800/433-7300
Continental Airlines, tel 808/523-3273 or 800/231-0856
Delta Airlines, tel 800/221-1212 go!, tel 808/838-7900 or 888/435-9462
Hawaiian Airlines, tel 808/838-1555 or 800/367-5320
Island Air, tel 808/484-2222
Japan Airlines, tel 800/525-3663
Mokulele Airlines, 808/326-7070 or tel 866/260-7070
Northwest Airlines, tel 800/225-2525
Pacific Wings, tel 888/575-4546, (for private charters)
Qantas, tel 800/227-4500
United Airlines, tel 800/225-5825

Airports
Honolulu International Airport is the gateway to Hawaii and the Pacific. There is an overseas terminal, an interisland terminal, and a commuter airline terminal. They are connected by the Wiki-Wiki Bus, a free shuttle. The Wiki-Wiki Bus takes you from your arrival gate to baggage claim if your flight has landed on the reef runway, built out into the ocean.

Renting a Car
Rental car agencies have vans to collect you at the airport to take you to their lot.

Taxis are outside the exit doorways. Fare to Waikiki is about $35.

Airport shuttles *(tel 808/539-9400)* operate 24 hours a day between the airport and Waikiki hotels and condos. No reservation necessary. You can board with two pieces of luggage and a carry-on at no extra charge, bicycles and surfboards at an additional fee. Fare is $8, tips appreciated, particularly if attendant helps you with bags.

TheBus *(tel 808/848-5555, thebus.org)* Nos. 19 and 20 run from the airport to Waikiki from 5:10 a.m. weekdays to 11:39 p.m. You may board only with a carry-on or small suitcase that will fit under your seat. A rack is available for bicycles only. Fare is $2, exact change only.

Lei Greeting
Unless you are being met by a friend or a tour company representative, you will not receive a traditional floral greeting. However, you can arrange for one from **Greeters of Hawaii** *(tel 808/836-0161 or 800/366-8559, $25–$50, depending on the lei).*

GETTING AROUND
By Air
The main way to travel from island to island is by plane. The major interisland carriers are Hawaiian Airlines, Mokulele Airlines, Island Air, and go!, a discount carrier. They operate a full schedule of jet flights daily, and offer a variety of discounts for multiple flights. Island Air flies turboprop aircraft and services the Islands' smaller airports. Oahu is the only island with a public transportation system: **TheBus** *(tel 808/848-5555 or visit www.thebus.org).* Taxi service is available at the airports. Many hotels provide airport transfers.

Hawaiian Airlines
From the U.S. mainland and neighbor islands, tel 800/367-5320. From Oahu, tel 808/838-1555. Cheaper fares can often be found at *hawaiianair.com.*

Island Air
From the U.S. mainland and neighbor islands. From Oahu, tel 808/484-2222, *islandair.com.*

By Car
Roads in Hawaii—except for those in Oahu—are well maintained and well marked. Freeways are part of the U.S. interstate network even though they connect with no other state. There are no toll roads. Rural roads can be little more than one lane or have one-lane bridges. Although highways are numbered, Islanders will usually direct you by the name of the road. Directions are rarely given by the points of the compass. You will be directed *mauka* (toward the uplands) or *makai* (toward the sea). It's difficult to get lost. Places of major tourist or historical interest are marked with the distinctive Hawaii Visitors and Convention Bureau sign featuring a warrior in a red cape.

Renting a Car
All major rental car agencies operate in Hawaii. Rates are among the most reasonable in the country. Airlines and hotels often have fly-drive or room-and-car deals. Inquire when making reservations. Reserve beforehand, as car companies are sometimes sold out, particularly on holiday weekends, when Islanders travel.

To rent a car you must be 25 years of age with a valid driver's license and credit card. There are rental desks at airports and hotels.

Motoring Regulations

All passengers must wear a seatbelt. Children aged seven and under must ride in a car seat (available by reservation from the car rental agencies at an additional charge). Pedestrians always have the right of way, even if they are not in a crosswalk.

Speed limits: highways, 55 mph, city streets, 25 mph.

Traffic lights: Some places don't have them. In the larger towns, the green light can get lost in exuberant foliage so be especially alert.

You may turn right on a red light from the right lane, providing you come to a full and complete stop, except if there is a sign specifically forbidding such a maneuver.

Drivers in Hawaii are courteous in the extreme. It is considered rude to block intersections or not allow a merging car to get in front of you. It is customary to wave a thank-you for traffic courtesies.

All distances on signposts are shown in miles.

Gasoline is sold by the gallon. 1 U.S. gallon is equal to 3.8 liters. 1.2 U.S. gallons is equal to 1 Imperial gallon.

Breakdown

Contact your rental car agency.

Accidents

See Emergencies p. 241.

Parking

Street parking is available, however check signs for tow-away times, usually during rush hour and strictly enforced. Parking in Waikiki and downtown Honolulu can be expensive. Restaurants will usually validate. Some hotels on all islands charge guests a per diem for parking. Inquire when reserving your accommodations.

Transportation in Waikiki & Honolulu

Taxis do not cruise for fares. Usually they must be called by telephone. **Charley's** (tel 808/531-1333) and **The Cab** (tel 808/422-2222) are two reliable companies. Your hotel will call a cab for you. There are extra charges for luggage. You are not allowed on city buses with luggage. TheBus routes traverse the island. You can make a circle of the island on one fare if you do not leave the bus. It's the cheapest circle-island tour.

PRACTICAL ADVICE
Communications
Post Offices

As a state, Hawaii uses U.S. postal service and the same rates apply as on the U.S. mainland. All first-class mail leaves Hawaii by air. **Airport Post Office** (3600 Aolele Street, Honolulu, tel 800/275-8777); **Waikiki Post Office** (330 Saratoga Road, Honolulu, tel 800/275-8777). Most hotels will take care of your mail for you.

Telephones

The area code for all Hawaii is 808. The international country code is 1. Underwater fiber-optic cables connect Hawaii to Asia and the U.S. Most long-distance calls can be dialed directly from any phone; however, hotels often attach high charges to outgoing in-room calls. To dial interisland, dial 1 plus 808 plus number; for the continental U.S. or Canada, dial 1 plus area code, plus the number. For international calls dial 011, country code, city code, and phone number. Directory assistance for all islands is 1-411. Mainland is 1-808/555-1212. They can also assist with mainland area codes.

Electricity

Electricity is standard U.S. 110–120 volts, 60 cycles AC.

Large hotels have voltage and plug converters, and often provide hair dryers and irons.

Etiquette & Local Customs

Aloha is said as hello or good-bye. Thank you is mahalo. People usually greet each other with a hug and a kiss. If you are given a lei, it will be slipped over your head and about your shoulders with part of the lei hanging in back. It will usually be bestowed with a kiss. You will see people waving a closed fist with the pinky and thumb extended. This is the "shaka," and means everything's "cool." When visiting someone's home or a hula school it is the custom to leave your shoes outside the door. It is a mark of affectionate respect to call an older person "auntie" or "uncle." Do not pat a child on the head as the head is sacred. Friday is "Aloha Friday," and the wearing of colorful Hawaiian clothing is encouraged. Many restaurants set the table with chopsticks. Most will provide forks upon request.

When visiting rural towns, be discreet when taking photographs. At sacred sites, such as temple ruins, do not climb on stone walls or platforms. Also, leave no offerings, as you do not know what might give offense.

Holidays

U.S. holidays are generally observed. All government offices are closed New Year's Day, January 1; Martin Luther King Jr. Day, third Monday in January; Presidents' Day, third Monday in February; Memorial Day, last Monday in May; Fourth of July; Labor Day, first Monday of September; Discoverers' Day (honoring both Christopher Columbus and the Polynesian discoverers of Hawaii), second Monday in October; Veterans' Day, November 11; Thanksgiving, fourth Thursday in November; and Christmas, December 25.

Hawaii holidays, when state and county offices are closed, are often celebrated with great enthusiasm. Kuhio Day, March 26, honors Prince Jonah Kuhio Kalanianaole, Hawaii's first delegate to the U.S. Congress; Kamehameha Day, June 11, celebrates the life of the warrior king who united the Hawaiian Islands; and Admissions Day, the third Friday in August, marks the admittance of Hawaii as the 50th state of the U.S., August 21, 1959.

Media
Newspapers
There is only one English-language newspaper with statewide circulation, *The Honolulu Star-Advertiser,* which publishes a morning edition. The *Hawaii-Hochi* is published on Oahu in English-Japanese. Neighbor Island newspapers are the *Hawaii Tribune Herald* and *West Hawaii Today* on the Big Island, the *Maui News* on Maui, and the *Kauai Times* and *Garden Island* on Kauai. The Catholic diocese of Honolulu publishes the *Hawaii Catholic Herald.* There are a wide variety of free tourist publications with maps, discount coupons, and good information available at airports, hotel lobbies, and street kiosks.

TV Channels
Hawaii receives a broad range of U.S. network and cable channels. There are ethnic stations and Hawaii Public Broadcasting Station (PBS). Channel numbers vary from island to island. Most hotels offer cable TV viewing.

Radio
The most popular morning drive-time show for adults 25–54 years old is "Perry & Price," KSSK FM 92.3 or AM 590. For adults 18–34 years old it's Hudson and Scotty B. at KUCD FM 101.9. For

Hawaiian music throughout the day it's KINE 105.1 FM. Hawaiian mixed with rock and reggae, sometimes called "Jawaiian" pops up on KCCN AM 1420. For contemporary hits spliced with surf reports, it's KIKI/HOT 1 on 94 FM; KQMQ AM 690 or FM 93.1; 97.5 The Edge; or 97.5 KPOI. Public radio stations on Oahu are KIFO AM 1380 for news, KIPO FM 89.3 for news, jazz, international, and classical; KHPR FM 88.1, for classical, news, and discussion. Maui's public radio is KKUA FM 90.7.

Money Matters
The currency is the U.S. dollar. Some stores in Waikiki and major Oahu malls accept Japanese yen. Currency can be exchanged in most banks. There are currency services at Honolulu International Airport but at no others. In Waikiki you may exchange currency at banks and larger hotels if a guest. Traveler's checks in U.S. denominations are widely accepted, but you must have a picture ID such as a driver's license.

Most major shopping malls and banks have ATMs for bank cards and international credit cards, typically accessible 24 hours a day.

Credit cards, especially Visa and MasterCard, are widely used.

Opening Times
Office hours are generally 8 a.m. to 4 p.m.
Banks: 8 a.m. to 3 p.m.
Post office: 8 a.m. to 4:30 p.m.
Stores: 9:30 a.m. to 9 p.m.
Grocery stores: many 24 hours
Gas stations: 7 a.m. to 6 p.m.
Museums: 9 a.m. to 3 p.m. See individual listings.

Senior Citizens
Public transportation, many attractions, and most movie theaters offer discounts for senior citizens.

Time Differences
Hawaii is located east of the International Dateline at Hawaiian Standard Time and never uses daylight-saving time. It uses the 12-hour, not the 24-hour, clock. Hawaii is:
—two hours behind Pacific Standard Time (PST);
—four hours behind Central Standard Time (CST);
—five hours behind Eastern Standard Time (EST);
—ten hours behind Greenwich Mean Time.

During daylight-saving time on the mainland, Hawaii is three hours behind PST, six hours behind EST, and so on.

For the correct local time, tel 808/643-8463.

Tipping
Tipping is expected in Hawaii. Local people tend to be generous tippers recognizing that many people rely on tips for survival because the cost of living is so high. At a minimum, tip porters $1 per bag; the same for hotel bellhops. Tip taxi drivers 15 percent of the fare, more if they handle baggage. Tip valet parkers $2 above any parking fee. Tip 15 to 20 percent in a fine restaurant. Tip room maids $1 to $2 per night. Tip hairdressers and barbers 15 to 20 percent. Tipping doormen, theater ushers, and gas station attendants is not expected.

Toilets
Stores and restaurants are required to have restrooms available to customers, including wheelchair clients. In addition, most malls and beach parks have restrooms. Usually picture signs designate men or women. Hawaiian is widely used: *kane* (men), *wahine* (women).

Tourist Offices

**Hawaii Visitors and
Convention Bureau Offices:**
2270 Kalakaua Ave.
Suite 801
Honolulu, Hawaii 96815
Tel 808/923-1811
Tel 800/GO-HAWAII
gohawaii.com

Travelers
with Disabilities

The Aloha State is accessible.
Most hotels are equipped with
wheelchair-configured rooms;
most intersections have ramped
curbs. **The Hawaii Center for
Independent Living** (*414 Kuwili
Street, Suite 102, Honolulu, HI
96817, tel 808/522-5400*) will
provide further information.
For $15 they have a book, *Aloha
Guide to Accessibility.* Check
their website at *hawaii.gov/health;*
e-mail: cpdppp@aloha.net.

A limited number of hand-
controlled rental cars are available
from **Avis** (*tel 800/331-1212*) and
Hertz (*tel 800/654-3131*). Handi-
capped parking placards from other
states are recognized. A recent court
decision has ruled that seeing-eye
dogs can now enter Hawaii without
the usual quarantine requirements.
Documentation must be presented
that the dog has been vaccinated
against rabies and that it is a trained
seeing-eye dog. For further information contact the **Animal Quarantine Station** (*tel 808/483-7171,
hawaii.gov*). For further information
on planning a trip for travelers with
disabilities from start to finish visit
access-able.com.

EMERGENCIES

Call 911 to summon police, report
a fire, or call an ambulance.
Because of liability concerns in
a litigious society, it is best to
summon police to the scene of a
traffic accident. Most hotels have
a physician on call.

Consulates

Australia, tel 808/524-5050
Japan, tel 808/543-3111
New Zealand, tel 808/595-2200
UK, tel 808/524-5050

For others, consult the local
telephone directory.

Lost Property

If you think you have lost
something in a taxi, bus, store,
or restaurant, notify the establishment (*TheBus Lost and Found,
tel 808/848-4444*). Report stolen
property to police (*tel 911*).
Keep a copy of the police report
for your insurance claim. Report
lost passports to the nearest
consulate or embassy. Lost credit
cards should be reported immediately to police and to the credit
card company.
American Express, tel 800/
528-4800
Diners Club, tel 800/234-6377
MasterCard, tel 800/826-2181
Visa, tel 800/336-8472

Health & Safety

For serious injuries, call 911.
Hawaii has one of the lowest
crime rates in the U.S., but crime
exists, particularly in Waikiki
and in the parking lots of tourist
attractions. Be as cautious and
prudent as you would be anywhere. Never leave valuables in
your car, even for a minute while
you take a photograph.

Water Safety

When surf is up, do not walk
close to the water's edge,
whether on a beach or rocky
ledge. Rogue waves commonly
sweep people out to sea. Obey all
signs warning of surf conditions
and riptides. Do not swim in the
ocean at sunrise, sunset, night, or
when the water is murky: These
are the times sharks may come
close to shore. They are also
attracted by blood. Do not dive
into streams, mountain pools,

or the ocean: Hidden rocks may
be just below the surface. Many
streams on Oahu are contaminated with leptospirosis. Never
drink the water in freshwater
streams and pools.

Land Safety

There are no known poisonous
snakes or insects whose bite
is fatal. When hiking, stay on
marked trails as volcanic soil
can be unstable. Never hike
alone. Always take water. Notify
someone of your plans and when
you expect to return. Bring a cell
phone, if you have one. If you get
lost, stay put until help arrives.
Obey all posted trail safety rules,
and never embark on a trail that
is closed.

Tanning

Remember, you are close to the
equator, and the sun's rays are
stronger. A fair-skinned person
can burn in ten minutes without
sunscreen. Dermatologists advise
applying sunscreen as soon as you
shower in the morning. Reapply
every two hours and after
swimming. Also wear a hat and
sunglasses. Many people get
sunburned while snorkeling; apply
waterproof sunscreen beforehand
and consider wearing a shirt over
your swimsuit in the water.

Smoking

It is against the law to smoke
in public buildings, such as
airports, restaurants, retail stores,
theaters, banks, government
offices, and hospitals. Most
hotels have nonsmoking rooms,
in fact, many smaller hotels
prohibit smoking completely.

Hotels & Restaurants

Excellent resorts, hotels, vacation condominiums, and bed-and-breakfast stays can be found all over Hawaii. Many of the world's leading hotel chains have Hawaii properties. Dining opportunities are multiethnic, varied in setting, and unusually good in overall quality of cuisine. All restaurants are smoke-free.

Hotels

Most establishments have designated nonsmoking rooms. If a property has a good restaurant, the restaurant symbol will be indicated in the listing even though the restaurant may not be reviewed separately. All hotels provide parking (many charge a per diem), and have air-conditioning unless otherwise noted. All swimming pools are outdoors.

Keep in mind that all beaches in Hawaii are public, so if you choose less expensive off-beach accommodations, you can plunk down on the sand right in front of the poshest hotel.

Major credit cards are accepted at hotels, except where noted. A sales and room tax of 13.71 percent will be added to your bill. When reserving, ask about possible room and car packages, family plans, or special interest packages such as golf or honeymoon deals.

Packages

Airlines often package flights with rooms and cars. Try:
American Airlines, tel 800/321-2121, aavacations.com
Continental, tel 800/634-5555, covacations.com
Delta, tel 800/872-7786, deltavacations.com
United, tel 800/328-6877, unitedvacations.com

Two packagers with excellent records for securing well-priced hotels and custom tours designed to suit your interests are:
American Express, tel 800/AXP-6898, americanexpress.com/travel
Pleasant Hawaiian Holidays, tel 800/448-3333, pleasant holidays.net

Bed & Breakfasts

Be&Bs provide a wonderful opportunity to meet local people, and stay in a real neighborhood rather than a resort enclave. The following agencies have multi-island listings:
Bed & Breakfast Hawaii, P.O. Box 449, Kapaa, HI 96746, tel 800/733-1632, fax 808/822-2723, www.bandb-hawaii.com.
Hawaii's Best Bed & Breakfast, 571 Pauku St., Kailua, HI 96734, tel 800/262-9912, fax 808/262-5030, bestbnb.com.

Multi-island Hotel Chains

Aston (tel 800/92-ASTON, fax 808/922-8785, resortquest hawaii.com) has a reputation for comfort and style in a broad range of prices. They count a number of lovely holiday condominiums in their portfolio. Package deals are a specialty.
Marc Resorts Hawaii (tel 800/535-0085, fax 800/633-5085, marc resorts.com) specializes in distinctive affordable accommodations and discounted packages on every island but Lanai.
Outrigger (tel 800/OUTRIGGER, fax 800/622-4852, outrigger.com) can be counted on for good rates and, as a regular customer said, "the kind of rooms I'd be happy to book my mother into." Outrigger is adding upscale properties to their chain so be sure and specify budget expectations.
Prince Hotels (tel 800/321-6248, fax 808/946-0811, princeresorts hawaii.com), with prime properties on Oahu, Maui, and the Big Island, offer quiet luxury and fine dining.
Sheraton (tel 800/325-3535, www.sheratonhawaii.com) has hotels on Oahu, Kauai, and Maui.

Organizations & Abbreviations

All sites are listed first by price, then in alphabetical order, with hotels preceding restaurants. The abbreviations used are:
L = lunch; D = dinner;
AE = American Express; DC = Diner's Club; DS = Discover;
MC = MasterCard; V = Visa

■ OAHU

HONOLULU

SOMETHING SPECIAL

🏨 **THE KAHALA**
🍴 **$$$$$**
5000 KAHALA AVE.
HONOLULU 96816
TEL 808/739-8888 OR
800/367-2525
FAX 808/739-8800
kahalaresort.com
Quiet elegance in Oahu's most exclusive neighborhood, Kahala, five minutes from Waikiki. Dolphin lagoon, canopy beds. Two excellent restaurants, indoor-outdoor Plumeria Beach Café and Hoku's for fine dining.
🛈 364 🏖 🍷

🏨 **MANOA VALLEY INN**
$$
2001 VANCOUVER DR.
HONOLULU 96822
TEL 808/947-6019 OR
800/535-0085
FAX 808/396-4664
manoavalleyinn.com
Tucked amid the big trees and gracious old houses of Manoa, this inn, once a private residence, is on the National Register of Historic Places. Each room has its own period decor.

🏨 Hotel   🍴 Restaurant   🛈 No. of Guest Rooms   🪑 No. of Seats   🅿 Parking   🕒 Closed   🛗 Elevator

---

PRICES

HOTELS

An indication of the cost of a double room in the high season is given by $ signs.

$$$$$	Over $240
$$$$	$160–$240
$$$	$110–$160
$$	$70–$110
$	Under $70

RESTAURANTS

An indication of the cost of a three-course meal without drinks is given by $ signs.

$$$$$	Over $65
$$$$	$50–$65
$$$	$30–$50
$$	$20–$30
$	Under $20

Includes continental breakfast.
🛏 8 units (3 with shared bath)

SOMETHING SPECIAL

🍽 CHEF MAVRO

$$$$

1969 S. KING ST.

TEL 808/944-4714

chefmavro.com

French/Hawaii Regional

Famed French chef George Mavrothalassitis pairs fine wines and courses in two prix-fixe menus, changed monthly. One of Chef Mavro's classics: *onaga* (snapper) baked in Hawaiian *alae* salt crust with a delicate sauce and *ogo* (a sea vegetable) paired with Marcel Deiss Pinot Blanc Alsace 1997. À la carte menu also.

🍴 68 🅿 Valet 🕐 Closed L 💳 All major cards

🍽 ALAN WONG'S RESTAURANT

$$$

1857 S. KING ST.

TEL 808/949-2526

Hawaii Regional

Master chef Alan Wong proves no fat doesn't mean no flavor. Dishes are so perfectly prepared, infused with herbs and spices, you won't miss the salt or pepper shakers. Try grilled lamb chops with coconut macadamia nut crust or pan-roasted salmon in soy balsamic sauce with Japanese eggplant.

🍴 100 🅿 Valet 🕐 Closed L 💳 All major cards

🍽 CHEF CHAI

$$$

1009 KAPIOLANI BLVD.

TEL 808/585-0011

Pacific Rim

Flavors of Thailand grace many of the dishes prepared by award-winning chef Chai Chaowasaree—from Thai chicken curry and vegetarian spring rolls to crab cakes and shredded green papaya salad.

🍴 90 indoors, 25 outdoors 🅿 💳 All major cards

🍽 INDIGO

$$

1121 NUUANU AVE.

TEL 808/521-2900

Eurasian

Make a meal of appetizers such as lemongrass chicken with peanut sauce or wontons filled with goat cheese, sweet peppers, and sun-dried tomatoes with a fruit sauce. Try for an outside table in a Balinese-style garden.

🍴 87 indoors, plus 55 in private room, 85 outdoors 🅿 Valet 🕐 Closed Sun. & Mon., L Sat. 💳 DC, MC, V

🍽 LEGEND SEAFOOD RESTAURANT

$$

CHINESE CULTURAL PLAZA

100 N. BERETANIA ST.

TEL 808/532-1868

Chinese

At lunch, carts laden with steaming bamboo baskets of dim sum dumplings cruise among the white-linen-dressed tables. Try taro puffs or vegetable dumplings. Dinner specializes in Chinese seafood dishes. Breakfast served on Saturday and Sunday.

🍴 190 🅿 💳 All major cards

🍽 SHOKUDO

$$

1585 KAPIOLANI BLVD.

TEL 808/941-3701

willowshawaii.com

Japanese Fusion

This wildly popular place has weird combos that are delicious. Try mochi gratin with mozzarella, sushi pizza, teriyaki salmon, served family style. Tofu is house-made and home style. Specialty bar drinks and fruity drinks. Noisy and trendy.

🍴 200 💳 All major cards

🍽 WILLOWS

$$

901 HAUSTEN ST.

TEL 808/952-9200

willowshawaii.com

Hawaii Regional

People wept when the Willows closed a few years ago. Now it's back and better than ever with thatched pavilions clustered around a pond and tropical gardens. The buffet format has everything from *lau lau* to macadamia nut cream pie. In between are stir-fry dishes, seafood, salads, Korean beef. Fine dining in a separate room at a higher price.

🍴 350 🅿 💳 All major cards

🍽 LITTLE VILLAGE

$

1113 SMITH ST.

TEL 808/545-3008

Chinese

Fine cuisine in an informal setting at reasonable prices—no wonder Jennifer and Kenneth Chan's small Chinatown restaurant is so successful. They arrived from China with $100 and a flair for innovative sauces. Try green onion pancake, honey walnut shrimp, stir-fry green beans, taro duck, or *daun-daun mein* noodles with peanut sauce.

🍴 120 💳 All major cards

🚭 Nonsmoking   ❄ Air-conditioning   🏊 Swimming Pool   🏋 Health Club   💳 Credit Cards

WAIKIKI

SOMETHING SPECIAL

🏨 HALEKULANI
🍴 $$$$$
2199 KALIA RD.
HONOLULU 96815
TEL 808/923-2311 OR
800/367-2343
FAX 808/926-8004
halekulani.com
Elegant, thoroughly modern
hotel built around a beautifully
restored gracious core, which
now serves as the restaurant
wing for acclaimed Orchids
(see p. 245) and La Mer (see
this page). This is the prestige
address in Waikiki. Go to
Honolulu Symphony, Bishop
Museum and Iolani Palace,
Contemporary Museum, and
Honolulu Academy of Arts
for free.
ⓘ 456 🛎 🍴

SOMETHING SPECIAL

🏨 ROYAL HAWAIIAN
🍴 HOTEL
$$$$$
2259 KALAKAUA AVE.
HONOLULU 96815
TEL 808/923-7311 OR
800/325-3535
FAX 808/931-7098
royal-hawaiian.com
The "Pink Palace" opened in
1927 and has hosted a long list
of celebrities. All rooms look
as if they could be in a tropical
home, but the nicest are in the
Historic Wing with its period
furnishings. Beachside restaurants, Mai Tai Bar, luau.

ⓘ 526 units 🛎

🏨 HILTON HAWAIIAN
🍴 VILLAGE BEACH
RESORT & SPA
$$$$
2005 KALIA RD.
HONOLULU 96815
TEL 808/949-4321 OR
800/HILTONS
FAX 808/951-5458

hawaiianvillage
.hilton.com
Three towers on 20 acres
of landscaping with waterfalls
and exotic wildlife. Shopping
complex with fast food. Six
restaurants including romantic
fine dining at Bali Steak &
Seafood (see this page). The
"Superpool" is 10,000
square feet.
ⓘ 3,000 🛎 3 🍴

🏨 MOANA SURFRIDER,
🍴 A WESTIN RESORT
$$$$
2365 KALAKAUA AVE.
HONOLULU 96815
TEL 808/922-3111
FAX 808/924-4799
sheraton.com/
moanasurfrider
Oldest hotel in Waikiki is in
mint condition and on the
National Register of Historic
Places. Victorian splendor amid
the new high rises. Ask for a
room in the old section where
the wallpaper is floral and the
armoires huge. Restaurant on
the beach.
ⓘ 793 units 🛎

🏨 ILIMA
🍴 $$$
445 NOHONANI ST.
HONOLULU 96815
TEL 808/923-1877 OR
800/801-9366
FAX 808/924-2617
ilima.com
Tasteful rooms are large
with kitchenette, bed, and
sleep-sofa. Staff is friendly and
helpful. Walk to beach.
ⓘ 99 units 🅿 Limited 🛎 🍴

🏨 NEW OTANI KAIMANA
🍴 BEACH HOTEL
$$$
2863 KALAKAUA AVE.
HONOLULU 96815
TEL 808/923-1555 OR
800/356-8264
FAX 808/922-9404
kaimana.com
By an uncrowded stretch of
sand at the foot of Diamond
Head on the quiet end of

Waikiki. Slip into a crisp cotton
robe and enjoy Japanese tea
service. Hau Tree Lanai (see
p. 245) is one of the few beachside restaurants in Waikiki.
ⓘ 124 units 🍴

🏨 ROYAL GARDEN
🍴 AT WAIKIKI
$$$
440 OLOHANA ST.
HONOLULU 96815
TEL 808/943-0202 OR
800/989-0971
FAX 808/945-7407
royalgardensatwaikiki.com
A gem for the money, with
impressive, marble lobby
and romantic, stylish rooms.
Continental breakfast included.
Walk to beach.
ⓘ 205 units 🛎 🍴

SOMETHING SPECIAL

🍴 LA MER
$$$$$
HALEKULANI HOTEL
2199 KALIA RD.
TEL 808/923-2311
French
Elegant, expensive, and
epicurean. It is Hawaii's only
five-diamond restaurant. Look
for fillet of *onaga* with truffles.
Desserts? You don't even have
to make a choice—get the
"Variation La Mer," which has
samplings of four excellent desserts. À la carte and masterfully
orchestrated prix-fixe dinners.
Jacket or long-sleeved, collared
shirt required.
🪑 100 🅿 🕐 Closed L
💳 All major cards

SOMETHING SPECIAL

🍴 BALI STEAK &
SEAFOOD
$$$$
HILTON HAWAIIAN VILLAGE
2005 KALIA RD.
TEL 808/941-2254
American/Hawaii Regional
Romance, ocean views, and
superb cuisine are hard to find
in one place, but Bali does it

🏨 Hotel 🍴 Restaurant ⓘ No. of Guest Rooms 🪑 No. of Seats 🅿 Parking 🕐 Closed 🛎 Elevator

with panache. This is American fare with Hawaii regional flair. Splurge on the three-course tasting menu. Choose macadamia nut butter glazed mahimahi with coconut rice, or filet mignon with Hamakua mushrooms and cognac sauce.

🛏 130 🅿 🌙 Closed L
🏧 All major cards

HOKU'S
$$$$
THE KAHALA HOTEL & RESORT
5000 KAHALA AVE.
TEL 808/739-8780
Pacific Fusion
An oceanside setting by the blue Pacific. Dining choices here range from Hoku's *ahi musubi* (fresh *ahi* riceball) to *kiawe*-smoked Tasmanian salmon. Dinners only, with one exception: Sunday brunch.

🛏 100 🏧 All major cards

ORCHIDS
$$$$
HALEKULANI HOTEL
2199 KALIA RD.
TEL 808/923-2311
Contemporary Seafood
Festive seaside dining with views of Diamond Head and banks of orchids. Mustard-herb crusted rack of lamb is an excellent choice.

🛏 97 indoors, 88 outdoors
🅿 🏧 All major cards

PRINCE COURT
$$$$
HAWAII PRINCE HOTEL
100 HOLOMOANA ST.
TEL 808/956-1111
Hawaii Regional
It's hard to find a seat on weekends when locals come for the sumptuous buffets. Sunday brunch is a legend. Look for richest bread pudding among 50 dishes. Or order from the gourmet seasonal menu. Big windows look out on Ala Wai Harbor.

🛏 180 🅿 🏧 All major cards

HAU TREE LANAI
$$$
NEW OTANI KAIMANA BEACH HOTEL
2863 KALAKAUA AVE.
TEL 808/921-7066
Hawaii Regional
From breakfast onward, this beachside terrace is a winner. Begin with eggs Benedict, scones, poi pancakes, and Belgian waffles. A sunset supper is ultra-romantic with torches. *Opakapaka* (pink snapper) steamed with Chinese vegetables in a ginger cilantro glaze is a good choice.

🛏 165 outdoors
🅿 🏧 All major cards

HY'S STEAK HOUSE
$$$
2440 KUHIO AVE.
TEL 808/922-5555
American
Ever wonder where the beef Wellington and chateaubriand went? Hy's has them. Also waiters in tuxes, and showy flames. Relax.

🛏 220 🅿 Valet 🌙 Closed L
🏧 All major cards

SOMETHING SPECIAL

LE BISTRO
$$$
NIU VALLEY CENTER
5730 KALANIANAOLE HWY.
TEL 808/373-7990
Eclectic Eurasian
A neighborhood attraction for locals who like the food and French casual atmosphere; special events are also celebrated here. Dine on a salad of gorgonzola, greens, and pear, a fricaseee of fresh Manila clams, or short ribs braised in wine, honey, and more.

🛏 55 🌙 Closed Tues.
🏧 All major cards

ROY'S
$$$
CORNER OF LEWERS ST. AND KALIA RD.
TEL 808/923-7697

Hawaii Fusion
Roy's Hawaiian fusion creations are a blend of fresh ingredients and Eurasian flavors with an emphasis on seafood, such as crab cakes and fresh *ahi* (tuna). This busy spot is open daily from 11 a.m. to 11 p.m.

🛏 160 indoors, 30 outdoors
🏧 All major cards

CAFÉ LAUFER
$$
3565 WAIALAE AVE.
TEL 808/735-7717
American
It's all about the desserts in this small modern café. Choose from at least a dozen specials a day. Dream of Black Forest torte, pear Danish, feathery coconut cake, cheesecakes. Start with a good homey meatloaf, a daily pasta, or the Thai satay chicken salad.

🛏 35 🏧 All major cards

DUKE'S CANOE CLUB
$$
OUTRIGGER WAIKIKI
2335 KALAKAUA AVE.
TEL 808/922-2268
American
On the beach, thatched umbrellas, Hawaiian music, drop-dead sunsets, steaks, great ribs, seafood, and well-stocked salad bar, including a made-for-you Caesar stand. What more can you want of Waikiki? Breakfast is served. Memorabilia of surfer legend and Olympic swim champ Duke Kahanamoku abound.

🛏 350 indoors, 150 outdoors
🅿 At Outrigger East
🏧 All major cards

GYOTAKU JAPANESE RESTAURANT
$$
1824 S. KING ST.
TEL 808/949-4584
Japanese
Lunches and dinners here attract aficionados of creative Japanese dishes, such as a sushi delicacy with a sense of humor

known as fuzzy wuzzy rolls. Or choose pokechos, the latter an Asian version of nachos complete with sprouts, avocado, seafood, and wonton strips.

🍴 200 💳 DC, DS, MC

🍴 HIMALAYAN KITCHEN
$$

1137 11TH AVE.
TEL 808/735-1122
Indian/Nepalese

It's a good thing the indoor/outdoor rooftop setting is so ethnically charming and the food is so good because the service is *slow*. Look for exquisitely prepared authentic dishes with freshly prepared spices. Try apricot/almond naan bread and a tandoori mixed grill, one of the many meat or vegetarian curries. BYOB.

🍴 Indoors, outdoors ⊕ Closed L Sat.–Mon. 💳 All major cards

🍴 KEO'S WAIKIKI
$$

AMBASSADOR HOTEL
2028 KUHIO AVE.
TEL 808/951-9355
Thai

Keo's introduced Thai food to Hawaii, among banks of orchids, small starry lights, and Siam art treasures. Indulge in Evil Jungle Prince sauced with coconut and basil, delectable curries, eggplant with peanut sauce. Exceptional desserts—mango sticky rice. Breakfast too.

🍴 260 🅿 💳 All major cards

WINDWARD OAHU

🏨 PARADISE BAY RESORT
$$$$$

47-039 LIHIKAI DR.
KANEOHE 96744
TEL 808/239-5711 OR
800/735-5071
FAX 808/239-6658
paradisebayresorthawaii.com
It's a stretch to call this rural motel a resort. Situated on beautiful Kaneohe Bay, close to water sports. Price depends on size of cottage and

proximity to the water.

ℹ️ 25 units, full kitchens or kitchenettes 🍴

🏨 PAT'S KAILUA BEACH PROPERTIES
$

204 S. KALAHEO AVE.
KAILUA 96734
TEL 808/261-1653
FAX 808/261-0893
patskailua.com
Agency has fully furnished home and cottage rentals on and near Oahu's most beautiful beach, Kailua Beach.

ℹ️ 39 units

🍴 BUZZ'S ORIGINAL STEAKHOUSE
$$

413 KAWAILOA RD. KAILUA 96734
TEL 808/261-4661
American
Rickety, casual place across from Kailua Beach. President Clinton dined here, and they're proud enough to have a plaque marking the table. Steaks, seafood, salad bar.

🍴 120 🅿 💳 No credit cards

NORTH SHORE

🏨 TURTLE BAY RESORTS
$$$$$

57-091 KAMEHAMEHA HWY.
KAHUKU 96731
TEL 808/293-6000 OR
800/203-3650
FAX 808/293-1286
turtlebayresort.com
A recreational resort offering golf, tennis, horseback riding, surfing, and a children's program. Safest swimming beach on the North Shore on one side of the peninsula; raging surf on the other in winter.

ℹ️ 443 units 🛎️

🍴 JAMESON'S BY THE SEA
$–$$$

62-540 KAMEHAMEHA HWY.
HALEIWA
TEL 808/637-4336
American
International beers are a

specialty at this seaview place. Dine on soups, burgers, appetizers such as Thai summer rolls or salmon pâté, and entrées including fresh fish and shrimp curry. The Fudge Works counter tempts with chocolate coconut macadamia fudge.

🍴 80 indoors, 55 outdoors 🅿 💳 All major cards

🍴 CHOLOS HOMESTYLE MEXICAN II
$

NORTH SHORE MARKETPLACE
66-250 KAMEHAMEHA HWY.
HALEIWA
TEL 808/637-3059
Mexican
They make their own salsa, the music is loud, tacky Mexican artifacts abound, the cooking is authentic, and the food is good and cheap. The fish taco plate uses fresh local seafood, and the vegetarian dishes such as spinach quesadilla are memorable. Seating is indoors and out. Surfers love the place. Lunch and dinner.

🍴 52 indoors, 22 outdoors 💳 All major cards

WAIANAE COAST

🏨🍴 JW MARRIOTT IHILANI RESORT & SPA AT KO OLINA
$$$$$

92-1001 OLANI ST.
KAPOLEI 96707
TEL 808/679-0079 OR
800/228-9290
FAX 808/679-0080
ihilani.com
Set in the manicured Ko Olina Resort, with sandy coves for swimming, Ihilani is like being on a neighbor island, but with Waikiki only 35 minutes away. Rooms are luxurious, with large lanai. The spa is state-of-the-art pampering with thalassic and hydro therapies plus some unique Hawaiian treatments.

ℹ️ 387 units 🍴 🛎️

🏨 Hotel 🍴 Restaurant ℹ️ No. of Guest Rooms 🍴 No. of Seats 🅿 Parking ⊕ Closed 🛗 Elevator

PRICES

HOTELS

An indication of the cost of a double room in the high season is given by **$** signs.

$$$$$	Over $240
$$$$	$160–$240
$$$	$110–$160
$$	$70–$110
$	Under $70

RESTAURANTS

An indication of the cost of a three-course meal without drinks is given by **$** signs.

$$$$$	Over $65
$$$$	$50–$65
$$$	$30–$50
$$	$20–$30
$	Under $20

■ MAUI

WEST MAUI

🏨🍽 HYATT REGENCY MAUI
$$$$$

200 NOHEA KAI DR.
LAHAINA 96761
TEL 808/661-1234 OR
800/223-1234
FAX 808/667-4498
maui.hyatt.com

A fantasy beach resort built in the 1980s on 40 acres with gardens, waterfalls, and pool. The restaurants are known for ambience as well as food.

ℹ 806 units 🏊 🏋

SOMETHING SPECIAL

🏨🍽 RITZ-CARLTON KAPALUA
$$$$$

ONE RITZ-CARLTON DR.
KAPALUA 96761
TEL 808/669-6200 OR
800/262-8440
FAX 808/669-1566
ritzcarlton.com

Quiet good taste and tropical style permeate every aspect

of this elegant hotel. The food is noteworthy (see p. 248), the beach is one of the best on Maui, and the hotel is committed to sharing the Hawaiian culture in a variety of programs. Three championship golf courses rise into the hills behind.

ℹ 548 units 🏊 🏋

🏨🍽 THE WESTIN MAUI
$$$$$

2365 KAANAPALI PKWY.
LAHAINA 96761
TEL 808/667-2525 OR
866/716-8112
FAX 808/661-5764
westinmaui.com

Two 11-story towers preside over an aquatic fantasyland. The beachside swimming pool is scalloped in heated pools, and a high waterslide, waterfalls, and swim-up grottoes.

ℹ 761 units 🏊 🏋

🏨🍽 NAPILI KAI BEACH RESORT
$$$$

5900 LOWER HONOAPIILANI RD.
LAHAINA 96761
TEL 808/669-6271 OR
800/367-5030
FAX 808/669-5740
napilikai.com

Traditional, charming low-rise units on 10 acres of lawn tucked in a cove on a beach. Rooms have shoji screens, lanai, cool colors, and rattan furniture. Attracts a loyal following of visitors.

ℹ 163 units 🚭 Some 🏊

🏨 THE WHALER ON KAANAPALI BEACH
$$$$

2481 KAANAPALI PKWY.
LAHAINA 96761
TEL 808/661-6000 OR
877/997-6667
FAX 808/661-8315
whalerkaanapali.com

People return to this well-run holiday condo year after year. Only a third of the units are available for vacation stays.

All have kitchens.

ℹ 360 units 🏊 🏋

🏨🍽 KAANAPALI BEACH HOTEL
$$$

2525 KAANAPALI PKWY.
LAHAINA 96761
TEL 808/661-0011 OR
800/262-8450
FAX 808/667-5978
kbhmaui.com

Aloha spirit abounds at this older hotel set among lawns and gardens. Super-friendly staff give lessons in Hawaiian crafts. Rooms sport wicker and rattan furnishings. Rates are lower than the neighbors'.

ℹ 430 units 🏊

🏨 KAPALUA VILLAS
$$$

200 VILLAGE RD.
LAHAINA 96761
TEL 808/665-5400 OR
800/545-0018
FAX 808/669-2702
kapaluavillas.com

A less expensive way to stay at exclusive Kapalua Resort. Units are individually decorated. Access to all resort features, shuttle to beach. Two-night minimum.

ℹ 266 units 🏊 🏋

🏨🍽 THE OLD WAILUKU INN AT ULUPONO
$$$

2199 KAHOOKELE ST.
WAILUKU 96793
TEL 808/244-5897
OR 800/305-4899
FAX 808/242-9600
mauiinn.com

Feel "old Hawaii" at a former plantation manager's home in a historic neighborhood. The rooms, with high ceilings, Hawaiian quilts, and ohia wood floors, are decorated with a 1930s theme, as if a sarong-clad Hedy Lamarr could show up at any time. Included is a breakfast prepared by chef Janice Fairbanks.

ℹ 10 🅿 🏧 MC, V

🚭 Nonsmoking ❄ Air-conditioning 🏊 Swimming Pool 🏋 Health Club 🏧 Credit Cards

🍴 GERARD'S

$$$

PLANTATION INN
174 LAHAINALUNA RD.
LAHAINA
TEL 808/661-8939
French

This is Lahaina's special-occasion restaurant, very French in cuisine, formality of service, wine list, and ambience—including Edith Piaf singing softly in the sound system. Try the perfectly done rack of lamb and finish with warm upside-down tarte of seasonal local fruit such as pineapple or mango served with vanilla ice cream and appropriate coulis. Dine on the veranda, in the garden or indoors at this award-winning restaurant.

🛏 50 indoors, 50 outdoors
🕐 Closed L ◈ All major cards

SOMETHING SPECIAL

🍴 HULA GRILL

$$$

WHALER'S VILLAGE SHOPPING
COMPLEX
2435 KAANAPALI PKWY.
LAHAINA
TEL 808/667-6636
Hawaii Regional

Celebrated chef and regional cuisine pioneer Peter Merriman offers fine dining, practically in the sand. Look for fresh grilled seafood with creative sauces and salsas, ribs steamed in banana leaves or crab/macadamia nut wontons. Finish with a giant ice cream sandwich: lush vanilla between two chocolate mac nut brownies. Outdoor barefoot area has a lighter menu of burgers and pizza. And what would a place called Hula Grill be without hula? Dancing nightly.

🛏 200 indoors, 120 outdoors
Ⓟ ◈ All major cards

SOMETHING SPECIAL

🍴 ROY'S KAHANA BAR & GRILL

$$

2290 KAANAPALI PKWY.
KAHANA
TEL 808/669-6999
Eurasian

Famed chef/owner Roy Yamaguchi's Maui restaurant has the high-decibel energy level that is his signature. Seafood is freshest, usually from Maui waters, and offered in almost a dozen preparations. It may be blackened *ahi* (tuna) or crusted mahimahi. If you're lucky, creamy polenta with spinach will be a special. Dessert is the hog wild chocolate souffle, runny with chocolate in the middle. Dinner only, from 5:30 p.m.

🛏 207 indoors
◈ All major cards

🍴 SANSEI RESTAURANT & SUSHI BAR

$$

KAPALUA SHOPS
600 OFFICE RD.
KAPALUA
TEL 808/669-6286
Japanese/Pacific Rim

A brilliant blend of cuisines results in delectables such as shrimp cake in ginger-lime chili butter with cilantro pesto, or lobster and crab ravioli. People drive from all over Maui for this one. Deep discounts for food ordered before 6 p.m. Late service and entertainment Thursday and Friday, with discounts after 10 p.m.

🛏 120 Ⓟ 🕐 Closed L
◈ All major cards

🍴 THE TERRACE

$$

RITZ CARLTON KAPALVA HOTEL
ONE RITZ-CARLTON DR.
TEL 808/665-7096
Pacific Regional

The indoor/outdoor restaurant has a Mediterranean feel, but the menu is definitely Pacific. Try the signature lemongrass soup and Maui onion–crusted *ahi* (tuna) topped with caramelized foie gras. Lunch and dinner.

🛏 63 ◈ All major cards

🍴 BEACH HOUSE

$

RITZ-CARLTON KAPALUA HOTEL
ONE RITZ-CARLTON DR.
TEL 808/669-6200
American

A great little find, all outdoors on a breezy lanai over the beach. Traditional Caesar salad, a plate with baby back ribs and grilled mahimahi, or Maui onion rings with buttermilk dressing.

🛏 50 Ⓟ 🕐 Closed D
◈ All major cards

CENTRAL MAUI

🍴 A SAIGON CAFÉ

$$

1792 MAIN ST., WAILUKU
TEL 808/243-9560
Vietnamese

An excellent place to explore this interesting cuisine, definitely influenced by French. Cooked-at-your-table vegetarian dishes, clay-pot chicken, fresh fish seasoned with lemongrass, ginger, and garlic, and *pho,* the classic Vietnamese soup with a mound of fresh basil.

🛏 65 Ⓟ ◈ MC, V

🍴 RESTAURANT MATSU

$

161 ALAMAHA ST.
KAHALUI 96732
TEL 808/871-0822
Japanese/Local Food

Islanders drive from far points for this low-key eatery with its daily specials, outstanding sushi, steaming noodle dishes, and fresh fish.

🛏 32 Ⓟ 🕐 Closed Sun.
◈ No credit cards

🏨 Hotel 🍴 Restaurant 🕐 No. of Guest Rooms 🛏 No. of Seats Ⓟ Parking 🕐 Closed 🛗 Elevator

EAST MAUI

🏨🍴 FAIRMONT KEA LANI MAUI
$$$$$
4100 WAILEA ALANUI
WAILEA 96753
TEL 808/875-4100 OR
800/659-4100
FAX 808/875-1200
fairmont.com
Like a Moorish apparition, stark white against blue sky. Decor in this resort may be the most consistently beautiful in the Islands, in tone-on-tone whites and creams. Luxury marble baths. Fine restaurants.
ℹ️ 450 units 🏊 🏋️

🏨🍴 FOUR SEASONS RESORT WAILEA
$$$$$
3900 WAILEA ALANUI
WAILEA 96753
TEL 808/874-8000 OR
800/334-MAUI
FAX 808/874-2244
fourseasons.com/maui
Expect the usual Four Seasons spacious rooms and deluxe marble baths. Almost all have ocean views. Furnishings look like refined Europe married to the tropics. Service is efficient, yet relaxed. Less expected: the warm Hawaiian hospitality and reliably dramatic sunsets. Restaurants are noteworthy.
ℹ️ 380 units 🏊 🏋️

SOMETHING SPECIAL

🏨🍴 GRAND WAILEA RESORT HOTEL & SPA
$$$$$
3850 WAILEA ALANUI
WAILEA 96753
TEL 808/875-1234 OR
800/888-6100
FAX 808/879-4077
grandwailea.com
A rare combination of luxe and looney fun. A $30-million art collection decorates a fantasy playground of aquatic antics—waterfalls, slides, a river pool, water elevator, restaurant in a man-made tide pool, a floating wedding chapel. Toss in Hawaii's grandest spa, fine dining, and a nightclub with laser lights. Children have their own program—even theater. Rooms are spacious.
ℹ️ 780 units 🏊 🏋️

🏨🍴 MAKENA BEACH & GOLF RESORT
$$$$$
5400 MAKENA ALANUI
MAKENA 96753
TEL 808/874-1111 OR
800/321-6284
FAX 808/879-8763
makenaresortmaui.com
An incredible setting on the edge of the Maui wilderness. Modern, breezy rooms. The central open-air atrium has a serene Japanese garden with stone paths and waterfalls flowing past exotic flowers.
ℹ️ 310 units 🅿️ 🏊 🏋️

🏨🍴 TRAVAASA HANA
$$$$$
5301 HANA HWY.
HANA 96713
TEL 808/820-1043 OR
800/321-4262
FAX 808/248-7202
travaasa.com/maui
On the edge of a 7,000-acre ranch, the units are charming, older cottages in gardens or newer Sea Ranch Cottages overlooking the ocean. Horseback riding along coast. Picnic lunches. Shuttle to a fine black-sand beach. Pleasant restaurant.
ℹ️ 66 units 🏊 🏋️

🏨 OLINDA COUNTRY COTTAGES & INN
$$$
2660 OLINDA ROAD
MAKAWAO 96768
TEL 808/572-1453
FAX 808/573-5326
mauibnbcottages.com
Cool and high on the slopes of Haleakala, this small inn looks like it's straight out of a Beatrix Potter tale with hollyhocks in the garden and roses climbing around doorways. Cottages are romantically secluded. It's 15 minutes from the hip cowboy town of Makawao, surrounded by forest and a protea farm. Furnishings could be shot for a *Country Living* magazine spread. Continental breakfast is artfully presented.
ℹ️ 5 units

🍴 FERRARO'S AT SEASIDE
$$$$
FOUR SEASONS HOTEL
3900 WAILEA ALANUI
TEL 808/874-8000
Italian
In the evening, the setting makes your heart soar—outdoors, overlooking the ocean with candles, torches, and impossibly romantic live violin music. All this, plus exquisite Italian cuisine with a tropical pinch. Taste the poached snapper with onion-orange marmalade. At lunch, the view is just as grand but the poolside crowd drops in for lobster salad, half-pound burgers, and mango margaritas.
🪑 145 seats, all outdoors
🅿️ 🚭 All major cards

🍴 SPAGO MAUI
$$$$
FOUR SEASONS HOTEL
3900 WAILEA ALANUI
TEL 808/879-2999
American
So sleek and sophisticated you barely notice the ocean views at Wolfgang Puck's Maui adventure. Look for 15-vegetable salad, wagyu rib eye steak, free-range chicken, and Hong Kong–style fish. There's even a training menu for junior gourmands. The kids proceed from amuse bouche through catch of the day to an ice cream sandwich.
🪑 130 indoors, 79 outdoors
🚭 All major cards

🍴 JOE'S BAR & GRILL
$$$
WAILEA TENNIS CLUB
131 WAILEA IKE PLACE

WAILEA
TEL 808/875-7767
American
Fresh fish or lamb chops are given a gourmet tweak. Signature dish: meat loaf and garlic mashed potatoes.
🔲 100 🅿 🕐 Closed L
🃏 All major cards

🍴 MAMA'S FISH HOUSE
$$$
799 POHO PLACE (MILE MARKER 8 ON THE HANA HIGHWAY)
PAIA
TEL 808/579-8488
American/Seafood
Tucked away in a picturesque cove, Mama's ambience is high-tiki and romantic. Famous seafood offerings include grilled tender octopus caught in a nearby bay, mahimahi baked in a macadamia nut crust, crab cakes, and opah stuffed with Hamakua mushrooms.
🔲 250 🃏 All major cards

🍴 NICK'S FISH MARKET MAUI
$$$
KEA LANI HOTEL
4100 WAILEA ALANUI
TEL 808/879-7224
American
Dine under the stars on exquisite seafood, Maine lobster, steak, or pasta.
🔲 100 indoors, 75 outdoors
🅿 🕐 Closed L
🃏 All major cards

SOMETHING SPECIAL

🍴 HALIIMAILE GENERAL STORE
$$
900 HALIIMAILE RD.
HALIIMAILE
TEL 808/572-2666
Hawaii Regional
Haute cuisine in the cane fields. Modern furnishings, original art in an old plantation store. Start with sashimi Napoleon, move on to baked salmon, or a green salad topped with oranges.
🔲 150 🅿 🃏 All major cards

🍴 STELLA BLUES CAFÉ
$$
1279 SOUTH KIHEI RD.
SUITE B201
KIHEI
TEL 808/874-3779
American
Everything's made from scratch at breakfast, lunch, and dinner, starting with banana macadamia nut pancakes. Salads, such as chicken curry, use Maui greens. The baby back ribs at dinner are simmered in mango-plum sauce. The turkey for sandwiches is roasted in Stella's oven.
🛈 50 indoors, 32 outdoors
🃏 D, MC, V

◼ BIG ISLAND

KONA-KOHALA COAST

SOMETHING SPECIAL

🏨 🍴 FOUR SEASONS HUALALAI
$$$$$
72-100 KAUPULEHU DR.
KAILUA-KONA
TEL 888/340-5662 OR
808/325-8000
FAX 808/325-8200
fourseasons.com/Hualalai
This one gets all the stars and diamonds and deserves them. Everything is low-rise and tucked into tropical flora with maximal ocean views. Strung along a half-mile white-sand beach, it has a spa and notable restaurants ranging from beachfront BBQ to Tuscan cucina rustica. It also has golf and most unusual of all, the King's Pond, a 1.8 million gallon aquarium carved into the lava coast. Snorkel among the 3,000 fish of 75 species. The serene decor includes local art from 1775 to the present. A cultural center offers interactive Hawaiian programs.
🛈 243 units 🃏 All major cards

🏨 🍴 HAPUNA BEACH PRINCE HOTEL
$$$$$
62-100 KAUNAOA DR.
KOHALA COAST 96743
TEL 808/880-1111 OR
888/977-4623
FAX 808/880-3142
hapunabeachhotel.com
Enter the open lobby and be greeted by views of sun-splashed ocean. Live music at sundown creates a vibrant atmosphere. Pale, modern rooms. Emphasis on activities. Outstanding cuisine (see p. 252, Hakone Steakhouse and Sushi Bar).
🛈 350 units 🏊 🎾

🏨 🍴 HILTON WAIKOLOA VILLAGE
$$$$$
69-425 WAIKOLOA BEACH DR.
WAIKOLOA 96738
TEL 808/886-1234 OR
800/HILTONS
FAX 808/886-2900
hiltonwaikoloavillage.com
Fantasy oceanside resort. Go to your room by boat or mini–bullet train. Swim with dolphins. Rooms in three towers. Pool with waterfalls, slides, grottoes. River pool.
🛈 1,240 units 🏊 🎾

🏨 🍴 MAUNA KEA BEACH HOTEL
$$$$$
62-100 MAUNA KEA BEACH DR.
KOHALA COAST 96743
TEL 808/882-7222 OR
866/977-4589
FAX 808/882-5700
maunakeabeachhotel.com
The grande dame of the luxe-on-lava hotels. Art treasures are scattered everywhere. Some families have been coming here for two and three generations. Superb swimming beach, fine restaurants, championship golf.
🛈 310 units 🏊 🎾

🏨 🍴 MAUNA LANI BAY HOTEL & BUNGALOWS
$$$$$

PRICES

HOTELS
An indication of the cost of
a double room in the high
season is given by **$** signs.

$$$$$	Over $240
$$$$	$160–$240
$$$	$110–$160
$$	$70–$110
$	Under $70

RESTAURANTS
An indication of the cost of
a three-course meal without
drinks is given by **$** signs.

$$$$$	Over $65
$$$$	$50–$65
$$$	$30–$50
$$	$20–$30
$	Under $20

68-1400 MAUNA LANI DR.
KOHALA COAST 96743
TEL 808/885-6622 OR
800/367-2323
FAX 808/881-7000
maunalani.com
Rooms are tropical modern.
Hotel is tucked in a quiet
sandy cove and built around a
network of ancient fishponds.
Outstanding cuisine is a
hallmark. Four ultra-luxe
bungalows at mega-rates offer
utmost privacy.
350 units

KANALOA AT KONA
$$$$
78-261 MANUKAI ST.
KAILUA-KONA 96740
TEL 808/322-9625 OR
800/688-7444
FAX 808/322-3818
outrigger.com
Spacious, elegant apartments
with koa cabinetry, bathroom
spas, located on Keauhou Bay.
Good restaurant.
166 units (87 rentals)
None

MAUNA LANI POINT
$$$$
68-1050 MAUNA LANI PT. DR.

KOHALA COAST 96743
TEL 808/885-5022 OR
800/642-6284
FAX 808/885-5015
maunalanipoint.com
Live in secluded luxury with
access to all the amenities of
Mauna Lani Resort. Dream
kitchen, spacious master bath,
designer furnishings, large lanai
with spectacular views of the
Kona coast.
116 units (56 rentals)

WAIKOLOA BEACH MARRIOTT RESORT & SPA
$$$$
69-275 WAIKOLOA BEACH DR.
WAIKOLOA 96738
TEL 808/886-6789 OR
800/922-5533
FAX 808/886-3601
waikoloabeachmarriott.com
This beachfront hotel boasts
sandstone flooring, off-white
tones, and a commitment
to keeping it Hawaiian in
ambience. Rooms reflect
tropical colors in greens and
bright yellows with bamboo
accents. Fantasy pool, full
Rainforest Spa.
545 units

KING KAMEHAMEHA'S KONA BEACH HOTEL
$$$
75-5660 PALANI RD.
KAILUA-KONA 96740
TEL 808/329-2911 OR
800/367-2111
FAX 808/329-4602
konabeachhotel.com
Right in Kailua-Kona town, on
the water. The hotel boasts
portraits of Hawaiian royalty
and historic artifacts. Walk to
important historical sites, and
dozens of shops and restau-
rants. Rooms are nothing fancy,
but reliable and clean.
458 units

ROYAL KONA RESORT
$$$
75-5852 ALII DRIVE
KAILUA-KONA 96740

TEL 800/222-5642
OR 808/329-3111
FAX 808/329-7230
royalkona.com
Two towers rise up from
a dramatic lava coastline
overlooking one of the state's
only private beaches and
a saltwater lagoon. Rooms
are large in this completely
remodeled older hotel right on
the edge of Kailua town. The
resort has four lighted tennis
courts, spa services, and Don
the Beachcomber Restaurant,
famous for its Sunday brunch
and sunset mai tais.
436 units

PAHUIA
$$$$$
FOUR SEASONS HUALALAI AT
HISTORIC KAUPULEHU
72-100 KAUPULEHU DR.
TEL 808/325-8000
From sunrise to sunset,
breakfast to dinner, dining here
means surrounding yourself
with sweeping ocean views and
the rolling surf. Signature items
include Keahole lobster and
fire-roasted Kona kampachi.
Selections are savory, spicy, or
sweet to please any palate.
180   All major cards

SOMETHING SPECIAL

CANOE HOUSE
$$$$
MAUNA LANI BAY HOTEL
68-1400 MAUNA LANI DR.
TEL 808/885-6622
Hawaii Regional
When the setting is as magnificent as this, with stars overhead and the ocean only feet
away, it's rare to find cuisine to
match, but Canoe House does
it. Freshest seafood from local
waters are cooked in a variety
of ways. Baby back ribs come
with a green papaya kimchi
sauce. For dessert, dare lychee
mousse with mango coulis.
184 indoors, 66 outdoors
P Closed L
All major cards

Nonsmoking   Air-conditioning   Swimming Pool   Health Club   Credit Cards

🍴 COAST GRILLE

$$$

HAPUNA BEACH PRINCE HOTEL
62-100 KAUNAOA DR.
TEL 808/880-1111
American/Hawaii Regional
A lively open-air place specializing in freshest seafood and trendy culinary styles. Try *moi*, the fish raised in aquaculture ponds, cold-water Big Island lobster, or oysters from the oyster bar. For a perfect finish indulge in the almost legendary chocolate macadamia nut caramel torte.

🪑 140 indoors, 100 outdoors
🅿 🕒 Closed L
🚫 All major cards

🍴 DON THE BEACHCOMBER

$$$

ROYAL KONA RESORT
75-5852 ALII DRIVE
TEL 808/329-3111
Pacific
Tangerine sunsets blaze just beyond your oceanside table as you toast with a big slushy mai tai, adorned with a paper parasol. Start with the pupu sampler featuring Kona crab cake and big spicy prawns. Order Big Island prime rib, baby back ribs, or Son-of-a-Beach filet with sizzling mushrooms, or for the timid, pick an entree salad. Daily breakfast buffet.

🪑 56 indoors, 50 outdoors
🕒 Closed L   🚫 All major cards

🍴 HAKONE STEAKHOUSE AND SUSHI BAR

$$$

HAPUNA PRINCE HOTEL
62-100 KAUNAOA DR.
TEL 808/880-1111
Japanese
If you've ever wanted to try fine Japanese cuisine but didn't know where to start, this is the place. The buffet is beautifully presented and each dish is tagged with an explanation. Choose from sushi, tempura, noodles, fish, sukiyaki, tender beef—and a very non-Japanese

enticement of pies and cakes.
🪑 140 🅿 🕒 Closed D Thurs.–Fri., & L   🚫 All major cards

🍴 HUGGO'S

$$$

75-5828 KAHAKAI RD.
TEL 808/329-1493
American
Surf 'n' turf with a bit of class, right on the water with manta rays gliding by. This is deservedly one of the most popular places in town. Big cocktails, live music, and smashing sunsets.

🪑 130 indoors, 75 outdoors
🅿 🚫 All major cards

🍴 KIRIN

$$$

HILTON WAIKOLOA VILLAGE
69-425 WAIKOLOA BEACH DR.
TEL 808/886-1234
Chinese
One-of-a-kind Chinese treasures highlight elegant decor. The menu is a reminder that Chinese is one of the world's great cuisines, here encompassing Hunan, Szechuan, Peking, and Canton. Dare to try the shredded jellyfish. Or try the crabmeat taro cup, live seafood including Maine lobster, or crispy-skinned Szechuan duck smoked over camphor wood and green tea leaves, served with plum sauce. Finish with a Western dessert: chocolate cake or lillikoi cheesecake with premium Chinese tea.

🪑 174 indoors, 25 outdoors
🕒 Closed L   🚫 All major cards

SOMETHING SPECIAL

🍴 THE TERRACE

$$$

MAUNA KEA BEACH HOTEL
62-100 MAUNA KEA BEACH DR.
TEL 808/882-7222
Buffet
Sunday brunch (the only meal served) is an extravagance of excellent food. On Tuesday evening the Terrace becomes a luau grounds, and on Saturdays

find an old-fashioned clam bake with complete seafood buffet. Eat outdoors overlooking the ocean.

🪑 160 outdoors
🅿 🚫 All major cards

🍴 BAMBOO

$$

HWY. 270
HAWI
TEL 808/889-5555
Hawaii Regional
The old Takata Store is dressed up in tropical mufti with wicker and bamboo. Try imupig quesadilla, and fresh local seafood. Many dishes have a Thai touch with coconut and lemongrass seasoning. Sunday brunch is served.

🪑 80 🅿 🕒 Closed D Sun. & Mon.   🚫 MC, V

🍴 THE COFFEE SHACK

$

HWY. 11 (1 MILE S OF
CAPTAIN COOK)
TEL 808/328-9555
American
This pink-and-white restaurant looks over old lava flows to the ocean. Sandwiches of fresh fish, or Reubens (grilled sandwiches) with tons of sauerkraut are enormous affairs on your choice of good bread. They grow their own coffee. Breakfast is served.

🪑 50 outdoors 🅿 🕒 Closed L
Sun. & D   🚫 D, MC, V

🍴 TESHIMA'S

$

HWY. 11 HONALO (15 MINUTES S
OF KAILUA-KONA)
TEL 808/322-9140
Japanese-American
This family-owned restaurant is a local favorite for the Japanese food developed on local plantations. Complete dinners, such as beef teriyaki or New York steak, come with soup and *tsukemono* (pickled vegetables). Japanese breakfast is a specialty.

🪑 75 🅿 🚫 All major cards

🏨 Hotel   🍴 Restaurant   ① No. of Guest Rooms   🪑 No. of Seats   🅿 Parking   🕒 Closed   🛗 Elevator

WAIMEA

⊞ WAIAKA HOMESTEAD
$$$
64-1664 WAIAKA ST.
KAMUELA, 96743
TEL 808/960-4027
waiaka.net

Classic Hawaiian-style atmosphere in a historic old Waimea home. Twenty minutes away from the beach or a nice hike.

ⓘ 4 suites 🅿 🗖 MC, V

⊞ AAAH, THE VIEWS
$
66-1773 ALANEO ST.
KAMUELA 96743
TEL 808/885-3455
FAX 808/885-4031
aaahtheviews.com

A sweet cottage beside a brook in an old-fashioned garden has stunning views from the slopes of Mauna Kea out to the distant ocean. You can also see Mauna Loa and Hualalae volcanoes.

ⓘ 3 🚫 None
🗖 No credit cards

SOMETHING SPECIAL

🍴 MERRIMAN'S
$$
65-1227 OPELU RD. (ON HWY. 19)
KAMUELA
TEL 808/885-6822
Hawaii Regional

A shrine for foodies. Pioneering chef Peter Merriman, a master with fresh local ingredients, hires farmers to grow what he wants. Lamb comes from nearby Kahua Ranch. Try it roasted with plum sauce and a papaya-mint relish.

🍴 130 🅿 🕐 Closed L Sat.& Sun. 🗖 All major cards

🍴 PANIOLO COUNTRY INN
$$
65-1214 LINDSEY RD.
KAMUELA
TEL 808/885-4377
American/Local Food

Guys with big boots and belt buckles mosey in for the great chow. Breakfast stars a mean Loko-Moko—local favorite of a hamburger patty on rice topped with a fried egg and gravy. The hollandaise on the eggs Benedict is exquisite. Or try the Belgian waffle with Waimea strawberries.

🍴 75 🅿 🗖 All major cards

🍴 WAIMEA COFFEE COMPANY
$
63-1279 KAWAIHAE RD., #114
KAMUELA
TEL 808/885-8915

Freshly baked delicacies for breakfast or lunch at reasonable prices. Try the croissants, scones, salads, soups, wraps, bagel sandwiches, and more.

🍴 30 🅿 🕐 Closed 4 p.m. Mon.–Fri., 3 p.m. Sat. & Sun.

EAST HAWAII

⊞ SHIPMAN HOUSE BED & BREAKFAST INN
$$$$
131 KAIULANI ST.
HILO 96720
TEL 808/934-8002 OR
800/627-8447
FAX 808/934-8002
hilo-hawaii.com

Queen Liliuokalani came to tea at this century-old Victorian manse with witch's hat turrets. Set amid lush gardens, the beautifully maintained house is on the National and State Registers of Historic Places. Rooms have vintage furnishings. Rates include breakfast.

🍴 5 units (with refrigerator)
🚫 None

⊞ VOLCANO HOUSE & 🍴 NAMAKANIPAIO CABINS
$$$$, $
CRATER RIM DR.
HAWAII VOLCANOES NATIONAL PARK 96718
TEL 866/536-7972
OR 808/441-7750
aquahospitality.com

You couldn't ask for a better location for exploring Hawaii Volcanoes National Park. Millions of dollars were spent to completely renovate the historic hotel ($$$$) and cabins ($) in 2013. The new dining room features local farm products. Diners have watched fiery volcanic activity over lunch.

ⓘ 33 hotel units, 10 cabins
🚫 None

⊞ HILO HAWAIIAN 🍴 HOTEL
$$$
71 BANYAN DR.
HILO 96720
TEL 808/935-9361 OR
800/367-5004
FAX 808/961-9642
castleresorts.com

This older hotel, in the leafy bowers of Banyan Drive on Hilo Bay, is nicely maintained. Rattan furniture against quiet backgrounds. Plantings are mature and views splendid.

ⓘ 286 units (with refrigerator)
🌊

⊞ KILAUEA LODGE 🍴
$$$
19-3948 OLD VOLCANO RD.
VOLCANO VILLAGE 96785
TEL 808/967-7366
FAX 808/967-7367
kilauealodge.com

A cozy inn just outside of Hawaii Volcanoes National Park, with a noteworthy restaurant (see this page). Rates include breakfast. Fireplaces, books, lush gardens.

ⓘ 14 units (with central heating) 🚫 None

🍴 KILAUEA LODGE RESTAURANT
$$
OLD VOLCANO RD.
VOLCANO VILLAGE
TEL 808/967-7366
Continental

Cozy up around the fireplace in the cool uplands just outside Hawaii Volcanoes National Park. All meals come with wonderful soups, salads, and a loaf of homemade bread. Specials might be fillet of antelope flambé, hasenpfeffer, or a vegetarian dish.

🔲 70 🅿 🕐 Closed L
🌊 AE, MC, V

SOMETHING SPECIAL

🍴 SEASIDE RESTAURANT & AQUAPONDS

$$

1790 KALANIANAOLE AVE.
HILO
TEL 808/935-8825
Pacific Rim

This rickety old local favorite was opened in 1921 by chef Colin Nakagawa's grandfather and wiped out twice by tsunamis. The restaurant is situated across from the ocean, on a network of aquaculture ponds. Order mullet, catfish, or *aholehole*—the staff nets it fresh. They also serve one of the best prime rib dinners anywhere. Go in time for sunset, when the egrets fly in from the sea and settle in the mangrove trees beside the ponds.

🔲 200 indoors 🅿 🕐 Closed L & Mon. 🌊 MC, V

SOMETHING SPECIAL

🍴 HANA HOU COFFEE RESTAURANT

$

95–1148 NAALEHU SPUR RD.
NAALEHU 96772
TEL 808/929-9717
American/Local Food

In a century-old building in a blink-and-you-miss-it town, you'll find a spotless place with fresh flowers on every table and home cooking at its finest. This multigenerational family operation serves comfort food—meat loaf, prime rib, fresh fish, and great potatoes. They bake their own bread, even the hamburger buns. People come for miles for the pies and brownies. Find good local arts and crafts in their gift shop. Breakfast and lunch daily.

🔲 50 🅿 🕐 Closed D Mon.– Wed. 🌊 All major cards

🍴 KEN'S HOUSE OF PANCAKES

$

1730 KAMEHAMEHA AVE.
HILO
TEL 808/935-8711
American

When all else fails, there's always Ken's, with reliably good burgers, hash, liver with bacon and onion, fish, and, of course, pancakes. Try *kalua* pig on a hoagie bun. Order lemon coconut custard pie whole or by the slice. Open 24 hours.

🔲 180 🅿 🌊 All major cards

🍴 NORI'S SAIMIN & SNACKS

$

688 KINOOLE ST.
HILO
TEL 808/935-9133
Local Food

Mountains of tasty food without fuss or fancy decor is what you get. Specialty is saimin, the unique local noodle soup. Add barbecued meat sticks to the order.

🔲 100 🅿 🌊 MC, V

■ KAUAI

LIHUE & ENVIRONS

🏨 KAUAI MARRIOTT
🍴 RESORT & BEACH CLUB

$$$$$

3610 RICE ST.
KALAPAKI BEACH
LIHUE 96766
TEL 808/245-5050 OR
800/220-2925
FAX 808/245-5049
marriott.com/lihhi

Everything comes on a grand scale—enormous swimming pool, network of lagoons and waterways, extravagant gardens, marble, statuary, columns. All this on lovely Kalapaki Beach in view of dramatic Nawiliwili Harbor. Restaurants (opposite).

ⓘ 356 units, 232 villas 🏊 🍴

🏨 KAUAI BEACH HOTEL
🍴 AND RESORT

$$$$

4331 KAUAI BEACH DR.
LIHUE 96766
TEL 866/536-7976
FAX 808/245-3956
kauaibeachresorthawaii.com

Low-rise with big aspirations. Waterfalls, caves, tiki torches, fantasy pool, even a nightclub. Rooms in wicker and pastels. Beach is breathtaking but unsafe for swimming.

ⓘ 341 units 🏊

SOMETHING SPECIAL

🍴 GAYLORD'S

$$$

KILOHANA SQUARE
3-2087 KAUMUALII HWY.
PUHI
TEL 808/245-9593
Continental Hawaii Regional

This is Kauai's special occasion place. Locals come in droves for the ribs and the homemade desserts such as authentic Linzer torte and Kilohana mud pie with mocha ice cream. Also find pastas, salads, seafood, all served on the lanai of a gracious sugar plantation manager's mansion. Sunday brunch.

🔲 143 outdoors
🅿 🌊 All major cards

🍴 BARBECUE INN

$$

2982 KRESS ST.
LIHUE
TEL 808/245-2921
Japanese/Pacific Rim

Popular family-owned place serves a wide variety of dishes: complete Japanese dinners, turkey dinner, catch of the day, good salads, and burgers. Complete dinners often combine local ethnic specialties.

🔲 96 🕐 Closed Sun. 🌊 MC, V

🏨 Hotel 🍴 Restaurant ⓘ No. of Guest Rooms 🔲 No. of Seats 🅿 Parking 🕐 Closed 🔲 Elevator

PRICES

HOTELS
An indication of the cost of
a double room in the high
season is given by **$** signs.

$$$$$	Over $240
$$$$	$160–$240
$$$	$110–$160
$$	$70–$110
$	Under $70

RESTAURANTS
An indication of the cost of
a three-course meal without
drinks is given by **$** signs.

$$$$$	Over $65
$$$$	$50–$65
$$$	$30–$50
$$	$20–$30
$	Under $20

🍴 CAFÉ PORTOFINO
$$
KAUAI MARRIOTT RESORT &
BEACH CLUB
3610 RICE ST.
TEL 808/245-2121
Italian
cafeportofino.com
Fine cuisine is served with
views of Nawiliwili Harbor and
dramatic mountain silhouettes.
They make their own gelati.
🪑 50 indoors, 50 outdoors 🅿
🚭 Closed L Sat.& Sun.
💳 All major cards

🍴 DUKE'S CANOE CLUB
$$
KAUAI MARRIOTT RESORT &
BEACH CLUB
3610 RICE ST.
TEL 808/246-9599
American
Great views, a lot of atmosphere, and live Hawaiian
music on Friday nights. Find
reliably good prime rib,
seafood, and noteworthy
salad bar.
🪑 250 indoors, 190 outdoors
🅿 💳 All major cards

🍴 HAMURA'S SAIMIN STAND
$
2596 KRESS ST.
LIHUE
TEL 808/245-3271
Local Food
Pull up at a tangerine Formica
counter for internationally
acclaimed saimin, Hawaii's
ubiquitous noodle soup. Add
barbecued teriyaki meat sticks
and a slab of pie for dessert.
A great experience.
🪑 50 🅿 💳 No credit cards

POIPU/KOLOA

SOMETHING SPECIAL

🏨 GRAND HYATT 🍴 KAUAI
$$$$$
1571 POIPU RD.
KOLOA 96756
TEL 808/742-1234 OR
800/233-1234
FAX 808/240-6598
grandhyattkauai.com
Gracious and relaxed is the
mood of this elegant hostelry
situated on 50 acres fronting
golden Shipwreck Beach. Fine
dining, a 25,000-square-foot
spa, and spacious rooms with
marble baths.
ℹ 602 units 🏊 🏋

🏨 SHERATON KAUAI 🍴 RESORT
$$$$$
2440 HOONANI RD.
KOLOA 96756
TEL 808/742-1661 OR
888/625-4988
FAX 808/742-9777
sheraton-kauai.com
Completely rebuilt in 1997, this
hotel is better than ever with lily
ponds, gardens, and a prime spot
on sunny Poipu Beach. It has
more Hawaiian atmosphere than
before, an excellent children's
program, and a spa overlooking the ocean. Restaurants have
sensational sunset views.
ℹ 414 units 🏊 🏋

🏨 KIAHUNA PLANTATION 🍴 **$$$$**
2253 POIPU RD.
POIPU 96756
TEL 808/742-6411 OR
800/688-7444
FAX 808/742-1698
outrigger.com
Lush gardens and a broad
expanse of lawn right on prime
Poipu Beach. Completely
rebuilt in 1994, after Hurricane
Iniki, units are fresh and
appealing. A notable garden
surrounds the vintage
plantation manager's home
that serves as the lobby and
restaurant (see p. 256).
ℹ 200 units (with kitchen)
🚭 None 🏊

🏨 PRINCE KUHIO
$
5061 LAWAI BEACH RD.
KOLOA 96756
TEL 808/245-4711 OR
800/767-4707
FAX 808/245-8115
prosserrealty.net
The best buy on Kauai's South
Shore. Not luxe, but pleasant
and recently renovated. You
get kitchens, ocean views,
garden pool, Beach House
restaurant. Across the street
from a fine surfing beach, and
adjacent to a great snorkeling
cove and swimming beach.
ℹ 72 units (11 rentals)
🚭 None 🏊

🍴 ROY'S POIPU BAR & GRILL
$$$
POIPU SHOPPING VILLAGE
2360 KIAHUNA PLANTATION DR.
POIPU
TEL 808/742-5000
Hawaii Regional
Another restaurant by famous
chef Roy Yamaguchi. Like the
others, it's hip, loud, and has a
cutting-edge daily menu that is
a fusion of East and West. Pray
for crab cakes.
🪑 220 indoors 🅿
💳 All major cards

🚭 Nonsmoking ❄ Air-conditioning 🏊 Swimming Pool 🏋 Health Club 💳 Credit Cards

🍴 **BRENNECKE'S BEACH BROILER**
$$
2100 HOONE RD.
POIPU
TEL 808/742-7588
American
Casual, breezy atmosphere in full view of Poipu Beach is perfect for this surf 'n' turf eatery that steps out with good vegetarian offerings.
🍴 100 indoors 🅿️
💳 All major cards

🍴 **PLANTATION GARDEN RESTAURANT & BAR**
$$
KIAHUNA PLANTATION
2253 POIPU RD.
POIPU
TEL 808/742-2121
California/Pacific Rim
Set in a historic home surrounded by a celebrated garden, they scarcely need good food. In fact, they serve very good Hawaiian fare. Seafood is freshest.
🍴 60 indoors, 124 outdoors
🅿️ 🕐 Closed L
💳 All major cards

COCONUT COAST

🏨 **ASTON ALOHA**
🍴 **BEACH HOTEL**
$$$
3-5920 KUHIO HWY.
KAPAA 96746
TEL 808/823-6000 OR
888/823-5111
FAX 808/823-6666
astonhotels.com
In 1998 this beachfront resort was totally remodeled, repositioned as a family-friendly place where children 19 and under stay free.
ℹ️ 216 units 🏊 🛗

🏨 **HOTEL CORAL REEF**
$$
4-1516 KUHIO HWY.
KAPAA 96746
TEL 808/822-4481 OR
800/843-4659
FAX 808/822-7705

hotelcoralreefresort.com
Cheap and cheerful on the beach, walk to shopping. Continental breakfast included.
ℹ️ 24 units 🚫 None 💳 MC, V

🍴 **THE BULL SHED**
$$
4-796 KUHIO HWY.
WAIPOULI
TEL 808/822-3791
American
Sage local carnivores make quiet pilgrimages to this oceanside dining room for macho-sized meals of steaks, chops, and ribs. Toss some pasta and seafood to the timid, or send them to the salad bar.
🍴 150 🅿️ 🕐 Closed L
💳 All major cards

🍴 **MEMA**
$$
4369 KUHIO HWY.
WAILUA
TEL 808/823-0899
Thai
Look for lemongrass soup, a wild variety of coconut-milk-based curries, vegetables with spicy peanut sauce.
🍴 60 🅿️ 🕐 Closed L Sat. & Sun. 💳 All major cards

🍴 **WAILUA MARINA RESTAURANT**
$$
5971 KUHIO HWY.
WAILUA
TEL 808/822-4311
American
Obviously designed for big riverboat crowds, this manages to be a truly nice restaurant by virtue of its setting beside the hauntingly beautiful Wailua River, and its satisfying menu, which ranges from signature stuffed pork chops to fresh seafood and teriyaki steak.
🍴 125 indoors, 175 outdoors
🅿️ 🕐 Closed Mon.
💳 AE, MC, V

🍴 **CAFFE COCO**
$
4-369 KUHIO HWY.
WAILUA
TEL 808/821-0066
Local Food
A funky little place lost among fruit trees has earned a big reputation for fresh tropical juices, fish wraps, salads, and vegetarian dishes. A good bet: The Pacific Rim platter with seared *ahi* (tuna) with mango sweet-sour sauce, tofu pot stickers, and noodle salad with peanut dressing. Dinner reservations required.
🍴 20 indoors, 60 outdoors
🅿️ 🕐 Closed L Sat.–Mon.
💳 MC, V

PRINCEVILLE-HANALEI AREA

SOMETHING SPECIAL

🏨 **PRINCEVILLE SAINT**
🍴 **REGIS RESORT KAUAI**
$$$$$
5520 KA HAKU RD.
PRINCEVILLE 96722
TEL 808/826-9644 OR
800/826-5000
FAX 808/826-1166
princevillehotelhawaii.com
Step into the lobby and look out at a grand vista of Hanalei Bay and magnificent mountains streaming with waterfalls. Serene swimming pool, wonderful restaurants (see Makana Terrace, opposite), outstanding rooms with handsome appointments, and views even from the bathroom shower. Two top-notch golf courses.
ℹ️ 252 units 🏊 🛗

🏨 **HANALEI BAY RESORT**
🍴 **& SUITES**
$$$$
5380 HONOIKI RD.
PRINCEVILLE 96722
TEL 808/826-6522 OR
800/827-4427

🏨 Hotel 🍴 Restaurant ℹ️ No. of Guest Rooms 🍴 No. of Seats 🅿️ Parking 🕐 Closed 🛗 Elevator

FAX 808/826-6680
hanaleibayresort.com
The landscaping is bright with flowers and leads the eye to the bay and mountains. Nicely furnished units are large with kitchens. Enjoy the romantic restaurant Bali Hai.

[1] 187 units 🏊

SOMETHING SPECIAL

🍴 MAKANA TERRACE
$$$
PRINCEVILLE SAINT REGIS RESORT
5520 KA HAKU RD.
PRINCEVILLE
TEL 808/826-2760
American/Continental
There is not a finer view on earth. Breakfast buffet with omelet stand. Lunch ranges from soups to salads and sandwiches, while dinner features fresh seafood. Thursday's Mailani Dinner Show is a luau gone gourmet.

[fork] 110 indoors, 70 outdoors
[P] 🅰 All major cards

🍴 KALYPSO
$$
5-5156 KUHIO HWY.
HANALEI
TEL 808/826-9700
Mixed
More microbrewed beer on the menu than food. Casual, happy, always packed. Flagrant tropical decor. Get tacos, burgers, fish, salads, chef's specials such as crusted *ahi* (tuna).

[fork] 90 indoors, 32 outdoors
[P] 🅰 MC, V

🍴 NANEA RESTAURANT & BAR
$$
WESTIN PRINCEVILLE OCEAN RESORT VILLAS
3838 WYLLIE RD.
PRINCEVILLE
TEL 808/827-8700
American/Healthy
This is the place to bring the kids. Children under 3 are free and 4- to 11-year-olds eat for half price. There are vegan and

gluten-free menus, in addition to daily seafood catch, ribs, and risotto. Dessert: tuck into the warm coconut cake with Grande Marnier strawberries and coconut ice cream.

[fork] 65 indoors, 70 outdoors
🅰 All major cards

🍴 POSTCARDS CAFÉ
$$
5-5075-A KUHIO HWY.
HANALEI
TEL 808/826-1191
Healthy
Best breakfasts on the island, but no bacon. It's a vegan's nirvana—with seafood for the backsliders. Vacationing Hollywood stars flock here. Look for taro fritters and prawns, and fish tacos.

[fork] 39 indoors, 21 outdoors
[P] 🅰 All major cards

WEST KAUAI

🏨🍴 WAIMEA PLANTATION COTTAGES
$$$$
9400 KAUMUALII HWY.
WAIMEA 96796
TEL 808/338-1625 OR
866/774-2924
FAX 808/338-2338
waimeaplantation
cottages.com
Plantation cottages with updated facilities and period furniture set beside the sea.

[1] 50 units 🚭 None 🏊

SOMETHING SPECIAL

🍴 THE BEACH HOUSE
$$$
5022 LAWAI RD.
KOLOA
TEL 808/742-1424
Regional
Locals and Kauai regulars flock here for the seaside setting, sunset views, and most of all, the exquisite cuisine, especially fresh seafood. Start with ceviche in a half coconut, move on to seafood pasta in a saffron cream broth or wasabi-crusted fresh catch with lilikoi/

lemongrass beurre blanc, and finish with old-fashioned bananas Foster. Island ingredients are featured, including local beef. There are also vegan and gluten-free menus.

[fork] 180 🅰 All major cards

▦ MOLOKAI

KAUNAKAKAI & EAST END

🏨 MOLOKAI SHORES
$$$
KAMEHAMEHA HWY.
KAUNAKAKAI 96748-1037
TEL 808/553-5954 OR
800/535-0085
FAX 808/553-3241
marcresorts.com
One- and two-room suites set beside the sea in lavish gardens. All have kitchenettes and ocean views.

[1] 100 units 🚭 None 🏊

🏨 PUU O HOKU RANCH
$$$
KAMEHAMEHA V HWY.
KAUNAKAKAI 96748
TEL 808/558-8109
FAX 808/558-8100
puuohoku.com
Extravagant scenery on a 14,000-acre ranch in the middle of glorious nowhere. Basic wicker furnishings.

[1] 17 units (6 in cottages, 11 in lodge) 🚭 None
🅰 No credit cards

🍴 MOLOKAI PIZZA CAFÉ
$$
KAHUA CENTER, OLD WHARF RD.
KAUNAKAKAI
TEL 808/553-3288
Italian/Local Food
Pizza, pasta, and pocket sandwiches are the staples in this casual, friendly gathering spot. Also daily themed menus such as Mexican and prime rib. Best-selling plate: barbecued baby back ribs.

[fork] 60 indoors, 12 outdoors
🅰 No credit cards

🚭 Nonsmoking ❄ Air-conditioning 🏊 Swimming Pool 🏋 Health Club 🅰 Credit Cards

🍴 KANEMITSU BAKERY & RESTAURANT

$

79 ALA MALAMA ST.
KAUNAKAKAI
TEL 808/553-5855
Local Food
Burgers, mahi burgers, sandwiches all come on the famous Molokai bread at this unpretentious diner. Good place to order a picnic lunch. Breakfast is served.
🔧 75 🕐 Closed D, & L Tues.
🚫 No credit cards

🍴 OVIEDO'S

$

145 ALA MALAMA
KAUNAKAKAI
TEL 808/553-5014
Filipino
Home-cooked Filipino specialties in a warm friendly atmosphere. *Adobos* (stews) are a specialty.
🔧 12 🕐 Closes 5:30 p.m. Mon.–Fri., 4 p.m. Sat. & Sun.
🚫 No credit cards

WEST END

🏨 KALUAKOI VILLAS
🍴 $$$

1121 KALUAKOI RD.
MAUNALOA 96770
TEL 808/552-2721 OR
800/367-5004
Conveniently located by the sea and a short drive from Maunaloa town, the world is left behind when you stay in a spacious studio, one-bedroom suite, or oceanfront cottage.
ⓘ 22 units 🚫 All major cards

SOMETHING SPECIAL

🏨 PANIOLO HALE RESORT CONDOMINIUMS
$$$
LIO PL.
MAUNALOA 96770
TEL 800/367-2984
molokai-vacation-rental.com
Simply furnished studios to 2-room condos with kitchens.

Most have ocean views. Two-night minimum.
ⓘ 77 units (16 rentals)
🚫 None 🏖

■ LANAI

SOMETHING SPECIAL

🏨 FOUR SEASONS RESORT
🍴 LANAI AT MANELE BAY
$$$$$
ONE MANELE BAY RD.
LANAI CITY 96763
TEL 808/565-2000 OR
800/321-4666
FAX 808/565-2483
fourseasons.com/manelebay
Elegant, relaxed, and breezy, overlooking Hulopoe Beach, the best on the island for swimming and snorkeling. Dining is exceptional.
ⓘ 249 units 🏖 🎾

🏨 FOUR SEASONS RESORT
🍴 LANAI, THE LODGE AT KOELE
$$$$$
ONE KEOMOKU HWY.
LANAI CITY 96763
TEL 808/565-4000 OR
800/321-4666
FAX 808/565-4561
fourseasons.com/koele
This baronial lodge in the cool uplands of Lanai City just misses being stuffy. English manor furnishings, fireplaces in the Great Hall, and wicker chairs on the porch. Known for its fine dining and visiting artists program. Courtesy shuttle to beach.
ⓘ 102 units 🚫 None 🏖 🎾

🏨 HOTEL LANAI
🍴 $$$
828 LANAI AVE.
LANAI CITY 96763
TEL 808/565-7211 OR
800/795-7211
FAX 808/565-6450
hotellanai.com
Graciously decorated in whites and pastels, this was once Lanai City's only hotel. The front

porch is still the local gathering place for impromptu music and "talk story." Restaurant.
ⓘ 11 units 🚫 None

SOMETHING SPECIAL

🍴 FORMAL DINING ROOM
THE LODGE AT KOELE
1 KEOMOKU HWY.
LANAI CITY
TEL 808/565-4580
$$$$
American
Eat Lanai game such as seared venison loin with cherry-cranberry sauce and parsnip-potatoes. This restaurant is a consistent award winner. Jackets required (available from concierge).
🔧 51 🅿 🕐 Closed L
🚫 All major cards

🍴 LANAI CITY GRILLE
$$$
HOTEL LANAI
828 LANAI AVE.
LANAI CITY
TEL 808/565-7211
American/Regional
Venison is featured here, with mushroom risotto and port–wine–fruit compote. Other star attractions are baby back ribs and green tea steamed fish. Desserts include lilikoi panna cotta with berries and coconut sabayon. Pau Hana Friday means you will be treated to Hawaiian music with dinner.
🔧 80 indoors, 50 outdoors
🚫 All major cards

🍴 BLUE GINGER CAFÉ
$
409 SEVENTH ST.
LANAI CITY
TEL 808/565-6363
American
It's plain and homey, the food reliable. Burgers, omelets, a few Filipino specialties, and saimin. Breakfast is served.
🔧 35 indoors, 16 outdoors
🚫 No credit cards

Shopping in Hawaii

You'll find an intriguing mix of European designer shops, Asian specialty stores, American chains, and a new wave of stores devoted to "made in Hawaii" goods, ranging from creamy coconut-based soaps scented with Hawaiian flora to fine art. Farmers' markets and craft fairs provide excellent shopping opportunities. Check local newspapers to see what's going on. Macy's department store is a reliable source for needs, whims, and gifts.

Hours

Hours vary widely by population density. Some supermarkets are open 24 hours. Most open at 7 a.m. and close at 9 p.m. Department stores and other retail outlets open between 9 and 10 a.m., and close at 9 p.m. Smaller stores in smaller towns close anywhere between 5 and 7 p.m. Most are open on Sunday.

Payment & Returns

Most stores, including supermarkets, accept credit cards. Few will accept an out-of-state personal check. If you have a complaint about a purchase, return it as soon as possible with the receipt. In case of serious dispute, contact the state **Consumer Resource Center,** tel 808/587-3222.

What to Buy

The most popular souvenir is a box of chocolate-covered macadamia nuts. Following the coffee craze, Kona coffee is hot. Check the label to see just how much Kona is in the blend; better yet, buy pure—expensive but worth it. Other good food bets are jams and jellies from tropical fruit, fresh pineapple, teas, such as mamake from Hawaiian plants, syrups, cookies, and taro chips. Good places to shop for these tasty treats are supermarkets, Longs Drugs throughout the Islands, and ABC stores in resort towns. Look for bowls and art objects carved from Hawaiian woods such as koa, and milo, also mango and Norfolk Island pine. Graphically strong Hawaiian quilts in spreads, pillows, and wall hangings blend with contemporary furnishings. Cheaper imitations are being sewn in developing nations. Ask about origins, or buy a kit and sew your own. Locally designed fashion goes way beyond aloha shirts and matching muumuu, although you will probably succumb and end up wearing a garden to dinner. Tropical flowers may be shipped around the globe. Hawaiian music CDs and tapes can warm a winter day back home. Good buys from Asia include jade, porcelain, interesting cooking utensils, vintage kimono, and obi (belts), which make good table runners.

The following is a list of the most interesting and characteristic shops, arranged by island.

◼ OAHU

Ala Moana Center (*1450 Ala Moana Blvd., 5 minutes from Waikiki*). Has more than 200 shops, including department stores such as Sears and Nieman Marcus. Housed in its own building with lots of parking, Nordstrom made an impressive Hawaii debut in 2008, with a full-scale department store. A whole new level is fragrant with new restaurants, mostly mainland chains such as **California Pizza Kitchen** (*tel 808/941-7715*), **Ruby Tuesday** (*tel 808/943-2525*), and **Bubba Gump Shrimp Company** (*tel 808/949-4867*). The Mai Tai Bar is the hip hub of the action with live Hawaiian music. At **Hyatt Regency Waikiki, Products of Hawaii Too** (*tel 808/923-7798*)

specializes in Hawaii-made gifts.

Aloha Flea Market (*99-500 Salt Lake Blvd. Halawa, tel 808/486-6704, closed Mon., Tues., Thurs., & Fri.*). More than a thousand vendors peddle everything from cheap T-shirts and extra luggage to carry home your treasures, to fashion, art, watches, and maybe an antique find. Go early, wear a hat. It's outdoors in the Aloha Stadium parking lot.

Aloha Tower Marketplace is a breezy gaggle of shops and restaurants beside the busy Honolulu Harbor.

Haleiwa Boutiques, art galleries, and surf shops offer fashionably outrageous clothing and accessories. Best bets are **Silver Moon Emporium** (*66-250 Kamehameha Hwy., tel 808/637-7710*) and **Oogenesis** (*66-249 Kamehameha Hwy., tel 808/637-4580*).

Hilo Hattie's (*700 N. Nimitz Hwy., Honolulu, tel 808/537-2926, hilohatties.com*). Still has touristy neon muumuus, but also quality aloha wear and souvenirs such as Kona coffee (free samples) and tropical jewelry. Free shuttles operate from Waikiki.

Hula Supply Center (*1050 Ala Moana Blvd., Honolulu, tel 808/941-5379*). Hula dancers come for their feathered gourd rattles and costume accessories. Find everything from cellophane skirts to shell jewelry. Great sarongs, woven lauhala bags, Hawaiian print backpacks, artistic T-shirts, and lots of fun kitsch.

Kapahulu Ave., Waikiki, is a string of interesting shops and restaurants in unpromising storefronts. **Bailey's Antique Clothing and**

Thrift Shop *(517 Kapahulu Ave., tel 808/734-7628)* is a hodgepodge of vintage "silky" aloha shirts with coconut buttons, smart reproductions of perennial favorites, and Hawaiian kitsch. At **Na Lima Mili Hulu Noeau** *(762 Kapahulu Ave., tel 808/732-0865)* buy prize feather lei or drop in for an inexpensive lei lesson. **Kilohana Square** *(1016 Kapahulu Ave.)* is a little group of shops, primarily quality Asian and European antiques, grouped around a picturesque courtyard.

The Little Hawaiian Craft Shop *(Royal Hawaiian Center, 2233 Kalakaua Ave., tel 808/926-2662).* The best place in Waikiki for quality Hawaiian gifts. Feather hatbands, Niihau shell lei, dried botanical collages, reproductions from the Bishop Museum's Hawaiian collection.

Victoria Ward Center This ever expanding center, at Ward Ave. and Auahi St. across from Ala Moana Beach Park, is a complex of two shopping centers, the 65-unit Ward Warehouse, and 30-unit Ward Center, plus a 16-screen megaplex and various strip mall shops and restaurants. Shops range from chains to local specialty stores. At **Native Books Na Mea Hawaii** *(Ward Warehouse, tel 808/596-8885),* look for reasonably priced petroglyph art by Lynn Cook, one-of-a-kind koa and milo lamps and bowls, lauhala placemats. **Honolulu Chocolate Co.** *(Ward Center, tel 808/591-2997)* carries locally made expensive gourmet candies. The **Mamo Howell** boutique *(Ward Warehouse, tel 808/591-2002)* carries the latest from this popular local designer's line of quality Hawaiian wear.

Waikele Shopping Plaza *(94-790 Lumiaina St., Waikele, tel 808/676-5656).* A 64-acre discount mall with everything from local surf wear to a Saks Fifth Avenue outlet. It's 20 miles from Waikiki. TheBus 48 passes by.

MAUI

Banyan Tree Craft Fair happens almost every weekend, presented by the Lahaina Arts Society and other arts and crafts groups beneath the historic banyan tree behind **Lahaina Courthouse** *(Wharf St., tel 808/661-0111).* It promotes local artists and Hawaiian crafts.

Front Street, Lahaina, has respectable boutiques in old grog shops. **Lahaina Scrimshaw** *(845A Front St., tel 808/661-8820)* carries both collectors' pieces and contemporary scrimshaw. **Lahaina Center** *(tel 808/667-9216)* features variety galore, from dining and hair salons to a nightclub and movie theater. **Lei Spa Maui** *(505 Front St., tel 808/661-1178)* concentrates on Maui-made soaps, masks, lotions, potions, candles, and perfumes.

Haimoff & Haimoff Creations in Gold *(130 Bay Dr., Kapalua Resort, tel 808/596-0090).* Imaginative, interesting original-design jewelry at good prices.

Makawao, Upcountry, draws shoppers from Honolulu who come for the off-beat chic and the arts. **Maui Hands** *(1169 Makawao Ave., tel 808/572-2008)* presents Maui art and collectibles. **Altitude** *(3660 Baldwin Ave., tel 808/573-4733),* a stylish boutique owned by a French-woman who plays Parisian golden oldies on her stereo, illustrates the bipolar nature of this former cow town.

For hip fashion, head into **Hurricane** *(3639 Baldwin Ave., tel 808/572-5076).* **Hui Noeau Visual Arts Center** *(2841 Baldwin Ave., tel 808/572-6560)* for a visual treat. **Mandalay Imports** *(Four Seasons Resort, Wailea, tel 808/874-5111)* has Thai silks, Asian treasures, and ethnic jewelry. **Maui Crafts Guild** *(69 Hana Hwy., Paia, tel 808/579-9697.)* On the cutting edge of Maui crafts. The selection is interesting and

reasonably priced for the quality.

Maui Swap Meet *(Hwy. 350 and S. Puunene Ave., Kahului, tel 808/877-3100).* Down-home Maui fun. Every Saturday from 7 a.m. until noon, about a hundred vendors peddle protea, veggies, antiques, arts, and crafts.

The Shops at Wailea *(3750 Wailea Alanui, tel 808/891-6770).* Upscale, breezy, and enticing, with mainly Mainland chains such as Tiffany, the Gap, and Louis Vuitton, but punctuated with good local shops such as Martin & MacArthur, purveyors of fine koa furniture and quality Hawaiian art and gifts.

Totally Hawaiian Gift Gallery *(Whalers Village Mall, tel 808/667-4070).* Locally made or inspired gift items include dolls in muumuus, sculptures from native woods, tropical perfumes and soaps, and rolls of Hawaiian-print paper to wrap your gifts.

BIG ISLAND

Blue Ginger *(Mamalahoa Hwy., Kainaliu, tel 808/322-3898).* You can't miss this eclectic shop (it's bright blue) with its original jewelry, Asian imports, local crafts, and unusual clothing.

Hilo Farmers Market *(Kamehameha Ave. & Mamo St., Hilo, tel 808/933-1000, Wed. & Sat. from 6 a.m. to 3 p.m.).* If you want the really good stuff, like Waimea strawberries, get there early. Other winners: pure home-extracted coconut oil (great for the hair), kapa, lauhala, homemade children's clothing.

Holualoa town Exceptional shops and galleries along its main street, Mamalahoa Hwy. Stop for freshest Kona coffee at **Holualoa Café** *(Mamalahoa Hwy., tel 808/322-2233).* **Studio 7** *(76-5920 Mamalahoa Hwy., tel 808/324-1335)* shows the work of respected Island artists, including gallery owners Setsuko and Hiroki Morinoue. More fine art at **Holualoa Gallery**

(76-5921 Mamalahoa Hwy., tel 808/322-8484). Of particular note: the raku pottery. Traditional Hawaiian lauhala weaving at **Kimura Lauhala Shop** *(77-996 Hualalae Rd., Hwy. 182, tel 808/324-0053).*

Kailua-Kona The main street, Alii Drive, is one long gaggle of shops and mini-malls mixed in with historical sites. The **Coconut Grove Market Place** features art galleries, jewelry stores, and T-shirt shops. The open-air **Alii Gardens Marketplace** is a happy collection of tents whose vendors sell everything from tacky souvenirs to fine Hawaiian crafts.

King's Shops *(Waikoloa Resort, 250 Waikoloa Beach Dr., Kohala Coast).* **Noa Noa** *(tel 808/886-5449)* has a distinctive line of clothing recognizable for ethnic Pacific prints, breezy fabrics, and easy, flattering lines. Spin-off shop **Kubuku** *(tel 808/886-8581)* is more into scarves, sarongs, and ethnic jewelry. Happy feet head for **Walking in Paradise** *(tel 808/886-2600)* for top walking shoes and salon styles from around the world.

Sig Zane Designs *(122 Kamehameha Ave., Hilo, tel 808/935-7077).* A very personal collection of art, aloha wear, and linens deeply rooted in the Hawaiian culture. Nearby **Hana Hou** *(164 Kamehameha Ave., Hilo, tel 808/935-4555)* has hip tropical fashions made from vintage Hawaiian fabrics.

Volcano Art Center *(Hawaii Volcanoes National Park, tel 808/967-7565).* In the old Volcano House Inn. Fine island art, much of it centered on a volcano theme. Look for ceramics, tiles, finest lauhala, paintings, prints.

KAUAI

Aunty Lilikoi *(9875 Waimea Rd., Waimea, tel 808/338-1296).* Tangy lilikoi, smoother than lemon, is the base for the jams, jellies, and award-winning salad dressings and mustards made

right here. Free tastings.

Hanapepe town has treasures in its restored plantation-era shops. Every Friday night, musicians stroll the streets and the 16 galleries have open houses. **Art of Marbeling** *(3890 Hanapepe Rd., tel 808/482-1472)* sells translucent wooden bowls and hand-marbled sarongs. At **Kauai Fine Arts** *(3905 Hanapepe Rd., tel 808/335-3778),* you can leaf through Victorian-era botanical prints, antique maps and prints of old Hawaii, and kapa art.

Kilohana Plantation *(3-2087 Kaumualii Hwy., Puhi, tel 808/246-8900).* Delightful shops crammed into every room of a former plantation manager's home. **Kilohana Gallery** *(tel 808/245-9352)* offers original paintings, affordable prints, gyotaku, jewelry, and ceramics, mostly by Kauai artists. Niihau shell lei turn up in the cloak room at the **Hawaiian Collection Room. Clayworks at Kilohana** *(tel 808/246-2529)* is a working ceramics gallery where you may choose pottery or sculptures, or create your own raku glaze and experience a firing on the spot.

Kong Lung *(Kilauea Rd., Kilauea, tel 808/828-1822),* housed in a historic old plantation store, draws faithful shoppers from other islands who come for the home furnishings, aloha wear, stationery, and just to look at the table settings.

Ola's *(5-5016 Kuhio Hwy., Hanalei, tel 808/826-6937).* Owned by an artist who paints, and makes, furniture—big imaginative pieces. They also carry the work of other fine artists in a variety of mediums including daring blown, hand-painted glass, innovative jewelry, and home furnishings.

Yellowfish Trading Company *(Hanalei Center, 5-5161 Kuhio Hwy., tel 808/826-1227).* Has a reputation among collectors and Hollywood stars for its depth of kitsch and breadth of vintage aloha shirts.

MOLOKAI

The Big Wind Kite Factory *(120 Maunaloa Hwy., Maunaloa, tel 808/552-2364)* is just that. They make and sell glorious kites that end up on walls as art. They have the latest aerodynamic kites, inexpensive paper kites, and colorful windsocks. You can tour the small factory and watch them stitch up flying hula girls and geckos.

Imamura Store *(Kaunakakai, tel 808/553-5615).* An old-fashioned Hawaiian general store with vintage print Hawaiian tablecloths, Japanese tea cups and relish dishes, kitsch, and sarongs.

Molokai Fish & Dive *(61 Ala Malama, Kaunakakai, tel 808/553-5926)* is like taking Philosophy 101. Just read the T-shirts and have a laugh at this sporting goods store.

Outpost Natural Foods *(70 Makaena Pl., tel 808/553-3377),* for reasonably priced fresh Molokai produce such as sweet potatoes and papayas. Salads, burritos, and mock meat loaf are among the many savory vegetarian foods for the health conscious.

Plantation Gallery *(120 Maunaloa Hwy., Maunaloa, tel 808/552-2364).* A jumble of Hawaiian handicrafts and whimsical imports from Bali and points east.

LANAI

Gifts with Aloha *(363 7th St., Lanai City, tel 808/565-6589).* Mix of aloha wear, jewelry, hanging art, candles, Lanai jams, and jellies.

Lanai Art Studio *(339 7th Ave., Lanai City, tel 808/565-7503).* Island artists, trained by visiting multimedia masters, show their wares—watercolors, ceramics, jewelry.

Mike Carroll Gallery *(443 7th St., Lanai City, tel 565-7122).* Vintage building houses fine art by Mike Carroll and guests artists. Find paintings, photography, wood bowls, jewelry, and Asian antiques.

Entertainment & Activities

Much of the fun of Hawaii is found in outdoor activities. Every Island offers excellent land and ocean options. Some, such as golf, have been covered in the main chapters. Here are the best contacts for walking, horseback riding, boating, diving, sports lessons. You'll also find sunset bars and after-dark entertainment.

▦ OAHU

AFTER DARK

Luau

Paradise Cove luau (tel 808/842-5911). Buses bring thousands to a remote beach for a well-done mass luau, with entertainment, games, pageantry.

Royal Hawaiian luau (Royal Hawaiian Hotel, 2259 Kalakaua Ave., tel 808/923-7311, Mon. eve.). Upscale luau on the seaside lawn with views of Diamond Head.

Shows

Cirque Hawaii (325 Seaside Ave., tel 808/922-0017, closed Wed.) is a multimillion dollar show that wows with aerialists, acrobats, clowns, dancers, contortionists, Hazers, Foggers, spangles, and edgy music. Twice nightly.

Hula Mound (Kuhio Beach, Waikiki, nightly). Free hula show and torch-lighting ceremony. Hula halau (schools) perform at sundown on this outdoor grassy stage on the beach beneath the giant banyan tree. This is the authentic hula, not Waikiki-ed.

Magic of Polynesia (Waikiki Beachcomber Hotel, 2300 Kalakaua Ave., tel 808/971-4321). A dramatic extravaganza of illusion and dance starring magician John Hirokawa.

Sunset

Alii Kai **Catamaran** (Pier 5, Aloha Tower, tel 808/539-9400). Polynesian-style catamaran sets sail with up to a thousand passengers for a well-organized sunset cruise, including an appetizing buffet and lively Hawaiian revue.

Banyan Veranda (Sheraton Moana Surfrider Hotel, 2365 Kalakaua Ave., tel 808/922-3111). Enjoy top-notch Hawaiian entertainment beneath the banyan tree on the ocean terrace of this Victorian grande dame.

House Without a Key (Halekulani Hotel, tel 808/923-2311). Hula and music under a century-old tree.

Mai Tai Bar (Royal Hawaiian Hotel, 2259 Kalakaua Ave., tel 808/923-7311) offers special pink beer.

Waikiki Beach Marriott Resort (Moana Terrace Café and Bar, 2552 Kalakaua Ave., Waikiki, tel 808/922-6611). Lineups of top Hawaiian entertainers including beloved singer Genoa Keawe, and slack key artists Martin Pahinui, George Kuo, and Aaron Mahi perform nightly in this outdoor space overlooking the ocean. This is a place to encounter authentic Hawaiian music.

ACTIVITIES

Hiking

Hawaii Department of Land and Natural Resources (1151 Punchbowl St., Room 130, Honolulu 96813, tel 808/587-0300). Trail information and camping permits. Trail maps available at small cost. Also camping permits.

Hawaiian Trail and Mountain Club (P.O. Box 2238, Honolulu 96804, htmclub.org). Weekly hikes on one of 80 Oahu trails. Website provides link to info on many hiking trails.

Sierra Club (P.O. Box 2577, Honolulu 96803, tel 808/538-6616). Regularly scheduled hikes at varied skill levels.

Kayaking

Twogood Kayaks Hawaii (345 Hahani St., Kailua, 96734, tel 808/262-5656). Paddle a kayak out to offshore islands.

Sailing

Navatek 1 (Pier 6, Honolulu Harbor, tel 808/973-1311, atlantis adventures.com) is the smoothest cruise in Hawaii. The 140' high-tech ship is the only one certified to sail beyond Waikiki and Diamond Head along the Kahala Gold Coast. They guarantee you won't be seasick, so enjoy the lobster and tenderloin dinner and the show. Or opt for the much cheaper prime rib buffet. Big windows, lots of open deck.

Tradewind Charters (796 Kalanipuu St., Honolulu 96825, tel 808/973-0311 or 800/829-4899, tradewindcharters.com). Private sunset, moonlight, daytime sails; also lessons, whale- watching, and deep-sea fishing.

Scuba Diving

Captain Bruce's Scuba Charters (on the pier, Waianae Boat Harbor, tel 808/373-3590, captain bruce.com). Experienced divers explore west Oahu waters. Also offers certification.

Surfing Lessons

Aloha Beach Service (2365 Kalakaua Ave., next to Sheraton Moana Surfrider, tel 808/922-3111, ext. 2341). Even grandmothers can be standing, riding the waves in one wet lesson.

Windsurfing

Naish Hawaii (155-A Hamakua Dr., Kailua 96734, tel 808/262-6068). World champion Robbie Naish and family run the operation. Lessons, rentals, sales, complete tours.

◼ MAUI

AFTER DARK

Shows

Ulalena (*Maui Myth and Magic Theater, 878 Front St., Lahaina, tel 808/661-9913, closed Sun. & Mon.*). A multimillion-dollar musical about Maui's legends and history.
Warren & Annabelle's (*900 Front St., Lahaina, tel 808/667-6244*). Magician and ghost pianist in intimate theater.

Sunset

Scotch Mist Charters (*Lahaina Harbor, tel 808/661-0386*). Champagne sail aboard a 25-passenger sloop.
America II Sunset Sail (*Lahaina Harbor, tel 808/667-2195*). Two-hour reasonably priced cruise on a 1987 America's Cup contender.

ACTIVITIES

Bicycling

Maui Easy Riders Bike Tours (*Baldwin Beach Park, Paia, tel 808/344-9489*). Owner/guide takes a maximum of eight riders down the slopes of Haleakala, with time to enjoy both Makawao and Paia towns. Offers a variety of bike sizes and comfy seats.

Boating

Makena Kayak Trips (*Makena, tel 808/879-8426*). Explore reefs and remote coves on Maui's wild eastern shore.
South Pacific Kayaks (*95 Halekuai St., Kihei 96753, tel 808/875-4848 or 800/776-2326, southpacific kayaks.com*). Tours, rentals, lessons, and snorkeling.
Trilogy Excursions (*Lahaina Harbor, tel 808/874-5649 or 888/225-6284, sailtrilogy .com*). Catamaran picnic sails to Molokini or Lanai.

Hiking

Hawaii State Department of Land and Natural Resources (*54 S. High St., Rm. 101, Wailuku 96793, tel 808/984-8109*). For trail information and camping permits.
Hike Maui (*tel 808/879-5270, hikemaui.com*). Expert guide Ken Schmitt plans several hikes a day from easy to strenuous.
Adatudes (*180 Dickenson St., #102, Lahaina, tel 808/661-7720 or 877/661-7720, ecomaui.com*). Guides trained in nature and culture have access to pristine trails and sites on private land. Choose rainforest trails, Haleakala, Hana, Kahakuloa, and more.

Horseback Riding

Lahaina Stables (*Hokiokio Rd., Puunoa, tel 808/667-2222, www .mauihorse.com*). Guided trail rides go into Kauaula Valley in the West Maui Mountains. Grand views of historic Lahaina.

Scuba Diving & Snorkeling

Ed Robinson's Diving Adventures (*Kihei, tel 808/879-3584 or 800/635-1273, www .mauiscuba.com*). Dive with masters at Makena, Molokini, and Lanai Caverns. Also sunset and night dives and aggressive three-tank dives.
Maui Dive Shop (*Cannery Mall, Lahaina, tel 808/661-5388*). Charters and instruction arranged from several locations around island.

Whale-Watching

Pacific Whale Foundation (*101 N. Kihei Rd., Kihei, tel 808/249-8811 or 800/942-5311, closed June–Nov.*). Sail with marine biologists who give lively and informative narrations.

Windsurfing

Maui Windsurfing Company (*520 Keolani Pl., Kahului, tel 800/872-0999*). Rentals, lessons for beginners to advanced.

◼ BIG ISLAND

AFTER DARK

Luau

Kona Village luau (*Queen Kaahumanu Hwy., Kaupulehu, tel 808/325-5555, Fri. only.*). There are many good luau on the Big Isle, but this is the best.

ACTIVITIES

Boating

Fair Wind Snorkeling and Diving Adventures (*tel 800/677-9461, fair-wind.com*). Two cruises daily aboard a 60-foot catamaran along the Kona Coast to Kealakekua Bay for snorkeling.
Hahalua Lele (*Orchid Beach Club, 1 North Kaniku Dr., Mauna Lani Resort, tel 808/887-7320*). Sail aboard Casey Cho's Polynesian-s tyle sailing canoe to remote coves for snorkeling and good Hawaiian stories.

Fishing

Humdinger Sportfishing (*P.O. Box 1995, Kailua-Kona, tel 808/325-3449, humdingersport fishing.com*). Captain Jeff has been fishing the deep waters off the Kona Coast for 40 years. He knows where to find mahimahi, tuna, and even the 1000-pound marlin.
Kona Charters Skippers Association (*74–857 Iwalani Pl., Kailua-Kona 96740, tel 800/762-7546, konabiggamefishing.com*). Will arrange deep-sea charters.

Hiking

Hawaii Department of Parks and Recreation (*101 Pauahi St., Hilo, 96720, tel 808/961-8311*).
Hawaii Forest and Trail (*74–5035B Queen Kaahumanu Hwy., Kailua-Kona 96740, tel 800/464-1993, www .hawaii-forest.com*). Founder Rob

Pacheco has organized hikes and a variety of outdoor adventures, including birding.
Hawaiian Walkways (*tel 808/775-0372 or 800/457-7759, www .hawaiianwalkways.com*). Owner/ guide Hugh Montgomery knows less traveled trails.
State Division of Forestry and Wildlife (*19 E. Kawili St., Hilo 96720, tel 808/974-4221*). Hiking information about various state-owned lands. Maps available.

Horseback Riding
King's Trail Rides (*tel 808/323-2388, konacowboy.com*). Two hours of riding and two hours of snorkeling make the day for four people. Trip goes to monument marking the site where Captain Cook was killed in a battle with the Hawaiians. Gear and lunch included.

Scuba Diving & Snorkeling
Fair Wind (*78–7130 Kaleio-papa St., Kailua-Kona 96740, tel 808/322-2788 or 800/677-9461, fair-wind.com*). Family-owned and operated catamaran or Zodiac cruises along Kona Coast.
Nautilus Dive Center (*382 Kame-hameha Ave., Hilo, tel 808/935-6939, nautilusdivehilo.com*). Advanced divers only.

Whale-Watching
Captain Dan McSweeney's Year-Round Whale Watching Adventures (*P.O. Box 139, Holualoa 96725, tel 808/322-0028 or 888/942-5376, ilovewhales.com*). Well-respected tours.

▓ KAUAI

AFTER DARK

Luau
Smith's Tropical Paradise (*174 Wailua Rd., Kapaa, tel 808/821-6895. Mon., Wed., & Fri.*).

ACTIVITIES

Boating
Captain Andy's Sailing Adventures (*P.O. Box 876, Eleele 96705, tel 808/335-6833 or 800/535-0830*). Sunset cruise, snorkel trip, Na Pali Coast tour.
Captain Zodiac Raft Expeditions (*P.O. Box 876, Eleele 96705, tel 808/335-6833 or 800/535-0830, napali.com*). Beautiful Na Pali Coast adventures.
Kayak Kauai (*5070-A Kuhio Hwy., Hanalei, tel 808/826-9844 or 800/437-3507*). Offers rentals and river trips.
Outfitters Kauai (*2827-A Poipu Rd., Poipu 96756, tel 808/742-9667*). Novice kayak river trips and advanced Na Pali excursions.
Smith's Motor Boat Service (*174 Wailua Rd., tel 808/821-6892*). Motor cruise to Fern Grotto at reasonable price.

Helicopter Tours
Island Helicopters (*tel 800/829-5999 or 808/245-8588, www .islandhelicopters.com*). Hour-long island overview includes Waimea Canyon, Na Pali Cliffs.

Hiking
Hawaii State Department of Land and Natural Resources (*3060 Eiwa St., #306, Lihue 96766, tel 808/274-3444*). Contact them to get hiking trail maps and camping permits.
Kauai Nature Tours (*P.O. Box 549, Koloa 96756, tel 808/742-8305 or 888-233-8365, kauainature tours.com*). Educational hikes to Sleeping Giant, Na Pali Coast, Waimea Canyon, and more.

Horseback Riding
CJM Country Stables (*end of Poipu Rd., Poipu, 1.6 miles east of Hyatt Regency Hotel, tel 808/742-6096*). Variety of rides including breakfast beach ride.

Surfing
Kauai Surf School (*Nukumoi Surf Shop, 2100 Hoone Rd., Poipu, tel 808/742-8019*). Classes taught by a champion surfer; classes for children also available.

▓ MOLOKAI

ACTIVITIES

Boating
Fun Hogs Hawaii (*meet at Slip 11, Kaunakakai Wharf, tel 808/567-6789*). Fish, dive, snorkel, and watch for whales.
Nature Conservancy (*P.O. Box 220, Kualapuu 96757, tel 808/553-5236*). Hikes to Moomomi Dunes and Kamakou Preserve.
Molokai Museum & Cultural Center (*located at Kalae, on the way to Kalaupapa Overlook, P.O. Box 269, Kalaupapa 96748, tel 808/567-6436*). Nineteenth-century Molokai comes alive with a visit to this restored R. W. Meyer Sugar Mill that was a center of plantation life.

▓ LANAI

AFTER DARK

Lanai Playhouse (*Lanai Ave., Lanai City, tel 808/565-7500*). Surprising state-of-the-art sound in this renovated old theater. First-run films and occasional plays and special events.

ACTIVITIES

Boating
Trilogy Excursions (*207 Kupuohi St., Lahaina 96761, tel 800/874-5649 or 888/225-6284, sailtrilogy.com*). Dive-snorkel aboard a trimaran. Excursions operate from Maui.

Horseback Riding
The Stables at Koele (*Lanai City, tel 808/565-4424*).

INDEX

ILLUSTRATIONS CREDITS

National Geographic

TRAVELER
Hawaii

Published by the National Geographic Society

John M. Fahey, *Chairman of the Board and Chief Executive Officer*

Declan Moore, *Executive Vice President; President, Publishing and Travel*

Melina Gerosa Bellows, *Executive Vice President; Chief Creative Officer, Books, Kids, and Family*

Lynn Cutter, *Executive Vice President, Travel*

Keith Bellows, *Senior Vice President and Editor in Chief, National Geographic Travel Media*

Prepared by the Book Division

Hector Sierra, *Senior Vice President and General Manager*

Janet Goldstein, *Senior Vice President and Editorial Director*

Jonathan Halling, *Design Director, Books and Children's Publishing*

Marianne R. Koszorus, *Design Director, Books*

Barbara A. Noe, *Senior Editor, National Geographic Travel Books*

R. Gary Colbert, *Production Director*

Jennifer A. Thornton, *Director of Managing Editorial*

Susan S. Blair, *Director of Photography*

Meredith C. Wilcox, *Director, Administration and Rights Clearance*

Staff for This Book

Hannah Lauterback, *Project Editor*

Ruth Ann Thompson, *Designer*

Carl Mehler, *Director of Maps*

Mike McNey & Mapping Specialists, *Map Production*

Olivia Garnett, *Text Editor*

Marshall Kiker, *Associate Managing Editor*

Judith Klein, *Production Editor*

Gary Colbert, *Production Manager*

Galen Young, *Rights Clearance Specialist*

Katie Olsen, *Production Design Assistant*

Production Services

Phillip L. Schlosser, *Senior Vice President*

Chris Brown, *Vice President, NG Book Manufacturing*

George Bounelis, *Vice President, Production Services*

Nicole Elliott, *Manager*

Rachel Faulise, *Manager*

Robert L. Barr, *Manager*

Drive maps drawn by Chris Orr Associates, Southampton, England

Illustrations drawn by Ann Winterbotham

The information in this book has been carefully checked and to the best of our knowledge is accurate. However, details are subject to change, and the National Geographic Society cannot be responsible for such changes, or for errors or omissions. Assessments of sites, hotels, and restaurants are based on the author's subjective opinions, which do not necessarily reflect the publisher's opinion.

The National Geographic Society is one of the world's largest nonprofit scientific and educational organizations. Founded in 1888 to "increase and diffuse geographic knowledge," the member-supported Society works to inspire people to care about the planet. Through its online community, members can get closer to explorers and photographers, connect with other members around the world, and help make a difference. National Geographic reflects the world through its magazines, television programs, films, music and radio, books, DVDs, maps, exhibitions, live events, school publishing programs, interactive media, and merchandise. *National Geographic* magazine, the Society's official journal, published in English and 38 local-language editions, is read by more than 60 million people each month. The National Geographic Channel reaches 440 million households in 171 countries in 38 languages. National Geographic Digital Media receives more than 25 million visitors a month. National Geographic has funded more than 10,000 scientific research, conservation, and exploration projects and supports an education program promoting geography literacy. For more information, visit www.nationalgeographic.com.

For more information, please call 1800-NGS LINE (647-5463) or write to the following address:

National Geographic Society
1145 17th Street N.W.
Washington, D.C. 20036-4688 U.S.A.

For information about special discounts for bulk purchases, please contact National Geographic Books Special Sales: ngspecsales@ngs.org

For rights or permissions inquiries, please contact National Geographic Books Subsidiary Rights: ngbookrights@ngs.org

National Geographic Traveler: Hawaii
(Fourth Edition)
ISBN: 978-1-4262-1250-5

Printed in Hong Kong

13/THK/1

18c 3/18 5/19